Companion Website and Pearson Test Prep Access Code

Access interactive study tools on this book's companion website, including practice test software, review exercises, a Key Term flash card application, a study planner, and more!

To access the companion website, simply follow these steps:

1. Go to www.ciscopress.com/register.

2. Enter the **print book ISBN:** 9780138213428.

3. Answer the security question to validate your purchase.

4. Go to your account page.

5. Click on the **Registered Products** tab.

6. Under the book listing, click on the **Access Bonus Content** link.

When you register your book, your Pearson Test Prep practice test access code will automatically be populated with the book listing under the Registered Products tab. You will need this code to access the practice test that comes with this book. You can redeem the code at **PearsonTestPrep.com**. Simply choose Pearson IT Certification as your product group and log into the site with the same credentials you used to register your book. Click the **Activate New Product** button and enter the access code. More detailed instructions on how to redeem your access code for both the online and desktop versions can be found on the companion website.

If you have any issues accessing the companion website or obtaining your Pearson Test Prep practice test access code, you can contact our support team by going to **pearsonitp.echelp.org**.

T0266546

Cisco Certified Support Technician CCST Networking 100-150

Official Cert Guide

RUSS WHITE, CCIE NO. 2635

Cisco Press

Cisco Certified Support Technician CCST Networking 100-150 Official Cert Guide

Russ White

Published by: Cisco Press

Hoboken, New Jersey

1 2023

Library of Congress Control Number: 2023943877

ISBN-13: 978-0-13-821342-8

ISBN-10: 0-13-821342-9

Warning and Disclaimer

This book is designed to provide information about the Cisco Certified Support Technician (CCST) Networking exam. Every effort has been made to make this book as complete and as accurate as possible, but no warranty or fitness is implied.

The information is provided on an "as is" basis. The authors, Cisco Press, and Cisco Systems, Inc. shall have neither liability nor responsibility to any person or entity with respect to any loss or damages arising from the information contained in this book or from the use of the discs or programs that may accompany it.

The opinions expressed in this book belong to the author and are not necessarily those of Cisco Systems, Inc.

Trademark Acknowledgments

All terms mentioned in this book that are known to be trademarks or service marks have been appropriately capitalized. Cisco Press or Cisco Systems, Inc., cannot attest to the accuracy of this information. Use of a term in this book should not be regarded as affecting the validity of any trademark or service mark.

Special Sales

For information about buying this title in bulk quantities, or for special sales opportunities (which may include electronic versions; custom cover designs; and content particular to your business, training goals, marketing focus, or branding interests), please contact our corporate sales department at corpsales@pearsoned.com or (800) 382-3419.

For government sales inquiries, please contact governmentsales@pearsoned.com.

For questions about sales outside the U.S., please contact intlcs@pearson.com.

Feedback Information

At Cisco Press, our goal is to create in-depth technical books of the highest quality and value. Each book is crafted with care and precision, undergoing rigorous development that involves the unique expertise of members from the professional technical community.

Readers' feedback is a natural continuation of this process. If you have any comments regarding how we could improve the quality of this book, or otherwise alter it to better suit your needs, you can contact us through email at feedback@ciscopress.com. Please make sure to include the book title and ISBN in your message.

We greatly appreciate your assistance.

Vice President, IT Professional: Mark Taub

Alliances Managers, Cisco Press: Jaci Featherly and Jim Risler

Director, ITP Product Management: Brett Bartow

Managing Editor: Sandra Schroeder

Development Editor: Christopher Cleveland

Senior Project Editor: Tonya Simpson

Copy Editor: Chuck Hutchinson

Technical Editor: Patrick Gargano

Editorial Assistant: Cindy Teeters

Cover Designer: Chuti Prasertsith

Composition: codeMantra

Indexer: Timothy Wright

Proofreader: Barbara Mack

Pearson's Commitment to Diversity, Equity, and Inclusion

Pearson is dedicated to creating bias-free content that reflects the diversity of all learners. We embrace the many dimensions of diversity, including but not limited to race, ethnicity, gender, socioeconomic status, ability, age, sexual orientation, and religious or political beliefs.

Education is a powerful force for equity and change in our world. It has the potential to deliver opportunities that improve lives and enable economic mobility. As we work with authors to create content for every product and service, we acknowledge our responsibility to demonstrate inclusivity and incorporate diverse scholarship so that everyone can achieve their potential through learning. As the world's leading learning company, we have a duty to help drive change and live up to our purpose to help more people create a better life for themselves and to create a better world.

Our ambition is to purposefully contribute to a world where

- Everyone has an equitable and lifelong opportunity to succeed through learning

- Our educational products and services are inclusive and represent the rich diversity of learners

- Our educational content accurately reflects the histories and experiences of the learners we serve

- Our educational content prompts deeper discussions with learners and motivates them to expand their own learning (and worldview)

While we work hard to present unbiased content, we want to hear from you about any concerns or needs with this Pearson product so that we can investigate and address them.

Please contact us with concerns about any potential bias at https://www.pearson.com/report-bias.html.

About the Author

Russ White has more than 20 years of experience in designing, deploying, breaking, and troubleshooting large-scale networks. Across that time, he has coauthored 48 software patents, has spoken at venues throughout the world, has participated in the development of several Internet standards, has helped develop the CCDE and the CCAr, and has worked in Internet governance with the ISOC. Russ is currently a senior architect at Akamai Technologies, where he works on next-generation data center designs, complexity, security, and privacy. His most recent books are *The Art of Network Architecture*, *Navigating Network Complexity*, and *Problems and Solutions in Network Engineering*.

MSIT Capella University, MACM Shepherds Theological Seminary, PhD Southeastern Baptist Theological Seminary, CCIE No. 2635, CCDE 2007:001, CCAr

About the Technical Reviewer

Patrick Gargano is a content developer and instructor on the Enterprise Technical Education team within Learning & Certifications at Cisco. Before that, he worked as a Cisco Networking Academy instructor; he has been an instructor-trainer since 2000 and a Certified Cisco Systems Instructor (CCSI) since 2005 for Fast Lane UK, Skyline ATS, and NterOne, teaching CCNA and CCNP courses. Recently, he was responsible for developing Cisco's official ENARSI and ENSDWI course content. He has published four Cisco Press books; is a regular speaker at Cisco Live; and holds CCNA, CyberOps Associate, and CCNP Enterprise certifications. He also holds BEd and BA degrees from the University of Ottawa and has a Master of Professional Studies (MPS) degree in computer networking from Fort Hays State University. He lives in Quebec, Canada, with his wife and son.

Dedication

I would like to dedicate this book to my wife, Adrianne.

Acknowledgments

Thanks for the editing efforts of Chris Cleveland and Patrick Gargano, who helped make this book great.

I'd also like to acknowledge all those across the years who have taught me networking, including Alvaro Retana, Don Slice, James Ng, and a host of others. I would also like to thank all those who have fed into sharpening my thinking skills, including Bruce Little and Doug Bookman. Knowing is useful, but knowing how to think is the most useful thing.

Contents at a Glance

Contents

Introduction

The Cisco Certified Support Technician (CCST) Networking certification is designed to be a first step into network engineering. The test is designed to validate an individual's skills and knowledge of computer network operation, as well as basic configuration and troubleshooting. The CCST is also a first step toward the CCNA certification, which can then lead into various expert-level certifications like the CCIE and CCDE.

Recommended Prerequisite Skills

While this text provides you with the information required to pass this exam, Cisco considers ideal candidates to be those who

- Understand standards and concepts related to computer networks.
- Are able to identify and work with IPv4 and IPv6 addresses, networks, and subnets.
- Identify cables, connectors, media types, and their uses.
- Identify and use ports, lights, and other physical attributes of network devices.
- Understand basic routing and switching concepts.
- Explain basic network management tools, techniques, and best practices.
- Configure and troubleshoot a simple computer network.
- Describe the function of packet filters, firewalls, and other security devices and measures.
- Describe foundational security concepts.
- Configure basic wireless security.

The Exam Topics

The Cisco Certified Support Technician (CCST) Networking exam is broken down into six major topic areas. The contents of this book cover each of the exam topic areas and the topics included in them as outlined in the table that follows.

Exam Topic Area/Topic	Covered in
1.0 Standards and Concepts	Chapters 1, 6, 7, 9, 12, 13, 14, 15, 16, 17
1.1 Identify the fundamental building blocks of networks.	Chapters 1, 6
TCP/IP model, OSI model, frames and packets, addressing	
1.2. Differentiate between bandwidth and throughput.	Chapter 9
Latency, delay, speed test vs. Iperf	
1.3. Differentiate between LAN, WAN, MAN, CAN, PAN, and WLAN.	Chapters 7, 12, 13
Identify and illustrate common physical and logical network topologies.	
1.4. Compare and contrast cloud and on-premises applications and services.	Chapter 17

Exam Topic Area/Topic	Covered in
Public, private, hybrid, SaaS, PaaS, IaaS, remote work/ hybrid work	
1.5 Describe common network applications and protocols.	Chapters 1, 5, 14, 15, 16
TCP vs. UDP (connection-oriented vs. connectionless), FTP, SFTP, TFTP, HTTP, HTTPS, DHCP, DNS, ICMP, NTP	
2.0 Addressing and Subnet Formats	Chapter 2
2.1 Compare and contrast private addresses and public addresses.	Chapter 2
Each IP address must be unique on the network	
2.2 Identify IPv4 addresses and subnet formats.	Chapter 2
Subnet concepts, Subnet Calculator, slash notation, and subnet mask; broadcasts do not go outside the subnet	
2.3 Identify IPv6 addresses and prefix formats.	Chapter 2
Types of addresses, prefix concepts	
3.0 Endpoints and Media Types	Chapters 4, 5, 7, 8, 11
3.1 Identify cables and connectors commonly used in local area networks.	Chapter 7
Cable types: fiber, copper, twisted pair; Connector types: coax, RJ-45, RJ-11, fiber connector types	
3.2 Differentiate between Wi-Fi, cellular, and wired network technologies.	Chapters 7, 8
Copper, including sources of interference; fiber; wireless, including 802.11 (unlicensed, 2.4GHz, 5GHz, 6GHz), cellular (licensed), sources of interference	
3.3. Identify types of endpoint devices.	Chapter 5
Internet of Things (IoT) devices, computers, mobile devices	
3.4. Demonstrate how to set up and check network connectivity on Windows, Linux, Mac, Android, and Apple mobile OS.	Chapters 4, 11
Networking utilities on Windows, Linux, Android, and Apple operating systems; how to run troubleshooting commands; wireless client settings (SSID, authentication, WPA mode)	
4.0 Infrastructure	Chapters 3, 10
4.1. Identify the status lights on a Cisco device when given instruction by an engineer.	Chapter 10
Link light color and status (blinking or solid)	
4.2. Use a network diagram provided by an engineer to attach the appropriate cables.	Chapter 10
Patch cables, switches and routers, small topologies	
4.3. Identify the various ports on network devices.	Chapter 10
Console port, serial port, fiber port, Ethernet ports, SFPs, USB port, PoE	

Exam Topic Area/Topic	Covered in
4.4. Explain basic routing concepts.	Chapter 3
Default gateway, layer 2 vs. layer 3 switches, local network vs. remote network	
4.5. Explain basic switching concepts.	Chapter 3
MAC address tables, MAC address filtering, VLAN (layer 2 network segment)	
5.0 Diagnosing Problems	Chapters 4, 21, 22, 23
5.1. Demonstrate effective troubleshooting methodologies and help desk best practices, including ticketing, documentation, and information gathering.	Chapter 21
Policies and procedures, accurate and complete documentation, prioritization	
5.2. Perform a packet capture with Wireshark and save it to a file.	Chapter 22
Purpose of using a packet analyzer, saving and opening a .pcap file	
5.3. Run basic diagnostic commands and interpret the results.	Chapter 4
ping, ipconfig/ifconfig/ip, tracert/traceroute, nslookup; recognize how firewalls can influence the result	
5.4. Differentiate between different ways to access and collect data about network devices.	Chapter 21
Remote access (RDP, SSH, telnet), VPN, terminal emulators, Console, Network Management Systems, Network Cloud Management (Meraki), scripts	
5.5. Run basic show commands on a Cisco network device.	Chapter 23
show run, show cdp-neighbors, show ip interface brief, show ip route, show version, show inventory, show switch, show mac-address-table, show interface, show interface x, show interface status; privilege levels; command help and auto-complete	
6.0 Security	Chapters 11, 18, 19, 20
6.1. Describe how firewalls operate to filter traffic.	Chapter 20
Firewalls (blocked ports and protocols); rules deny or permit access	
6.2. Describe foundational security concepts.	Chapters 18, 19
Confidentiality, integrity, and availability (CIA); authentication, authorization, and accounting (AAA); Multifactor Authentication (MFA); encryption, certificates, and password complexity; identity stores/databases (Active Directory); threats and vulnerabilities; spam, phishing, malware, and denial of service	

Exam Topic Area/Topic	Covered in
6.3. Configure basic wireless security on a home router (WPAx).	Chapter 11
WPA, WPA2, WPA3; choosing between Personal and Enterprise; wireless security concepts	

Steps to Becoming a Cisco Certified Support Technician (CCST)

The CCST Networking certification demonstrates an individual's skills and knowledge of entry-level networking concepts and topics. The certification demonstrates foundational knowledge and skills needed to show how networks operate, including the devices, media, and protocols that enable network communications. The CCST Networking exam is 50 minutes long and tests your knowledge of: Standards and Concepts, Addressing and Subnet Formats, Endpoints and Media Types, Infrastructure, and Diagnosing Problems.

Signing Up for the Exam

The steps required to sign up for the Cisco Certified Support Technician (CCST) Networking exam:

1. Create a Certiport account at https://www.certiport.com/portal/SSL/Login.aspx.

2. Once you have logged in, make sure that "Test Candidate" from the drop-down menu is selected.

3. Click the **Shop Available Exams** button.

4. Select the **Schedule exam** button under the exam you wish to take.

5. Verify your information and continue throughout the next few screens.

6. On the **Enter payment and billing** page, click the **Add Voucher or Promo Code** button if applicable. Enter the voucher number or promo/discount code in the field below and click the **Apply** button.

7. Continue through the next two screens to finish scheduling your exam.

Facts About the Exam

The CCST Networking exam will be delivered by Certiport and can be administered through Certiport Authorized Testing Centers (CATCs).

The exams will also be available through Certiport's OnVUE platform, their online testing platform, which offers online proctoring for individual candidates.

TIP   Refer to the Cisco Certification site at www.cisco.com/c/en/us/training-events/training-certifications/certifications/entry/ccst/faqs.html for more information regarding this certification.

About the *Cisco Certified Support Technician CCST Networking 100-150 Official Cert Guide*

This book maps directly to the topic areas of the exam and uses a number of features to help you understand the topics and prepare for the exam.

Objectives and Methods

This book uses several key methodologies to help you discover the exam topics on which you need more review, to help you fully understand and remember those details, and to help you prove to yourself that you have retained your knowledge of those topics. This book does not try to help you pass the exam only by memorization; it seeks to help you to truly learn and understand the topics. This book is designed to help you pass the Cisco Certified Support Technician (CCST) Networking exam by using the following methods:

- Helping you discover which exam topics you have not mastered

- Providing explanations and information to fill in your knowledge gaps

- Supplying exercises that enhance your ability to recall and deduce the answers to test questions

- Providing practice exercises on the topics and the testing process via test questions on the companion website

Book Features

To help you customize your study time using this book, the core chapters have several features that help you make the best use of your time:

- **Foundation Topics:** These are the core sections of each chapter. They explain the concepts for the topics in that chapter.

- **Chapter Review:** After the "Foundation Topics" section of each chapter, the "Chapter Review" section lists a series of study activities that you should do at the end of the chapter:

  - **Review All the Key Topics:** The Key Topic icon appears next to the most important items in the "Foundation Topics" section of the chapter. The Review All Key Topics activity lists the key topics from the chapter, along with their page numbers. Although the contents of the entire chapter could be on the exam, you should definitely know the information listed in each key topic, so you should review these.

  - **Key Terms You Should Know:** Although the exam may be unlikely to ask a question such as "Define this term," the exam does require that you learn and know a lot of related terminology. This section lists the most important terms from the chapter, asking you to write a short definition and compare your answer to the glossary at the end of the book.

  - **Concepts and Actions:** Confirm that you understand the content that you just covered by completing the Concepts and Actions exercise, which you can find in the online Appendix B.

- **Web-based practice exam:** The companion website includes the Pearson Cert Practice Test engine that allows you to take practice exam questions. Use it to prepare with a sample exam and to pinpoint topics where you need more study.

How This Book Is Organized

This book contains 23 core chapters—Chapters 1 through 23. Chapter 24 includes preparation tips and suggestions for how to approach the exam, and Chapter 25 is a "living document" that will be updated online should any of the certification coverage and parameters change. Each core chapter covers a subset of the topics on the Cisco Certified Support Technician (CCST) Networking exam. The core chapters map to the Cisco Certified Support Technician (CCST) Networking exam topic areas and cover the concepts and technologies that you will encounter on the exam (see the table in "The Exam Topics" section for coverage of each topic by chapter).

The Companion Website for Online Content Review

All the electronic review elements, as well as other electronic components of the book, exist on this book's companion website.

To access the companion website, which gives you access to the electronic content with this book, start by establishing a login at ciscopress.com and register your book.

To do so, simply go to ciscopress.com/register and enter the ISBN of the print book: 9780138213428. After you have registered your book, go to your account page and click the Registered Products tab. From there, click the Access Bonus Content link to get access to the book's companion website.

Note that if you buy the Premium Edition eBook and Practice Test version of this book from Cisco Press, your book will automatically be registered on your account page. Simply go to your account page, click the Registered Products tab, and select Access Bonus Content to access the book's companion website.

Please note that many of our companion content files can be very large, especially image and video files.

How to Access the Pearson Test Prep (PTP) App

You have two options for installing and using the Pearson Test Prep application: a web app and a desktop app. To use the Pearson Test Prep application, start by finding the registration code that comes with the book. You can find the code in these ways:

- **Print book:** You can get your access code by registering the print ISBN (9780138213428) on ciscopress.com/register. Make sure to use the print book ISBN regardless of whether you purchased an eBook or the print book. Once you register the book, your access code will be populated on your account page under the Registered Products tab. Instructions for how to redeem the code are available on the book's companion website by clicking the Access Bonus Content link.

- **Premium Edition:** If you purchase the Premium Edition eBook and Practice Test directly from the Cisco Press website, the code will be populated on your account page after purchase. Just log in at ciscopress.com, click Account to see details of your account, and click the digital purchases tab.

NOTE   After you register your book, your code can always be found in your account under the Registered Products tab.

Once you have the access code, to find instructions about both the PTP web app and the desktop app, follow these steps:

Step 1.   Open this book's companion website, as shown earlier in this Introduction under the heading "The Companion Website for Online Content Review."

Step 2.   Click the **Practice Exams** button.

Step 3.   Follow the instructions listed there both for installing the desktop app and for using the web app.

Note that if you want to use the web app only at this point, just navigate to pearsontestprep.com, log in using the same credentials used to register your book or purchase the Premium Edition, and register this book's practice tests using the registration code you just found. The process should take only a couple of minutes.

Customizing Your Exams

Once you are in the exam settings screen, you can choose to take exams in one of three modes:

- **Study mode:** Allows you to fully customize your exams and review answers as you are taking the exam. This is typically the mode you would use first to assess your knowledge and identify information gaps.

- **Practice Exam mode:** Locks certain customization options, as it is presenting a realistic exam experience. Use this mode when you are preparing to test your exam readiness.

- **Flash Card mode:** Strips out the answers and presents you with only the question stem. This mode is great for late-stage preparation when you really want to challenge yourself to provide answers without the benefit of seeing multiple-choice options. This mode does not provide the detailed score reports that the other two modes do, so you should not use it if you are trying to identify knowledge gaps.

In addition to these three modes, you will be able to select the source of your questions. You can choose to take exams that cover all of the chapters, or you can narrow your selection to just a single chapter or the chapters that make up specific parts in the book. All chapters are selected by default. If you want to narrow your focus to individual chapters, simply deselect all the chapters and then select only those on which you wish to focus in the Objectives area.

You can also select the exam banks on which to focus. Each exam bank comes complete with a full exam of questions that cover topics in every chapter. The two exams printed in the book are available to you as well as two additional exams of unique questions. You can have the test engine serve up exams from all four banks or just from one individual bank by selecting the desired banks in the exam bank area.

There are several other customizations you can make to your exam from the exam settings screen, such as the time of the exam, the number of questions served up, whether to randomize questions and answers, whether to show the number of correct answers for multiple-answer questions, and whether to serve up only specific types of questions. You can also create custom test banks by selecting only questions that you have marked or questions on which you have added notes.

Updating Your Exams

If you are using the online version of the Pearson Test Prep software, you should always have access to the latest version of the software as well as the exam data. If you are using the Windows desktop version, every time you launch the software while connected to the Internet, it checks if there are any updates to your exam data and automatically downloads any changes that were made since the last time you used the software.

Sometimes, due to many factors, the exam data may not fully download when you activate your exam. If you find that figures or exhibits are missing, you may need to manually update your exams. To update a particular exam you have already activated and downloaded, simply click the **Tools** tab and click the **Update Products** button. Again, this is only an issue with the desktop Windows application.

If you wish to check for updates to the Pearson Test Prep exam engine software, Windows desktop version, simply click the **Tools** tab and click the **Update Application** button. This ensures that you are running the latest version of the software engine.

Figure Credits

Figure 7-7: Courtesy of Russ White

Figure 7-13A: Alehdats/123RF

Figure 7-13B: Artush/123RF

Figure 7-15A: Evgeny Martynov/Shutterstock

Figure 7-15B: https://en.wikipedia.org/wiki/XFP_transceiver

Figure 10-1: Arjuna Kodisinghe/Shutterstock

Figure 10-9A: Wavebreakmedia/Shutterstock

Figure 10-9B: White78/Shutterstock

Figure 10-10: Hxdyl/123RF

Figure 11-4: Flegere/Shutterstock

Figure 11-6: John Crowe/Alamy

Figure 12-2: Courtesy of Russ White

Figure 12-4: ©TeleGeography

Figure 13-4: 2009fotofriends/Shutterstock

Part I

Foundations

Computer networks are almost magical: you send an image from this device, and it appears on some other device almost instantly, even when there is no apparent physical connection between the two devices. The reality is far more commonplace that it appears from the outside.

Thinking About Moving Packets

There is, in fact, a direct physical connection between all the devices on planet Earth (and network-connected devices in space!) over which signals are carried between devices, no matter how remote. The magic has, as it turns out, a physical connectivity infrastructure just as real as roads.

This book begins the process of untangling the magic behind computer networking, from the physical through the logical.

Because shipping packages is similar to shipping packets—an idea suggested by Rick Graziani—the first chapter begins by describing transporting packets as if they were physical packages.

Just like a shipping network, however, a computer network does not end with physical connections, whether optical, copper, or radio transmissions through the air. It takes a lot of information to transfer stuff from one place to another. For the shipping network, the information required to get a package from one place to another is cleanly separated from the package itself.

Before we can dive into computer networking proper, however, there are a few topics worth mentioning—words, thinking, and change.

Thinking About Words

Computer networks are messier than the physical supply chain. In computer networks, the packages being shipped are, themselves, made of information. This makes the words we use to talk about computer networks difficult; marketing often takes over where technology ends, leaving us with multiple, overlapping meanings attached to a single word.

These overlapping meanings often makes it hard to talk to one another clearly. The first part of almost every technical discussion will be spent clarifying what words mean.

This book will try to avoid the mess of terminology by adopting *technical terms*. A technical term is not one that is technical, but rather a word for which a single meaning, out of the total range of possible meanings, has been chosen as "the" meaning. Each time you see the word *switch*, for instance, throughout this book, it will have a single, definite meaning.

This approach makes it easier for me, the author, to communicate clearly to you, the reader—but the real world does not work this way. In the real world, once you are outside this book, you will need to remember that words in computer networking—even simple ones—might have a range of meanings.

It's important to be sensitive to this reality.

Each time a word is defined in the text, two definitions will be given. The first will be the single (technical) meaning used throughout this book. A second part of the definition will describe a range of definitions used within the world of computer networking.

Thinking About How to Think

As you dive into this book, working toward this certification in computer networking, it's important to know how to think about computer networks. Learning two basic concepts will help you on your journey toward understanding networks.

Abstraction is a way of dealing with complexity. As a way of thinking, abstractions group things in some way—because they are alike, different, chronologically ordered, or something else. No one says, "I'll meet you out in the area with thousands of grass blades, many kinds of flowers, and trees along the edges." Everyone says, "I'll meet you at the field."

Engineers must be able to see groups of things as abstractions, and then to break groups of things apart into their components—mentally—to deal with complexity.

The *problem and solution mindset* is the second critical thinking skill engineers must have. Quickly finding the problem, understanding the kind of problem it is, knowing the broad set of solutions available for the problem, and then being able to pinpoint the best solution for the problem—these things are the hallmark of good engineering.

Thinking About Change

Technology is always changing. Networking technologies are not an exception.

In some ways, change is good. There is always something interesting or exciting going on the world of technology. There are new inventions, new ideas, and new ways of doing things. Things are always getting faster, more efficient, or easier.

On the other hand, constant change is bad. After a while, change itself becomes monotonous and boring. It's hard to find a foothold on a constantly pitching deck.

One way of countering the constant movement is to separate the fundamentals—the problems and solutions, the ways of thinking—from their implementations in the real world. This book will give you the foundations you need to understand the basics, and to ask the right questions to build on those basics, achieving excellence as a network engineer.

Laying the Foundation

Computer networks are as vital to the modern world as any other kind of network—the transportation system, the supply chain, and the organization.

Let's begin by looking at the basic problems a computer network must solve to transport data between two devices: packaging things for shipment and finding the path to reach the destination.

The chapters in this part of the book are as follows:

Chapter 1: Shipping Things

Chapter 2: Addresses

Chapter 3: Routing and Switching

Chapter 4: Wired Host Networking Configuration

Chapter 5: What's in a Network?

Chapter 6: Network Models

Shipping Things

This chapter covers the following exam topics:

1. **Standards and Concepts**

   1.1 **Identify the fundamental building blocks of networks.**

   TCP/IP model, OSI model, frames and packets, addressing

   1.5 **Describe common network applications and protocols.**

   TCP vs. UDP (connection-oriented vs. connectionless), FTP, SFTP, TFTP, HTTP, HTTPS, DHCP, DNS, ICMP, NTP

Let's say you have something to ship to a friend—a necklace, a book (like this one), a poster, or a dog. Okay, maybe you don't want to ship a dog, but the process is the same for just about everything else. You

1. Put the item in a box.
2. Seal the box.
3. Put an address on the box.
4. Take the box to a shipper (the post office, a commercial shipper, etc.).

Shipping an item is a simple process from the outside, but simple and easy are not the same thing. Packages are delayed, damaged, and lost; someone must figure out how to track each package. Each address must be at least somewhat unique, and someone must know how to relate a person to a location. Someone must figure out how to move the package along well-known routes and what kind of transportation to use (boat, train, truck, airplane, or bicycle?).

And all these things must happen at a hard-to-imagine scale. Millions of packages must be sealed, addressed, shipped, and received daily.

Because the physical process of packaging data to carry it through a network is similar enough to shipping a physical item halfway across the world, it is helpful to start with material things.

"Do I Know This Already?" Quiz

Take the quiz (either here or use the PTP software) if you want to use the score to help you decide how much time to spend on this chapter. Appendix A, "Answers to the 'Do I Know This Already?' Quizzes," found at the end of the book, includes both the answers and explanations. You can also find answers in the PTP testing software.

Table 1-1 "Do I Know This Already?" Foundation Topics Section-to-Question Mapping

Section	Questions
The Purpose of Packaging	1, 2
Addressing	3, 4, 5
Packaging Data	6, 7, 8
Tunnels	9

CAUTION   The goal of self-assessment is to gauge your mastery of the topics in this chapter. If you do not know the answer to a question or are only partially sure of the answer, you should mark that question as wrong for purposes of the self-assessment. Giving yourself credit for an answer you incorrectly guess skews your self-assessment results and might provide you with a false sense of security.

1. What is packaging a piece of data called to add an address and other metadata?

   a. Packet

   b. Encapsulation

   c. Labeling

   d. Packaging

2. What is metadata?

   a. Virtual data; used in computer networks to describe a virtual interface

   b. Information about Information; used in computer networking to describe the source, destination, and other information about a frame, packet, or segment

   c. Tunnel data; used in computer networks to describe the path a packet should take through the network

   d. Data that does not exist

3. What is a physical address?

   a. An address identifying a single physical interface

   b. An address identifying a single logical interface

   c. An address identifying a single host or device

   d. An address identifying a single application

4. What is an interface address?

   a. An address identifying a single physical interface

   b. An address identifying a single logical interface

   c. An address identifying a single host or device

   d. An address identifying a single application

5. What is a port?

   a. An address identifying a single physical interface

   b. An address identifying a single logical interface

   c. An address identifying a single host or device

   d. An address identifying a single application

6. What is a frame?
   a. Data packaged to be moved from one host to another
   b. Data packaged to be moved from one application to another
   c. Data packaged to be moved from one physical interface to another
   d. Data packaged to be moved from one application to a physical interface

7. What is a packet?
   a. Data packaged to be moved from one host to another
   b. Data packaged to be moved from one application to another
   c. Data packaged to be moved from one physical interface to another
   d. Data packaged to be moved from a host to a physical interface

8. What is a segment?
   a. Data packaged to be moved from one host to another
   b. Data packaged to be moved from one application to another
   c. Data packaged to be moved from one physical interface to another
   d. Data packaged to be moved from a host to an application

9. What does a tunnel hide in a computer network?
   a. The contents of the packet
   b. The source and destination physical interfaces
   c. The original destination addresses
   d. The original packet's protocol

Foundation Topics

The Purpose of Packaging

Packaging is the first step in shipping. Let's look at packaging in the physical world and then consider how packaging in networking is similar and different.

The Physical World

Most people package things to protect them during shipment. We usually place an item in at least two packages—the commercial packaging, which tells us about the item, and an outer package protecting the inner packaging and the item itself.

Packaging, however, is not limited to protecting things.

A second purpose for packaging is to hide what we're shipping. When you ship a present to a friend, you will place the commercial packaging inside another box, then wrap the box so your friend cannot see what's inside until they rip the wrapping off. This wrapped package is placed inside a shipping box—so we now have three layers of packaging.

Packages might also be placed inside packages to keep related items together. If you buy a computer, it is likely to come in one large box. When you open the large box, you find separate boxes for the keyboard, processing unit, etc.

Finally, packages are placed inside other packages to make them easier to handle. Putting them all on a pallet is easier if you have several hundred packages to load into a container (for transport via ship, truck, or train). Moving one pallet is easier than moving a hundred separate boxes.

Figure 1-1 illustrates these layers of packaging.

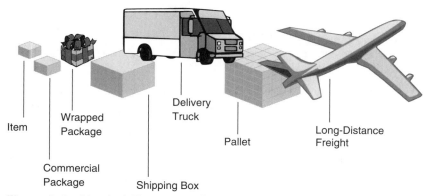

Figure 1-1   *Physical Shipping Packages*

In Figure 1-1:

1. The manufacturer wraps the item in commercial packaging.
2. The shipper wraps the commercial packaging in gift wrap.
3. The shipper wraps the gift-wrapped package in a shipping box.
4. A driver picks up the shipping box and delivers it to a warehouse or shipping facility.
5. The shipping company adds the shipping box to a pallet with other shipping boxes addressed to recipients in the same geographic area.
6. The shipping company places the pallet on a flight, train, ship, or other transport.

Each container is broken down at the other end until the recipient gets to the item.

Computer Networks

We tend to think of networks as being somehow "not connected to the real world." We put a picture in over here, and it pops out over there—but data is still physical. Pictures are encoded in physical signals of some kind, the physical bits need to be moved to the receiver, and the receiver needs to display the image based on the bits received.

We use different words to describe the packaging. Figure 1-2 illustrates the transmission process for computer networks.

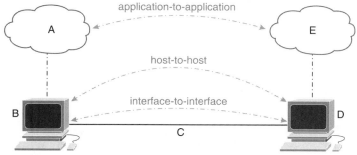

Figure 1-2   *Packaging in Computer Networks*

As you do when shipping physical packages, you start with something to send—in this case, data. Application *A* wants to send data to application *E*. To do this, it puts the data in a package, or *encapsulates* it, and hands it off to the host, *B*.

Host *B* then puts the data into a second package and hands it off to a local network interface. The local interface then puts the data into a third package and transmits it across the physical link *C* toward the interface on host *D*.

Once the interface on host *D* receives the data, it removes the outer package and hands off the inner package to the host (or the software within the host—the operating system). The host software then removes the outer package (once again) and sends the innermost package to application *E*.

Application *E* then removes the innermost package and uses the data.

The words used in this process are not the same as physical shipping; let's go through a few.

Encapsulating is putting data inside a new package. When you take an existing data package and put it into another package—a larger box, in other words—you are encapsulating it. The box the data is put into is called **encapsulation**.

Much like there are commercial packaging, shipping boxes, and pallets in physical shipping, each encapsulation has a name in computer networking:

- A **frame** is data encapsulated with the information needed to move from one physical interface to another physical interface.

- A **packet** is data encapsulated with the information needed to move from host to host.

- A **segment** is data encapsulated with the information needed to move from application to application. A segment may also be called a *datagram*.

Sometimes you have several related items to send that will not fit into a single box. You can send them as a set of shipments, each somehow marked, so they are received and "processed" in the same order. In computer networking, applications often send information this way: an image or song will not fit into a single packet. It might take tens of thousands of packets to send a single piece of information or a set of interrelated pieces of information.

Some protocols allow two applications to form a *session* to transfer information in *streams*, which supports breaking large pieces of data into smaller chunks for transmission or even collecting related information into a single group. Part III of this book, "Services," will consider the idea of a transport service that carries data streams in more detail.

Looking at Figure 1-2, you might notice what looks like layers—the applications communicate to one another across the top, the hosts communicate to one another in the middle, and the interfaces communicate to one another along the bottom. These are called just that—*layers*—in a computer network.

These layers are the basis for models of computer network operation. Chapter 6, "Network Models," will consider models more fully.

NOTE   While *frame* is rarely substituted for *packet*, *packet* is often substituted for *frame* or *segment*. Engineers often call data moving through the network packets regardless of the encapsulation or layer.

Addressing

Packaging also gives us a place to put the origin and destination addresses. The address tells the shipper *to whom* and *where* a package should be delivered.

The Physical World

It's not so obvious the address on a package might change over the shipping process; Figure 1-3 illustrates.

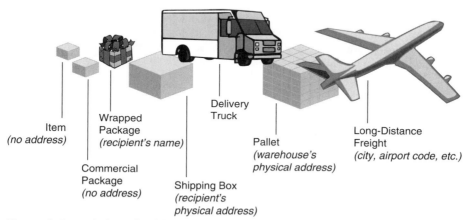

Item
(no address)

Wrapped
Package
(recipient's name)

Commercial
Package
(no address)

Shipping Box
*(recipient's
physical address)*

Delivery
Truck

Pallet
*(warehouse's
physical address)*

Long-Distance
Freight
(city, airport code, etc.)

Figure 1-3   *Labels and Addresses Through the Shipping Process*

The item itself does not have an address. Because it is used by whoever happens to own or have physical possession of it, there is no real need for an address here (although you sometimes see people put their names on toys, serving dishes, and other items). The commercial package, likewise, does not have an address.

The wrapped gift, however, will normally have a name or some form of identification. It's long been a tradition in our house to wrap Christmas presents so each person has their own "wrapping paper," which eliminates the need for tags.

However, this use of wrapping paper as an identifier is a good example of the importance of context when reading an address. There isn't any need for any address other than a name when the package is destined for someone in the same house.

The context of an address is its *scope*—the range in which the address makes sense without any other information. The scope of a gift tag is within a single household, office, or other small groups of people.

Once the package has been placed in a shipping box, the recipient's physical address is attached to the outside in some way. The recipient's address is not always clear-cut; the address may include a "care of" indicating a business or caretaker.

When we move from the gift tag to the shipping label, the scope of the address changes. The scope contains a lot more possible people and locations. Because of this, the label must have a lot more information.

The scope changes once again when the shipping box is combined with many other boxes and placed on a pallet. The shipping company will address the pallet to a warehouse or shipping facility. Again, this address represents a physical location within the shipping network.

Finally, the entire airplane itself acts as a shipping container. The destination, in this case, is not on the airplane but rather in the flight plan, and the destination is a city or airport.

Moving from the gift tag to the shipping box increased the scope *and* the amount of information on the label simultaneously. More information is needed because the package no longer has the context of a small group of people.

Moving from the shipping label to the pallet label, however, *reduces* the information on the label. Why is this?

Because the person moving the pallet around does not want (or need) to know the shipping address of every box on the pallet. Knowing the destination address of every box on the pallet would be confusing rather than helpful. Forcing the person moving the pallet to read all those addresses would also waste time and energy, so it would be inefficient.

Addressing the pallet to a shipping facility rather than the destination of every box on the pallet is a form of *abstraction*; just the name of the city represents all the addresses within a city, a postal code, an airport code, or the location of a shipping warehouse. Abstraction is one of the most important concepts in network engineering.

Computer Networks

Data moving through a network also has a hierarchy of labels, much like physical shipping; Figure 1-4 illustrates.

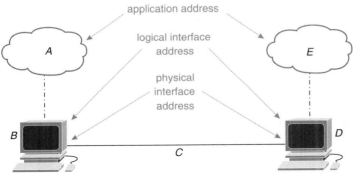

Figure 1-4 *Host Addresses*

For historical reasons, the names of the different addresses used in computer networks often overlap.

A **physical interface address** was originally tied to an individual, physical computer interface.

As computers became more powerful and new applications developed, the direct relationship between physical interface addresses and physical interfaces ended.

First, *virtual* interfaces, which *emulate* physical interfaces, were invented. Virtual interfaces are like a pen or stage name; a single (physical) person has multiple identities, each of which is "used" in a different situation, and each of which can have a different "personality." Aliases and multiple usernames across social media and gaming sites are another instance of the same kind of thing. A single person represents themselves using multiple identities, each of which might have slightly different characteristics.

A virtual interface may also be called a *logical* or *software* interface. While these three have slightly different meanings, in this book, all three will be called an interface or virtual interface.

Second, a single physical interface may also have multiple physical addresses—like an apartment building with multiple physical addresses within the same physical space or multiple businesses with offices in the same building.

Physical interface addresses are

- Often shortened to **physical address**.

- Called *Media Access Control (MAC)* addresses. The Institute of Electrical and Electronics Engineers (IEEE) uses this term to describe the address of an interface that controls access to a physical transmission medium, such as a copper, optical, or wireless link. Part II of this book discusses physical links in more detail.

- Called the *Layer 2 address*. The name "Layer 2" is taken from the second layer of the Open Systems Interconnection (OSI) model. Chapter 6 will consider the OSI model in more detail; for now, note the *Layer 2 address* is the address of a physical or virtual interface.

NOTE   I use the term *physical address* throughout this book to refer to these kinds of addresses.

The **logical interface address** was originally tied to a logical interface. The *network stack* or *network software*, which is part of the host's operating system, manages this logical interface.

As with the physical address, the meaning and use of the logical interface address have expanded and changed. Logical interface addresses can identify a virtual interface, and a single interface may have multiple addresses (in fact, most logical interfaces have multiple addresses).

Logical interface addresses are

- Often shortened to **interface address**.

- Called a *host address*. Some networking technologies identify an entire host with a single address (often called an *identifier*), and some devices have only a single interface.

- Called an *Internet Protocol (IP)* address. In most networks, the logical interface address will be an Internet Protocol (IP) address of some type, so this address is also called the *IP address*. There are many other kinds of logical interface addresses than IP.

- Called a *Layer 3 address* because these addresses are at the third layer of the OSI model. Chapter 6 describes the OSI model in detail.

- Because the third layer of the OSI model is called the *network layer*, these addresses are also sometimes called *network addresses*. The term *network address* has a different meaning, described in a later chapter—terms in networking often have multiple meanings, which can be confusing.

> **NOTE** A logical interface address is called an *interface address* or *IP address* throughout this book.

Applications have addresses too—addresses that only make sense within the context of an individual host. These addresses are called **ports**, **sockets**, or sometimes *service identifiers*. From the network's perspective, the application is represented as a port or service identifier. The application is represented as a socket from the perspective of the software running on the host.

> **NOTE** Applications running on individual hosts are identified using *ports* throughout this book.

Table 1-2 provides a quick reference to all the different names of addresses and how they are related.

Table 1-2 Addresses

Name	Description	Alternate Names
Physical address	A media access address associated with a physical or virtual computer interface	Layer 2 address MAC address
Interface address	An address associated with a logical software interface	Layer 3 address Logical interface address Host address IP address System ID or NET
Port	A communication channel to an application running on a host	Socket

Hosts and Devices

Before we move more deeply into packaging, it is worth mentioning two other words used in computer networking with overlapping meanings: *host* and *device*.

When computers were large enough to be shared resources, the *host* "hosted," or ran, software, while the *terminal* allowed users to access the computer. *Devices*, on the other hand, were things like printers and keyboards. When desktop computers (called *microcomputers* at the time) became commonplace, they were called hosts for the same reason: they hosted (ran) software applications.

Embedding computers in more (and smaller) devices blurs the line between the host and device. No clear line between the two kinds of devices any longer exists.

I will use the term *host* throughout this book to describe what most people consider a standard computer, like a desktop or laptop. *Device* describes anything connected to a network, like printers, tablets, doorbells, and toasters.

Packaging Data

Physical packaging is intuitive; cardboard boxes, plastic bags, bubble bags, envelopes, pallets, and crates are all common. What about data? You cannot put a digital image in a cardboard box and push it through a copper wire, so how do you package data?

What does encapsulation do in a computer network, and what does it look like?

Encapsulation is putting a *header* in front of the data describing

- The source of the data, the *source address*
- The destination, the *destination address*
- The service this data needs to be passed to when it reaches its destination to be processed
- Any other information needed for the network to forward the data from the source to the destination

Information about the packet is always added to the front of the packet, so it is carried in a *packet header*. A new header is added with the correct information to encapsulate a packet, as shown in Figure 1-5.

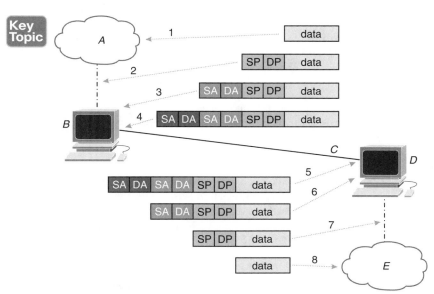

Figure 1-5 *Encapsulation Process*

Each step in the process is shown as a number on the illustration:

1. Application *A* creates some data it would like to send to application *E*. The data might be an image, text message, emoji, or any kind of digital data.
2. Application *A* encapsulates the data in a header containing (at least) source and destination ports (*SP* and *DP* in the illustration).

3. Host *B*'s network stack will determine the correct interface address to send the data. Host *B*'s network stack will determine the correct destination is an interface address on host *D* and add a new header on the packet with the correct source and destination addresses (SA and DA in the illustration). Host *B* will also add a *protocol number* indicating which process on host *D* should process the information. The protocol number is just like a socket, but it is an address for a network stack rather than an application.

4. Host *B*'s network stack will send the newly encapsulated data to the physical interface through which host *D* can be reached. The physical interface will add another header containing host *B*'s physical address as the source and host *D*'s address as the destination (SA and DA in the illustration). At this point, the data is contained inside a packet, which is then contained inside a frame.

5. When host *D* receives the frame, the physical interface software will recognize "this frame is for me" by examining the outermost header's destination address. After determining whether it should process the packet, host *D*'s physical interface software will use information in the outer header to determine which process should process the information contained in the frame using the *protocol number*. Once the physical interface software at host *D* determines where it should send the packet on the local host, it strips the outer header, *de-encapsulating* the frame.

6. The network stack at host *D* receives the packet and uses the socket number to determine which application running on the local host should receive this information. Once it has determined the correct application, the network stack strips the outer header, de-encapsulating the packet, and leaving just the application's header on the data.

7. Application *E* receives the packet, examines the remaining header for useful information, then strips this final header and processes the data.

One additional encapsulation layer—the transport protocol—has been left out of this description for clarity (step 8 in Figure 1-5). Chapter 14, "Network Transport," examines transport protocols in more detail.

What Is a Protocol?

If you were to meet the queen or president of some country, you would need to follow a **protocol**—when to speak, when to bow, when to curtsy, when to leave, etc. When you read a book, you read from left to right in some languages and from right to left in others. You introduce yourself when you attend a gathering the first time, such as a church or bingo game.

All of these are *protocols*.

A protocol is nothing more than a way of doing things. Communications protocols have a dictionary—what symbols mean—and a grammar—the proper ordering of elements like nouns and verbs, or even the way the context of a symbol changes its meaning.

Computers are communication networks, so they have protocols. Network protocols, for instance, determine how 0s and 1s translate into numbers, letters, and actions.

All the protocols in computer networks fall into one of two categories—*transport* and *routing*—both of which are covered in more detail later in this book.

NOTE *Transport* protocols are also sometimes called *routed* protocols, which should not be confused with a *routing protocol*. This book uses the term *transport protocol* rather than *routed protocol*, because not all transport protocols are routed, and routable transport protocols are not always routed.

What Is Metadata?

Data is straightforward: it is just knowledge about something. For instance, if you know someone's favorite color, music group, or car, you have data about them.

Metadata is just as easy to define: *metadata is data about data (or information about information).*

Defining something is not the same thing as making sense of (or understanding) it. Perhaps a real-world example will help.

The batting average of a baseball team and the scoring average of a football team are both data—information about the team. The *trend* of the batting and scoring averages can be considered metadata. While the trend is information about the team, it is also about the batting and scoring averages. In many situations, classifying a piece of information as either data or metadata is a matter of perspective.

The difference between data and metadata is more apparent in building packets to carry through a computer network.

An address is data when used to describe an interface or host.

An address is metadata when used to describe where a piece of data needs to be delivered. The delivery address is something you know about the data; hence, it is metadata.

Tunnels

Tunnels are one of the most challenging concepts to understand in computer networks because there are few real-world examples and because so many things seem to be tunnels—but they are not.

The word *tunnel* evokes a tunnel through a mountain or under a body of water—like the Lincoln Tunnel crossing under the Hudson River between New Jersey and New York. Tunnels in computer networks do not go under something else; instead, they usually go *over* something else.

The sense we can bring from real-world tunnels to a computer network is they *hide* things. If you are sitting on a boat on the Hudson River directly above the Lincoln Tunnel, you would not have any idea there are hundreds of people driving along under you.

In the same way, a computer network tunnel hides packets being carried through the network from the underlying network by encapsulating it. Specifically, a tunnel hides the original source and destination from the network over which the tunnel passes.

Another way of understanding a tunnel is through the *head-end* and *tail-end*. The head-end of a tunnel is where the encapsulation is added, and the tail-end is where the encapsulation is removed.

This description makes it sound as though the encapsulation of a packet into a frame is a form of tunneling, though, and it is not. Why not? Because tunnels go *over* in a network rather than *under*. Physical interfaces are logically *under* logical interfaces; encapsulating packets into frames so one physical interface can transmit the data to another physical interface is *under*.

Figure 1-6 illustrates tunneling.

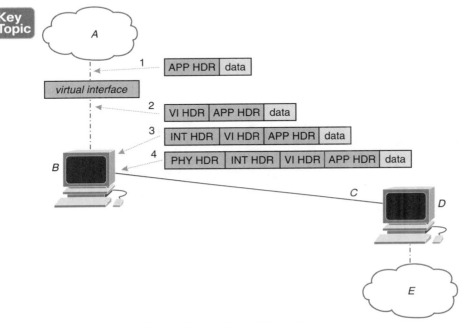

Figure 1-6   *A High-Level Overview of Tunneling*

In Figure 1-6,

1.   The application, *A*, encapsulates some data (*APP* HDR in the illustration) and sends it to a local interface.

2.   The interface application *A* sends the data to is virtual. From application *A*'s perspective, there is no difference between the physical and virtual interfaces. The virtual interface processes the packet the same way any other interface would, encapsulating the packet into a new header (*VI HDR* in the illustration). This VI HDR hides the original destination from lower layers by adding a second set of addresses to the packet.

3.   Host *B*'s network stack treats this packet like any other, processing it and sending it to the destination address provided in the outermost header. In this case, the outermost address will be a tunnel endpoint rather than host *D*'s interface address.

4.   Host *B*'s physical interface software will (finally) encapsulate the packet with a header containing host *D*'s physical address.

The critical point here is not the kind of header used by the virtual interface to encapsulate the packet but rather the *destination address*. If the destination address is a type of interface that would normally be *below* the virtual interface, and the destination must de-encapsulate the packet before discovering its "true destination," the packet is being tunneled.

Later chapters will discuss tunneling in more detail. The critical point to remember here is the protocol used is not what determines whether a packet is tunneled. The destination of the packet and whether the final destination is being hidden from underlying network elements determine whether a packet is being tunneled.

Chapter Review

This chapter used physical world examples to explain the importance and uses of packaging—or *encapsulation*—and addressing in computer networks. You should also have learned about what a protocol is, what metadata is, and what a tunnel is.

One point to remember: addresses in computer networks can refer to many things, including a physical interface, a logical interface, a host (device), or even an application. Clearly differentiating these different kinds of addresses will help you lay a solid foundation for understanding computer networks.

Now that you understand the purpose of addresses, the next chapter will discuss how to work with addresses in computer networks.

One key to doing well on the exams is to perform repetitive spaced review sessions. Review this chapter's material using either the tools in the book or interactive tools for the same material found on the book's companion website. Refer to the online Appendix D, "Study Planner," element for more details. Table 1-3 outlines the key review elements and where you can find them. To better track your study progress, record when you completed these activities in the second column.

Table 1-3   Chapter Review Tracking

Review Element	Review Date (s)	Resource Used
Review key topics		Book, website
Review key terms		Book, website
Repeat DIKTA questions		Book, PTP
Review concepts and actions		Book, website

Review All the Key Topics

Table 1-4 lists the key topics for this chapter.

Table 1-4   Key Topics for Chapter 1

Key Topic Element	Description	Page Number
Paragraph	Encapsulating and encapsulation	10
List	Distinction between a frame, packet, and segment	10
Paragraph	Sessions and streams	10
Paragraph	Physical interface addresses	12
Paragraph	Virtual interfaces	12

Key Topic Element	Description	Page Number
Paragraph	Logical interface addresses	13
Paragraph	Application addresses: ports, sockets, service identifiers	14
Figure 1-5	Encapsulation process	15
Paragraph	Protocol definition	16
Paragraph	Metadata definition	17
Paragraph	Computer network tunnel definition	17
Figure 1-6	Tunneling process	18

Key Terms You Should Know

Key terms in this chapter include

encapsulation, frame, packet, segment, physical interface address, physical address, logical interface address, interface address, port, socket, protocol, metadata, tunnel

Concepts and Actions

Review the concepts considered in this chapter using Table 1-5. You can cover the right side of this table and describe each concept or action in your own words to verify your understanding.

Table 1-5 Concepts and Actions

Encapsulate	Adding a header to data to carry metadata such as the source and destination addresses
Frame	Data encapsulated to be carried from interface to interface
Packet	Data encapsulated to be carried from host to host
Segment	Data encapsulated to be carried from application to application
Address context	The scope in which the address uniquely describes a receiver or set of receivers
Physical interface	A physical point of connection where electrical or optical signals are converted to and from data
Virtual interface	A logical point of connection that acts like a physical interface; no physical hardware is associated with a virtual interface
Media Access Control	Official IEEE name for a physical interface address
Logical interface	A higher-layer interface defined in software and related to a physical or virtual interface
Port	The address of an individual application running on a host
Host	A device that can host or run applications
Header contents	At a minimum, the source address, destination address, and some way to indicate a service

Protocol	A way of doing things that enables communications
Metadata	Data about a collection of data
Tunnel	Hiding packet contents and headers from intermediate devices by adding a layer of encapsulation
Head-end	Where packets are encapsulated to be carried through a tunnel
Tail-end	Where packets are de-encapsulated and removed from a tunnel

1

CHAPTER 2

Addresses

This chapter covers the following exam topics:

    2. Addressing and Subnet Formats

        2.1 Compare and contrast private addresses and public addresses.

            Each IP address must be unique on the network

        2.2 Identify IPv4 addresses and subnet formats.

            Subnet concepts, Subnet Calculator, slash notation, and subnet mask; broadcasts do not go outside the subnet

        2.3 Identify IPv6 addresses and prefix formats.

            Types of addresses, prefix concepts

The overview of shipping in the previous chapter assumed at least an addressing scheme and a physical transport system. Later chapters will look at the physical infrastructure of networking; this chapter focuses on addresses.

There are four kinds of addresses you will normally encounter in networking:

- Physical or Media Access Control (MAC) addresses

- Internet Protocol version 4 (IPv4) addresses

- Internet Protocol version 6 (IPv6) addresses

- Port numbers

This chapter begins by considering the two dimensions of an address's scope and then discusses each kind of address in a separate section.

"Do I Know This Already?" Quiz

Take the quiz (either here or use the PTP software) if you want to use the score to help you decide how much time to spend on this chapter. Appendix A, "Answers to the 'Do I Know This Already?' Quizzes," found at the end of the book, includes both the answers and explanations. You can also find answers in the PTP testing software.

Table 2-1   "Do I Know This Already?" Foundation Topics Section-to-Question Mapping

Section	Questions
Address Scope	1, 2
Internet Protocol version 4	3, 4
Why Two Addresses?	5

Section	Questions
Internet Protocol version 6	6
Network Prefixes	7
Ports and Sockets	8
Network Address Translation	9

CAUTION The goal of self-assessment is to gauge your mastery of the topics in this chapter. If you do not know the answer to a question or are only partially sure of the answer, you should mark that question as wrong for purposes of the self-assessment. Giving yourself credit for an answer you incorrectly guess skews your self-assessment results and might provide you with a false sense of security.

1. What does the scope of an address refer to? (Choose two.)
   a. The physical distance the packet may travel before being discarded
   b. The host or set of hosts that should receive the packet
   c. The parts of the network topology where the packet should be sent
   d. The number of devices that may receive and process the packet
2. Broadcast, unicast, and anycast packets should be transmitted to which of the following?
   a. Every host in the world, a single host, the closest instance of a service
   b. Every host in a broadcast domain, a single host, the closest instance of a service
   c. Every host in a broadcast domain, a group of hosts, the closest instance of a service
   d. Every host in a broadcast domain, a single hose, the closest host
3. What is the size and format of IPv4 addresses?
   a. 32 bits, written as four decimal numbers
   b. 64 bits, written as four hexadecimal numbers
   c. 48 bits, written in groups of hexadecimal numbers
   d. 128 bits, written in groups of hexadecimal numbers
4. The prefix of an IP address refers to which of the following?
   a. The last part of the address
   b. The first part of the address
   c. A number placed before the address to indicate the service
   d. The part of the IP address that differentiates subnets from one another
5. What does an IP address represent? (Choose two.)
   a. An application
   b. A logical interface
   c. A physical interface
   d. A host
   e. A group of hosts or networks

6. What is the size and format of an IPv6 address?

    a. 32 bits, written as four decimal numbers

    b. 64 bits, written as four hexadecimal numbers

    c. 48 bits, written in groups of hexadecimal numbers

    d. 128 bits, written in groups of hexadecimal numbers

7. What is publicly routable IP address space?

    a. Addresses that can be used by any network

    b. Well-known addresses

    c. Addresses that can be routed on the global Internet

    d. Addresses used by public entities, like governments

8. What is a well-known port?

    a. A physical port on a host or network device that is easy to identify

    b. Port assigned through standardization to an individual application

    c. The most commonly used port on a network device

    d. The primary service port through which a host is connected

9. What do most Network Address Translation implementations modify?

    a. The source address

    b. The destination address

    c. The source address and source port number

    d. The destination address and destination port number

Foundation Topics

Address Scope

An address has two different kinds of *scope*:

- Who should receive and process the packet

- Where the packet should be sent

Each of these will be considered in the following sections.

Receiver Set

The first kind of scope might be called the audience or *receiver set*. The recipients of a packet can be

- **Unicast:** One individual host should receive and process this packet.

- **Multicast:** A group of hosts should receive and process this packet.

- **Broadcast:** Every host within a given part of the network should receive and process this packet.

- **Anycast:** The closest host with a given service should receive and process this packet.

2

Each of these four scopes can be illustrated using a room full of people.

Starting a conversation with one person is *unicast*: you are talking to one other person. It does not matter if a lot of people can hear the conversation. Even if you are sitting on a stage at the front of the room so everyone can hear the conversation, your words are intended for the one person you are talking to.

Telling a story to a group of friends within the larger group, you are using *multicast*. Everyone in the room might be able to hear you, but your story is intended for a small group within the larger group.

If you stand on a stage or yell "fire," you probably mean for everyone in the room to hear what you have to say. This is a *broadcast*; everyone in the room should hear and act on what you are saying. Broadcast does *not* mean "everyone in the world." It means "everyone who is in this local area." The scope of a broadcast could be an entire city, region, or even the entire world, but information intended for everyone within a single room is still a broadcast.

While unicast, multicast, and broadcast are generally intuitive, *anycast* is a bit harder. If your friend collapses while you are talking to them, you might shout out: "My friend needs help! Is anyone a doctor?"

The anycast is *like* a broadcast in this situation because everyone in the room can hear your cry for help. Once someone answers your cry, however, the conversation between you and that person is unicast, or the conversation between the various people trying to help your friend is multicast.

Anycast always has these two attributes:

- You are looking for a *service* instead of a *specific person* (or *host* in the case of a network). You are looking for a doctor rather than a specific person.

- Once you have found the service, person, or host, the conversation becomes unicast.

Anycast in networks operates a little differently than in the real world because of the physical nature of the network in this one way: the initial packet that sets up the following unicast conversation is sometimes directed to the closest instance of a service rather than being broadcast. We'll discuss this difference more fully when we discuss *routing* in the next chapter.

The format of the address does not always determine its scope; sometimes you can tell the differences between unicast, multicast, broadcast, and anycast addresses; sometimes you cannot.

Topological Reach

The second kind of scope is *topological*. The network topology is like the geography of the real world, but they don't always match. Figure 2-1 illustrates.

Houses *A*, *B*, and *C* are located on two different islands. *A* and *B* use the same service provider, which has an underwater cable connecting the two islands; when *A* sends a packet to *B*, it travels through this underwater cable. On the other hand, *B* and *C* have chosen to use different service providers. These two service providers do not have a physical cable connecting them because of a chain of mountains running down the center of the island, but rather only communicate via a satellite connection.

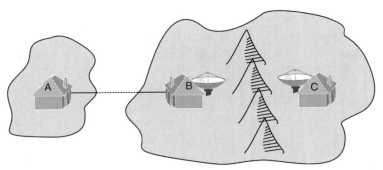

Figure 2-1   *Topological Distance*

A and *B* can be said to be physically distant but topologically close; *B* and *C* can be said to be physically close but topologically distant. Topological distance relates to the distance packets travel rather than the distance between two points.

Just as with physical addresses, network addresses can describe anything from a host to a topological region. Returning to the shipping example from the previous chapter, a package follows a portion of the address rather than the entire address during any part of its journey. Figure 2-2 illustrates.

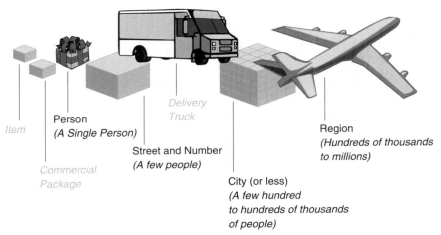

Figure 2-2   *Address Scope*

Moving from the gift tag to a street (or house) address means moving from one person to a small group of people. A city represents many street addresses, and a region might represent a few cities. We can say the street address is an **abstraction** of the people who live there—it isn't the real people; it just tells you where to find those people. In the same way, the city is an *abstraction* of all the street addresses within the city, and the region is an *abstraction* of the cities within the region.

Abstraction is one of the most difficult concepts in computer networking to understand, but it is also one of the most important. An abstraction represents a collection of things. Figure 2-3 illustrates abstraction in relation to network addresses.

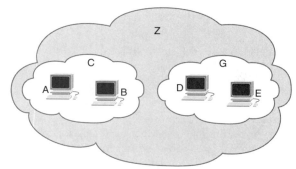

Figure 2-3 *Topological Reach*

Hosts *A*, *B*, *D*, and *E* all have individual (interface) addresses. The network *C* represents, or abstracts, hosts *A* and *B*. The network *G* represents, or abstracts, hosts *D* and *E*. The network *Z* represents, or abstracts, networks *C* and *G*.

Computer networks can have as many layers of abstraction of this kind as you like; the only logical limit is the size of the address. In practice, most computer networks have just two or three layers of abstraction.

When *A* sends a packet toward *E*, the packet follows a path determined by *routing* to reach *E*. Routing will be discussed in more detail in the next chapter; for now you just need to know *A*'s path to *E* is called a *route* or a *reachable destination*.

This route can be aggregated just like physical addresses can be. *A* may only know how to reach *Z*, and *Z* may only know how to reach *G*. The specific route to *E* may only exist within *G*. In other words, *Z* may only know of an *aggregate route* that contains *E*, but any details about *E* itself.

This example is like knowing which city your friend lives in but not their street address. When you get into their city, you can call them so they can give you their actual physical address.

There is one special reachable destination in computer networks, as well—the *default route*. Host *A* may not know how to reach *E*; it just knows *E* is somehow reachable through the network. Because *A* has no specific information, it can just send packets out into the network following the default route.

When a network device sends traffic along the default route, it assumes some other device will know more about how to reach the destination.

This explanation all sounds very complicated; let's simplify by classifying addresses into four groups based on their **topological reach**:

- **Within this segment or broadcast domain:** The segment is sometimes also called *on this wire*. Any host that receives a broadcast packet sent by this host is considered "on the same wire" as the local host. In real-world terms, this is like everyone in the room where you are speaking loudly enough for everyone to hear. People in other rooms are not going to hear you, so they are not within your broadcast domain.

- **On this network:** This address belongs to a host that is not physically connected to the same wire but is connected someplace within the same network I am connected to.

- **On another network:** This address belongs to a group of addresses representing some other physical network. I am not connected to that network, but I do know what direction to go to reach that group of networks, and I assume some device within that group of networks will know how to deliver my packets to the destination host.

■ **Out there "somewhere":** This is the default route. This host exists, but I have no idea what network it is connected to or how to reach it.

Physical Addresses

As the first chapter noted, **physical addresses** originally represented a single physical interface on a host or other network device. As computing power increased, developers built several *virtual computers*, or *virtual machines (VMs)*, on top of a single physical computer.

These VMs needed their own physical addresses so they could send and receive network frames, so virtual interfaces were created. The idea of a virtual interface, once invented, was applied to many other problems; virtual interfaces are now ubiquitous in computer networks.

> **NOTE**   VMs were originally developed to allow many different users to time-share on a single large-scale computer, such as a mainframe or minicomputer. Developers transferred the idea of VMs from these larger computers to smaller computers (microcomputers, which we call desktop computers today) to build sandboxes and emulators. To play an arcade game on a computer, you need an emulator, which is essentially a VM. If you want to test code to make certain it does not contain a virus, running it in a sandbox, another kind of VM, is a good idea.
>
> The term *mainframe* originated in the telephone industry. Engineers constructed large frames to hold the massive wiring, crossbar switches, and Strowger switches, required to build a telephone exchange. The frame at the center of a region was called the main frame and housed in the central office. Smaller frames called building distribution frames (BDFs) might be placed in larger buildings as well. The first large-scale computers relied on massive wiring and hence were built using frames like those used in building telephone networks; hence, the term *mainframe* bled over from the telephone to the computing world.

There are many kinds of physical hardware addresses, but the most common is the Institute of Electrical and Electronics Engineers (IEEE) **EUI-48** format, illustrated in Figure 2-4.

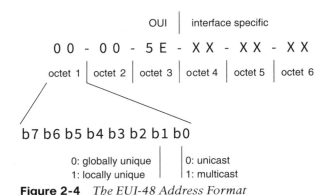

Figure 2-4   *The EUI-48 Address Format*

> **NOTE**   You might see the term *MAC-48 address* from time to time. MAC-48 is an older name for EUI-48; the IEEE has declared MAC-48 obsolete.

Key Topic

The EUI-48 address is 48 bits or 6 octets. Each octet is encoded as a pair of hexadecimal digits and often (though not always) displayed in sections divided by dashes.

> **NOTE**   *Octet* and *byte* are often used interchangeably in information technology, but they are not always the same thing. A byte is the number of bits a given processor can hold in internal registers or can process at one time. In an 8-bit processor, a byte is 8 bits; in a 32-bit processor, a byte is 32 bits. An octet, on the other hand, is always exactly 8 bits. Byte, however, is often used to mean exactly 8 bits, regardless of the processor. Because these terms have overlapping meaning, you might need to verify which meaning is intended. Byte almost always means a set of 8 bits in networking documentation and standards.

A physical shipping address has multiple parts: recipient, house number, street name, city, region, and state. As noted in the first chapter, part describes a different geographic region.

The EUI-48 address format is broken up in the same way, but rather than describing different geographic regions, each part describes something about the address.

The eighth bit of the first octet is called the *I/G bit*. The I/G bit tells you what the scope of this address is. If the I/G bit is set to *0*, this is a unicast address—an address of a single physical interface. If the I/G bit is set to *1*, this is the address of a group of physical interfaces, or a *multicast group*.

Interfaces are never assigned an EUI-48 multicast address. Interfaces are programmed to listen to these addresses by software; any individual host might or might not be listening to a particular multicast address.

The seventh bit of the first octet is called the *U/L bit*. The U/L bit tells you if the address is globally or locally unique. Globally unique means just what it sounds like: no other device in existence, even in space, should have this same address. Locally unique addresses were often assigned by network administrators way back in the mists of time.

The first half, or three octets, of the address, is the *organizationally unique identifier (OUI)*. While the OUI is divided into a few different *registries*, the main thing you need to know is the OUI tells you who—the organization—assigned the address. If the U/L bit is set to 0, this address was assigned by the device's manufacturer.

Globally unique numbers are globally unique because each manufacturer is given a block of addresses. Manufacturers assign a number from their pool of addresses to each device they build. So long as these manufacturers assign each number in their pool to precisely one device, every device made will have a unique address.

> **NOTE**   Could we run out of EUI-48 addresses? In theory, yes, but it does not seem likely any time soon. Even with the two reserved—U/L and I/G—bits removed from the calculation, the EUI-48 address space has some 70 trillion possible addresses. If we do reach the end of the EUI-48 address space, it is possible to recycle older addresses, because devices generally have some expected lifetime. Most devices will be thrown away within 10 or 15 years of being manufactured.

Because the I/G and U/L bits are placed at the end of the first octet, you can always tell what kind of EUI-48 address you are working with by looking at the last digit of the first octet:

- If the first octet ends in a 0, 4, 8, or C, this is a globally unique unicast address.

- If the first octet ends in 1, 5, 9, or D, this is a globally unique multicast address.

There is a longer version of the EUI-48 address called, naturally enough, EUI-64. The EUI-64 address has the same format as an EUI-48 address, only two octets longer—or 64 bits.

Internet Protocol Version 4

The physical address is just the first of (at least) three layers of addresses used in networking. The next layer up is the interface address, which describes the topological location of the host on the network. There are many kinds of interface addresses, but the two most common are Internet Protocol version 4 (**IPv4**) and Internet Protocol version 6 (**IPv6**). This section considers IPv4; the following section will consider IPv6.

Back in 1966, when computer networks were just being developed, Vinton Cerf and Robert E. Kahn started working on the *Transmission Control Program* to transfer data. They soon realized having a single protocol to control errors, control data flow, provide the information needed to carry data through the network, and insulate host-to-host data transmission from the physical medium would be too large and inflexible. To resolve this problem, they divided the protocol into two protocols called the *Transmission Control Protocol (TCP)* and the *Internet Protocol (IP)*.

NOTE Chapter 14, "Network Transport," considers IP and TCP in more detail; this section just considers IP addresses.

An IPv4 address is 32 bits and is split into four decimal sections for ease of writing and reading, as shown in Figure 2-5.

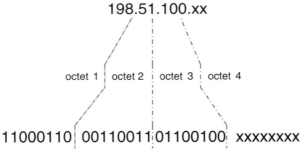

Figure 2-5 *IPv4 Address*

The IPv4 address is divided into two parts: the **prefix** and the **subnet**. The division between these two parts was originally set by the first octet of the address itself:

- If the first octet was between 0 and 127, the address was in the *class A* range. For class A addresses, the prefix is one octet (the first section of the address), and the subnet part is the remaining three octets of the address.

- If the first octet was between 128 and 191, the address was in the *class B* range. For class B addresses, the prefix is two octets, and the subnet part is the two remaining octets.

- If the first octet was between 192 and 223, the address was in the *class C* range. For class C addresses, the prefix is three octets, and the subnet part is the remaining octet.

In 1993 these address classes were replaced with *Classless Interdomain Routing (CIDR)*. Individual IPv4 addresses are always given with a *prefix length* indicating the dividing point between the prefix and the subnet.

NOTE   You will hear the parts of the IPv4 address called many different things. The prefix is often called the *network* or *reachable destination*, and the subnet is often called the *subnetwork*, *network*, or *host*. The host address can mean the subnet, or the individual address assigned to an interface. Some of these terms have meaning within specific historical contexts that generally do not apply to classless IPv4 addresses. Others have overlapping—and hence confusing—meanings.

To avoid confusion, the two parts of both IPv4 and IPv6 addresses will be called the *prefix* and *subnet* throughout this book.

To understand the difference between the prefix and subnet, let's go back to the four groups of addresses based on their topological reach:

- An interface (or host) with the same IPv4 prefix and prefix length is within the same segment or broadcast domain.

- An interface (host) with a different IPv4 prefix or prefix length is not in the same segment. These hosts are someplace else on this network or they are in a group of networks outside this network.

From the perspective of the host, there is no way to tell the difference between addresses someplace else on this network and addresses outside this network because of **aggregation**, discussed in a later section of this chapter.

We can define the prefix and subnet as

- The prefix indicates *which subnet*.

- The subnet is a group of interfaces, hosts, or subnets.

The prefix length is just what it sounds like—the number of bits in the prefix. For IPv4 addresses, the prefix length can only be between 1 and 32 because there are only 32 bits in an IPv4 address. For example:

- **10.0.0.0/8:** The first 8 bits, or the first octet, are the prefix; the remaining three octets are addresses within the subnet. The first address in the subnet is 10.0.0.0; the last address in the subnet is 10.255.255.255.

- **10.1.0.0/16:** The first 16 bits, or the first two octets, are the prefix; the remaining two octets are the subnet. The first address in the subnet is 10.1.0.0; the last address in the subnet is 10.1.255.255.

- **10.1.1.0/24:** The first 24 bits, or the first three octets, are the prefix; the remaining octet is an address within the subnet. The first address in the network is 10.1.1.0; the last address in the network is 10.1.1.255.

The prefix and subnet parts of the address are not always conveniently divided at a dot like the ones in these examples. For example:

- **192.0.2.64/27:** The first 27 bits, or the first three octets and 3 of the bits in the fourth octet, are the prefix; the remaining 6 bits are addresses in the subnet. The first address in the subnet is 192.0.2.64; the last address in the subnet is 192.0.2.91.

- **10.128.192.0/18:** The first 18 bits, or the first octet and 2 bits of the third octet, are the prefix; the remaining 14 bits are addresses in the subnet. The first address in the subnet is 10.128.192.0; the last address in the subnet is 10.128.192.255.

As shown in the example of 192.0.2.64/27, an IPv4 prefix can contain 0s. In the subnet portion of the address, however, all 0s and all 1s addresses are considered *broadcast addresses* or *subnet broadcast* addresses. Sending a packet to either of these broadcast addresses means every host within the segment or broadcast domain should receive and process the packet. The broadcast addresses for these examples are

- **10.0.0.0/8:** 10.0.0.0 and 10.255.255.255

- **10.1.0.0/16:** 10.1.0.0 and 10.1.255.255

- **10.1.1.0/24:** 10.1.1.0 and 10.1.1.255

- **192.0.2.64/27:** 192.0.2.64 and 192.0.2.91

- **10.128.192.0/18:** 10.128.192.0 and 10.128.255.255

Key Topic

The broadcast addresses are the first and last addresses in the prefix.

NOTE The all 0s address, or the subnet address itself, is almost never used as a broadcast address. While you should be aware this broadcast address exists, and how to calculate it, when you see "broadcast address," you should almost always interpret this to mean the all 1s address, or the last address in the prefix.

The all 0s and all 1s addresses, 0.0.0.0 and 255.255.255.255, are also broadcast addresses.

There are at least three ways to find the prefix and subnet addresses. Each section explains one of these three methods, starting from the most difficult to calculate and easiest to understand.

Why Two Addresses?

If every host, camera, television, and toaster already has unique physical addresses, why should we assign interface addresses as well?

The physical address identifies the host, while the interface address describes the topological location of the host. The physical address is a permanent, fixed address every other host attached to the same physical network can use to communicate with it. The interface address, on the other hand, tells other devices where the host is connected to the network or where to send packets if they are not attached to the same physical link.

Another way this might be expressed is the physical address is the address *on this wire*, while the interface address is the host's location *on this network*. The meanings of *on this wire* and *on this network* have, as with most terms in the computer network, broadened over time.

Yet another way to express the difference between the physical and interface addresses is using the idea of network stack layers, a topic that will be considered in more detail in Chapter 6, "Network Models." The physical address is commonly called a *Layer 2 address*, and the interface address is often called a *Layer 3 address*.

Why not make the physical interface match the interface address? There are network systems where both the physical and interface address are the same. The *Open Systems Interconnection* network protocol suite, which includes *Connectionless Network Protocol (CLNP)* and the *Intermediate System to Intermediate System (IS-IS)* protocols, is designed so a single manually assigned address is used for all the interface and physical addresses.

On the other hand, most network protocols, such as IP, assume a host will need to *discover* interface addresses once it is attached to the network. If the interface address must be configured to create the physical address, the interface address must be configured before the host can communicate *at all*—not even with an automatic configuration system. Figure 2-6 illustrates the problem.

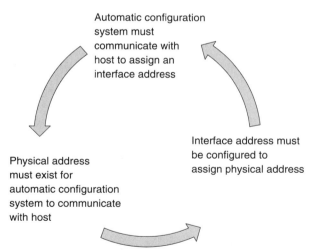

Automatic configuration system must communicate with host to assign an interface address

Interface address must be configured to assign physical address

Physical address must exist for automatic configuration system to communicate with host

Figure 2-6   *Address Assignment Bootstrap Problem*

There are many ways to solve this *bootstrap problem*, but the simplest is to make certain the physical address of each device attached to a network is globally unique.

Why not make the interface address match the physical address? Because the interface address is topological, it must also be *hierarchical*. Rather than being a single flat address space, there must be something like the equivalent of a street number, street name, city, etc., so the address can be aggregated or summarized. Without some form of aggregation, the address of every host in the world would need to be known to every other host in the world—a completely unworkable situation.

Instead, just like in physical shipping, a packet is carried toward its destination in stages, with different parts of the interface address used at different places.

What an IP Address Represents

Throughout most of the computer networking world, the host and interface addresses are used interchangeably, but they are not really the same thing. In fact, *host addresses do not exist in IP networks*:

- Each host on an interface has an independent IP address.

- Each interface is (generally) on a separate segment or in a different broadcast domain.

Many protocols and applications will use one of the available IP addresses as a unique identifier. Hosts with only one interface will have only one interface address, and that interface address may be used to identify the host.

When you read or hear the term *host address* in an IP networking context, it is probably describing an interface address.

Calculating Prefixes and Subnets Using Subnet Masks

The earliest use of IPv4 addresses relied on the *subnet mask* rather than the prefix length to differentiate the prefix from the subnet address. Figure 2-7 illustrates.

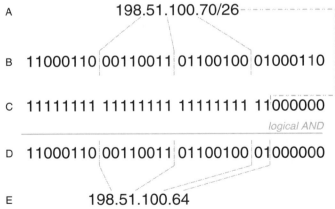

Figure 2-7   *The Subnet Mask*

An IPv4 address and prefix length are shown on *A* in Figure 2-7. *B* is this same IPv4 address translated to four binary octets. *C* is 32 binary digits laid out as four octets, just like *A*. In *C*, the number of 1s, starting at the left, is given by the prefix length, so there are twenty-six 1s, leaving six 0s. The 1s are the network part of the address or prefix; the 0s are the subnet part of the address.

To find the prefix, use a Boolean logical *AND*, setting the digit in the result, *D*, to 1 when the digits in both *B* and *C* are 1, and setting the digit in *D* to 0 if the two digits do not match. The resulting four octets in *D* are converted to a standard decimal IPv4 address.

The prefix—and the network address—in this example is 198.51.100.64.

Seeing the address laid out in binary helps make more sense of the meaning of all the 1s and all the 0s broadcast addresses. If we set the entire subnet portion of the address to 0s, the resulting IPv4 address is 198.51.100.64. This is not only the prefix but also the first of the two broadcast addresses. Setting the subnet portion to 1s results in the last octet translating to 127, so the second broadcast address is 198.51.100.127.

Calculating Prefixes and Subnets Using a Skip Chart

Converting numbers to binary, running Boolean operations, and then converting them back to decimal is time-consuming; using a skip chart to calculate the prefix and broadcast addresses is much faster. Table 2-2 will be used to illustrate the process.

Table 2-2 IPv4 Networks by Prefix Length

Prefix Length	Skip	Working Octet
8	1	First
9	128	Second
10	64	Second
11	32	Second
12	16	Second
13	8	Second
14	4	Second
15	2	Second
16	1	Second
17	128	Third
18	64	Third
19	32	Third
20	16	Third
21	8	Third
22	4	Third
23	2	Third
24	1	Third
25	128	Fourth
26	64	Fourth
27	32	Fourth
28	16	Fourth
29	8	Fourth
30	4	Fourth
31	2	Fourth

Let's use the same address—198.51.100.70/26—to calculate the prefix and broadcast address:

1. Find the prefix length by going down the left column.

2. Divide the number in the *skip* column next to the prefix length into the number in the *working octet* indicated in the third column. In this case, the *skip* is 64, and we are working in the fourth octet, so we divide 70 by 64.

3. Ignoring any remainder, multiply the result by the number in the *skip* column. In this case, 64 goes into 70 once, so we multiply 64 by 1, with a result of 64.

4. Make the working octet the result; this is the network address. In this case, the network address is 198.51.100.64.

5. Add the *skip* to the resulting number and subtract 1; this is the broadcast address. In this case, the *skip* minus 1 is 63, so we add 63 to 64. The result is 127, so the broadcast address is 198.51.100.127.

Using a skip chart requires a little practice, but it is much faster. If you memorize the chart, you can probably calculate IPv4 prefixes and broadcast addresses without any paper, pen, or computer.

Calculating Prefixes Using Skips

You do not need to memorize the chart, however, if you add one more bit of math to the process we used to calculate the prefix and broadcast address in the preceding section. To understand this method, you need to understand why the skip chart works. Figure 2-8 illustrates.

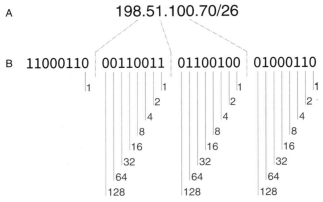

Figure 2-8 *Binary Places in the IPv4 Address*

Notice the numbers below each bit; these are the binary *places*, which are just like the 1s, 10s, 100s, etc., in the decimal number system everyone learns in school. If any of these change to either a 0 or 1, the entire number changes value by the amount shown below:

These numbers are the powers of two from 2^0 to 2^7.

Counting over the number of bits in the prefix length—26—we come to the second bit in the fourth octet, which is a 1. If this bit changes to a 0, the value of the number changes by

64, so 64 is the skip value. Networks with a 26-bit prefix length can exist only on boundaries of 64—0, 64, 128, and 192—with a 26-bit prefix length. Because the 26th bit is in the fourth octet, the networks will count by 64s in the fourth octet.

If you can find the correct octet from the prefix length and then figure out what the skip is, you can calculate the prefix and broadcast address without the chart. Using 198.51.100.70/26 as an example again:

1. Divide 8 into the prefix length; ignore the remainder and add 1. In this case, 26/8 is 3; we add 1 and find we are working in the fourth octet of the IPv4 address.

2. Multiply the working octet by 8; subtract the prefix length. In this case, 8*4 is 32, and subtracting 26 from 32 gives us 6.

3. Find the power of 2 of this number; in this case, 2^6 is 64. Find the prefix. In this case, 64 will go into 70 once, and we're working in the fourth octet, so the prefix is 198.51.100.64.

4. Subtract 1 from the skip and add it to the prefix to find the broadcast address. In this case, the skip is 64. Subtracting 1, we get 63, and adding to 64, we get 127, so the broadcast address is 198.51.100.127.

Again, this method takes some practice to remember all the steps, but it reduces the entire problem to some simple division (without remainders), multiplication, addition, and subtraction. With some practice, you can use this technique to quickly find prefixes and broadcast addresses.

Internet Protocol Version 6

By the 1980s, the global Internet was growing quickly enough that it became obvious more IP address space would be needed. While several schemes to resolve this problem were proposed, only two are widely deployed today: IPv6 and **Network Address Translation (NAT)**.

> **NOTE**   IPv6 is completely different than IPv4, but we are only concerned with the changes in addressing here. Other changes between IPv4 and IPv6 will be considered in Chapter 14.
> The term *IP* is used when both IPv4 and IPv6 are intended throughout this book.

IPv6 was initially accepted as a draft standard by the Internet Engineering Task Force (IETF) in December 1998, and the first IPv6 addresses were allocated in July of 1999. IPv4 and IPv6 will likely co-exist in most networks for a long time.

In designing IPv6, the IETF quadrupled the address space. Rather than 32 bits divided into four one octet sections, the IPv6 address is 128 bits divided into 16 sections. Each section, sometimes called a *quartet*, represents two octets of the address using four hexadecimal digits. Figure 2-9 illustrates an IPv6 address.

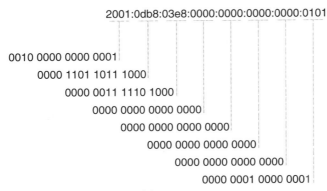

Figure 2-9   *An IPv6 Address*

IPv6 addresses include a prefix length to differentiate between the prefix and subnet addresses—just like IPv4—but the maximum prefix length is now /128 rather than /32. Longer addresses are more difficult to work with, but IPv6 addressing is also simplified in some ways:

- Individual hosts always receive a /64 address, and links between network devices normally receive a /128 address. Prefix lengths between /64 and /128 are extremely uncommon.

- The shortest prefix most networks will be allocated will be a /48. Larger companies and service providers may have access to address space with a prefix length as short as a /29, but most of the addresses you will be working with daily will have prefix lengths longer than /48.

- Any *single* long string of 0s can be replaced with a double colon or :: (you can use the :: only once in an address).

- All leading 0s are omitted.

These simplifications mean you will mostly work with addresses with prefix lengths between a /48 and a /64, or about 16 possible lengths. Much like IPv4 addresses, the simplest way to work with IPv6 prefix lengths—if you insist on working with IPv6 addresses by hand—is by using skips, as shown in Table 2-3.

Table 2-3   IPv6 Address Skips

PL	Skips in the Fourth Section	Examples
49	By eights in the first digit	0, 8
50	By fours in the first digit	0, 4, 8, c
51	By twos in the first digit	0, 2, 4, 6, 8, a, c, e
52	By ones in the first digit	0, 1, 2 … c, d, e, f
53	By eights in the second digit	00, 08, 10, 18 … e0, e8, f0, f8
54	By fours in the second digit	00, 04, 08, 0c … f0, f4, f8, fc
55	By twos in the second digit	00, 02, 04, 06, 08, 0a, 0c … f0, f2, f4, f6, f8, fa, fc
56	By ones in the second digit	00, 01, 02, 03, 04 … f0, f1, f2, f3, f4 …

PL	Skips in the Fourth Section	Examples
57	By eights in the third digit	000, 008, 010, 018 … f00, f08, f10, f18, f20 …
58	By fours in the third digit	000, 004, 008, 00c, 010, 014, 018 …
59	By twos in the third digit	000, 002, 004, 006, 008, 00a, 00c, 010, 012 …
60	By ones in the third digit	000, 001, 002, 003 …
61	By eights in the fourth digit	0000, 0008, 0010, 0018 …
62	By fours in the fourth digit	0000, 0004, 0008, 000c, 0010, 0014, 0018, 001c …
63	By twos in the fourth digit	0000, 0002, 0004, 0006, 0008, 000a, 000c, 0010 …
64	By ones in the fourth digit	0000, 0001, 0002, 0003, 0004, 0005, 0006 …

For instance, for 2001:db8:3e8::/48 prefix:

- You can create two /49 subnets, 2001:db8:3e8::/49 and 2001:db8:3e8:8000::/49.

- You can create four /50 subnets, 2001:db8:3e8::/50, 2001:db8:3e8:4000::/50, 2001:db8:3e8:8000::/50, and 2001:db8:3e8:c000::/50.

- 2001:db8:3e8:500::/54 is not a valid prefix; you count by fours in the second digit for /54s, and 5 is not a multiple of 4.

Just like in IPv4, the first and last address of the subnet are broadcast addresses.

Three further points:

- After working with IPv6 addresses for a while, you will probably recognize common prefix lengths and where their prefixes begin and end.

- Most network operators carefully plan their addressing so only a few prefix lengths are used; this simplifies becoming familiar with them and makes spotting mistakes easy.

- While working with IPv6 addresses, you should use a subnet calculator and/or cheat sheet to prevent mistakes.

Aggregation

A physical address has different amounts of detail in its different parts: the street number indicates an individual house, the street indicates a street with many houses, and the city indicates a geographic area with hundreds (or thousands) of streets and thousands (or millions) of individuals. Each level of detail is used at different points in shipping a package from a sender to a receiver.

IP addresses can also represent different levels of detail; just as a city contains or represents many streets, streets contain or represent many houses (each with its own number), and each house can contain or represent many residents, an IP address can represent many different topological regions of a network. Figure 2-10 illustrates.

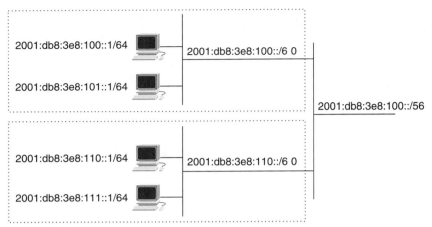

Figure 2-10   *Aggregation*

The four hosts in Figure 2-10 have been assigned /64 IPv6 addresses. Each host is connected to a single segment (broadcast domain); these segments are assigned /60 IPv6 addresses. The segment address is much like a street address in the physical world: it contains a group of houses. If you want to find a specific house, you must first find the street; if you want to find a specific host, you must first find the segment.

The two /60 segments are contained within a larger network with a shorter prefix length, /56. This is like the city in a physical address, representing or containing many different streets.

Shortening the prefix length to describe a larger part of the network is called *aggregation*. We can say

- 2001:db8:3e8:100::1/64 and 2001:db8:3e8:101::1/64 are *components* or *subnets* of 2001:db8:3e8:100::/60.

- 2001:db8:3e8:100::/60 is an aggregate containing 2001:db8:3e8:100::1/64 and 2001:db8:3e8:101::1/64.

- 2001:db8:3e8:110::1/64 and 2001:db8:3e8:111::1/64 are *components* or *subnets* of 2001:db8:3e8:110::/60.

- 2001:db8:3e8:110::/60 is an aggregate containing 2001:db8:3e8:110::1/64 and 2001:db8:3e8:111::1/64.

- 2001:db8:3e8:100::/60 and 2001:db8:3e8:110::/60 are *components* or *subnets* of 2001:db8:3e8:100::/56.

- 2001:db8:3e8:100::/56 is an aggregate containing 2001:db8:3e8:100::/64 and 2001:db8:3e8:110::/64.

When addresses are aggregated, an address can be reachable even though no host is attached to the network with that address. For instance, suppose some host wanted to send a packet to 2001:db8:3e8:100::2. Outside of the 2001:db8:3e8:100::/60 network, it might seem as though the ::2 address is a valid reachable destination, but the host does not exist. What happens in this situation? Packets destined to a nonexistent address will be carried as close to the destination as possible and then dropped.

> **NOTE** *Aggregation* is used interchangeably with *summarization* in the field of computer networking. To avoid confusion, this book will use *aggregation* throughout, and avoid using the term *summarization*.
>
> Chapter 3, "Routing and Switching," will consider how aggregation relates to packet forwarding. Using aggregation in network design is outside the scope of this book.

> **NOTE** You might see the term *supernet* from time to time. The term originated in classful IPv4 addresses, and meant a prefix with a length larger than its class; for instance, 203.0.13.0 is a class C address, so the classful prefix length is /24. If an operator used 203.0.00/16 in their network, this would be considered a supernet. Over time, the meaning of supernet has been extended to mean the same thing as an aggregate. To avoid confusion, this book will not use the term *supernet*.

Network Prefixes

You need an IP prefix to build a network. There are two sources for these addresses, described in the following sections.

Private Address Space

Several ranges of addresses are set aside as *private* for IPv4:

- 10.0.0.0/8

- 172.16.0.0/12

- 192.168.0.0/16

These addresses are considered *bogons* by service providers, and therefore not routable on the public internet. You can use these addresses to build any kind of network that will not be connected to the global internet (unless the connection is through network address translation, described in a later section).

There is no explicit **private address space** set aside for ipv6; the ip community generally assumes ipv6 addresses are so readily available that there is no point in using an address that is not globally routable. However, many people use the 2001:db8::/32 address space set aside for documentation and examples to build private networks.

> **NOTE** The fc007::/7 IPv6 address space is reserved for unique local addressing (ULA). In some situations, these addresses can be used to build a private network so long as it is a pure IPv6 network. The interaction between IPv4 addresses and IPv6 ULA addresses can be surprising.

Publicly Routable Address Space

Publicly routable addresses are obtained through a service provider or a Regional Internet Registry (RIR). Figure 2-11 illustrates the flow of IP addresses on the global Internet.

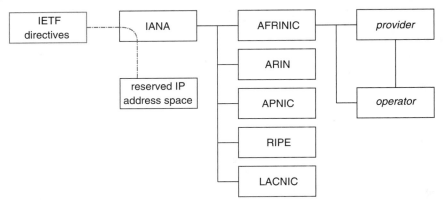

Figure 2-11   *IP Address Assignment Flow in the Global Internet*

The Internet Assigned Numbers Authority (IANA), an international nonprofit, controls the distribution of all number and name resources used on the Internet. One part of IANA's job is to control the distribution of IP addresses.

IANA can receive requests for address space from the IETF to reserve blocks of addresses, such as the private addresses discussed in the previous section.

IANA can also receive requests for publicly routable address space from a Regional Internet Registry. There are currently five RIRs, each of which assigns addresses within a region:

- The African Network Information Center (AFRINIC) serves Africa.

- The American Registry for Internet Numbers (ARIN) serves the United States, Canada, parts of the Caribbean, and Antarctica.

- The Asia-Pacific Network Information Center (APNIC) serves East, South, and Southeast Asia.

- The Latin American and Caribbean Network Information Center (LACNIC) serves most of the Caribbean and all of Latin America, including South America and North America up to Mexico.

- The Réseaux IP Européens Network Coordination Centre (RIPE) serves Europe, Central Asia, and West Asia.

Large organizations can request addresses directly from one of these RIRs; however, it is almost impossible to get IPv4 address space. Most of the RIRs have run out of free IPv4 space. Organizations can also purchase IPv4 addresses from specialized resellers.

RIRs are more willing to assign IPv6 addresses to organizations. Requirements vary by RIR, so it is best to check the RIR for your region to find out how to obtain an IPv6 network address.

Operators and end users can also get addresses from their service provider when they purchase Internet access; this is the most common way to obtain IP addresses.

Reserved Addresses

Some addresses should never be used either for private networks or for connecting to the global Internet. These are called **reserved addresses**, and they are considered unroutable bogons by service providers. Table 2-4 lists some of these addresses.

Table 2-4   Reserved IP Addresses

Address Space	Usage
10.0.0.0/8	Private networks
100.64.0.0/10	Assigned by service providers using Carrier Grade Network Address Translation (CGNAT)
127.0.0.0/8::1/128	Loopback; most host network software implementations will send any packets sent to an address in this address range back to the host itself
169.254.0.0/16	Link local addresses; not widely used
172.16.0.0/12	Private networks
192.0.2.0/24	Documentation
192.88.99.0/24	No longer used, but still reserved
192.168.0.0/16	Private networks
198.18.0.0/15	Benchmarking
198.51.100.0/24	Documentation
203.0.113.0/24	Documentation
224.0.0.0/4	Multicast distribution
233.252.0.0/24	Documentation
240.0.0.0/4	Reserved
::ffff:0:0/96 ::ffff:0:0:0/96 64:ff9b::/96 64:ff9b:1::/48 2002::/16	IPv4 to IPv6 translation services; not widely used and/or deprecated
100::/64	Discard prefix; any packets sent to this address will be discarded
2001:0000::/32 2001:20::/28	Special applications like Toredo
2001:db8::/32	Documentation
fe80::/64	Link local addresses
ff00::/8	Multicast

You should always check on the Internet for the most recent list of reserved addresses when you are setting up a network.

Ports and Sockets

The final kind of address in a network is a port (or socket) number. Port numbers are not normally considered their own kind of address, but they are often included in the *five-tuple*, which uniquely identifies a communication *session* between two applications (running on two hosts).

> **NOTE**   The five-tuple is described more fully in Chapter 14.

Figure 2-12 illustrates the *network stack*, and the place of port numbers in the stack.

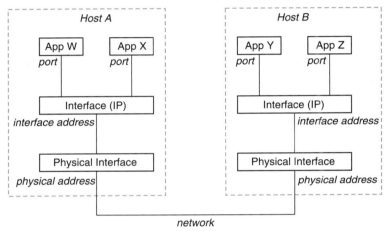

Figure 2-12   *Communication Path Between Two Applications*

In Figure 2-12:

- The physical address, at the bottom, is used to identify the interface (or host) on a single segment.

- The interface address will normally be an IP address. This address identifies the interface on the network.

- The port number identifies the application among all the applications running on the host.

> **NOTE**   We add another layer to this diagram for transport protocols when we discuss models in Chapter 6. Chapter 14 discusses transport protocols in more detail.

The port number is a simple 16-bit number that translates to a decimal number between 0 and 65,536. There are two classes of port numbers:

- **Well-known or registered:** These ports are registered to particular applications by IANA or are so widely used by an application that they have become well known.

- **Ephemeral:** These ports are not assigned to any application.

When *app* W wants to communicate with *app* Y, it will

- Build a packet with the data it wants to send to *app* Y.
- Set the destination address in the packet to *host* B's interface (IP) address.
- Set the destination port to the **well-known port** for *app* Y.
- Set the source address to *host* A's interface (IP) address.
- Set the source port to an **ephemeral port** number.

When *app* Y wants to reply to *app* W, it will

- Build a packet with the data it wants to send to *app* W.
- Set the destination address in the packet to *host* A's interface (IP) address.
- Set the destination port to the ephemeral port that *app* W used as its source port.
- Set the source address to *host* B's interface (IP) address.
- Set the source port to the well-known port number for *app* Y.

The combination of source address, ephemeral source port, destination address, and well-known destination port is an (almost) unique identifier for the session between the two applications.

The port is sometimes called a *service or service access point (SAP)*. These terms are not as common as they once were, but they are still used from time to time.

Network Address Translation

When IPv4 addresses started becoming scarce, John Mayes and Paul Tsuchiya—independently—designed a way to extend the IPv4 address space into the port number space through *Network Address Translation (NAT)*.

NOTE   *NAT* and **Port Address Translation (PAT)** are slightly different technologies, but the terms are used interchangeably. Most NAT implementations and deployments are PAT. To reflect current usage, this book uses *NAT* for both.

Figure 2-13 illustrates the way NAT extends the IPv4 address space.

In Figure 2-13:

- *App* W sends a packet from *host* A toward *app* Y on *host* B. This packet is transmitted by *host* A with a source address of 192.0.2.1 and a source port of 49170.
- *App* X sends a packet from *host* C toward *app* Y on *host* B. This packet is transmitted by *host* C with a source address of 192.0.2.2 and a source port of 49170.

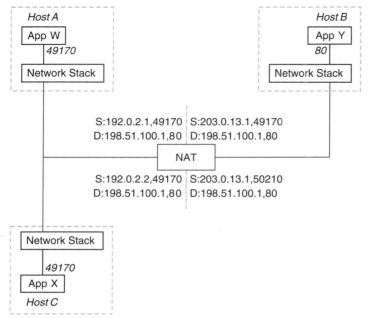

Figure 2-13 *NAT Translation*

There is, however, only one source address available on *host B*'s side of the NAT. How will these two different packets, sourced from two different hosts, be separated?

The *NAT* translates the source address on both packets to 203.0.13.1, giving each packet a different source port (49170 versus 50210). Now when *app Y* responds to these two packets, *host B* will send

■ Packets for *host A* to 203.0.13.1 with a destination port of 49170

■ Packets for *host C* to 203.0.13.1 with a destination port of 50210

When the *NAT* device receives these packets, it can translate the destination address and port *host B* used to the correct ports, and the packets will be delivered to the correct hosts.

Chapter Review

This chapter dove deeply into the three most common kinds of addresses you will encounter in a network: physical, Internet Protocol, and ports. Each one of these addresses has different semantics, or ways of formatting and representing information. Unlike physical addresses, these kinds of addresses represent a topological location on a network with a single number, using different parts of the address to indicate different kinds of information.

Learning and understanding what these addresses look like, where they come from, and how to work with them, are all critical to learning how to build, design, operate, and troubleshoot computer networks.

Addresses are only part of getting a package or packet from one place to another. There also needs to be some way to decide where the packet needs to go next in its journey. Directing a package through a shipping network is called *routing*. Directing a packet through a computer network is also called *routing*, and there is a similar concept called *switching*. The next chapter considers how packets are routed and switched through a computer network.

One key to doing well on the exams is to perform repetitive spaced review sessions. Review this chapter's material using either the tools in the book or interactive tools for the same material found on the book's companion website. Refer to the online Appendix D, "Study Planner," element for more details. Table 2-5 outlines the key review elements and where you can find them. To better track your study progress, record when you completed these activities in the second column.

Table 2-5   Chapter Review Tracking

Review Element	Review Date (s)	Resource Used
Review key topics		Book, website
Review key terms		Book, website
Repeat DIKTA questions		Book, PTP
Review concepts and actions		Book, website

Review All the Key Topics

Table 2-6 lists the key topics for this chapter.

Table 2-6   Key Topics for Chapter 2

Key Topic Element	Description	Page Number
List	Address scopes	24
Paragraph	Address scope receiver set	24
Paragraph, Figure 2-1	Address scope topological reach	25
Paragraph, Figure 2-3	Abstraction	26
List	Address classification based on topological reach	27
Paragraph	Physical addresses	28
Paragraph	Virtual interfaces	28
Paragraph	EUI-48 address	29
Paragraph, Figure 2-5	IPv4 addresses	30
Paragraph	Prefix vs. subnet	31
Paragraph	Prefix length	31
Paragraph	Broadcast addresses	32
Paragraph, Figure 2-9	IPv6 addresses	37
Paragraph, Figure 2-10	Aggregation	39
List	IPv4 private addresses	41
Paragraph, Figure 2-11	Publicly routable addresses	42
Paragraph, Table 2-4	Reserved IP addresses	43
List	Classes of port numbers	44

Key Terms You Should Know

Key terms in this chapter include

unicast, multicast, broadcast, anycast, abstraction, topological reach, physical address, EUI-48, IPv4, IPv6, prefix, subnet, aggregation, broadcast address, Network Address Translation (NAT), private address space, reserved addresses, well-known port, ephemeral port, Port Address Translation (PAT)

Concepts and Actions

Review the concepts considered in this chapter using Table 2-7. You can cover the right side of this table and describe each concept or action in your own words to verify your understanding.

Table 2-7   Concepts and Actions

Unicast	One individual host should receive and process this packet
Multicast	A group of hosts should receive and process this packet
Broadcast	Every host within a given part of the network should receive and process this packet
Anycast	The closest host with a given service or application running should receive and process this packet
Topological distance	The distance a packet must travel to move between two hosts
Topological reach	The topological area within a network where a network makes sense without any further context
Four topological reaches	Within this segment, within this network, on another network, "out there"
Virtual machine	A logical computer running on top of a physical computer that appears to be a "real computer"; there can be many virtual machines running on a single physical computer
EUI-48 address	A physical address format standardized by the IEEE
The I/G bit of the EUI-48 address	Indicates whether an EUI-48 address is globally unique or locally significant
The U/L bit of the EUI-48 address	Indicates whether an EUI-48 address is unicast or multicast
EUI-64 address	A longer version of the EUI-48 address; 64 bits instead of 48
Classless Internet Domain Routing	The prefix length of an address is determined by the prefix length rather than the class of the address
IPv4 broadcast address	The all 0s and all 1s address within a subnet; the first and last address in a subnet's address range
Bootstrap problem	A host needs a physical address to communicate on a network, but to autoconfigure a physical address, it needs to communicate on the network
Subnet mask	Binary representation of the prefix length
Size of an IPv4 address	32 bits, written as four decimal numbers
Size of an IPv6 address	128 bits, written as eight hexadecimal numbers

Aggregate	A collection of subnets
Component	A subnet contained within an aggregate address
Bogon	Addresses that cannot be routed on the global Internet
Reserved addresses	Addresses that cannot be routed on the global Internet
Port	The address of an application running on a host
Well-known port	A port number assigned to an application (such as a web server) through standardization
Ephemeral port	A random port
Network Address Translation	Translating a range of IP addresses into a single IP address, and using ephemeral port numbers to differentiate between the addresses
Topological distance	The distance a packet must travel to move between two hosts; not the same as the geographical distance
Virtual machine	A virtual computer running on top of a physical computer; there can be many virtual machines running on a single physical computer
EUI-48 address	A 48-bit physical address format standardized by the IEEE
Subnet	A group of hosts or networks
Broadcast address	The broadcast addresses are the all 0s address, or the first address in the subnet and the all 1s address, or the last address in the subnet
Addressing bootstrap problem	The physical address is required to communicate on the network, but communication on the network requires a physical address
IP address aggregation	Shortening the prefix length to represent a larger set of interfaces (hosts) or subnets
10.0.0.0/8 is …	An IPv4 private address space
Reserved IP address	A range of addresses set aside for a special purpose, such as multicast or documentation
Ephemeral port	Random port selected for communication between two applications
Port Address Translation	Using ephemeral ports to extend the IPv4 address space

For practice, find the prefix and all 1s broadcast address for each of the following addresses. You can cover the right side of Table 2-8 to calculate each problem and uncover the right column to check your answer.

Table 2-8   IP Subnetting Problems

Address	Prefix	Broadcast
192.0.2.1/24	192.0.2.0	192.0.2.255
198.51.100.251/25	198.51.100.128	198.51.100.255
203.0.113.47/26	203.0.113.0	203.0.113.63
192.0.2.55/27	192.0.2.32	192.0.2.63

Address	Prefix	Broadcast
198.51.100.130/28	198.51.100.128	198.51.100.143
203.0.113.72/29	203.0.113.72	203.0.113.79
192.0.2.201/30	192.0.2.200	192.0.2.203

For practice, calculate the longest aggregate that will cover the supplied subnets. You can cover the right side of the chart to calculate each problem and uncover the right column to check your answer.

Table 2-9   IP Aggregation Problems

Prefixes	Aggregate
192.0.2.0/25, 192.0.2.128/25	192.0.2.0/24
192.0.2.0/26, 192.0.2.64/26, 192.0.2.192/26	192.0.2.0/24
192.0.2.128/26, 192.0.2.192/26	192.0.2.128/25
192.0.2.32/27, 192.0.2.80/27	192.0.2.0/25
192.0.2.32/27, 192.0.2.64/27	192.0.2.0/26

CHAPTER 3

Routing and Switching

This chapter covers the following exam topics:

4. **Infrastructure**

4.4. **Explain basic routing concepts.**

Default gateway, layer 2 vs. layer 3 switches, local network vs. remote network

4.5. **Explain basic switching concepts.**

MAC address tables, MAC address filtering, VLAN (layer 2 network segment)

The address on a physical item must be read by someone (or something), packaging may need to be adjusted, and the package needs to be physically transported to the next stop in the journey toward its destination. Packets, like packages, must also be carried from one place to another in the network.

This chapter begins with the assignment of an interface address to a host. It might not be intuitive, but incorrectly assigned addresses will make adjusting moving packets from a source to a destination impossible. Each host must have an interface address unique within the network (for the global Internet, this means globally unique), and these addresses must be assigned to enable aggregation.

After looking at assigning interface addresses, we look at *switching* packets and *routing* packets. *Routing* might be a familiar term because it is also used in creating physical world directions (for roads and trails), and it is used by shipping companies to describe the path a delivery vehicle takes. The idea of routing in the computer networking world is similar: finding a path through the network and then carrying the packet along that path to its destination.

"Do I Know This Already?" Quiz

Take the quiz (either here or use the PTP software) if you want to use the score to help you decide how much time to spend on this chapter. Appendix A, "Answers to the 'Do I Know This Already?' Quizzes," found at the end of the book, includes both the answers and explanations. You can also find answers in the PTP testing software.

Table 3-1 "Do I Know This Already?" Foundation Topics Section-to-Question Mapping

Section	Questions
Assigning IP Address to Hosts	1, 2
Host-to-Host Communication and Address Resolution on a Single Wire	3, 4
Switching Packets	5, 6
Routing Packets	7, 8
Redirects and Relays	9

1. How far will packets destined to an address in fe80::/48 travel through a network?

    a.   To the destination host, even if it is connected multiple hops away

    b.   To all the hosts connected to a single segment

    c.   To all the hosts within a range of addresses

    d.   To a single host connected to the same local segment

2. How can a host find or calculate a publicly routable IPv6 address? (Choose two.)

    a.   Dynamic Host Configuration Protocol (DHCP)

    b.   Stateless Address Autoconfiguration (SLAAC)

    c.   Address Resolution Protocol (ARP)

    d.   IPv6 Neighbor Discovery (ND) protocol

3. How can a host discover the mapping between a physical address and an IPv4 interface address?

    a.   Dynamic Host Configuration Protocol (DHCP)

    b.   Stateless Address Autoconfiguration (SLAAC)

    c.   Address Resolution Protocol (ARP)

    d.   IPv6 Neighbor Discovery (ND) protocol

4. How can a host discover the mapping between a physical address and an IPv6 interface address?

    a.   Dynamic Host Configuration Protocol (DHCP)

    b.   Stateless Address Autoconfiguration (SLAAC)

    c.   Address Resolution Protocol (ARP)

    d.   IPv6 Neighbor Discovery (ND) protocol

5. How does a switch discover which physical addresses are reachable through each interface?

    a.   By receiving a frame with a host's physical source address

    b.   The Spanning Tree Protocol (STP)

    c.   Using ping to interrogate each connected host

    d.   Through a link-state routing protocol

6. Switching forwards packets based on

    a.   The destination physical (MAC) address.

    b.   The metric to each destination.

    c.   The destination logical (IP) address.

    d.   The set of ports blocked based on the Spanning Tree Protocol (STP).

7. Routing forwards packets based on
    a. The destination physical (MAC) address.
    b. The metric to each destination.
    c. The destination logical (IP) address.
    d. The set of ports blocked based on the Spanning Tree Protocol (STP).

8. When a router has multiple routes that could be used to forward a packet, what is the first rule for deciding which entry to use?
    a. The lowest route metric will be used.
    b. The shortest hop count will be used.
    c. The route through the nonblocked interface will be used.
    d. The route with the longest prefix length will be used.

9. What will happen if a host tries to use DHCP to get an IP address on a segment without a DHCP server?
    a. The host will not be able to get an IP address.
    b. The system administrator will be notified and can configure an address manually.
    c. The router will forward the DHCP request packets out every interface as a broadcast.
    d. The router may relay the DHCP request packet toward the DHCP server (if configured).

Foundation Topics

Assigning IP Addresses to Hosts

Once the network has a block of IP addresses, how can these addresses be translated into addresses for each host? There are three basic techniques for assigning an address to an interface:

- Manual configuration

- Calculate an address

- Assign an address through a protocol

Let's look at each of these techniques in a little more detail.

Manual Configuration

Manual configuration is just what it sounds like—using the tools available on an individual host to configure an IP address on each interface. Because this topic is covered in more detail in Chapter 4, "Wired Host Networking Configuration," we will not consider it here.

Calculate an IP Address

Many older network protocols similar to IP calculated their addresses by combining a physical address with a network prefix:

- Novell NetWare calculated an interface address for each interface by combining a four-octet network number assigned by the operator with the EUI-48 address, creating a 10-octet interface address.

- The OSI protocol suite and DECnet Phase V both use a variable-length address that can take an EUI-48 address as a host identifier within a prefix.

IPv4 was designed for efficient forwarding on existing hardware, hence the four-octet address. Since most forwarding decisions are made in the first or second pair of octets, depending on the prefix length, even processors with 16-bit registers could process IPv4 addresses efficiently. A 32-bit interface address cannot contain a 48-bit physical address, so there is no practical way to calculate an interface address from a physical address.

IPv6, however, was designed with the EUI-64 physical address space in mind; this is why every host receives an address with a 64-bit (/64) prefix length.

Computing a Link Local Address

IPv6 implementations calculate a **link local address** for each interface by combining the *fe00* prefix with the EUI-48 physical address. Figure 3-1 illustrates.

A   00-00-FE-11-22-33

B   02-00-FE-11-22-33

C   02-00-FE-FF-EE-11-22-33

D   (FE80::)(02-00-FE-FF-FE-11-22-33)(/64)

E   fe80::200:feff:fe11:2233/64

Figure 3-1 *Computing an IPv6 Link Local Address*

In this illustration:

- *A* shows the existing EUI-48 physical address; this address is chosen from among the addresses programmed into the physical interface chipset by its manufacturer.

- At *B*, the IPv6 software sets the seventh bit in the first octet—the U/L bit—of the physical address to 1. This indicates the address is unique only within this segment.

- The IPv6 implementation then adds *FF-FE* in the center of the address, as shown at *C*.

- The resulting 64-bit address—an EUI-64 address—is combined with *FE80::* on the front and the prefix length, /64, at the end. This is shown in step *D*.

- The resulting address is shown at *E*: fe80::200:feff:fe11:2233/64.

Two hosts on the same segment may have been configured with the same physical address, so two hosts may end up calculating the same link local address using this process.

To make certain the link local address is not a duplicate, the IPv6 software will run *Duplicate Address Detection (DAD)*.

This link local address can be used to communicate with any other device within the same broadcast domain but not outside the broadcast domain (as the name *link local* implies).

Computing a Global Address

Once the link local address is calculated, a host running IPv6 can use *Stateless Address Autoconfiguration (**SLAAC**)* to calculate a globally routable address. To calculate a global address using SLAAC,

1. The IPv6 software sends a *Router Solicitation (RS)* message to a special router-only multicast address.

2. A router on the link will respond with a *Router Advertisement (RA)*. The RA contains the segment prefix.

3. The IPv6 software combines the EUI-64 address, calculated above, with the segment prefix.

4. It performs duplicate address detection with this new address to make certain no other host on the segment has the same address.

5. It sets the default gateway address on the local host to the RA message source.

> **NOTE**   If the host does not receive an RA in response to its RS message, there are no routers on the segment; hence, there is no way to communicate with any hosts on some larger network or the global Internet. If there are no routers, the host can assume every other host it can reach will be reachable using the link local address.

SLAAC is widely but not always used for configuring IPv6 interface addresses. Operators often note three problems with SLAAC:

- Naming services cannot be configured through SLAAC.

- It is difficult to relate an IPv6 address to an individual user or host in network management systems.

- SLAAC reveals potentially private information in some situations.

It is worth looking at the last item in this list in a little more detail.

Physical Addresses and Privacy

Suppose you have a host—a laptop, mobile phone, or some other device—you use in several locations; Figure 3-2 illustrates.

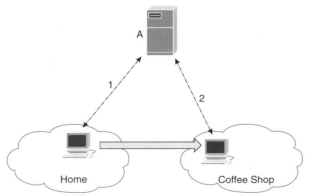

Figure 3-2   *Privacy and Host Movement*

In Figure 3-2, a host moves from a home network at *1* to a coffee shop at *2*. If the host uses SLAAC to calculate an IP address at both locations, server *A* can tell this is the same host in two locations because the lower 64 bits of the address will be the same.

In fact, no matter where you take this host, if you attach it to the global Internet and access this same server, server *A* will be able to know this is the same host. It is possible to track an individual user by noting their IPv6 address everywhere they go. This is a violation of the user's privacy.

One solution to this problem is configuring the host to use a random physical address. Chapter 11, "Local Area Networks," discusses this solution in more detail.

A second solution is to assign hosts addresses rather than calculating the interface address from the physical address.

Assign an Address Through a Protocol

Many operators deploy the **Dynamic Host Configuration Protocol (DHCP)** to

- Support IPv4 hosts, which do not have any way to automatically calculate interface addresses
- Support naming services (DNS)
- Log and control the mapping of interface IP addresses, including controlling who can be assigned an IP address on the network
- Control the assignment of the default gateway
- Ensure the same IP address is not used in multiple places

IPv4 DHCP

Figure 3-3 illustrates the IPv4 DHCP process.

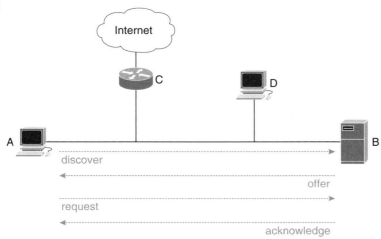

Figure 3-3 *IPv4 DHCP Operation*

In this figure, host *A* is connected to the network and needs to obtain an IPv4 address. *A*, the *DHCP client*, sends a *discover* message to determine whether a DHCP server is connected to the network. If no DHCP server answers, *A* will not be able to obtain an IPv4 address.

A sends this discovery message to a broadcast address, so router *C* and host *D* also receive the message. Since neither is a DHCP server, they will not respond to the message.

Most routers can be configured as DHCP servers; the two functions have been separated in this figure for clarity.

The DHCP server *B* will examine its local DHCP table for *A*'s physical address. If the server has assigned *A* an address in the recent past, it will have a record associating *A*'s physical address with an already assigned IPv4 address. If so, *B* will use the existing assignment. Otherwise, *B* will look for an unassigned address in its address pool and create an entry for *A*.

Server *B* offers this IPv4 address to *A*; the offer message is sent to the broadcast address. Both *D* and *C* receive this message, but the physical address of the requesting host (*A* in this case) is carried in the offer packet, so *C* and *D* ignore this message.

When it receives the offer message, *A* will probe the network using the Address Resolution Protocol (**ARP**), discussed in more detail in the next section, to verify the address is not in use by another host. After verifying the proposed address is unused, *A* will send a request message to the DHCP server, *B*.

The request message is also a broadcast, so *C* and *D* receive the packet. Since neither one of these devices is a DHCP server, however, they will ignore the request message.

The DHCP server will then respond with an acknowledgment sent directly (not as a broadcast) to the client, *A*.

This final acknowledgment message contains other information, such as the default gateway the host should use, the prefix length for this segment, a list of name (DNS) servers available on the network, and a *lease time*.

The lease time allows IP addresses to be reused if a host has not been active for some time—usually measured in hours or days. Just before a lease expires, the client can request an extension. Timing out IP address assignments allows addresses to be reused once a host moves permanently to another location in the network.

IPv6 DHCP and Router Advertisements

The original design of IPv6 did not include DHCP; all hosts would use SLAAC to calculate their IPv6 address. As noted previously, operators discovered there are still reasons to have a lightweight protocol that supports interface address configuration.

There are some minor differences between DHCP for IPv4 and DHCP for IPv6 (often called DHCPv6):

- Instead of broadcasting responses, the server can send packets to the client's link local address, thus eliminating all server broadcasts.

- Instead of broadcasting packets intended for the DHCP server, the client sends these packets to a multicast group.

- A server can assign an address to a host based on a *DHCP unique identifier (DUID)*, which is calculated by the client. If the host's physical address changes, it can keep or recover its previous IPv6 address.

- Many unnecessary and unused options from DHCP for IPv4 have been removed in DHCPv6.

- The *discover* message in IPv4 DHCP is the *solicit* message in DHCPv6.

- The *offer* message in IPv4 DHCP is the *advertise* message in DHCPv6.

- The acknowledge message in DHCP for IPv4 is the *reply* message in DHCPv6.

One major difference between DHCP for IPv4 and DHCPv6 is the prefix length and default gateway are not included in the DHCPv6 reply message. Instead, these are carried in a separate IPv6 protocol called *Router Advertisements (RAs)*.

IPv6-capable routers send RAs to each segment to

- Inform hosts connected to the segment the router can be used as a default gateway.

- Indicate whether hosts connected to this segment should automatically compute their IPv6 addresses via SLAAC or should ask for an address through a DHCPv6 server.

- Inform hosts connected to the segment about the maximum packet size (or *maximum transmission unit [MTU]*).

NOTE   The chapters in Part II explore MTU in more detail.

Host-to-Host Communication and Address Resolution on a Single Wire

Once all the hosts connected to a single segment have physical and interface addresses, they can begin to communicate. Figure 3-4 will be used to explain the process.

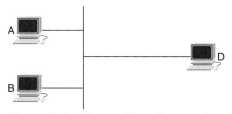

Figure 3-4   *Host-to-Host Communication*

In the figure, each host has *two* addresses: a physical address and an interface address. Host A could send packets destined to host D to the correct interface and broadcast physical addresses. Host D would certainly receive and process the packet in this case, but host B would need to receive the packet, examine it, determine it does not need to accept or process it, and then discard it. If every host on the segment must receive and process every packet—even if the processing is just to discard the packet—this would be a huge waste of resources.

It is much more efficient if host *A* can send packets to host *D*'s correct interface and physical addresses. To do this, however, *A* must know the relationship between these two addresses; it must *resolve* host *D*'s interface address to a physical address reachable on this segment.

IPv4 and IPv6 use different address resolution techniques.

IPv4 Address Resolution

If *A*, *B*, and *D* are running IPv4, the Address Resolution Protocol (ARP) maps physical to interface addresses. When host *A* wants to send a packet to *D*:

1. Host *A* examines its local ARP cache to see whether it already knows the physical and interface addresses for *D*.

2. Given *A* does not have an existing mapping, it will send an *ARP request* to the physical broadcast address, so both *B* and *D* receive this packet.

3. The ARP request will have host *D*'s interface address in the *Target Protocol Address* field of the ARP packet and host *A*'s physical address in the *Sender Hardware Address* field.

4. When *B* receives this packet, it will determine its local interface address does not match the target protocol address, so it will discard the ARP packet.

5. When *D* receives this packet, it will determine its local interface address matches the target protocol address, so it will build a response.

6. In its response, host *D* will include its interface address in the *Sender Protocol Address* field, and the physical address for the correct interface in the sender hardware address field.

When *A* receives this response, it can add the mapping between *D*'s interface and physical addresses, allowing it to send unicast packets to *D*.

ARP can also be used to notify all the hosts on a segment about an address change or to announce the connection of a new host to the segment. This is called a *gratuitous ARP* because it is an ARP response that does not correspond to any ARP request. Most hosts will send a gratuitous ARP when they connect to a segment so that all the other hosts will have their interface to physical address mapping in their local cache, saving time and effort in transmitting packets.

Duplicate Address Detection is another function of ARP in an IPv4 network. A host can send an *ARP probe* to determine whether any host on the segment is already using an IP address. If the host does not receive an answer, it can assume the IP address is not in use.

IPv6 Address Resolution

If *A*, *B*, *D*, and *E* are running IPv6, the *Neighbor Discovery (ND)* protocol maps physical interface addresses. One major difference between IPv4 and IPv6 is that IPv6 hosts do not assume every other host on the segment uses the same prefix. Figure 3-5 illustrates.

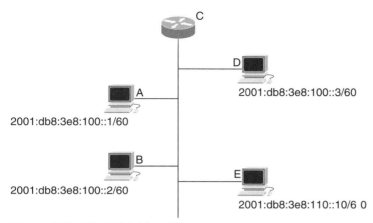

Figure 3-5 *IPv6 Neighbor Discovery*

Because of the role the router plays in IPv6 address resolution, we have to start a few steps back from where we started with IPv4:

1. Router *C* sends an RA with a list of prefixes.
2. Each prefix in use on this segment is marked with the *L* bit.
3. Each host on the segment—*A*, *B*, *D*, and *E*—keeps a list of the prefixes in use on this segment based on all the RAs they have received.

When host *A* wants to send a packet to *B*:

1. Host *A* examines its local list of prefixes in use on this segment.
2. If host *B*'s IPv6 address is contained within one of the prefixes on this segment, *A* sends a *Neighbor Solicitation* packet to a multicast address.
3. Host *B* responds with a *Neighbor Advertisement* packet linking its IPv6 and physical addresses.
4. Host *A* receives the neighbor advertisement and uses it to build a local cache of IPv6 to physical address mappings.

Switching Packets

Up to this point, we have considered hosts connected to a single segment. What if you want to connect multiple segments (or broadcast domains or wires)? There are three ways to connect segments in a computer network:

- Switches
- Routers
- Gateways

Switches act on the physical (Layer 2) interface. Routers act on the interface (Layer 3) address. Gateways or proxies act on some higher-level address, including the protocol identifier and port number. Gateways are outside the scope of this book.

Switches are the simpler of the two kinds of devices we want to look at, so we'll start there. Figure 3-6 and the list that follows help to illustrate how a switch works.

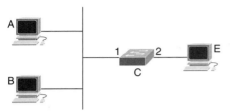

Figure 3-6   *Switching Packets*

In Figure 3-6, if host *A* does not have any information on *E*, but *A* wants to send a packet to *E*:

1. Host *A* sends an address discovery packet for *E*. For IPv6, this will be a neighbor solicitation, and the packet's destination address will be a multicast. For IPv4, this will be an ARP, and the packet's destination will be a broadcast.

2. Switch *C* receives this packet. Because *C* receives this packet on *port 1*, *C* will learn *A* is connected to (or reachable by) *port 1*. A switch learns about which hosts are connected where by examining packets it receives in the normal course of the network's operation. This is called **bridge learning**.

3. Switch *C* examines the destination address and discovers it is either a multicast (IPv6) or broadcast (IPv4). Broadcast and multicast packets should be forwarded out all unblocked ports, so *C* forwards this packet through *port 2*.

4. Host *E* receives the address resolution packet and responds.

5. When *C* receives *E*'s response on *port 2*, it learns *E* is reachable through *port 2*.

6. Switch *C* forwards *E*'s responses back through *port 1*, where *A* receives the response and builds a local table mapping *E*'s interface address to *E*'s physical address.

NOTE   Switches can decide not to forward a multicast packet out through a port if the switch knows there are no hosts listening to the multicast group. How the switch knows this is outside the scope of this book, but it involves the switch snooping on Internet Group Message Protocol (IGMP) packets.

When *A* sends a packet toward *E*, it will place *E*'s interface and physical addresses into the packet and transmit it onto the segment. When *C* receives this packet, it will examine its local table, called a **bridge** or *forwarding table*, and find *E* is reachable through *port 2*. Because the destination is on a different port than where *C* received the packet, *C* will forward the packet out the correct port (*port 2* in this case).

NOTE   Hosts will receive and process all packets with a broadcast physical address, some packets with a physical multicast address, and unicast packets only if the destination address matches the physical address of the interface. Switches, on the other hand, receive packets promiscuously, which means they receive and process every packet transmitted on the physical wire or segment.

The process of sending a packet from *A* to *E* seems to be just the same as it was without switch *C* in the network, so what purpose does the switch serve? Let's walk through the process of *A* sending packets to *B* to see the difference:

1. Host *A* sends an address discovery packet for *B*. For IPv6, this will be a neighbor solicitation, and the packet's destination address will be a multicast. For IPv4, this will be an ARP, and the packet's destination will be a broadcast.

2. Switch *C* receives this packet. Because *C* receives this packet on *port 1*, *C* will learn *A* is connected to (or reachable by) *port 1*. A switch learns about which hosts are connected where by examining packets it receives in the normal course of the network's operation. This is called *bridge learning*.

3. Switch *C* examines the destination address and discovers it is either a multicast (IPv6) or broadcast (IPv4). Broadcast and multicast packets should be forwarded out all unblocked ports, so *C* forwards this packet through *port 2*.

4. Host *E* receives the address resolution packet and does not respond because the packet request does not contain *E*'s interface address.

5. Host *B* receives the address resolution packet and responds with a unicast packet directly to host *A*.

6. When *C* receives *B*'s response on *port 1*, it learns *B* is reachable through *port 1*.

7. Host *A* receives *B*'s response and creates a local cache entry mapping *B*'s physical and interface address.

When *A* sends packets to *B*, switch *C* will receive these packets. When *C* looks up the packet's destination in its local forwarding table, it will find *B* is reachable through *port 1*, which is the same port *B* itself is reachable through. Because the packet is received on the same port through which the destination is reachable, *C* does nothing with the packet.

Because *C* ignores the packet, *E never receives it*. For a single packet, the reduction in processing load might be small. Breaking up the network into parts greatly impacts the size of buildable networks—or the possible *scale*.

Multiple Hops and Switching

NOTE This section describes what the Spanning Tree Protocol accomplishes and why it is important. The operation of SPT is outside the scope of this book.

A single switch might be useful in some situations, but to build a large network, you are going to need more than one. How do hosts communicate when there are multiple switches in a network, as Figure 3-7 illustrates?

Suppose host *A* wants to send a packet to *G*. We'll simplify the example by assuming *A* already knows the mapping between *G*'s physical and interface addresses.

1. Host *A* will build a packet with *G*'s destination physical and interface addresses and transmit it.

2. When switch *C* receives this packet, it will learn *A* is reachable on port *C1*.

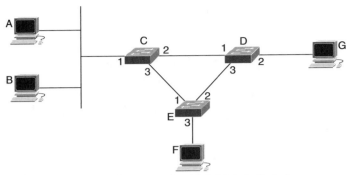

Figure 3-7 *A Single Network with Multiple Switches*

Assume switches *D* and *E* have also received traffic in the past, so *D* knows *G* is reachable via port *D2*, and *E* knows *F* is connected to port *E3*.

Which port will *C* forward the packet through to reach *G*? What if

- Switch *C* chooses to forward the packet through port *C3*?

- When switch *E* receives the packet, it decides to forward the packet through *E2*?

- When switch *D* receives the packet, it decides to forward the packet through *D1*?

The traffic would travel around in a loop...forever! To prevent this from happening, switches need to decide which ports they will forward traffic on, and which packets they will not (which ports they will *block*).

Spanning Tree Protocol (**STP**) is used in most *switched* computer networks to decide which ports to use and block, preventing loops of this kind from forming. To prevent loops, STP

- Chooses a root bridge.

- Blocks ports not on the *shortest path* to or from the root bridge.

The shortest path is chosen based on **metrics** assigned to each link in the network. While metrics are often assigned based on the bandwidth of each link, all links might also be assigned the same metric, or the network operator might assign metrics based on some other method.

> **NOTE** Why use the shortest path? Because the shortest path can never be a loop. Loops will always contain some part of a given path twice, so they will always be longer than some alternate path that does not loop. The shortest path test is too strict because it eliminates non-looping paths. In advanced routing techniques, the shortest path test is relaxed, and methods are used to discover loop-free paths that are the shortest path. In traffic steering and engineering, packets are carried past the point where they would otherwise loop in tunnels. These techniques are beyond the scope of this book.

If STP chooses switch *E* as the root, for instance:

- Switch *C*'s shortest path to reach *E*, the root, is through port *C3*. Switch *C* will leave *C3* in a forwarding state and block *C2*, so no traffic will be forwarded through that port.

- Switch *D*'s shortest path to reach *E*, the root, is through port *D3*. Switch *D* will leave *D3* in a forwarding state and block *D1*, so no traffic will be forwarded through that port.

- Switch *E* will leave all its ports in forwarding state.

When *A* sends a packet to *G*:

- Switch *C* will forward the packet destined to *G* through port *C3* because this is the only other port in a forwarding state.

- When *E* receives this packet on port *E1*, it will learn *A* is reachable through this point.

- Since *E* does not yet know which port to use when forwarding traffic to *G*, it will forward the packet out ports *E2* and *E3*.

- Host *F* will ignore the packet because the destination does not match *F*'s physical address.

- When switch *D* receives the packet on port *D1*, it learns *A* is reachable through this port.

- Switch *D*'s only other port in forwarding mode is *D2*, so it forwards the packet through this port.

- Host *G* will receive the packet and process it.

In the opposite direction, when host *G* sends a response to *A*:

- Switch *D* will learn *G* is reachable through port *D2*.

- Switch *D* will have a table entry stating *A* is reachable through port *D3*, so it will forward the packet through port *D3*.

- Switch *E* will have a table entry stating *A* is reachable through port *E1*, so *E* will forward the packet through *E1*.

- Switch *C* will have a table entry stating *A* is reachable through port *C1*, so it will forward the packet through *C1*.

- Host *A* will receive the packet and process it.

Two key points to remember about STP are

- STP builds a tree of the entire network regardless of where each host is and forwards traffic along the tree. For instance, in Figure 3-7, the shortest path between *A* and *G* is through *C* and *D* rather than through *C*, *E*, and *D*. The tree may take some packets along the more optimal path and other packets along less-than-optimal paths to prevent loops from forming.

■ Any time the topology of the network—the switches and links—changes, the switches must relearn how to reach each host connected to the network.

Routing Packets

Switches determine where to forward a packet based on physical interface addresses. Because physical interfaces are often called *Layer 2 addresses*, switches are often called *Layer 2 switches* or *Layer 2 network devices*. Routing, on the other hand, uses interface, or IP, addresses to forward traffic through a network.

Figure 3-8 illustrates routing.

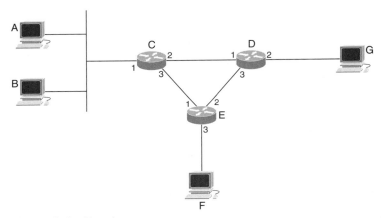

Figure 3-8 *Routing*

Let's consider what happens in this network when host *A* sends a packet to *G*.

1. Host *A* determines *G* will not receive any broadcast addresses it sends. Because of this, *A* cannot use ARP, ND, or any other mechanism to discover *G*'s physical address.

2. Because host *A* has only an interface (IP) address to send the packet to, it will send the packet to the default gateway. The default gateway is learned from DHCP for IPv4, learned from RAs for IPv6, or manually configured. In this case, router *C* is the default gateway.

3. Host *A* builds the packet with *G*'s interface address and *C*'s physical address. *A* needs to build the packet with *C*'s physical address because routers—unlike switches—do not operate in promiscuous mode. Routers only accept and process packets destined to one of their physical addresses. It is also important for *A* to build the packet with *G*'s interface address since router *C* knows where the packet is ultimately destined.

4. Router *C* examines its local **routing table** to determine the *next hop* toward *G*. Let's assume the shortest path through the network toward *G*, from *C*'s perspective, is via router *D*.

5. Router *C* strips the outer encapsulation (or physical layer header) off the packet and adds a new physical layer header with *D*'s physical address. Router *C* leaves *G*'s address in place as the final interface address so *D* can determine where to forward the packet.

6. Router *D* processes the packet because the destination physical address matches one of its local interfaces. *D*'s routing table indicates *G* is directly connected through port *D2*.

7. Router *D* strips the outer encapsulation and adds a new one with *G*'s physical address. The interface address remains *G*'s. *D* then transmits the packet on the segment toward *G*.

If router *C* does not know the correct physical address for port *D1*, or router *D* does not know *G*'s physical address, they will use the normal protocols and processes described previously to build this mapping—IPv4 ARP and IPv6 ND.

Key points to remember about routing:

- Routers (unlike switches) do not forward packets transmitted to physical broadcast segments. This means traditional mapping protocols like DHCP will not work through a router (although some protocols can be made to work, as described in a later section).

- Two hosts connected only through a router are not on the same segment or broadcast domain. Breaking networks into multiple segments is important for scaling. Imagine if 10,000 hosts were all connected to the same broadcast domain, and each host sent one broadcast packet each second. Every host on the network would need to process 10,000 broadcast packets per second—a huge amount of traffic for very little (or no) gain.

- Hosts send packets directly to the physical interface address of the router, rather than the physical interface address of the destination host or a broadcast address. A router is more like a host in this regard than a switch.

- Routers decide where to send packets based on the interface, or IP, address, rather than the physical address. The table routers use to determine where to forward packets is called the *routing table*, or the *IP routing table*.

This description of how routing works leads to other questions, such as

- How is the routing table used to forward packets?

- How is the routing table built?

- What is the difference between a router and a switch?

- What happens inside a router or switch? How do these devices forward packets?

Each of these questions will be discussed in the following sections.

> **NOTE**   Breaking networks into multiple segments also reduces the size of the failure domain by reducing the scope of broadcast packets. Controlling failure domains falls under network design, and so is outside the general scope of this book.

Using the Routing Table to Forward Packets

The router uses an IP routing table, or *routing information base (RIB)* to forward packets. The RIB is a table of

- Destination network

- Port to forward traffic through

- Next hop information

Figure 3-9 illustrates a network and corresponding routing tables.

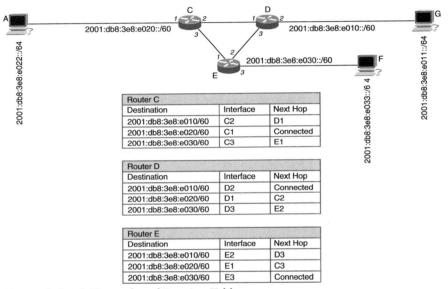

Figure 3-9 *A Network and Routing Tables*

From router *C*'s perspective, there are two paths to 2001:db8:3e8:e010::/60—one through *E* and another through *D*. How does *C* choose between these two paths? Based on the *metric* or *weight* of each path. The shortest or lowest cost path *cannot be a loop*.

Figure 3-9 uses the number of *hops*, or routers, along a path as the metric. The path to 2001:db8:3e8:e010::/60 through *D* only passes through *D* itself—one hop—while the path through *E* passes through *E* then *D* to reach the destination—two hops.

When *A* sends a packet toward *G*:

1. Router *C* receives and processes the packet because *A* built the packet with the interface address of *C1*.

2. Router *C* examines its routing table to discover the correct route to reach *G*. Notice *C* does not have a route to *G*'s interface (IP) address, which is 2001:db8:3e8:e011::/64. Instead, *C* only has a route to the network *G* is connected to, 2001:db8:3e8:e010::/60. Routers will always forward to the network address *containing* the packet's destination.

3. After finding the network *containing G*, router C finds the corresponding output interface, C2, and the correct next hop, D1, to reach the packet's destination.

4. Router C builds a physical layer (Layer 2) encapsulation with the physical interface address of D1, leaves the IP header, which contains G's interface address, alone, and queues the packet for transmission by interface C2.

When host A sends a packet toward F:

1. Router C receives and processes the packet because A built the packet with the interface address of C1.

2. Router C examines its routing table to discover the correct route to reach F. Router C will use the entry for 2001:db8:3e8:e030::/60 to reach F.

3. After finding the network containing F, router C finds the corresponding output interface, C3, and the correct next hop, E1, to reach the packet's destination.

4. Router C builds a physical layer (Layer 2) encapsulation with the physical interface address of E1, leaves the IP header, which contains F's interface address, alone, and queues the packet for transmission by interface C3.

In these two examples, router C does not have an entry for the destination host address; it uses the network containing the host address to forward traffic. The idea of one address containing another, like a state containing a city or a city containing a street, is a part of address aggregation. To forward to aggregated addresses, routers follow a rule called the *longest prefix match*. Figure 3-10 illustrates.

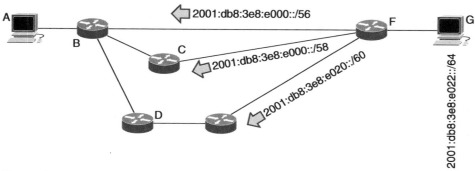

Figure 3-10 *Longest Prefix Match*

In Figure 3-10, host A sends a packet toward G with a destination address of 2001:db8:3e8:e022::/64. When router B receives this packet, it will have three different ways to forward the packet:

■ Along a one-hop route through F using the route to 2001:db8:3e8:e000::/56

■ Along a two-hop route through C using the route to 2001:db8:3e8:e000::/58

■ Along a three-hop route through D using the route to 2001:db8:3e8:e020::/60

Router *B* will send the packet through *D*—even though this is the longest path (three hops instead of one) because of the longest prefix match rule. Specifically:

- Routes with different prefix lengths are treated as different destinations in the routing table.

- The route with the longest prefix length that covers the destination interface (IP) address is preferred.

In Figure 3-10, *B* treats the three available paths as separate destinations, and the route with the longest prefix, a /60 instead of a /56, is preferred.

When you are looking at a routing table and trying to decide which path the router will send packets, you always need to consider the longest prefix match rule.

Building the Routing Table

Routers build routing tables from a variety of sources, but the primary ones are

- Including the IP address of each connected interface

- Manual configuration, or *static routes*

- Dynamic routing protocols

Including the connected interfaces is obvious: the router knows about these networks because it has direct local configuration information.

Static routes are a little more difficult, but still simple. Since the network operator in Figure 3-10 has a drawing of the network (a *network diagram*) and all the IP addresses, they can manually configure routing table entries in *B*'s routing table. These are called *static routes*.

The third option is the most complex and most common. Each router in the network is a specialized computer. Routers, like all other computers, can run software of various kinds, even though they do not normally have keyboards and monitors attached to them. One of the pieces of software almost all routers run is an application called a **routing protocol**.

The various methods used to build routing tables, all combined, are often called the *control plane*.

Let's return to the real world for a few moments to understand how routing protocols work; Figure 3-11 illustrates.

In Figure 3-11, there is a small network of paths with labeled intersections. We are trying to find a path between *Y* and *Z*, each located in a cul-de-sac. The idea is someone standing at *Y* should be able to get a package to *Z* without moving. The person can hand off the package to one of the runners illustrated at each intersection, who can then hand off the package to another runner at an adjacent intersection, etc., until the package is delivered.

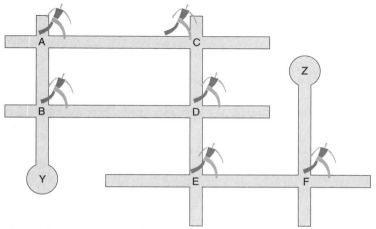

Figure 3-11   *A Physical World Routing Protocol Illustration*

There are many different ways we could find a route through this network of paths; for instance:

■ Because we have a picture (a network diagram), we can just trace out the route and tell each runner where they should go and to whom they should hand off the package.

■ We can have one runner, say at the beginning, wander down every possible path, recording where they end up, and use this information to tell each of the runners stationed at an intersection where to take the package when they receive it.

NOTE   Some routing systems do, in fact, send a packet (called an *explorer*) through every path in the network. The originator, *Y* in this illustration, can then choose a path through the network. This is called *source routing*.

We are going to use a slightly different method, though, because we would prefer not to have any single runner move farther away from their intersection than an immediately adjacent intersection. Runner *A* should only ever go to *B* and *C*, runner *C* should only ever go to *A* and *D*, etc.

Each runner is given a way to record and copy notes—a pad of note paper and a copying machine, in effect. Once equipped, every runner will carry a copy of what they know about the network to the intersections they can reach. There are two different versions of this information.

For **distance-vector routing protocols**, the runner carries information about destinations they can reach and the cost, from their perspective of reaching that destination. In Figure 3-11, assuming the cost is the hop count:

■ Runner *F* tells *E* they know how to reach *Z*, which is directly connected.

■ Runner *E* tells *D* it knows how to reach *Z* with a cost of 1.

- Runner *D* tells *C* and *B* it can reach *Z* with a cost of 2.

- Runner *C* tells *A* it can reach *Z* with a cost of 3.

- Runner *A* tells *B* it can reach *Z* with a cost of 4.

At the end of this process, *B* knows it can reach *Z* in two ways: through *D* with a cost of 2 and *A* with a cost of 4. Because the path through *D* is the shorter path (and therefore cannot be a loop), the runner at *B* will give the package to *D* when they receive a package from *Y*.

This same process can be performed for the path from *Z* back to *Y*, and for any other pair of points in the networks. In network engineering, this algorithm is called *Bellman-Ford*, after the names of its inventors. A variant of Bellman-Ford is called the *diffusing update algorithm (DUAL)*.

For *link-state protocols*, the runner carries information about who the neighboring intersections are and any directly connected destinations. In Figure 3-11:

- Runner *A* tells runners *B* and *C* their adjacent intersections (neighbors) are *B* and *C*.

- Runner *B* tells runners *A* and *D* their neighbors are *A* and *D*, and they can reach *Y*.

- Runner *C* tells runners *A* and *D* their neighbors are *A* and *D*.

- Runner *D* tells runners *B*, *C*, and *E* their neighbors are *B*, *C*, and *E*.

- Runner *E* tells runners *E* and *F* their neighbors are *D* and *F*.

- Runner *F* tells runner *E* it has one neighbor, *E*, and it can reach *Z*.

Each runner keeps a copy of this information on their pads; this is called the *Link State Database (LSDB)*. Using the information in their LSDB, each runner can use an algorithm called *Dijkstra's Shortest Path First* to find the lowest cost (in this case least number of hops) through the network. Dijkstra's Shortest Path First is often called *Dijkstra* or *Shortest Path First (SPF)*. The graph of the network resulting from running SPF is called the *Shortest Path Tree (SPT)*.

Essentially, runner *B* can see it is connected to *D*, *D* is connected to *E*, *E* is connected to *F*, and *F* is connected to the destination they are trying to reach, *Z*.

It might seem a little odd that the runners tell a neighbor they can reach that neighbor. Why does runner *A* care *B* can reach *A*? There are two reasons:

- It is simpler to implement a **link-state routing protocol** when every router tells all its neighbors the same thing.

- If *A* knows *B* can reach *A*, then *A* can be certain the link (or path) between *A* and *B* is working correctly, so packages can be carried over the path. This is called the *back-link check*.

For *path-vector* protocols:

- Runner *F* tells *E* they can reach *Z*.

- Runner *D* tells *C* and *B* they can reach *Z* via the path *[F]*.

- Runner *C* tells *A* they can reach *Z* via the path *[D,E,F]*.

- Runner *A* tells *B* they can reach *Z* via the path *[C,D,E,F]*.

Runner *B* now has two paths, neither of which can be a loop because they pass through different nodes to reach the destination. *B* can choose one of the two paths based on local policy, such as "choose the path with the shortest hop count."

Some common routing protocols are

- *Routing Information Protocol (RIP)*, which has two versions: RIPv1 and RIPv2. RIP is a distance-vector protocol and uses the Bellman-Ford method of finding the routes through a network.

- *Enhanced Interior Gateway Routing Protocol (EIGRP)*, which is a distance-vector protocol using the DUAL method of finding the routes through the network.

- *Open Shortest Path First (OSPF)*, which has two versions: OSPFv2 and OSPFv3. OSPF is (surprisingly enough!) a link-state protocol and uses Dijkstra's SPF to find routes through the network.

- *Intermediate System to Intermediate System (IS-IS)*, which uses Dijkstra's SPF to find routes through the network.

- *Border Gateway Protocol (BGP)*, currently in version 4 (BGPv4), which is a path-vector protocol. BGPv4 currently provides routing information for the global Internet.

Metrics

Up to this point the illustrations have all used hop count as the only metric. Most routing protocols use some more sophisticated metrics, such as

- RIP uses the hop count as its metric.

- EIGRP uses the bandwidth of the slowest link in the path as one element of its metric.

- EIGRP uses the sum of the delays across every link in the path as one element of its metric.

- OSPF uses the sum of the inverse of the bandwidths of every link in the path.

- IS-IS uses a metric like the hop count by default, but most implementations can be configured to use the sum of the inverse of the bandwidths of every link in the path.

- BGP uses the operator's preference on how packets should exit the provider's network as one metric. This is called the *local preference*.

- BGP uses the operator's preference on how packets should enter the provider's network as one metric. This is called the *multiple exit discriminator*.

- BGP uses the number of networks (a network is close to an *autonomous system*, or *AS*) a packet will pass through to reach a given destination as a metric. This is called the *AS Path Length*.

What Happens Inside a Router?

Routers and switches are opaque boxes to most network operators and engineers. To better understand how these devices forward packets, and the relationship between the physical interfaces, the routing table, and the applications (like routing protocols), it is useful to peek inside. Figure 3-12 illustrates.

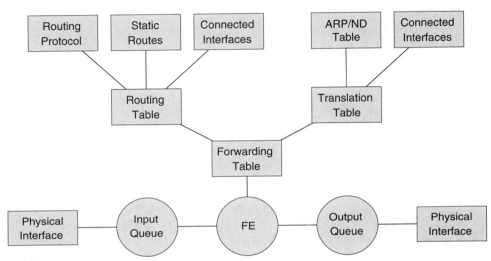

Figure 3-12   *Router Components*

Figure 3-12 is a simplified version of the internal components of a router; as you gain experience in computer networking, you will probably want to do a deeper study on the components and operation of routers and switches.

The path of a packet through a router is simple:

1   The packet is received as electrical or optical signals on the physical interface. These signals are decoded and copied into the router's memory by the *serial/deserializer (SerDes)* and *Phy* chipset.

2.   The packet is (sometimes) copied into an input queue. Some routers and switches do not have an input queue; they process packets directly as the physical interface is copying them into memory.

3.   The *forwarding engine (FE)* processes the packet. FEs are also called *switching engines*, *switching chipsets*, and *Ethernet chips*. A common name used for these processors is the *application-specific integrated circuit (ASIC)*, because most FEs are also ASICs. There are many other kinds of ASICs than FEs, however.

4.   The FE strips off the outer (physical header), finds the correct entry in the forwarding table (also called the *forwarding information base*, or *FIB*), builds a new physical layer header, and places the packet on the output queue.

5.   The physical interface converts the packet from internal memory locations to electrical or optical signals for its journey to the next hop.

The forwarding table supplies the FE with the three pieces of information it needs to forward a packet:

- A destination interface (IP) address

- The interface this packet should be transmitted on

- The correct physical interface address to use when forwarding the packet

The forwarding table, in turn, is built by combining the various translation tables available in the router—tables relating the IP address of each next hop device (whether a host or another router) to a physical address. There normally is not a separate table, as shown here (for clarity), but rather the ARP and ND tables are consulted directly.

The routing table is built from information provided by routing protocols, static (manually configured) routes, and information about connected interfaces.

Routers versus Switches

While this chapter describes the function of routers and switches separately, *router* and *switch* are often used interchangeably in computer networking. To use the words absolutely properly:

- *Routers* should refer to devices that switch (or route) each packet based on the interface or IP destination address.

- Routers break up broadcast domains; two hosts connected to two different ports on a router are not on the same segment or broadcast domain.

- *Switches* should refer to devices that switch each packet based on the physical address.

- Switches do not break up broadcast domains; two hosts connected to two different ports on a switch are still on the same segment or broadcast domain.

A further major difference between routing and switching is IP packets have a *time-to-live (TTL)*, while physical frames normally do not. Each time a router processes an IP packet, it reduces the TTL by 1; when the TTL reaches 0, the packet is discarded.

The confusion in naming these two devices stems from the early days of networks, when

- Routers processed or switched all packets in software. Because routers processed packets in software, their switching speed was limited by the general-purpose processor, which means routers could not switch packets very quickly.

- Switches processed or switched all packets in hardware. Because switches processed packets in hardware, they could switch packets nearly as fast as their interface speeds.

When the first routers with hardware-based switching were designed and deployed, no one really wanted to call it a router because routers were slow. No one really wanted to call it a switch either because it routed packets based on the destination IP address rather than switching them.

A compromise developed: they were called *Layer 3 switches*. Over time, however, the *Layer 3* part of the *Layer 3 switch* was dropped, and now routers are called switches.

Calling both of these kinds of network devices a *switch* can cause confusion. Make certain that when you hear someone say the word *switch*, you understand which of the two kinds of devices they are discussing.

> **NOTE**   One of the first routers, if not the first, with hardware-based forwarding was the Cisco 7000 with a Silicon Switching Engine (SSE).

Routing Loops

It is possible, from time to time, for a **routing loop** to form in a network. Figure 3-13 illustrates.

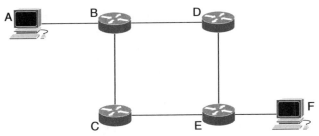

Figure 3-13   *A Routing Loop*

If host *A* sends a packet toward *F*, then

1.   Router *B* forwards the packet to *D*.
2.   Router *D* forwards the packet to *E*.
3.   Router *E* forwards the packet to *C*.
4.   Router *C* forwards the packet to *A*.

This is called a *routing* or *forwarding loop*. This loop can happen for a few moments when a link or device either fails or is added to the network—called a *microloop*. This can also happen because of misconfigurations.

IP packets carry a time-to-live (TTL). Routers decrement the TTL by 1 when processing a packet; if a packet is received with a TTL of 0, it is discarded. The TTL prevents a packet from being forwarded around in the network "forever."

Physical frames do not have a TTL, so a forwarding loop in a switched network is more likely to cause a network failure in a switched network than a routed network.

Asymmetric Paths

IP networks are *packet-based*, meaning each packet can travel a different path, or packets between two hosts can travel on two different paths. Figure 3-14 illustrates.

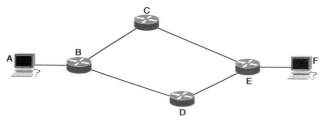

Figure 3-14 *Asymmetric Routing*

In Figure 3-14, packets traveling from host *A* to *F* can travel along the *[B,C,E]* path or the *[B,D,E]* path. Every other packet *A* sends to *F* could travel along a different path, or router *B* could choose to send all the packets traveling to host *F* along one of these two paths. Normally, in IP routing, router *B* will choose one path because splitting the traffic along two paths will reduce the performance of the host *A* to *F* communication.

When host *F* sends packets to *A*, it may also travel on either of the available paths. There is no particular reason for routers *B* and *E* to choose the same path, however. In fact, these two routers are not even aware of which path the other router has chosen. It is often true, then, that packets will travel consistently on one path in one direction and consistently on another path in the opposite direction.

Using different paths in each direction is called **asymmetric routing**; it is very common for two hosts to communicate over an asymmetric path of this kind.

Redirects and Relays

What if you have a network like the one illustrated in Figure 3-15? If host *A* has its default gateway set to router *B*, it does not seem as though it can ever send any packets to *E*.

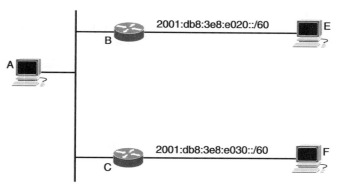

Figure 3-15 *Redirects*

Router *B* is configured as host *A*'s default gateway. When *A* sends a packet toward *F*, it will send the packet to *B*, which will either route the packet back out the same interface, toward *C*, or it will drop the packet (if *B* has been configured not to forward traffic back out the interface on which it arrived).

To resolve this point, router *B* can send a **redirect** to *A*, telling the host it should send traffic destined to 2001:db8:3e8:e030::/60 toward router *C*. Redirects are transmitted through the *Internet Control Message Protocol (ICMP)* in both IPv4 and IPv6.

Host *A* will insert this information into its local routing table. Hosts also have routing tables but do not normally run a routing protocol to populate them. Host routing tables will be considered in the next chapter.

We can use the same illustration to consider one final host configuration problem and its solution. If *A* is the only configuration server attached to this network, then *E* is going to run into a problem trying to lease an address and retrieve other configuration information. DHCP relies on local segment broadcast packets. If *E* sends a DHCP request to the physical address broadcast address, *A* will never receive this request because router *B* breaks up the broadcast domain; *B* will not forward broadcast packets from one segment to another.

To resolve this problem, router *B* can be configured as a DHCP **relay**. When *B* receives a broadcast DHCP interface on any interface, it will forward the DHCP request—as a unicast—to host *A*'s IP address.

Chapter Review

Addresses are complex; they must be defined, formatted, and assigned. This chapter discussed address assignment and mapping in detail. Addresses are not enough for moving packets through a network, however. Network devices like routers and switches need to know where and how hosts are attached to the network and where to send packets so they can be delivered.

This chapter considered calculating, assigning, and mapping IP addresses. Routing and switching are also explained here at a high level, and we pulled the lid off a router to get a better idea of how it really works.

Now that you have a general idea of how addresses are used to move packets from a source host to a destination host and how addresses are assigned to a host, it is time to look at how to configure a few different kinds of hosts. The next chapter considers how to configure Windows, Apple Macintosh, and Linux hosts for network connectivity.

One key to doing well on the exams is to perform repetitive spaced review sessions. Review this chapter's material using either the tools in the book or interactive tools for the same material found on the book's companion website. Refer to the online Appendix D, "Study Planner," element for more details. Table 3-2 outlines the key review elements and where you can find them. To better track your study progress, record when you completed these activities in the second column.

Table 3-2   Chapter Review Tracking

Review Element	Review Date (s)	Resource Used
Review key topics		Book, website
Review key terms		Book, website
Repeat DIKTA questions		Book, PTP
Review concepts and actions		Book, website

Review All the Key Topics

Table 3-3 lists the key topics for this chapter

Table 3-3   Key Topics for Chapter 3

Key Topic Element	Description	Page Number
Paragraph	Link local addresses	55
Paragraph	Duplicate Address Detection (DAD)	55
Paragraph	Using Stateless Address Autoconfiguration (SLAAC) to calculate a globally routable address	56
Figure 3-3, Paragraphs	Dynamic Host Configuration Protocol (DHCP)	57
Paragraph	Address Resolution Protocol (ARP)	60
Paragraph, Figure 3-5	Neighbor Discovery (ND) protocol	60
Figure 3-6, list	Bridge learning	62
Paragraph	Bridge/forwarding table	62
Paragraph	Preventing loops with Spanning Tree Protocol (STP)	64
Paragraph, Figure 3-8	Routing packets	66
Paragraph	Routing information base (RIB)	68
Paragraph	Sources from which routing tables are built	70
Paragraphx	Static routes	70
Paragraph	Routing protocol	70
Paragraph	Control plane	70
Paragraph	Asymmetric routing	77

Key Terms You Should Know

Key terms in this chapter include

IPv6 link local address, IPv6 SLAAC, DHCP, ARP, bridge learning, bridge table, STP, metrics, routing table, routing protocol, distance-vector routing protocol, link-state routing protocol, routing loop, asymmetric routes, redirect, relay

Concepts and Actions

Review the concepts considered in this chapter using Table 3-4. You can cover the right side of this table and describe each concept or action in your own words to verify your understanding.

Table 3-4   Concepts and Actions

Physical address used to calculate an IPv6 link local address	EUI-48
Significance of the fe80:: IPv6 address prefix	This is a link local address automatically calculated by the host
Two protocols a host uses to calculate a globally routable IPv6 address	Neighbor Discovery (ND) and Router Discovery (RD)
Private information can leak through SLAAC-generated IPv6 addresses	The physical interface portion of the address does not change, potentially allowing a host to be tracked across multiple locations
Three things DHCP supplies to a host	An IP address, a default gateway, a name server
Lease time	The amount of time a host may use an address assigned through DHCP without renewal
Duplicate address detection	Sending an ARP or ND request to ensure some other host on the same network is not using the same address as a local interface
Gratuitous ARP	A host sends an ARP on connecting to a network so all the other hosts can prepopulate their neighbor discovery/resolution tables
Forwards packets based on physical addresses	Switch
Bridge learning	A switch learns a given physical address is reachable on a given port by examining the source addresses of frames it receives
Forwards all broadcast frames out all nonblocked ports or interfaces	Switch
Elects a root bridge to prevent forwarding loops	Spanning Tree Protocol
Builds a spanning tree per destination	Routing
Forwards packets based on the interface (IP) address	Routing
Does not forward broadcast packets out all ports	Router
Distance-vector routing	Each router advertises the destinations it can reach, and its cost to reach those destinations, to its neighbors
Link-state routing	Each router advertises what it is connected to, to all other routers in the network (flooding domain)
Path-vector routing	Each router advertises the destinations it can reach, and its path to reach those destinations, to its neighbors
Common metric types	Hop count, inverse of the bandwidth, the sum of the delays along the path

Forwarding table	The correct output port and physical encapsulation for each destination; built from the routing table and translation or neighbor tables
Sources of information for the routing table	Routing protocols, static (manually configured) routes, connected interfaces
Redirect	When a router informs a host to use a different router to send traffic to a destination
DHCP Relay	When a router forwards DHCP packets to a DHCP server, so hosts connected to a segment can use DHCP to configure local network parameters
DHCP	Dynamic Host Configuration Protocol; assigns an IP address, a default gateway, and a name server to a host
Root bridge	The switch (or bridge) used to determine which ports are blocked in spanning tree
Link-state routing protocol	Computes loop-free paths through the network by every router sending information about what they are connected to, to every other router in the network
Receive ring	Where packets are copied (or clocked) off physical media into a router's memory
Forwarding engine	A specialized chip designed to forward packets

3

CHAPTER 4

Wired Host Networking Configuration

This chapter covers the following exam topics:

3. **Endpoints and Media Types**

    3.4. **Demonstrate how to set up and check network connectivity on Windows, Linux, Mac, Android, and Apple mobile OS.**

    Networking utilities on Windows, Linux, Android, and Apple operating systems; how to run troubleshooting commands; wireless client settings (SSID, authentication, WPA mode)

5. **Diagnosing Problems**

    5.3. **Run basic diagnostic commands and interpret the results.**

    ping, ipconfig/ifconfig/ip, tracert/traceroute, nslookup; recognize how firewalls can influence the result

The previous three chapters discussed how computer networks use addresses and control planes to carry traffic from one host to another. This chapter is a more practical examination of configuring individual hosts to connect to and use an IP network.

We work through

- Verifying the physical interface address.
- Configuring and verifying the IP address.

NOTE Chapter 15, "Application Transport," considers DNS operation. Chapter 8, "Wireless Networks," considers connecting to a wireless network.

This chapter also touches on the host routing table. Each section considers a single operating system.

NOTE The instructions given here may not be correct for the version of the operating system you are using, and they may not be correct for future versions of these operating systems. Vendors change the way these options are accessed and configured regularly.

NOTE Chapter 7, "Wired Networks," considers the operation of Ethernet, the typical interface type you will encounter when working with hosts.

"Do I Know This Already?" Quiz

Take the quiz (either here or use the PTP software) if you want to use the score to help you decide how much time to spend on this chapter. Appendix A, "Answers to the 'Do I Know This Already?' Quizzes," found at the end of the book, includes both the answers and explanations. You can also find answers in the PTP testing software.

Table 4-1 "Do I Know This Already?" Foundation Topics Section-to-Question Mapping

Section	Questions
Windows	1, 2, 3
macOS	4
Linux	5
Verifying Connectivity	6, 7, 8, 9
Finding Your Public IP Address	10

CAUTION The goal of self-assessment is to gauge your mastery of the topics in this chapter. If you do not know the answer to a question or are only partially sure of the answer, you should mark that question as wrong for purposes of the self-assessment. Giving yourself credit for an answer you incorrectly guess skews your self-assessment results and might provide you with a false sense of security.

1. What tools can you use to view and manage the IP addresses of interfaces on Windows 11?

    a. System Information app, Control Panel, command-line utilities

    b. Control Panel, System Information app

    c. Settings app, Control Panel, command-line utilities

    d. Command-line utilities, Control Panel

2. What Windows 11 application can you use to view the amount of information transmitted and received on an interface? (Choose two.)

    a. Control Panel network configuration dialog

    b. System Information app interface information

    c. Settings app Network & Interface

    d. Control Panel Interface Status dialog

3. What is one primary difference between command-line interfaces (CLIs) for configuration and monitoring rather than graphical user interfaces (GUIs) when configuring and monitoring network interfaces?

    a. The CLI always provides more information than the GUI.

    b. The GUI always uses fewer system resources than the CLI.

    c. The CLI is easier to use with scripts and automation tools.

    d. The GUI tends to respond more quickly to user commands than a CLI.

4. What tools can you use to view and manage the IP addresses of interfaces on Apple's OS/X?

a. Control Panel, Finder, command line

b. Settings application, System Information app, command line

c. Control Panel, System Information app, command line

d. Settings application, Finder, command line

5. What are the most common commands used for discovering the IP address in Linux?

a. Powershell and **ifconfig**

b. **ipconfig** and **ip**

c. **ifconfig** and **ip**

d. Powershell and **ip**

6. What kinds of packets do **ping** applications transmit?

a. User Datagram Protocol (UDP)

b. Transmission Control Protocol (TCP)

c. QUIC

d. Internet Control Message Protocol (ICMP)

7. What kinds of packets do **traceroute** applications normally transmit? (Choose two.)

a. User Datagram Protocol (UDP)

b. Transmission Control Protocol (TCP)

c. QUIC

d. Internet Control Message Protocol (ICMP)

8. What characteristic of an IP packet does **traceroute** use to find each hop in a path?

a. Destination address

b. Source address

c. Packet size

d. Time-to-live

9. What does an asterisk (*) in **traceroute** mean? (Choose two.)

a. The router or host at this hop in the network does not send ICMP responses.

b. The packet passed through a tunnel.

c. The path ends at this point.

d. The network has blocked the ICMP response packet.

10. Why might your public and private IP addresses be different?

a. The host operating system displays your private IP addresses to preserve the user's privacy.

b. The private IP address is only known to the user, while everyone knows the public IP address.

c. If the network operator runs out of address space, they will sometimes use private IP addresses they own for hosts.

d. Your local network assigns your host a private IP address that is translated to a public IP address for use on the global Internet.

Foundation Topics

Windows

There are three ways to examine, verify, and configure wire interface information in Windows 11: the **Settings app**, the **Control Panel**, and the command line.

The Settings App

To find and verify the network configuration in Windows 11 using the graphical user interface (GUI), open the **Settings** app and the **Network & Internet** section. A host may have several interfaces; you must select an individual interface to find its addresses and other information. Figure 4-1 illustrates the *Network & internet* section for a wired (Ethernet) interface.

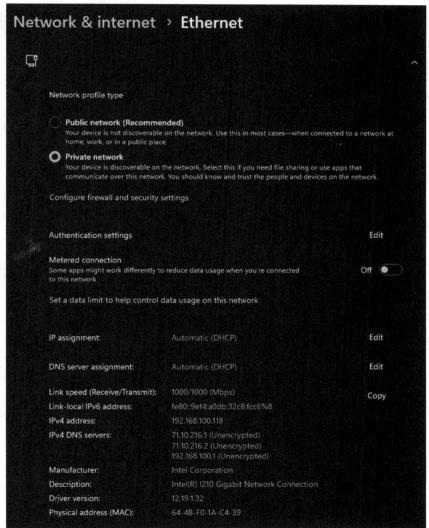

Figure 4-1 *Network Section of the Windows 11 Settings App*

Several lines are of interest here:

- **IP assignment:** Indicates whether the host's address was assigned manually or through DHCP.

- **DNS server assignment:** Indicates whether the host's DNS server address was assigned manually or through DHCP.

- **Link speed:** Indicates the speed of the physical connection. Chapter 9, "Bandwidth, Delay, and Jitter," will consider bandwidth in more detail.

- **Link-local IPv6 address:** Computed as described in Chapter 3, "Routing and Switching."

- **IPv4 address:** Indicates the IPv4 address assigned to the Ethernet interface.

- **IPv4 DNS servers:** DNS servers used to translate (resolve) domain names to IPv4 addresses.

- **Physical address (MAC):** Indicates the physical address assigned to the interface by the manufacturer.

There are several lines with an Edit button to their right. Clicking the button to the right of *IP assignment* will allow you to manually assign an IP address rather than depending on a DHCP server. Once you have selected manual, rather than DHCP, assignment, you can change the *IPv4 address* field.

The Control Panel

A second place you can see the physical and interface addresses on Windows 11 is through the *Control Panel*. Once you have opened the Control Panel, select **Network & Internet**, then **View Network Status and Tasks**. Following this process opens a screen with the label *View your basic network information and set up connections* at the top.

Once there, select the **Ethernet** port to see the wired interface information.

> **NOTE**   There might be a number after Ethernet; this indicates this host has multiple physical interfaces. If so, each interface will have separate physical and interface addresses.

Selecting the interface will cause a dialog to appear with some basic information, as shown in Figure 4-2.

This dialog shows some basic information about the interface, including

- **IPv4 Connectivity, IPv6 Connectivity:** Whether this host has Internet connectivity via IPv4 or IPv6

- **Media State:** Whether the interface is enabled or disabled

- **Duration:** How long this interface has been active and connected

- **Speed:** The speed of the connection

- **Bytes Sent:** The number of octets of data this host has transmitted on this interface

- **Bytes Received:** The number of octets of data this host has received on this interface

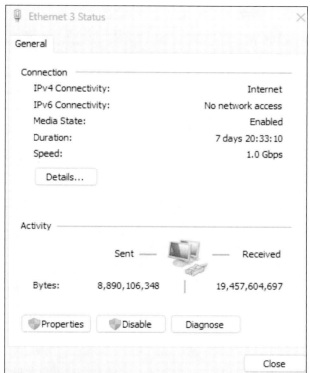

Figure 4-2 *Windows 11 Interface Status Dialog*

The **Disable** option does precisely what it sounds like: disables this interface.

The **Diagnose** option runs the *Windows Network Troubleshooter*. The troubleshooter checks the interface's status and whether the interface has a connection and then tries to *ping* various addresses. If the interface does not appear connected, the troubleshooter will attempt to reset the interface, release and renew any addresses assigned through DHCP, and take other actions.

The **Properties** option brings up another dialog, shown in Figure 4-3.

Figure 4-3 shows two different dialogs. On the left is the Properties dialog for the wired information. Clicking some items in the list will only enable the **Install** and **Uninstall** options, while others will also enable the **Properties** option.

If you select **Internet Protocol Version 4**, the dialog on the figure's right will pop up. This dialog allows you to configure how the interface obtains an IPv4 address and DNS server information—automatically or manually. You can configure an IPv4 address in the provided space if the manual option is selected.

Returning to the Ethernet Status dialog, selecting the **Details** option will cause a dialog to pop up containing the current interface physical address, interface address, DHCP lease information, DHCP server, and DNS server. This dialog will also display the subnet mask on some versions of Windows.

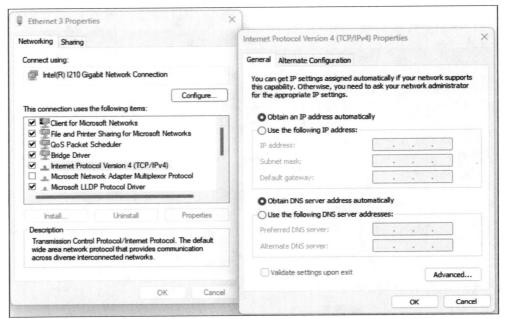

Figure 4-3 *Control Panel Interface and Properties Dialogs in Windows 11*

The Command Line

A command-line interface (**CLI**) is interactive: the user types commands and the host returns some response, usually text. Network engineers tend to work with CLIs more than GUIs because

- CLIs tend to respond more quickly.

- CLIs require fewer resources, so they can be implemented in a broader range of devices.

- Text output typically contains a higher density of textual information than GUIs.

- CLIs are more amenable to automation.

Powershell is the best tool on a Windows 11 host to access a command line. Most Windows hosts have Powershell installed, but it is available in the Microsoft Store if not. To display the physical interface from Powershell, use the command **getmac /v** from the CLI prompt, as shown in Figure 4-4.

```
PS C:\Windows\System32> getmac /v

Connection Name Network Adapter Physical Address     Transport Name
=============== =============== ==================== ===============================================
Ethernet 4      ExpressVPN TAP  00-FF-00-C7-B6-70    Media disconnected
Local Area Conn ExpressVPN TUN  N/A                  Media disconnected
Wi-Fi           Intel(R) Wi-Fi  E4-FD-45-90-B5-82    \Device\Tcpip_{2714C24A-CB0A-4DC8-B870-32C4CDD55B65}
Ethernet 3      Intel(R) I210 G 64-4B-F0-1A-C4-39    \Device\Tcpip_{492A8CAC-AE87-4A03-8654-429AD5866201}
Bluetooth Netwo Bluetooth Devic E4-FD-45-90-B5-86    Media disconnected
```

Figure 4-4 *Displaying the Physical Interface Address from Powershell*

Each interface has a single line of output with the following:

- **Connection Name:** Matches the interface name in GUI

- **Network Adapter:** Identifies the Interface manufacturer

- **Physical Address:** Indicates whether the interface has a physical interface

- **Transport Name:** Indicates the name of the protocol running over (or *bound to*) this interface

IPv4 and IPv6 information can be discovered by running a different command, **ipconfig /all**, as shown in Figure 4-5.

Key Topic

```
PS C:\> ipconfig /all

Windows IP Configuration

   Host Name . . . . . . . . . . . . : WinHst
   Primary Dns Suffix  . . . . . . . :
   Node Type . . . . . . . . . . . . : Hybrid
   IP Routing Enabled. . . . . . . . : No
   WINS Proxy Enabled. . . . . . . . : No

Ethernet adapter Ethernet 3:

   Connection-specific DNS Suffix  . :
   Description . . . . . . . . . . . : Intel(R) I210 Gigabit Network Connection
   Physical Address. . . . . . . . . : 64-4B-F0-1A-C4-39
   DHCP Enabled. . . . . . . . . . . : Yes
   Autoconfiguration Enabled . . . . : Yes
   Link-local IPv6 Address . . . . . : fe80::9ef4:a0db:32c8:fcc6%8(Preferred)
   IPv4 Address. . . . . . . . . . . : 192.168.100.118(Preferred)
   Subnet Mask . . . . . . . . . . . : 255.255.255.0
   Lease Obtained. . . . . . . . . . : Thursday, January 19, 2023 17:34:26
   Lease Expires . . . . . . . . . . : Friday, January 27, 2023 16:35:00
   Default Gateway . . . . . . . . . : 192.168.100.1
   DHCP Server . . . . . . . . . . . : 192.168.100.1
   DHCPv6 IAID . . . . . . . . . . . : 660884464
   DHCPv6 Client DUID. . . . . . . . : 00-01-00-01-2A-CF-A2-3B-64-4B-F0-1A-C4-39
   DNS Servers . . . . . . . . . . . : 71.10.216.1
                                        71.10.216.2
                                        192.168.100.1
   NetBIOS over Tcpip. . . . . . . . : Enabled
```

Figure 4-5 *Interface Configuration Information on Windows 11*

The same basic information (IPv4 address, IPv6 address, subnet mask, etc.) is available here as the GUI, but additional information is also available. In particular:

- The IPv6 DUID, described in Chapter 2, "Addresses"

- The physical interface address

- The default gateway

In most situations, starting Powershell and running **ipconfig /all** is the quickest way to find all the network information you need about a host. The **ipconfig** command can be used for more than showing current configuration information; it can also be used to

- **/release:** Release DHCP-learned IPv4 addresses

- **/renew:** Renew the DHCP-learned IPv4 addresses

- **/release6:** Release DHCP-learned IPv6 addresses

- **/renew6:** Renew DHCP-learned IPv6 addresses

- **/flushdns:** Flush the local DNS cache

NOTE   Chapter 15, "Application Transport," considers the **ipconfig** DNS commands in more detail.

NOTE   You can change the host's IP address from Powershell using the **netsh** command. Using **netsh** is outside the scope of this book.

Two other pieces of network information available from Powershell are difficult to find in any GUI display: the local ARP cache and routing table. To see the local ARP cache, use the **arp -a** command, as shown in Figure 4-6.

```
PS C:\Windows\System32> arp -a

Interface: 192.168.100.118 --- 0x8
  Internet Address      Physical Address      Type
  192.168.100.1         60-a4-b7-74-9a-38     dynamic
  192.168.100.77        00-11-32-a2-f0-73     dynamic
  192.168.100.101       58-ce-2a-da-80-ae     dynamic
  192.168.100.103       e4-fd-45-90-b5-82     dynamic
  192.168.100.106       ae-06-67-2c-8c-1b     dynamic
  192.168.100.108       cc-6a-10-2a-79-85     dynamic
  192.168.100.110       b0-5c-da-fd-ee-dd     dynamic
  192.168.100.111       00-11-32-59-6c-93     dynamic
  192.168.100.112       c8-cb-9e-4b-18-c4     dynamic
  192.168.100.116       bc-d0-74-59-2e-3a     dynamic
  192.168.100.117       b4-6c-47-18-cc-fb     dynamic
  192.168.100.255       ff-ff-ff-ff-ff-ff     static
  224.0.0.22            01-00-5e-00-00-16     static
  224.0.0.251           01-00-5e-00-00-fb     static
  224.0.0.252           01-00-5e-00-00-fc     static
  239.192.5.8           01-00-5e-40-05-08     static
  239.255.102.18        01-00-5e-7f-66-12     static
  239.255.255.250       01-00-5e-7f-ff-fa     static
  255.255.255.255       ff-ff-ff-ff-ff-ff     static
```

Figure 4-6 *Showing the ARP Cache in Powershell*

Each IP address is shown with its matching physical address in the table. Addresses marked *dynamic* were learned using ARP. Addresses marked *static* are embedded in the operating system software; for instance, the IP broadcast address (255.255.255.255) is always mapped to the physical interface broadcast address (ff-ff-ff-ff-ff-ff).

Figure 4-7 illustrates the Windows 11 host routing table, as displayed using the **Get-NetRoute** command from Powershell.

```
PS C:\Windows\System32> Get-NetRoute

ifIndex DestinationPrefix   NextHop   RouteMetric ifMetric PolicyStore
------- -----------------   -------   ----------- -------- -----------
22      255.255.255.255/32  0.0.0.0   256         25       ActiveStore
17      255.255.255.255/32  0.0.0.0   256         25       ActiveStore
5       255.255.255.255/32  0.0.0.0   256         30       ActiveStore
15      255.255.255.255/32  0.0.0.0   256         5        ActiveStore
10      255.255.255.255/32  0.0.0.0   256         65       ActiveStore
8       255.255.255.255/32  0.0.0.0   256         25       ActiveStore
2       255.255.255.255/32  0.0.0.0   256         5        ActiveStore
1       255.255.255.255/32  0.0.0.0   256         75       ActiveStore
```

Figure 4-7   *The Windows Host Routing Table*

Several fields are of interest in the output shown in Figure 4-7:

- **ifIndex:** Indicates which interface to send packets through when following this route.

- **DestinationPrefix:** Indicates the destination network.

- **NextHop:** Identifies where to send packets to reach this destination; 0.0.0.0 means "this device" or the local host.

- **RouteMetric:** Indicates the metric, or cost to reach this destination. Windows hosts use the hop count as a metric.

- **ifMetric:** Indicates the default metric for routes reachable through this interface.

macOS

Apple's macOS is the operating system used by every Macintosh computer. There are three ways to display physical and interface addresses on macOS computers: the GUI, the CLI, and the *System Information* application.

System Preferences

Open the System Preferences app and select the **Network** icon. Figure 4-8 illustrates the resulting dialog.

Select either the Ethernet port or a port labeled *LAN (Local Area Network)* for the wired connection. Fields of note include

- **IPv4 Address:** The IPv4 address assigned to the interface.

- **Subnet Mask:** The subnet mask, which indicates the network prefix. In this case, the subnet mask is 255.255.255.0, so the prefix length is /24.

- **Router:** The default gateway.

- **DNS Server:** The IP address of the server this host will use to resolve domain names.

Figure 4-8 *The macOS Network Configuration Dialog*

If you remember the reserved IP addresses from Chapter 2, you will recognize the address 127.0.0.1 as a loopback address; any packets sent to this address loop back to the host. Some hosts set the DNS server to a loopback address and then use an internal process to capture and process DNS packets.

If you select the dropdown next to *Configure IPv4*, you can select to configure the IPv4 address either *Using DHCP* or

- **Using DHCP with a manual address,** which means you will manually configure an IP address on this interface, but DHCP will be used to discover the correct DNS server and default gateway.

- **Using BootP,** which uses an older, largely deprecated protocol called *BootP* to configure the IP address, default gateway, etc.

- **Manually,** which means you will insert the correct IP address, default gateway, and other information in the fields in the dialog.

Selecting the **Advanced** option and then the **Hardware** tab results in the dialog shown in Figure 4-9.

Figure 4-9 *The Advanced Hardware Tab*

The Hardware tab shows the physical address for this interface.

The Terminal Command Line

Like most other hosts, Apple Macintosh computers have a command line you can use to examine and configure network parameters. You can typically find an application called Terminal under Applications, Utilities in the Finder app. Once you have launched the terminal, you can display the network configuration using **ifconfig**, as shown in Figure 4-10.

```
rwhite ~ % ifconfig

en0: flags=8863<UP,BROADCAST,SMART,RUNNING,SIMPLEX,MULTICAST> mtu 1500
options=6463<RXCSUM,TXCSUM,TSO4,TSO6,CHANNEL_IO,PARTIAL_CSUM,ZEROINVERT_CSUM>
ether bc:d0:74:59:2e:3a
inet6 fe80::1426:fd9e:684c:b6be%en0 prefixlen 64 secured scopeid 0xd
inet 192.168.100.116 netmask 0xffffff00 broadcast 192.168.100.255
nd6 options=201<PERFORMNUD,DAD>
media: autoselectstatus: active
```

Figure 4-10 *macOS* ifconfig

A lot of information here will not look familiar because macOS provides a lot more information from the physical interfaces than Windows does (there are ways to get this information in Windows, but they involve using different commands than **ifconfig**). Most of this information, however, is not very useful for the average operator.

The important fields are

- **en0** is the *service name* of the interface.

- **ether bc** contains the physical address.

- **inet6** contains the IPv6 interface address and prefix length.

- **inet** contains the IPv4 interface address and subnet mask.

The output does not include the default gateway.

If you need to release and renew the DHCP-assigned IP address in macOS, you use a pair of commands:

> **sudo ipconfig set en0 BOOTP; sudo ipconfig set en0 DHCP**

Make sure you replace **en0** with the correct interface name. This first command sets the interface to retrieve a new IP address via the bootp protocol and forces the interface to release the DHCP learned address. Since bootp is no longer widely used, the interface will (most likely) not have an address once the first command is run.

The second command tells the host to request a new DHCP address from the server.

> **NOTE**   Because DHCP servers store mappings between host physical addresses and assigned IP addresses, a host will probably receive the same address after the renewal as it had before.

In macOS, unlike Windows 11, you can use the **ifconfig** command to set the IP address for an interface manually. However, because macOS manages IP addresses as part of a central configuration system *configd*, any address you set using **ifconfig** will be overwritten by configd.

You can tell configd to change the IP address on an interface using the command **networksetup.**

System Information

Finally, you can find information about network configuration in the *System Information* application, customarily located under Utilities in Finder. Two sections contain information on wired network interfaces: Ethernet and Network Locations.

Figure 4-11 shows the information in the System Information Ethernet section.

The Ethernet section of System Information displays information about the physical connection. This Ethernet port connects through a USB port, has a physical interface (MAC) address, and can support up to a 5 Gb/s data rate and the physical interface (MAC) address.

```
USB 10/100/1000 LAN:
Bus:USB
Vendor Name:Realtek
Product Name:USB 10/100/1000 LAN
Vendor ID:0x0bda
Product ID:0x8153
USB Link Speed:Up to 5 Gb/s
Driver:com.apple.DriverKit.AppleUserECM
BSD Device Name:en7
MAC Address:00:e0:4c:0c:00:a6
AVB Support:No
```

Figure 4-11 *Ethernet Section of System Information*

NOTE Why is this Ethernet port listed as a USB port? Because, like many laptops, this particular Macintosh does not have a physical Ethernet port. This port is a USB to Ethernet adapter plugged into the laptop.

4

Figure 4-12 shows the correct section of the Locations tab, located under the Network portion of the System Information app.

```
USB 10/100/1000 LAN:
Type:Ethernet   BSD Device
Name:en7
Hardware (MAC) Address:00:e0:4c:0c:00:a6
IPv4:   Configuration Method:DHCP
IPv6:   Configuration Method:Automatic
DNS:   Server Addresses:127.0.0.1
Proxies:
Exceptions List:*.local, 169.254/16
FTP Passive Mode:Yes
```

Figure 4-12 *Network Locations Section of System Information*

The information displayed here is like that displayed in other places in macOS.

Linux

While the average user does not encounter the Linux operating system very often, Linux is widely used to support web-based enterprise-grade applications. If you work in a data center environment, in software development, or with automation, you will almost certainly encounter and use some variant of the Linux operating system.

NOTE Each version (distribution or distro) and each version of each distro of Linux has slightly different commands for displaying and setting the network configuration on a host. This section will use examples from Ubuntu 22.04.

Linux's most common commands used to display network configuration are **ifconfig** and **ip**. Figure 4-13 illustrates **ipconfig** on Ubuntu Linux.

```
eth0: flags=4163<UP,BROADCAST,RUNNING,MULTICAST>  mtu 1500
        inet 192.168.154.207  netmask 255.255.240.0  broadcast 192.168.159.255
        inet6 fe80::215:5dff:fe24:2bb  prefixlen 64   scopeid 0x20<link>
        ether 00:15:5d:24:02:bb  txqueuelen 1000   (Ethernet)
        RX packets 69977  bytes 395750691 (395.7 MB)
        RX errors 0  dropped 0  overruns 0  frame 0
        TX packets 27821  bytes 2015983 (2.0 MB)
        TX errors 0  dropped 0 overruns 0  carrier 0  collisions 0

lo: flags=73<UP,LOOPBACK,RUNNING>  mtu 65536
        inet 127.0.0.1  netmask 255.0.0.0
        inet6 ::1  prefixlen 128   scopeid 0x10<host>
        loop  txqueuelen 1000   (Local Loopback)
        RX packets 0  bytes 0 (0.0 B)
        RX errors 0  dropped 0  overruns 0  frame 0
        TX packets 0  bytes 0 (0.0 B)
        TX errors 0  dropped 0 overruns 0  carrier 0  collisions 0
```

Figure 4-13 ipconfig *Output on Ubuntu Linux*

The fields of interest are

- **inet:** The IPv4 address.

- **netmask:** The subnet mask. Here, it is 255.255.240.0, so the prefix length is /28.

- **inet6:** The IPv6 address.

- **prefixlen:** The prefix length.

- **scope:** Whether this is a link-local or global address. Since the IPv6 address begins with fe80, this is a link-local address.

- **ether:** The physical address.

- **RX packets:** The number of packets received, dropped, etc.

- **TS packets:** The number of packets transmitted, dropped, etc.

Figure 4-14 shows the output of the **ip addr** command.

```
6: eth0: <BROADCAST,MULTICAST,UP,LOWER_UP> mtu 1500 qdisc mq state UP group default qlen 1000
    link/ether 00:15:5d:24:02:bb brd ff:ff:ff:ff:ff:ff
    inet 192.168.154.207/20 brd 192.168.159.255 scope global eth0
        valid_lft forever preferred_lft forever
    inet6 fe80::215:5dff:fe24:2bb/64 scope link
        valid_lft forever preferred_lft forever
```

Figure 4-14 ip addr *Command on Ubuntu Linux*

The output of **ip addr** shows the physical address, the IPv4 address (**inet**), and the IPv6 address (**inet6**). This output also includes some DHCP information: **alid_lft forever preferred_lft forever** means the DHCP lease lifetime is forever.

Configuring a static interface address requires editing **/etc/netplan/01-netcfg.yaml**, as Figure 4-15 illustrates, and then restarting the network software.

```
network:
  version: 2
  renderer: networkd
  ethernets:
    enp0s3:
     dhcp4: no
     addresses: [203.0.113.4/24]
     gateway4: 203.0.113.1
     nameservers:
        addresses: [8.8.8.8,8.8.4.4]
```

Figure 4-15   *01-netcfg.yaml File in Ubuntu Linux*

You can edit the file in any text editor, such as VI or Emacs, replacing the **addresses: 203.0.113.4 /24** with the correct address and the default gateway, 203.0.113.1, with the correct default gateway address. The **nameservers** should also be replaced with their correct values.

Verifying Connectivity

Once network parameters are configured, you must verify the configuration is correct. **ping** and **traceroute** are the two most widely used utilities. The network in Figure 4-16 will be used throughout this section to illustrate tools commonly used to verify connectivity and their use.

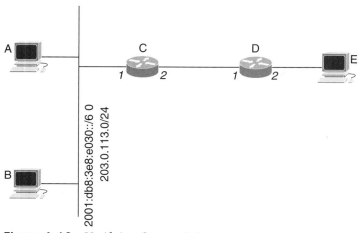

Figure 4-16   *Verifying Connectivity*

Ping

The first application to use when verifying connectivity is ping. The ping application sends a series of ICMP packets, called the *ICMP echo request*, to the indicated IP address. The host should respond with an ICMP echo reply packet if it receives these packets.

> **NOTE**   This example assumes *C* is the default gateway for *A* and *B*, while *D* is *E*'s.

For instance, you could verify connectivity from host *A* in the network illustrated in Figure 4-16 by

- Pinging *B*'s interface address, verifying local connectivity on the segment is working correctly.

- Pinging the interface address of *C1*, verifying connectivity to the default gateway is working correctly.

- Pinging the interface address of *C2*, verifying connectivity to the default gateway *and* the default gateway is configured correctly to route packets back to *A*.

- Pinging the interface address of *E* to verify connectivity is working across the entire network (or Internet) to the destination host.

You can also ping local broadcast and multicast addresses. For instance, pinging 203.0.113.255 (the network broadcast address) should elicit a response from every device connected to the segment. If you ping 203.0.113.255 from *A*, you should receive replies from *B* and *C*. Pinging a broadcast or multicast address can be especially useful to clear and rebuild a host's IPv4 ARP cache and IPv6 neighbor table.

Ping is a versatile application with many options. Options for the **ping** application on Ubuntu Linux include

- **-4**: Use IPv4 packets only.

- **-6**: Use IPv6 packets only.

- **-b**: Allow pinging to a broadcast address (as described previously).

- **-c**: Send a specific number of ICMP echo packets; the default usually is 5 or 10 for most ping applications.

- **-f**: Flood ping, which provides a quick way to determine how many packets are being dropped between the source and destination.

- **-i**: Use a specific source address or interface.

- **-p**: "Pad" the ICMP echo packets with a specific pattern. This can be good for catching problems with the network transmitting packets of all 1s, all 0s, or some other specific content.

- **-s**: Pad the ICMP packets transmitted to a specific size; this can be good for determining if larger or smaller packets can be carried through the network.

- **-t**: Set the TTL to a specific number.

The source interface can be handy when verifying local connectivity if you cannot access a specific host. If you have access to router *C* but not to host *B*, you can ping *B* from *C* twice, using

- A source address of interface *C1*

- A source address of interface *C2*

If host *B* answers the ping sourced from *C1* but not *C2*, the likely problem is *B*'s default gateway configuration.

Traceroute

Traceroute is another helpful piece of network diagnostics software installed on most hosts. Traceroute takes advantage of the TTL in each IP packet to find the path between the local host and a destination.

If you run a traceroute from host *A* in Figure 4-16 toward *E*:

1. The traceroute application at *A* will send an IP packet with a TTL of 1 and *E*'s destination address.

   a. Router *C* will receive this packet, decrement the TTL, discard the packet, and send an *ICMP TTL expired* response to *A*.

   b. The traceroute application at *A* has now discovered the first hop, or the first router on the path to *E* is *C*.

2. The traceroute application at *A* will send an IP packet with a TTL of 2 and *E*'s destination address.

   a. Router *C* will receive this packet, decrement the TTL to 1, and forward the packet to *D*.

   b. Router *D* will receive the packet, decrement the TTL to 0, discard the packet, and send an *ICMP TTL expired* response to *A*.

   c. The traceroute application at *A* has now discovered the second hop, or the second router on the path to *E* is *D*.

3. The traceroute application at *A* will send an IP packet with a TTL of 3 and *E*'s destination address.

   a. Router *C* will receive this packet, decrement the TTL to 2, and forward the packet to *D*.

   b. Router *D* will receive this packet, decrement the TTL to 1, and forward the packet to *E*.

   c. Host *E* will receive this packet, decrement the TTL to 0, discard the packet, and send an *ICMP TTL expired* response to *A*.

4. Because the traceroute application at *A* now has a response from the destination IP address, it will stop sending packets.

Figure 4-17 shows a typical traceroute output.

If you traceroute to a domain name (such as *rule11.tech*), most applications will resolve the name into a destination IP address.

```
$ traceroute rule11.tech
traceroute to rule11.tech (194.1.147.98), 64 hops max
   1    192.168.144.1   0.003ms    0.148ms    0.101ms
   2    192.168.100.1   0.710ms    0.541ms    0.446ms
   3    *   *   *
   4    96.34.68.148    12.100ms   10.015ms   8.794ms
   5    96.34.119.58    13.776ms   15.666ms   13.749ms
   6    96.34.13.234    23.770ms   22.794ms   24.848ms
   7    96.34.13.230    23.409ms   39.905ms   23.983ms
   8    96.34.15.19     30.809ms   24.590ms   31.041ms
   9    96.34.0.37      50.090ms   48.061ms   47.917ms
  10    96.34.0.14      48.384ms   49.866ms   241.704ms
  11    96.34.0.12      53.719ms   55.738ms   53.843ms
  12    96.34.3.11      58.935ms   63.786ms   59.977ms
  13    *   *   *
  14    *   *   *
```

Figure 4-17 *Typical Traceroute Output*

NOTE   Chapter 15 considers DNS in more detail.

Each output line describes a set of packets transmitted at the TTL indicated. Line 1 represents three packets sent with a TTL of 1; line 2 represents three packets sent with a TTL of 2, etc. Traceroute keeps track of how much time elapses between sending the packet and receiving an *ICMP TTL expired* response.

The address given for each device is generally (but not always) the interface address closest to the source of the traceroute packets. In Figure 4-17, if *A* sent a traceroute to host *E*, router *C* would respond from interface *C1*'s address, and router *D* would respond from interface *D1*'s address. It is important to remember you are not seeing the *entire* path in traceroute results; you cannot see the *outbound* interface from each device forwarding the packet.

An asterisk in the output, such as those shown in Figure 4-17, can mean one of several things:

- The device 13 hops away from the local host is configured not to send *ICMP TTL expired* replies.

- Some device between the local host and the device 13 hops away is configured to filter or block *ICMP TTL expired* replies.

Hosts sometimes do not send ICMP replies, and network operators sometimes block ICMP replies to improve network security.

NOTE   Chapter 22, "Troubleshooting," and Chapter 23, "Configuring a Network," consider filters and tools for network security.

Traceroute implementations vary in the kind of packet they send to discover the path. For instance, Windows sends *ICMP echo request* packets with various TTL settings to perform a traceroute, while most Linux implementations and Apple Macintosh macOS send *User Datagram Protocol (UDP)* packets.

> **NOTE**   Chapter 14, "Network Transport," discusses UDP in more detail.

Traceroute does not always detail the path from a host to a destination; Figure 4-18 illustrates.

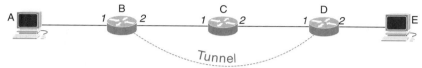

Figure 4-18   *Traceroute and Tunnels*

In Figure 4-18, routers *B* and *D* are connected by a tunnel:

- Router *B* encapsulates packets inside a second header with interface *D1*'s address as the destination.

- When router *D* receives these packets, it removes the outer header and forwards them based on the inner header toward host *E*.

Because router *C* only receives a packet with a destination address of interface *D1*, it does not examine the internal packet nor process it in any other way; it just receives the packet. It forwards it to router *D*. This means router *C* will not decrement the TTL in the original packet transmitted by host *A* nor respond.

Router *C* will not be in the traceroute results from host *A* to *E* in this situation.

> **NOTE**   Chapter 6, "Network Models," discusses tunnels in more detail.

Finding Your Public IP Address

Network Address Translation (NAT), described in Chapter 2, can sometimes make verifying the connection between a host and servers on the Internet difficult. Figure 4-19 illustrates.

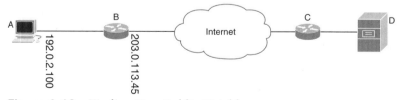

Figure 4-19   *Finding Your Public IP Address*

In Figure 4-19, host *A* communicates with server *D* using its local interface address 192.0.2.100. Unknown to *A*, router *B* has NAT configured and is translating 192.0.2.100 to 203.0.113.45 (and some port number, but the port number is not essential for this example).

In this example, 192.0.2.100 is the *private IP address*, and 203.0.113.45 is the **public IP address**.

If there is a problem with the host *A* to server *D* communication, and the user would like to know what the network looks like from server *D*'s perspective, the user needs to know what IP address *D* is using to reach *A*—or rather, *A*'s public IP address.

The simplest way to discover *A*'s public IP address is to open a web browser and use a service. Several are available on the Internet, including

- If you type "what is my IP address" into Google search, the search engine will show the public IP address for your host on a web page.

- If you open the web page at https://checkip.amazonaws.com, it will display the public IP address of your host.

- If you open the web page at https://infoip.io, it will display information about the public IP address and location of your host.

Some hosts, particularly those running Linux, may not have a web browser installed. You can use many of these same sites to find your public IP from the command line, such as

```
$ curl -s http://tnx.nl/ip
<97.95.136.20>
$ curl -s https://checkip.amazonaws.com
97.95.136.20
```

Chapter Review

This chapter took a break from the theory of how networks work and focused on how to configure three different kinds of hosts—Windows 11, macOS, and Linux—to connect to a wired network. There are multiple ways to configure these hosts, including GUI and CLI options. Network engineers tend to prefer CLIs for configuring and managing devices.

This chapter also considered two of the most important tools for verifying connectivity: ping and traceroute. Part V of this book will return to verifying connectivity and troubleshooting networks.

At this point, we have covered the basic process of sending a packet through a network. You should now understand IP addressing, routers, switches, and basic host wired network configuration. In the next chapter, we will take a break from operational internals and look at an overview of the various kinds of devices making up a computer network.

One key to doing well on the exams is to perform repetitive spaced review sessions. Review this chapter's material using either the tools in the book or interactive tools for the same material found on the book's companion website. Refer to the online Appendix D, "Study Planner," element for more details. Table 4-2 outlines the key review elements and where you can find them. To better track your study progress, record when you completed these activities in the second column.

Table 4-2   Chapter Review Tracking

Review Element	Review Date (s)	Resource Used
Review key topics		Book, website
Review key terms		Book, website
Repeat DIKTA questions		Book, PTP
Review concepts and actions		Book, website

Review All the Key Topics

Table 4-3 lists the key topics for this chapter.

Table 4-3   Key Topics for Chapter 4

Key Topic Element	Description	Page Number
Section	The Settings App	85
Figure 4-1, list	Information in the Network section of the Windows 11 Settings app	85
Section	The Control Panel	86
Figure 4-2, list	Windows 11 Interface Status dialog information	87
List	Characteristics of CLIs	88
Figure 4-5	Interface Configuration Information on Windows 11	89
Figure 4-6	Showing the ARP Cache in Powershell	90
Figure 4-8	The macOS Network Configuration Dialog	92
Figure 4-10	macOS **ifconfig**	93
Paragraph	Linux **ipconfig** and **ip**	95
Section	Ping	97
Section	Traceroute	99
Section	Finding Your Public IP Address	101

Key Terms You Should Know

Key terms in this chapter include

Settings app, Control Panel, CLI, Powershell, **ipconfig**, **ifconfig**, ping, traceroute, public IP address

Concepts and Actions

Review the concepts considered in this chapter using Table 4-4. You can cover the right side of this table and describe each concept or action in your own words to verify your understanding.

Table 4-4   Concepts and Actions

Field to change from DHCP to manual address assignment in the Windows Setting app	IP Assignment
Total amount of data sent from and received by an interface in Windows 11	Interface Status dialog, accessible from the Control Panel
Discovering the IPv6 DUID in Windows 11 from the command line	**ipconfig /all**
Release a DHCP assignment in Windows 11 from the command line	**ipconfig /release**
Show the local host routing table in Windows 11	**Get-NetRoute**
bootp	Deprecated protocol; replaced by DHCP
Discovering the IP address in macOS from a command line	**ifconfig**
Discovering the IP address in Linux from a command line	**Ifconfig**
ping with a source address	Discover if a host's default gateway is configured correctly
Finding your public address	Primarily only possible through websites and public services

CHAPTER 5

What's in a Network?

This chapter covers the following exam topics:

> 3. **Endpoints and Media Types**
>
> > 3.3. **Identify types of endpoint devices.**
> >
> > > **Internet of Things (IoT) devices, computers, mobile devices**

Up to this point, we have been looking at network control plane concepts and configurations: addresses, routing, switching, and wired host configuration. Throughout this discussion, we have limited the universe of things you can attach to a computer network to hosts, routers, and switches. Before moving to the physical infrastructure of computer networks, we need to look at the other kinds of devices you can connect to a computer network. After looking at the kinds of devices used in computer networks, this chapter explains the overall combination of services and organizations that create the global Internet.

"Do I Know This Already?" Quiz

Take the quiz (either here or use the PTP software) if you want to use the score to help you decide how much time to spend on this chapter. Appendix A, "Answers to the 'Do I Know This Already?' Quizzes," found at the end of the book, includes both the answers and explanations. You can also find answers in the PTP testing software.

Table 5-1 "Do I Know This Already?" Foundation Topics Section-to-Question Mapping

Section	Questions
Hosts and Virtual Hosts	1, 2, 3, 4, 5
Mobile Devices	5
Things	6
Middle Boxes	7
The Global Internet	8, 9

> **CAUTION** The goal of self-assessment is to gauge your mastery of the topics in this chapter. If you do not know the answer to a question or are only partially sure of the answer, you should mark that question as wrong for purposes of the self-assessment. Giving yourself credit for an answer you incorrectly guess skews your self-assessment results and might provide you with a false sense of security.

1. What is a host?
   a. A large-scale computer, such as a mainframe
   b. A computer (because it can host applications)
   c. A lot of computers connected in a single facility (a host of computers)
   d. Any network connected device

2. What is the kernel?
   a. The critical parts of an operating system
   b. A simple bit of code a computer uses to boot
   c. A set of critical applications running on a computer
   d. A shared set of services running in a single memory space

3. What is true of applications running in user space?
   a. They are accessible by the user, unlike applications running in the kernel.
   b. Each application has its own memory pool.
   c. They can directly access system hardware resources, such as a video card.
   d. A single-user space application crashing will cause the entire computer to crash.

4. What is the purpose of the Linux masquerade?
   a. It allows a user to pose as the root user for certain operations.
   b. It allows one virtual host to pose as another virtual host.
   c. It provides Network Address Translation services for virtual hosts.
   d. It allows the entire host to appear as a router on the network.

5. What kind of kernel do Android devices use?
   a. Windows 11
   b. Apple's macOS
   c. Linux
   d. Mach microkernel

6. What does an IoT gateway do?
   a. Translates IoT protocols into IP for transmission across the Internet
   b. Prevents unauthorized users from accessing IoT devices connected to the network
   c. Monitors IoT devices for proper operation
   d. Aggregates data produced by IoT devices

7. What are common services implemented by a firewall?
   a. NAT, packet filtering, routing
   b. NAT, data exfiltration detection, packet filtering
   c. NAT, session termination, routing
   d. NAT, packet filtering, stateful packet filtering

8. What organization manages the names and numbers used on the global Internet?

   a. The Internet Engineering Task Force

   b. The United States government

   c. The Internet Corporation for Assigned Names and Numbers

   d. The International Telecommunications Union

9. What role do Internet Exchange Providers play in the global Internet?

   a. Connecting large-scale transit providers to each other

   b. Connecting local providers within a region to one another and to global providers

   c. Connecting large-scale cloud services to transit providers

   d. Connecting individual users to large-scale cloud services

Foundation Topics

Hosts and Virtual Hosts

From the outside, it is easy to treat a **host** as "one thing"—a single object used to run software, connect to the Internet, etc. A host has many software components, just like it has many hardware components. Figure 5-1 illustrates some of the essential components of a host.

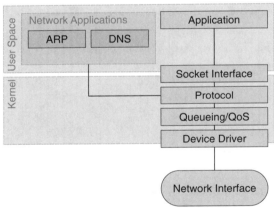

Figure 5-1 *Host Networking Stack*

You can break host operating systems roughly into two parts: the **kernel** and **user space**. Each application in the user space has (what appears to be) its own memory space, a set of sockets to send and receive packets, access to the video subsystem, etc. In reality, these things are all shared among multiple applications, but from each application's perspective, each resource is wholly dedicated to its use.

The kernel is a set of functions shared among all the applications running on the host.

All the applications running in the kernel space (generally) share the same memory and processor space; they do not have dedicated resources. Because one application's mistake (or bug) can cause another application sharing the same memory resources to crash, the kinds of applications allowed to run in the kernel are limited.

An application sends a packet by placing it into a *socket queue*. The *protocol* application inside the kernel will take the packet off the socket queue, process the packet through any queueing, and then hand off the packet to the device driver. This *protocol* application is an implementation of the TCP/IP *protocol stack*.

The device driver will then pass the packet to the physical interface chipset, which will convert the packet from the internal computer system representation to the external network representation and send the packet.

> **NOTE** Converting a packet from the internal to external format is often called *clocking the packet* onto the wire, and is often performed by a serial/deserializer (SerDes) chip combined with an electrical/electrical or electrical/optical interface chip.

Suppose the protocol stack does not have all the information it needs to send the packet, such as the mapping between the destination's interface and physical addresses. In that case, it can call the *ARP*, *ND*, or another process. These applications, residing in user space, use a socket interface like any other application to build ARP packets and discover the information needed to send a packet.

When the network interface receives a packet destined for the physical interface, it will convert the electrical or optical signals into memory locations, and in a format host applications know how to process. The network interface will then trigger an *interrupt*, which lets the protocol stack know there is a packet to process.

The protocol stack will take over the processor for a few moments. During this time, the protocol stack will examine the destination interface address to make certain the host itself is supposed to receive and process the packet. Finally, after some preliminary processing, the protocol stack will place the packet into the socket queue for the application to retrieve and process the next time it runs.

The port number indicates the application receiving the packet, as discussed in Chapter 2, "Addresses."

What kinds of applications run on hosts? Everything you are familiar with, from games to word processors. Each of these uses access to the global Internet in similar ways, including

- Saving files to a cloud storage service

- Sending emails

- Retrieving web pages, videos, etc.

- Receiving, processing, and displaying streaming video

- Interacting with a server in a near real-time massive online game

Everything you do on a computer today touches the network somehow, so the protocol stack running through the user space into the kernel tends to be very busy.

Virtual computers add another layer of complexity, as shown in Figure 5-2.

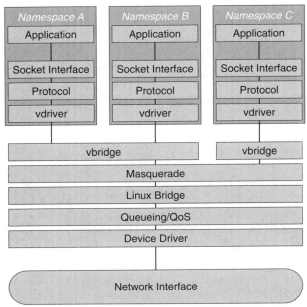

Figure 5-2   *Virtual Namespaces in Linux*

You can configure a Linux host with several **namespaces** to create multiple **virtual hosts** (or containers). Each namespace has its socket interface, protocol stack, and virtual driver (*vdriver*). The vdriver is a class of processes called a **hardware abstraction layer (HAL)**. From the protocol stack's perspective, the virtual driver acts like a network interface.

The primary difference between the virtual driver and the external network driver is where processed packets are sent for processing. The vdriver transmits packets on an internal virtual bridge (*vbridge*). Like in a physical switch, every namespace connected to the same vbridge can receive and process packets. For instance, if namespace *A* sends a packet to a destination in namespace *B*, the packet will cross the vbridge between these two processes in the same way it would cross a physical network connection, although the packet is never transmitted through the external network interface.

Multiple virtual bridges can exist on a Linux host, and different namespaces can be connected to different vbridges. If namespace A transmits a packet to namespace *C*, the packet would need to flow down through the vbridge, through the **masquerade**, onto the *Linux bridge*, and then back up through the masquerade, onto the second vbridge, and finally through the vdriver and protocol stack in namespace *C*.

There is, in effect, an entire network *behind* the Linux bridge in a host configured to support multiple virtual hosts.

The masquerade is a virtual switch performing Network Address Translation (NAT). By placing the masquerade in the path, each virtual host has a separate IP address space.

Packets destined to host connected through an external network pass through the queuing process, then through a device driver, and finally onto a network interface.

When a packet is received at the network interface, it follows the same process as a packet received at the network interface of a conventional host. The destination packet is examined and placed in a queue for processing by the masquerade. Once the masquerade has translated the external interface address and port number into their correct internal counterparts, the masquerade will pass the packets across the correct vbridge into the queue of the correct vdriver. The vdriver, in turn, will hand off the packet to the correct protocol stack, socket interface, and, finally, application.

Types of hosts include

- Desktop computers, whether all-in-ones, computers with separate processor units and monitors, gaming computers, business workstations (like those you might see when you walk through a grocery store checkout line), graphics workstations, and many other kinds of devices. These devices likely (though not always) connect through a wired interface.

- Laptop and "two-in-one" computers can connect through a wired or wireless interface, although they will most likely be connected through a wireless interface. These devices tend to be designed to be carried from one location to another and then set on a stable surface for use. Laptops were once considered much less powerful than desktop computers, but as processor technology has advanced, the difference between these two has narrowed.

- Servers, which run the software that drives websites, cloud services, and on-premises computing services. You usually will not see servers unless you enter a data center.

Other devices are considered hosts, but these are the main categories.

Mobile Devices

Any small, handheld, battery-powered device used for general communications and running lightweight applications is considered a **mobile device**.

Mobile device use has been growing since the use of analog radio communications in the early 1900s. The ability to use small, handheld radios for individuals to communicate across long distances—globally—had been a dream since the first use of telegraph systems.

When telephone companies first installed wired telephone services, people used them like a local mail system. An executive would dictate some information to a secretary, who would then go to the mail room and have someone there call the correct receiver in some other mailroom. The receiver would then transcribe the message and hand it off to someone who would hand it to the recipient.

As telephones became more common, they were installed in houses (through the *party line*) and directly in the secretaries' offices, who then screened calls directed at their managers.

In the early 1920s, *amateur radio operators* worldwide proved the power of person-to-person, rather than organization-to-organization, communication. These hams, as they are widely called, developed (and drove the development) of ever smaller radios, reaching handheld size in the 1960s–70s.

The importance of person-to-person communication proven in the real world, telephone companies began working on deploying similar systems in the mid-1940s in cars. The first car phone calls were made in Chicago in 1946. Sweden launched the first commercial service for car telephones in 1956. Several other attempts were made at creating a commercially successful mobile (car) phone network, but they generally failed because of the small range of frequencies available and inefficient use of the available frequencies.

In 1987, the technical specifications were standardized for Europe's first large-scale mobile-phone network. The first text message followed quickly in 1992, and the first downloadable content—a ringtone—in 1998.

All these early phones, however, were modeled on the desk phones everyone already knew. There was a small keypad to make calls and doubling to thumb-type messages through the *Simple Messaging Service (SMS)*. In 2007, Apple debuted the iPhone with its single large screen, driving the perception of the mobile phone from a small desk phone to a small hand-held computer.

Part of what made the original iPhone and commercial cellular mobile networks successful was the radical improvement in bandwidth use represented by *voice over IP (VoIP)*, which paved the way for converting analog voice signals into a digital format so they could be carried over packet-switched networks like the Internet. The histories of packet-based switching, like the Internet and telephone networks, are deeply intertwined.

NOTE   Chapter 8, "Wireless Networks," describes the operation of cellular networks.

The mobile device market expanded into tablets in the mid-2000s into the *phablet*, straddling the cellular telephone and tablet devices.

Mobile devices now create and consume a large portion of the traffic on computer networks. From a computer networking perspective, one of the interesting things about mobile devices is they are rarely connected via a wired interface. Instead, they use Wi-Fi or cellular networks (sometimes both) to connect to the Internet.

Two operating systems dominate the mobile device market: **Apple's iOS** and **Android**. Apple's iOS is proprietary, so very little information is available about how Apple's mobile devices interact with computer networks. Android, however, is open-source and based on a standard Linux kernel. Figure 5-3 illustrates the basic Android operating system network architecture.

The kernel under the hardware abstraction layer (HAL) is a standard Linux kernel, making it easier for developers to adapt new processors and interfaces to Android devices. Above the HAL, however, many of the components are Android-specific, such as native libraries and runtime.

Most of the previous section's description of networking in the Linux kernel applies to the Android operating system.

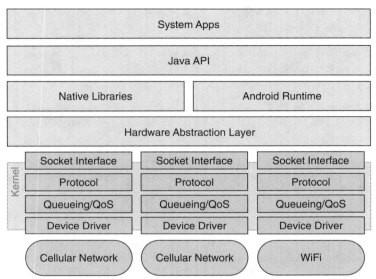

Figure 5-3   *Android System Architecture Overview*

Things

The idea of connecting *things* to the Internet started when a Coca-Cola vending machine at Carnegie Mellon University was modified so the inventory and temperature of drinks could be monitored. From these humble beginnings, connecting things to the Internet has become a significant new area of the growth of the Internet—the Internet of Things (**IoT**).

A *thing* is any device designed to monitor or control real-world systems (air conditioners, cars, etc.) connected to a network.

In 2003, about 10 times more people (using hosts, of course) connected to the Internet. In 2010, there were about twice as many things connected to the Internet as people using hosts.

What is a thing, exactly? Things in the IoT can be almost any electrical or electronic device that can be tracked or can provide environmental information. For instance:

- A vehicle can be connected as a single thing. Each vehicle component can also be connected to a *car area network (CAN)*, providing internal and external telemetry. This includes the depth of the brake pads, current oil pressure, external temperature, coolant temperature, and many other environmental factors to find and predict failures.

- Homes have many different places where IoT can be useful. Refrigerators can be connected to the Internet to monitor internal temperatures and potentially provide camera views into their interior to help residents figure out when they need to purchase items. Thermostats are an obvious use case for IoT, allowing complex and self-learned programming of usage habits.

- Medical care is another area where the IoT can drive improved results. Hearing devices can be connected to the Internet to monitor battery levels and operational conditions. Insulin pumps can be connected to the Internet to adjust the amount of insulin required in specific situations automatically. Sleep and fitness trackers can help people understand their habits and improve their lifestyle.

■ Farms can benefit from IoT by embedding computing devices to provide direction and control for more efficient plowing of fields. IoT devices can monitor soil moisture and nutrients, making irrigation and fertilization more effective and efficient.

■ Industrial manufacturing can benefit from IoT by enabling close environmental control. Sensors can track physical changes in manufactured devices through tool wear, feeding back into auto-adjustment capabilities to keep quality more consistent.

IoT potentially has millions of uses in the real world. Figure 5-4 illustrates an IoT ecosystem.

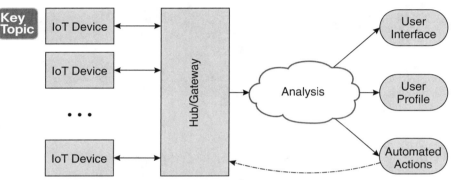

Figure 5-4 *IoT Ecosystem Example*

Points to note about Figure 5-4:

■ The *hub* or **IoT gateway** converts the communication protocols used by IoT devices into IP—or encapsulates these protocols on IP—so this information can be carried through the Internet or a standard IP network for analysis.

■ Some form of analysis process. Most IoT devices do not have the local computing and memory capacity to analyze and act on input.

■ Most IoT systems have several different user interfaces. For instance, a robotic vacuum will have one interface for the end user, showing floor maps, vacuum status, last cleaning, and other information. A second user interface will provide information for the vacuum's manufacturer, showing how often the vacuum has been used, how the vacuum is performing, developing problems, and so on. A third user interface will be used to troubleshoot the vacuum, showing internal component status, vacuum levels, and so on.

■ Input from IoT devices is used to build a *user profile*, including information such as when the user is home or away, what temperature the user likes to keep their residence at different hours of the day, sleeping patterns, and so on. This information can be used to provide better service for the end user, but it can also be sold to third parties to build a fuller picture of each end user's life and preferences.

NOTE   The chapters in Part IV of the book consider privacy.

IoT devices generally have four components:

- Some means of communication. While some IoT devices may use Wi-Fi and IP— standard network protocols—many others use low-power wireless systems of other kinds, such as *personal area networks (PANs)*, *CANs*, *Bluetooth*, *ZWave*, and others.

- Processing and memory to support gathering and formatting information. Local processing and memory might also be used to take actions, such as changing the temperature setting on a thermostat and storing recurring actions.

- Sensors to detect temperature, movement, humidity level, and other environmental conditions.

- A power supply. Some IoT devices are small enough to capture power from the environment using solar or other sources. Other IoT devices may draw power from the larger system (such as a sensor in a vehicle), whereas others will have batteries.

An interesting variant of IoT is *fog computing*, which distributes processing among local devices rather than relying on a centralized processing facility.

Middleboxes

Computer networks rely on a variety of *middleboxes* to transport and process packets. We have previously examined two middleboxes: the router and switch. This section provides an overview of *firewalls*, *intrusion detection systems*, *proxies* (or *gateways*), and *load balancers*, four other kinds of middleboxes important to network operation.

The Firewall

A **firewall** is a collection of services, including (but not limited to)

- Network Address Translation (NAT)

- Packet filtering

- Stateful packet filtering

- Intrusion detection systems

- Domain Name filtering

NOTE   The chapters in Part IV of the book describe firewall operation and configuration in more detail.

Many routers designed for use in residences or small business locations have some form of firewall functionality included. Many anti-virus software programs also have some of these functions.

While each of these services can exist as standalone applications or as part of another application, a firewall draws them all together into one physical or virtual device, making network administration simpler.

Operators have historically deployed firewalls at the edge of a network, such as a residence or a small business location. Virtual firewalls are often deployed in public cloud services or between segments in a large-scale data center.

> **NOTE**   Chapter 17, "Cloud Computing," considers cloud services.

The Intrusion Detection System

An **IDS** examines the traffic passing through a network for

- Malware, such as computer viruses, being carried in packets through the network

- Evidence that someone is exfiltrating data from the network or improperly copying data from hosts in the network to a host outside the network

- Evidence that someone is using a host in the network to attack other hosts

These systems almost always use traffic and packet content patterns developed through years of research. An IDS can be implemented as a standalone appliance wired into the network, as a virtual service, or embedded in a router or firewall.

The Proxy or Gateway

Some network engineers consider proxies and gateways different, although they are similar enough in their operation to treat them in a single description.

> **NOTE**   This book uses the term *proxy* when describing a proxy or gateway.

Figure 5-5 illustrates the basic function of a proxy.

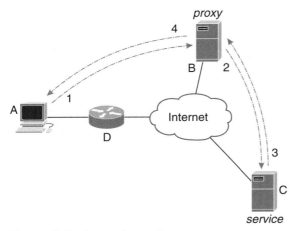

Figure 5-5   *Proxy Operation*

In Figure 5-5, host *A* is configured to send packets to the proxy running on host *B*. The connection terminates at *B*, and the proxy process initiates a separate connection to *C*, acting on host *A*'s behalf. In Figure 5-5:

1. Host *A* sends a packet with *B*'s IP address.

2. The proxy service receives this packet and removes the IP encapsulation. The proxy service encapsulates the data in a new IP packet destined to *C*'s IP address.

3. The service (running on host *C*) processes the packet and responds as needed, using a packet sent to *B*'s IP address.

4. The proxy service replaces *C*'s encapsulation, sending a new packet to host *A*.

An application might want to connect through a proxy rather than directly to the service because

- The user at host *A* does not want the service to know their location or interface address.

- The service on host *C* does not support encrypted connections, and the user at *A* would prefer router *D* not to be able to observe the information it sends to *C*.

- The service running at host *C* does not accept direct connections for security or privacy reasons.

NOTE   Chapter 22, "Troubleshooting," considers virtual private networks (VPNs), which are similar, in some ways, to proxies.

The Load Balancer

The simplest way to think of a load balancer is as an intelligent *reverse proxy*. There are two primary differences between a proxy and a reverse proxy:

- When users connect to a proxy, they intentionally do not send packets directly to the service. Instead, they send their packets to an intermediate device—a middlebox—that acts like the originating host when communicating with the service.

- On the other hand, users are unaware they are connecting to a reverse proxy instead of the actual service.

- The traffic flow is bidirectional through a proxy. The traffic from the host to the service and from the service to the host passes through the proxy.

- The traffic is asymmetrical through a reverse proxy. The initial connection, and potentially all the packets sent to the service, pass through the reverse proxy. However, traffic from the service to the user does not pass through the reverse proxy.

Figure 5-6 illustrates the operation of a reverse proxy.

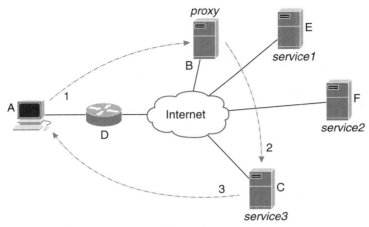

Figure 5-6   *Reverse Proxy Operation*

In Figure 5-6:

   1.   Host *A* sends initial packets to start a session with a service to an IP address. From *A*'s perspective, the destination IP address is the interface address of some physical or virtual host running the service.

   2.   In reality, the IP address host *A* sends these packets to the interface address of host *B*, a proxy server. The proxy service will choose one of several servers running the service—in this case, host *C*.

   3.   When *C* receives this packet, it will process the data as needed and respond to host *A*, whose address is still in the original packet.

Unlike a proxy server, the reverse proxy service does not modify the packet's source and destination addresses. The reverse proxy service can load balance by sending service requests to different servers running the same service.

> **NOTE**   Chapter 17 looks at reverse proxies in more detail in the context of content services.

The Global Internet

We have covered a lot of information in these first five chapters; it is time to back up and look at the bigger picture. Operators build computer networks based on the addressing, routing, and devices covered previously, but how are all these things put together to create the global Internet? Figure 5-7 provides a basic overview of the components of the Internet.

Later chapters will cover some of these organizations in more detail; this section provides an overview of how all these pieces fit together.

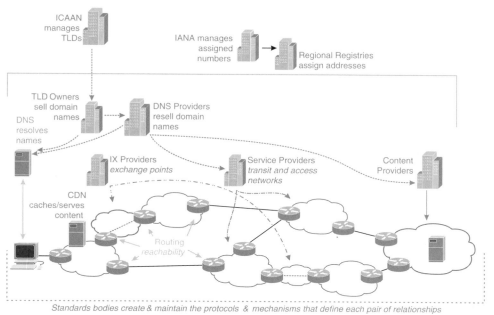

Figure 5-7 *An Overview of the Global Internet*

Internet Assigned Numbers Authority

The Internet Assigned Numbers Authority (**IANA**) manages the numbers and names needed to make the global Internet work. While the ICAAN tends to focus on the names used in Domain Name Service (DNS), IANA focuses on numbers, like IP addresses, protocol numbers, and port numbers.

IANA is often directed by standards bodies such as the Internet Engineering Task Force (IETF) to set aside blocks of addresses (like the reserved IP addresses discussed in Chapter 2) and other resources.

Internet Corporation for Assigned Names and Numbers

The Internet Corporation for Assigned Names and Numbers (**ICANN**) manages the numbers (like IP addresses and port numbers) required to make the global Internet work under the supervision of IANA. The ICAAN mainly focuses on policy around the names used in the DNS.

Regional Internet Registries

IANA gives blocks of addresses and other resources to the five **Regional Internet Registries (RIRs)** to manage. Each RIR supports a geographic region:

- The African Network Information Center (AFRINIC)
- The American Registry for Internet Numbers (ARIN)
- The Asia-Pacific Network Information Center (APNIC)
- The Latin America and Caribbean Network Information Center (LACNIC)
- The Réseaux IP Européens Network Coordination Centre (RIPE)

Each of these five RIRs assigns address blocks and other resources to organizations such as *Internet service providers (ISPs)*.

Top-Level Domain Owners

Top-level domains (TLDs) are the far-right portion of the domain name, such as *.com* and *.org*.

TLD owners sell the right to use subdomains of their TLD to organizations of all kinds through *Domain Name Service providers*.

Transit Providers

Transit providers focus on carrying packets across cities, regions, nations, continents, and the world. These providers make up what is generally considered the "core" of the global Internet.

> **NOTE** There are few "pure" transit, access, or content providers; more providers have moved into multiple markets to support their business models.

Access Providers

Access providers connect individual users and organizations to the global Internet. Examples of access providers are

- Cellular telephone companies, such as AT&T and Claro

- Cable television companies, such as Time Warner and Rogers

- Telephone companies, such as Verizon and Orange

- Satellite providers, such as Starlink and Hughes

- Regional providers, such as ATMC

- Wireless Internet service providers (WISPs), such as Array Communications

Large telecommunications companies provide Internet access as a part of a larger business, while others focus only on individual regions or unique access technologies.

Content Providers

Content providers are the "endpoints" of the Internet, where content is hosted. The vast majority of Internet traffic is either sent to or retrieved from a content network. Content providers include

- Cloud services, such as Amazon, Google, and Linode

- Compute and storage services, such as Seagate and Digital Ocean

- Social media, such as Twitter and LinkedIn

- Information, like blogs, newspapers, magazines, and journals

- Services and shopping, such as FedEx and Amazon

Content providers can be local or global and can sell just about anything; the critical point, though, is they sell a service or good to others. These organizations use computer networks as strategic assets, integral to their business, rely on the Internet to communicate with their customers, and often rely on the Internet to deliver a product.

Content Distribution Networks

Content distribution networks (CDNs) add value to the Internet at the intersection of two problems:

- Positioning content closer to users improves user experience, driving business.

- Many content providers do not have the physical infrastructure to position content close to users.

CDNs provide storage and compute resources globally to position content as close to users as possible.

Internet Exchange Providers

Internet exchange providers (or points, also called IXPs, or sometimes just IXs) provide the filler "glue" that holds regional portions of the Internet together. Figure 5-8 illustrates.

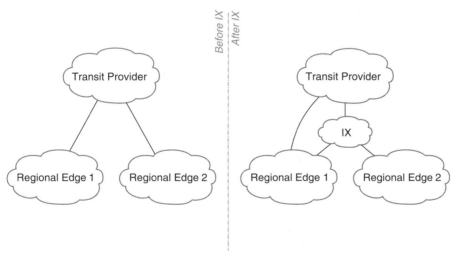

Figure 5-8 *Internet Exchange Providers*

On the left side of Figure 5-8, marked *Before IX*, two regional edge providers communicate only through a transit provider. The disadvantages to this kind of connectivity are

- Both regional providers pay the transit provider to carry traffic between them, even though they are in the same geographic area.

- If the transit provider's connection point is geographically distant, pushing all the traffic through the transit provider introduces long delays and lots of jitter. For instance, if the two regional providers are in Brazil and the transit provider's closest cross-connect point is in Miami, the user experience between the two regional providers will be poor.

To remedy this situation, regional providers can cooperate to build an IX where they can cross-connect locally, as shown in the *After IX* portion of Figure 5-8. Suppose several regional providers and other large businesses connect through the IX. Because of the existing connectivity, transit providers will also find connecting to the IX attractive because they can reach more customers with fewer cable runs.

Over time, cloud providers will also find connecting to the IX attractive, and CDNs will station equipment on the IX fabric to increase user perception of performance in the region. The IX can become a "community gathering point" for global Internet connectivity in a region.

Chapter Review

Hosts, virtual hosts, middleboxes, and things all use the Internet to communicate. Each plays a different (and important) role in the Internet. These roles can be broken down into four basic functions: creating information, carrying information, processing information, and consuming information. So long as you can fit any device into one of these four roles, you can quickly understand what problems the device must solve and also the components required to solve that problem.

All these devices connect to the global Internet, but what is the Internet, anyway? The Internet is a group of organizations that work together to create and transport data across the globe. Carrying data requires a set of global names and numbers, as well as organizations filling niches in a larger ecosystem.

You will encounter many of these terms and organizations again and again as you move through this book.

One key to doing well on the exams is to perform repetitive spaced review sessions. Review this chapter's material using either the tools in the book or interactive tools for the same material found on the book's companion website. Refer to the online Appendix D, "Study Planner," element for more details. Table 5-2 outlines the key review elements and where you can find them. To better track your study progress, record when you completed these activities in the second column.

Table 5-2   Chapter Review Tracking

Review Element	Review Date (s)	Resource Used
Review key topics		Book, website
Review key terms		Book, website
Repeat DIKTA questions		Book, PTP
Review concepts and actions		Book, website

Review All the Key Topics

Table 5-3 lists the key topics for this chapter.

Table 5-3 Key Topics for Chapter 5

Key Topic Element	Description	Page Number
Paragraph	Kernel	108
Paragraph	Socket queue	109
Paragraph	vdriver	110
Paragraph	Masquerade	110
List	Types of hosts	111
Paragraph	Mobile devices	111
Paragraph	Mobile device operating systems	112
Paragraph	Internet of Things (IoT)	113
Figure 5-4, list	IoT ecosystem	114
List	Firewall services	115
List	What IDS examines traffic for	116
Section	Internet Assigned Numbers Authority	119
Section	Internet Corporation for Assigned Names and Numbers	119
Section	Regional Internet Registries	119
Section	Top-Level Domain Owners	120
Section	Transit Providers	120
Section	Access Providers	120
Section	Content Providers	120
Section	Content Distribution Networks	121
Section	Internet Exchange Providers	121

Key Terms You Should Know

Key terms in this chapter include

host, kernel, user space, namespace, virtual host, hardware abstraction layer (HAL), masquerade, mobile device, Apple iOS, Android, IoT, IoT gateway, firewall, IDS, IANA, ICAAN, Regional Internet Registries (RIR), transit provider, access provider, content provider, content distribution network (CDN), Internet exchange

Concepts and Actions

Review the concepts considered in this chapter using Table 5-4. You can cover the right side of this table and describe each concept or action in your own words to verify your understanding.

Table 5-4 Concepts and Actions

Kernel space	A space where all applications and processes share the same memory, scheduler, and other resources
User space	A space where each application has its own memory space, and accesses hardware interfaces through sockets or a HAL
vbridge	A virtual bridge connecting Linux namespaces

Masquerade	A virtual Network Address Translation device in the Linux networking stack
Mobile device operating systems	Apple iOS and Android
Android kernel	Android uses a standard Linux kernel
IoT devices	Sensors and robotic devices connected to the global Internet
IoT gateway	Converts IoT protocols to IP so the data can be carried across the global Internet
Firewall	A collection of services including NAT, packet filtering, stateful packet filtering, etc.
Proxy	Terminates a session and sends the data from the sender to the destination on behalf of the sender
ICANN	Manages the assignment of numbers and names in the global Internet
IANA	Manages the assignment of numbers, like IP addresses, in the global Internet
Regional Internet Registry	Manages the assignment of numbers, like IP addresses, in a region, like Africa
Transit providers	Carry packets across diverse geographic regions
Access providers	Sell Internet access to individual users and organizations
Content providers	Endpoints of the Internet; store and process data, provide services
IX	Internet Exchange; provides local connectivity between access providers, and a regional hub of Internet activity

CHAPTER 6

Network Models

This chapter covers the following exam topics:

1. **Standards and Concepts**

    1.1 Identify the fundamental building blocks of networks.

        TCP/IP model, OSI model, frames and packets, addressing

Because models are an abstraction of the way computer networks work, they are often hard to understand. It is also often hard to understand why you should memorize a model of computer network operation. Why not just understand the protocols themselves?

Because having a good mental model of how network protocols work helps you

- Ask the questions required to understand any individual protocol.

- Understand what a protocol should be doing so you can troubleshoot effectively when it is not.

- Understand what a protocol does so you can effectively use the available protocols in your network designs.

A second objection to learning network models is that it may not seem as though network protocols have enough in common to build a model of how each one works. In fact, modeling network protocols is going to become more complex in future chapters as we add another layer of protocols into the stack. It is possible to build network operation models regardless of the differences in the protocols because there is only a small range of problems to be solved and a small range of solutions to each of these problems. These similarities will become more apparent as you move through this chapter.

"Do I Know This Already?" Quiz

Take the quiz (either here or use the PTP software) if you want to use the score to help you decide how much time to spend on this chapter. Appendix A, "Answers to the 'Do I Know This Already?' Quizzes," found at the end of the book, includes both the answers and explanations. You can also find answers in the PTP testing software.

Table 6-1 "Do I Know This Already?" Foundation Topics Section-to-Question Mapping

Section	Questions
Why Are Models Important?	1
The OSI Seven-Layer Model	2, 3, 4, 5, 6
The TCP/IP Model	7
The Recursive Internet Architecture	8

1. Why is understanding network models important?

    a. So you can place protocols in their proper context within a computer network

    b. So you can understand "Layer 2," "Layer 3," etc.

    c. So you can quote the layers of each model when asked

    d. So you can understand network management displays

2. What is the correct order of the seven layers of the OSI model, from lowest to highest?

    a. Data link, physical, transport, network, presentation, session, application

    b. Session, application, presentation, physical, data link, network

    c. Physical, data link, network, transport, session, presentation, application

    d. Application, presentation, session, transport, network, data link, physical

3. What are two significant things about Layer 2—the data link layer—of the OSI model? (Choose two.)

    a. Data is carried in frames.

    b. Data is carried in packets.

    c. Routers operate at this layer.

    d. Switches operate at this layer.

4. What are two significant things about Layer 3—the network layer—of the OSI model? (Choose two.)

    a. Data is carried in frames.

    b. Data is carried in packets.

    c. Routers operate at this layer.

    d. Switches operate at this layer.

5. What kinds of addresses are used in Layer 3 of the OSI model?

    a. MAC addresses

    b. EUI-48 addresses

    c. Internet Protocol addresses

    d. Port numbers

6. Why is it sometimes difficult to map OSI model layers to protocols in the TCP/IP suite?

    a. Every function provided by protocols in the TCP/IP suite of protocols is not described in the OSI model.

    b. Every function described in the OSI model is not provided in the TCP/IP suite of protocols.

    c. Some functions described in the OSI model are either repeated by multiple protocols or fall into protocols outside the specified layer.

    d. Some functions in the TCP/IP suite of protocols do not exist in the OSI model.

7. What are the layers of the DoD model, in the correct order from lowest to highest?

    a. Internet, network interface, application, transport

    b. Network interface, internet, transport, application

    c. Physical, data link, internet, transport

    d. Network interface, data link, internet, session

8. What are the four functions described in the RINA model?

    a. Error control, flow control, multiplexing, marshaling

    b. Physical access, logical access, error control, flow control

    c. Network interface, data link, session control, flow control

    d. Error control, flow control, session control, logical access

Foundation Topics

Why Are Models Important?

Suppose you decided to become a master car mechanic, and start by memorizing the way everything under the hood of your car looks. You note the oil filter, for instance, is painted green. Just after you take your car in for service, you are stranded on the roadside because the engine stops running.

You open the hood and immediately spot the problem: the oil filter is red. Maybe the oil filter changes color to show it needs to be replaced? Or perhaps the people at the service center put the wrong oil filter into your car?

This example might be ludicrous to anyone who knows what oil filters do and knows manufacturers paint them different colors. But this example is very close to what happens when you try to understand how a network works by memorizing how to configure different protocols.

You might even cut the old and new oil filters apart, noting the differences, but you still will not understand what an oil filter does or how it relates to the rest of the engine. Again, this is the same as memorizing the packet format for a protocol or looking at packets captured off the wire. Just because you understand the internal format of a protocol does not mean you completely understand how the protocol works.

You need to understand the oil filter and know how it works, how it is built, and what it does in the larger system of your car's engine. What you need to understand about a protocol is how it works, how it is formatted, configured, and what it does in the larger computer network system.

State machines and descriptions explain how a protocol works. Protocol specifications explain how a protocol is formatted. Configuration guides and user manuals explain how to configure a protocol to achieve different results. Models explain *what a protocol does*.

Just like you cannot troubleshoot a car engine by looking at the color of an oil filter, you cannot troubleshoot a network by just looking at a particular protocol's bits on the wire. It would help if you had some larger context so you understand how to interpret those bits. Just like you cannot design a car engine by knowing which color of oil filter to use, you cannot design a network by just looking at the protocol configuration guide or specification. It would help if you had some larger context to understand how to *use* the protocol in a network.

Rather than memorizing the various models of network stacks, learn how to use them to improve your network engineering skills.

The OSI Seven-Layer Model

The network engineering community is (largely) united behind the Internet Protocol (IP) and protocols related to IP, but things were different in the early days of computer networks. In the late 1970s and early 1980s, networks used a lot of different protocols, such as Netware's Internet Packet Exchange (IPX) and Banyan's VINES Internetwork Protocol (VIP).

There was even some disagreement over whether an end-to-end system of protocols should be standardized or if

- Lower-layer protocols describing how to send data over a link should be standardized

- Upper-level protocols describing how to send data between applications should not be standardized

If every application needs to move data differently, standardizing a single protocol suite would be a fruitless quest and harm competition. During this time—the mid-1970s—*X.25* and the *High-Level Data Link Control (HDLC)* protocols were standardized. Through various political maneuvers, a subgroup of the *International Organization for Standardization (**ISO**)* was formed to work on packet-based network protocols called *Open Systems Interconnection (OSI)*.

Over the next several years, through the late 1970s, this group moved from working on link-level protocols to end-to-end protocol standards by Charles Bachman, Hubert Zimmerman, and others. Bachman believed that protocol standardization should focus on host interfaces because of his experience with database systems.

In 1978, this new committee met and proposed a seven-layer reference model, now known as the **OSI seven-layer model**. The specification for the OSI model became a working paper in 1979 and then an international draft standard.

6

Figure 6-1 shows the OSI model.

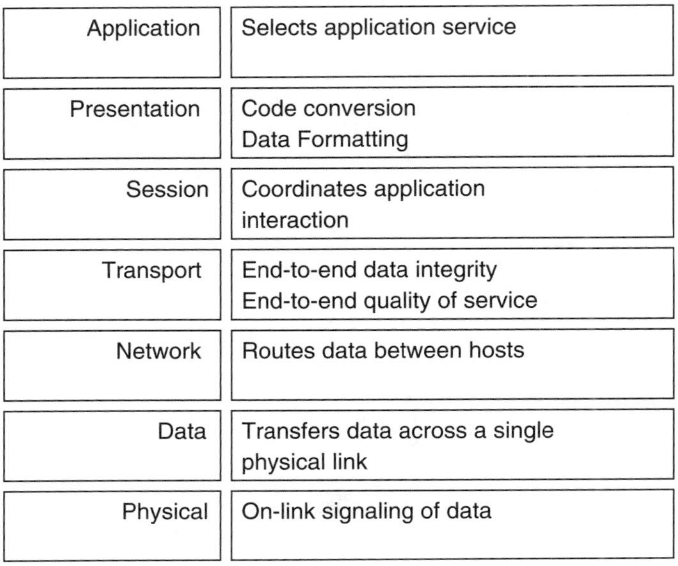

Application	Selects application service
Presentation	Code conversion Data Formatting
Session	Coordinates application interaction
Transport	End-to-end data integrity End-to-end quality of service
Network	Routes data between hosts
Data	Transfers data across a single physical link
Physical	On-link signaling of data

Figure 6-1 *The OSI Model*

The original meaning of each OSI model layer was precise, designed to fit into the way operating systems and computer hardware functioned then. As network theory has developed since then, the OSI model has been retained by generalizing and expanding some layers' meanings and minimizing others' functions. Specifically:

- The application and presentation layers' functions are generally handled in a single protocol rather than two separately specified protocols.

- The functions of the session and transport layers are generally handled in a single protocol rather than two separately specified protocols.

- End-to-end quality of service (QoS) is often provided through packet markings in network layer protocols rather than being handled in the transport layer.

- The data (or *data link*) layer is often thought of as being combined with the physical layer, although there often are two different protocols or functions here.

Designers and operators now often stack protocols on top of one another within a single layer. For instance, the QUIC protocol runs over the *User Datagram Protocol (UDP)*, although both are within the transport layer of the OSI model.

> **NOTE**   Chapter 14, "Network Transport," considers transport protocols in detail. The chapters in Part II of this book consider physical transport.

It is possible to map the Internet Protocol (IP) protocols onto the OSI model, as Figure 6-2 illustrates.

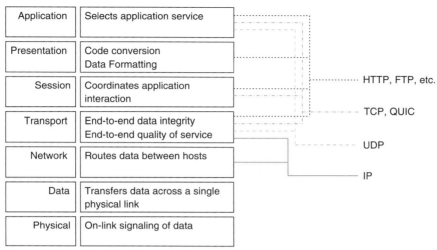

Figure 6-2   *The Complexity of Mapping Protocols in the IP Suite to the OSI Model*

Figure 6-2 shows the complexities of mapping a modern protocol suite onto a model designed for a different environment. For instance:

- The port number selects an application service and is carried in IP transport protocols.

- End-to-end QoS is partly handled in IP transport protocol and partly in IP.

- Application layer protocols in the IP suite, such as the Hypertext Transfer Protocol (HTTP), ensure end-to-end integrity, a function IP and IP transport layer protocols like TCP also support.

Most network engineers simplify the OSI to TCP/IP mapping problem by equating each layer in the model with a small set of protocols, as Figure 6-3 shows.

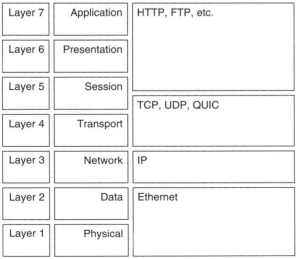

Figure 6-3   *Simplified IP Protocol Suite to OSI Model Mapping*

While the mapping shown in Figure 6-3 is not perfectly accurate, it is still useful:

- A *Layer 1* protocol is the physical signaling that carries data on a wire or wireless channel.

- A *Layer 2* protocol relates to physical addresses, multicast techniques, and switching protocols.

- A *Layer 3* protocol relates to IP, IP addresses, and IP routing.

- A *Layer 4* protocol relates to transport protocols like TCP and QUIC.

These layers do not precisely match because the various TCP/IP protocols were designed for a different model altogether. The remaining layers tend to be bundled into the application space.

The OSI model is helpful today because

- It provides a basic breakdown of the protocols required to carry data from one host to another.

- The layering scheme—Layer 1–7—provides a helpful frame of reference to discuss protocols and network functionality. If you say, "This is a Layer 2 switch," everyone in computer networking will understand the device forwards based on physical addresses.

The OSI model is also important to abstracting and understanding the process of sending data from one host to another across the network, as Figure 6-4 illustrates.

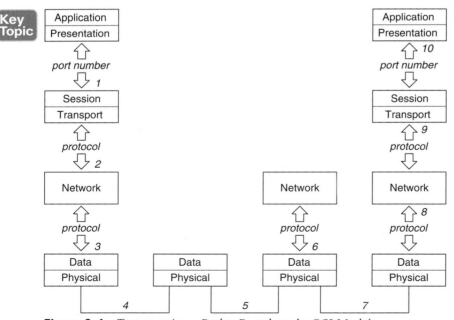

Figure 6-4 *Transporting a Packet Based on the OSI Model*

Based on the numbered steps in Figure 6-4:

1. An application sends a data block to the transport protocol through a socket interface.

2. The application protocol encapsulates the data into a segment and sends the segment to the network layer—the IP protocol.

3. The network protocol (IP) encapsulates the segment into a packet and attaches the source and destination interface addresses. The network protocol then sends this packet to the physical interface.

4. The physical interface encapsulates the packet into a frame and attaches the source and destination physical addresses. The physical interface then transmits the frame onto the wire connecting the host to the network.

5. When a switch receives this frame, it forwards the frame based on the physical interface address.

6. When a router receives this frame, it removes the physical interface encapsulation and sends the packet from inside the frame to the forwarding engine. The router determines the correct output interface and physical interface and sends the packet to the correct physical interface.

7. The physical interface encapsulates the packet into a frame, adding the correct source and destination physical addresses.

8. The host interface receives the frame, strips off the outer physical encapsulation, and determines which local protocol software to send the packet for further processing. In this case, the correct process will be the IP protocol stack.

9. The network software will strip off the outer packet encapsulation, leaving the segment. The protocol will forward this segment to the correct transport protocol process using the protocol number.

10. The transport protocol will determine which application should receive this data based on the port number. The transport protocol will strip off the outer segment encapsulation, leaving the data itself, and forward this data to the correct application.

The OSI model helps engineers visualize this entire process.

The TCP/IP Model

You might have noticed that mapping the IP protocol suite into the OSI model results in four layers rather than seven. These four layers are not an accident. Developers originally developed the IP protocol suite using a four-layer model called the Department of Defense (DoD) or the **TCP/IP model**. Figure 6-5 illustrates the TCP/IP model.

The TCP/IP model is like the OSI model, except the TCP/IP model is less specific. Since the TCP/IP model was developed before the OSI model, before the community recognized more complex computer network problems and before the early attempts to standardize physical network interfaces, its simplicity makes sense.

The DoD model is no longer widely used, but it is still helpful to know and understand.

Layer 4	Application	Establishes and manages application-to-application connections	HTTP, FTP
Layer 3	Transport	Establishes and manages host-to-host connections	TCP, UDP, QUIC
Layer 2	Internet	Routes packets between hosts	IP
Layer 1	Network Interface	Sends and receives frames from the physical network	Ethernet

Figure 6-5 *The DoD Network Model*

The Recursive Internet Architecture

The original group of engineers developing and standardizing the OSI model never intended for seven layers to be carved in stone, as they are often treated today. Many engineers believed more layers would be added as new problems were discovered and solved.

In a sense, more layers have been added through tunneling. Figure 6-6 illustrates.

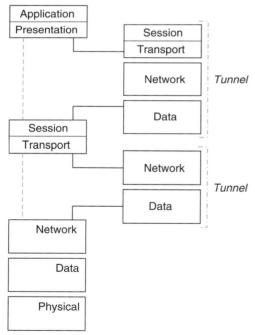

Figure 6-6 *Tunneling in the OSI Model*

A tunnel can be modeled as a second set of **protocol layers** inserted into the OSI model's protocol stack. One of the original developers of the OSI model, John Day, went on to develop another kind of model for network protocols called the *Recursive InterNetwork Architecture (RINA)*. Figure 6-7 illustrates the **RINA model**.

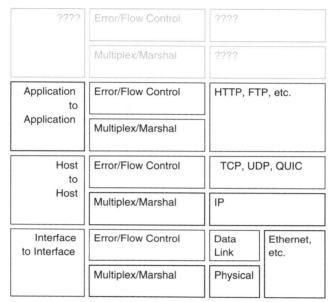

Figure 6-7 *The RINA Model*

The concept behind RINA is four fundamental problems need to be solved to carry data across a network:

- **Error Control:** Data must be delivered without error.

- **Flow Control:** The transmitter cannot transmit data more quickly than the receiver can accept it, nor so slow the receiver is starved of data.

- **Multiplexing:** There must be some way for multiple devices to share the same physical wire or transmission medium. Addressing and routing would be included as solutions for multiplexing.

- **Marshaling:** Data must be formatted by the sender so the receiver will understand it.

According to the RINA model, each protocol will accomplish two things. Protocol designers generally implement error and flow control in one protocol and marshaling and multiplexing in another. Protocols come in pairs, with each protocol in the pair solving two of the four problems.

While the OSI model focuses on the interfaces and interactions between the software and hardware in the process of sending data, the RINA model focuses on what each component is doing. The RINA model is important because this shift in focus allows network engineers to ask different kinds of questions.

Rather than asking "How does this protocol fit into the protocols around it?" the RINA model asks "What should this protocol be accomplishing?" When you are designing or troubleshooting a network, both kinds of questions are helpful.

The RINA model is not just another networking model but is an entire project designed to change the fundamental design and operation of computer networks. Vendors have not developed the ideas behind RINA into widely available protocol implementations, and operators have not deployed RINA-based protocols.

Because the RINA model is *recursive*, there is no reason a network should have two, four, six, or eight layers. Dr. Day argues networks should have eight layers, illustrated as two grayed-out layers in Figure 6-7. His argument has been proven true, at least in some sense, by the widespread use of tunnels in modern computer networks.

Chapter Review

Network models might seem impractical and distant when you first encounter them, but they are built into the language of computer network engineering. Models provide more than a common language set, though. Models also provide a way of thinking about how networks work.

You should study the OSI and RINA models, in particular, and understand how these two models map to what protocols do and what problem is being solved at each stage in carrying a packet from one application to another. Using models will get you into the mindset of clarifying and solving problems.

This is not the end of our journey through the logical concepts of network technology like the control plane, addresses, protocols, and models. For the next part, however, we will focus on the physical aspects of transmitting data across wires and optical fibers and building network topologies.

One key to doing well on the exams is to perform repetitive spaced review sessions. Review this chapter's material using either the tools in the book or interactive tools for the same material found on the book's companion website. Refer to the online Appendix D, "Study Planner," element for more details. Table 6-2 outlines the key review elements and where you can find them. To better track your study progress, record when you completed these activities in the second column.

Table 6-2   Chapter Review Tracking

Review Element	Review Date (s)	Resource Used
Review key topics		Book, website
Review key terms		Book, website
Repeat DIKTA questions		Book, PTP
Review concepts and actions		Book, website

Review All the Key Topics

Table 6-3 lists the key topics for this chapter.

Table 6-3 Key Topics for Chapter 6

Key Topic Element	Description	Page Number
Paragraph, Figure 6-1	OSI model	129
Figure 6-2	The Complexity of Mapping Protocols in the IP Suite to the OSI Model	131
Figure 6-4, list	Transporting a Packet Based on the OSI Model	132
Section	The TCP/IP Model	133
List	Four problems behind the RINA concept	135
Paragraph	RINA model vs. OSI model	135

Key Terms You Should Know

Key terms in this chapter include

ISO, OSI seven-layer model, TCP/IP model, protocol layers, RINA model, error control, flow control, multiplexing, marshaling

Concepts and Actions

Review the concepts considered in this chapter using Table 6-4. You can cover the right side of this table and describe each concept or action in your own words to verify your understanding.

Table 6-4 Concepts and Actions

Network models describe	What protocols do
Seven OSI model layers	Physical, data, network, transport, session, presentation, application
Network layer function	Routes data between hosts; routers operate at this layer
Data layer function	Transfers data across a single physical link; switches operate at this layer
Network layer protocols	The Internet Protocol (IP)
Original TCP/IP model	DoD model
Four TCP/IP model layers	Network interface, internet, transport, application
Tunneling in the OSI model	Tunnels can be seen as repeating the layers between layers
Four RINA functions	Error control, flow control, marshaling, multiplexing

6

Part II

Infrastructure

The first part of this book started with a physical world shipping example, working through the problems, solutions, and implications of addresses on shipping packets. One tiny detail (okay, it is not so tiny) we skipped over from the original shipping in the real world is how packages are physically carried from one place to another. The physical trucks, vans, airplanes, ships, and trains must have equivalents in computer networks. Even if the signals are digital, there must be some physical path between the sender and receiver.

What does this path look like, and how does it work?

Part II of this book will aim to answer these questions by looking at the infrastructure of computer networks.

The first chapter in this part will provide some mild electronic engineering background and then consider wired network connectivity. The second chapter will move into the wireless realm, including Wi-Fi, cellular networks, and configuring hosts for Wi-Fi connectivity. The third chapter will look at bandwidth, delay, and their measurement in the real world. The fourth chapter will look at network hardware's physical layout and lights. The fourth, fifth, and sixth chapters move into the way wires are connected to build a physical network—what are called *topologies* in the computer networking world.

The chapters in this part of the book are as follows:

Chapter 7: Wired Networks

Chapter 8: Wireless Networks

Chapter 9: Bandwidth, Delay, and Jitter

Chapter 10: Basic Network Hardware

Chapter 11: Local Area Networks

Chapter 12: Wide Area Networks

CHAPTER 7

Wired Networks

This chapter covers the following exam topics:

1. **Standards and Concepts**

    1.3. **Differentiate between LAN, WAN, MAN, CAN, PAN, and WLAN.**

    Identify and illustrate common physical and logical network topologies.

3. **Endpoints and Media Types**

    3.1 **Identify cables and connectors commonly used in local area networks.**

    Cable types: fiber, copper, twisted pair; Connector types: coax, RJ-45, RJ-11, fiber connector types

    3.2 **Differentiate between Wi-Fi, cellular, and wired network technologies.**

    Copper, including sources of interference; fiber; wireless, including 802.11 (unlicensed, 2.4GHz, 5GHz, 6GHz), cellular (licensed), sources of interference

Even with the knowledge of packets, addresses, and routing, the Internet—and computer networks more broadly—might seem a little...magical. After all, packets somehow leave your computer or cellular telephone and make it to another host, which then processes the data and sends a packet back from some distant location to your host for processing. Because packets are not really packages, what is the physical process for sending and receiving packets across long distances?

The process of sending packets and packages is similar in some ways and different in others. For instance:

- Even though we say a packet leaves one host and travels to another, the packet your host sends is not the same *physical* packet received. Packets are read into memory and re-created at every hop—every router, switch, and gateway. Even though the *data is the same*, the electrical signals carrying the data are not the same.

- There is a direct physical path between the sender and the receiver. While millions of hosts, routers, switches, and other devices cannot share a single physical path, there is still a physical path between every pair of hosts connected to the Internet.

Just like a physical package might travel over roads, tracks, through the atmosphere, or across the surface of water, packets are carried across copper wires, optical fibers, and through the air when transmitted from one location to another.

This chapter looks at two kinds of physical wiring: copper (or electrical) and optical.

Before jumping into copper wiring, we learn about *electromagnetic transmission* because this will clarify interference in copper cabling and the *maximum transmission unit (MTU)*.

"Do I Know This Already?" Quiz

Take the quiz (either here or use the PTP software) if you want to use the score to help you decide how much time to spend on this chapter. Appendix A, "Answers to the 'Do I Know This Already?' Quizzes," found at the end of the book, includes both the answers and explanations. You can also find answers in the PTP testing software.

Table 7-1 "Do I Know This Already?" Foundation Topics Section-to-Question Mapping

Section	Questions
Electrical Transmission and Interference	1, 2
The Maximum Transmission Unit	3
Ethernet over Copper	4, 5, 6
Fiber	7, 8
Pluggable Interfaces	9

CAUTION The goal of self-assessment is to gauge your mastery of the topics in this chapter. If you do not know the answer to a question or are only partially sure of the answer, you should mark that question as wrong for purposes of the self-assessment. Giving yourself credit for an answer you incorrectly guess skews your self-assessment results and might provide you with a false sense of security.

1. What is the frequency of an electronic signal or wave?

    a. How often the signal shuts on and off

    b. How often the signal's power changes

    c. How often the signal changes polarity

    d. How often the signal changes from a 0 to a 1

2. What is far-end crosstalk?

    a. The amount of interference between two optical fibers

    b. The amount of interference between two copper wires carrying different signals

    c. The amount of interference measured at a point farthest from the equipment

    d. The amount of interference between two wireless signals

3. What is the maximum transmission unit?

    a. The longest amount of time a transmitter can use the network

    b. The shortest possible packet a sender can transmit on a segment or through a network

    c. The largest file a sender can transmit over a network

    d. The largest packet, in bits, that can be transmitted over a segment or through a network

4. What is coax?

   a. A type of copper cable with an inner conductor and outer shield

   b. A type of fiber-optic cable containing two optical strands

   c. A type of copper cable carrying two wires twisted together

   d. A type of copper connector with two prongs

5. The 100BASE-T standard describes?

   a. A method for transmitting 100 Mb/s over an optical cable

   b. A method for transmitting 100 Mb/s over a twisted pair of copper wires

   c. A method for transmitting 100 Mb/s over a coaxial cable

   d. A method for transmitting files containing less than 100 MB of data

6. What is an RJ-45 connection?

   a. A small round connection used for fiber-optic networks

   b. A small round connection used for twisted-pair copper networks

   c. A rectangular connector with 8 wires used for twisted-pair Ethernet

   d. A rectangular connector with 4 wires used for twisted-pair Ethernet

7. What is single mode?

   a. An Ethernet mode where only one host can transmit data at a time

   b. An optical fiber connection using high-power laser transmitters

   c. An optical fiber cable with a single optical strand

   d. An Ethernet cable with a single strand of wire, rather than a twisted pair

8. What is an SC connector?

   a. A square twisted-pair Ethernet connector

   b. A small round connector used as an alternate to the RJ-45

   c. A common round fiber-optic connector

   d. A common square fiber-optic connector

9. Why are pluggable interfaces popular?

   a. Deployment flexibility.

   b. They are less expensive.

   c. The profit margin is higher for vendors.

   d. They always support many different interface speeds.

Foundation Topics

Electrical Transmission and Interference

Perhaps the simplest way to think of electrical signals moving through a copper wire is like water in a pipe. Of course, this comparison is crude and will only take you so far in understanding electrical transmission, but the similarities allow this comparison a reasonable place to start. For instance, we can define some common electrical terms as they might relate to water in a pipe, such as

- Voltage is like the pressure of the water being pushed through the pipe.

- Amperage is like the amount of water being pushed through the pipe.

- Wattage is like multiplying the pressure times the amount to measure the power of the water moving through the pipe

Assume you and a friend are on either end of a water pipe, and you want to find some way to communicate through the pipe. You could, for instance, vary the water pressure in some way. If you increase and decrease the water pressure 10 times in a second, you send a 0. If you increase and decrease the water pressure 20 times a second, you send a 1.

Suppose you can send a string of 0s and 1s over the pipe in an hour; if you had a way to translate a string of 0s and 1s to a character, image, or something else, you would have a communication system. The rate at which you pulse the water—10 or 20 times each second in this simple example—is called the *frequency*. Frequency is measured in *hertz*, the number of cycles in a second.

Pulling these terms into electrical signaling, we have

- **Voltage** is the pressure of the electrical signal passing through the wire.

- **Amperage** is the amount of electricity passing through the wire.

- **Wattage** is the power, or the combined pressure and volume, of electricity.

- **Frequency** is how often the *polarity* of the electrical signal changes direction.

Imposing a signal onto an electronic signal is called **modulation.** Signaling data by shifting the signal's frequency is a form of **frequency modulation.** The signal onto which data is modulated is called the *carrier*, and the signal frequency when no data is being modulated is called the **carrier frequency.**

Computer networks use copper wires roughly the same way as you can a water hose to communicate (although it is much more complex than this simple description). Figure 7-1 illustrates a wave of electrons passing through a wire.

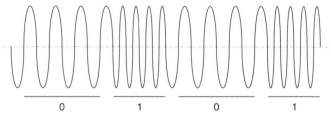

Figure 7-1   *A Simplified View of Converting Frequency into Binary*

To get closer to how things really work, we need to add another detail to the example: the electricity in the wire is *polarized* as it travels or moves in two different directions. When the wave shown in Figure 7-1 is above the gray dashed center line, the power moves (or is polarized) in one direction. When the wave is below the gray dashed center line, the power moves (or is polarized) in the opposite direction.

When the electrical signals move in one direction through the wire, they create a magnetic field with the north pole facing in one direction and the south pole facing in the opposite direction. When the power level crosses the center gray dashed line, the magnetic field collapses, so there is no magnetic field. When the electrical signal moves in the opposite direction, the magnetic field rebuilds, with the north and south poles facing opposite directions.

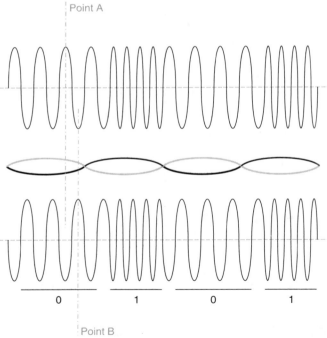

This magnetic field to electrical signal effect also works in the opposite direction. Placing a wire into a constantly shifting magnetic field causes electrical signals in the wire. The frequency and direction of these signals will correspond to the ebb and flow of the magnetic field.

Transferring signals from one wire to another through magnetic fields is called *inductive reactance*. Inductive reactance is the cause of most **interference** in transmitting wired (and wireless) electrical signals.

Imagine, for instance, two cables running near one another. Each of the wires in these two cables will produce and react to the magnetic fields generated by the other cable. Laying a power cable too close to a data cable can sometimes allow magnetic fields from the power cable (which would be much stronger than the fields generated by the data cable) to generate signals in the data cable.

High-power radio transmitters can cause this same effect. For instance, running a data cable near a microwave oven may allow signals from the oven to change the signal transmitted through the wire.

How do engineers prevent this kind of interference between cables? The two primary methods are *twisting* and *shielding*. Figure 7-2 illustrates how twisting conductors for the signal's return path in a cable acts as a countermeasure to interference.

Figure 7-2   *Twisting Conductors and Inverting the Signal to Reduce Interference*

Assume each of the signals shown in Figure 7-2 is transmitted on one of the two wires twisted together in the image. At *Point A*, as one signal is at its maximum—creating its maximum possible magnetic field polarized in one direction—the signal traveling along the second wire creates a magnetic field polarized in the opposite direction.

These two magnetic fields will cancel one another out, effectively creating *no magnetic field* around the wires.

This process is imperfect: the two signals cannot be paired perfectly, the wire will have spots where the twist is just slightly different than what it should be, etc. Of course, when you untwist the wires at either end to insert them into a connector, you break the intended effect and allow interference, particularly between pairs of wires in the same cable. You should be careful to untwist the amount of wire specified by the connector when attaching a connector to avoid disturbing this countermeasure against interference.

The second way to protect a cable from external electrical and magnetic signals is through shielding. Figure 7-3 illustrates.

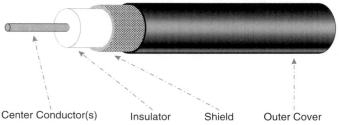

Center Conductor(s)   Insulator   Shield   Outer Cover

Figure 7-3   *Shielded Cable*

Shielded cable contains an inner core containing one or more cables and an outer shield. The outer shield is either a mesh or thin grounded foil—literally attached to something able to absorb all the signal generated in the shield. Since the shield is absorbing and (in theory) blocking the magnetic and electrical signals from nearby transmitters and cables, external interference should not affect cables in the shield's center.

The signal travels from the transmitter through the coax to the receiver. The return path for the power from the receiver to the transmitter is along the shield.

Coax has one conductor in the center. Cables can have more than one twisted set of wires in the center of shielding, called a *shielded* **twisted pair**.

When working with shielded cables, it is important to strip the correct amount of shielding when installing a connector and to connect the shield to a ground.

Measuring Interference

Network engineers care about two distinct measures of interference when working with cable: *near-end crosstalk (**NEXT**)* and *far-end crosstalk (**FEXT**)*. Both of these are called *crosstalk* because the kind of interference described previously was first noticed back in the analog telephone days. Crosstalk in analog telephones happens when you can hear the conversation from another cable pair in the background of your conversation.

NEXT measures how much external noise a cable can reject or how noisy an environment a cable can be used in without compromising the signal passing through the cable. NEXT is measured at the *near end*, where the transmitter connects to the cable.

FEXT measures how much external noise is interfering with a signal in an existing cable. FEXT is a "real-world" measurement used to determine the quality of an in-place existing cable run. You measure FEXT at the *cable's far end or the opposite end* where the transmitter is attached.

Other Cable Ratings

There are other kinds of ratings you should care about as a network engineer—specifically whether the cable is **plenum** or *direct-bury* rated.

Plenum is just a fancy name for an air return for an air conditioner or heating system. If there is a fire in a building, these air returns are the primary way oxygen makes it to people who happen to be inside the building, helping to keep them alive. If a cable run through a plenum releases poisonous gasses when it burns, those gasses will be released into the return air system and directly into the lungs of the people inside the building.

Dumping poison gas into the air during a fire would not be a good thing, to say the least.

Caution is required because the space above the drop ceiling in many commercial buildings is the air return or plenum.

Direct-bury rating is just what it sounds like: these cables can be directly buried underground instead of being placed inside a conduit or some other protective cover. If you are running cables between two buildings, the direct-bury rating of the cable might be an important factor to consider.

The Maximum Transmission Unit

Assume you are sitting around a campfire (or table) with friends. A discussion about a really important topic breaks out, but one person (or a couple of people) dominates the conversation. One way of solving this is the "speaking stick." An object is chosen (like a stick) and passed around the room. Only the person who has the stick can talk.

But what if the person with the stick talks for too long, and they still dominate the conversation? One way to solve this situation is to set a timer when someone gets the stick. Once the timer times out (*wakes up* in computer programming terms), the person holding the stick must hand the stick to the next person in line.

The problem solved by the speaking stick is many people in the same physical space want to share the same medium—the air in the room—and the listener's attention.

Computer networks are designed so multiple hosts share the same physical wire (called *multiplexing*) and have the same problem as a group of friends sitting around a table trying to have a coherent conversation. If any one computer is "talking," no other computers can talk at the same time; otherwise, their signals will *collide*, and none of the other computers will be able to understand the signal.

The maximum packet size—the *maximum transmission unit (MTU)*—is set on each link to help prevent these collisions. Because each bit takes a specific amount of time to transmit, setting the number of bits a host can send at once controls how long the host can use the network before being required to allow some other host to (try to) transmit.

About MTUs

The MTU also relates to how long it takes for the signal to traverse the longest permitted wire for a particular kind of wire. The transmission should last long enough for every host on the wire to know another host is transmitting before it tries to transmit.

The smallest MTU across an entire path between two hosts in a network is called the path MTU. While this is similar to, and based on, the MTU of a single link, these two concepts should not be confused.

Ethernet over Copper

When Ethernet was first developed and deployed by Xerox in the mid-1970s, operators built networks using Token Ring, ARCnet, X.25, and circuits designed to carry voice. Even in the late 1980s, operators deployed large-scale installations of inverse multiplexers, combining several lower-speed telco-based lower-speed T1 links into a single circuit, and token bus networks.

By 1985, however, 3Com had sold some 100,000 Ethernet adapters for personal computers, and Ethernet interfaces 150 times faster than the fastest telephone-based circuit were available (10 Mb/s versus 64 Kb/s). Since the mid-1980s, the speed and capacity of Ethernet have increased, and virtually every wired circuit deployed uses some form of Ethernet standards.

Standards set the speed and kind of Ethernet standards; Table 7-2 gives some examples.

Table 7-2 Typical Ethernet Designations

Designation	Description
10BASE-2	10 Mb/s over thin coaxial cable; *thinnet*
10BASE-5	10 Mb/s over thick coaxial cable; *thicknet*
10BASE-F	10 Mb/s over fiber optics
10BASE-T	10 Mb/s over a single twisted pair of unshielded copper wire (*category 3*)
100BASE-T	100 Mb/s over a single twisted pair of unshielded copper wire (*category 5*)
100BASE-T2	100 Mb/s over two pairs of unshielded twisted pairs of copper wire (*category 3*)
1000BASE-T	1 Gb/s over four pairs of unshielded twisted pairs of copper wire (*category 5*)

Ethernet was initially designed to run over a thick coaxial cable called *thicknet*. Technicians connected hosts to a thicknet cable by drilling a hole through the outer layers to reach the inner conductor, then attached a *vampire tap* with two spikes. The longer center spike contacts the inner conductor, and the shorter spikes contact the outer shield. *Thinnet* was much easier to work with because the cable was much thinner and easier to handle, and you connected to it using T- and soldered end-connectors.

Ethernet Bus Topologies

All the hosts are attached to a single segment of wire when using thicknet and thinnet, as shown in Figure 7-4.

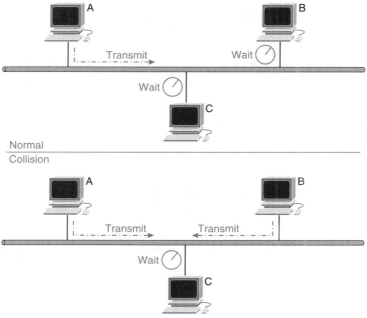

Figure 7-4 *Ethernet Shared Medium Access*

Because only one host can transmit onto the shared medium at a time, every host waits for a predetermined amount to see if the wire is empty before transmitting. The wait time required depends on the minimum packet size allowed on the segment and the amount of time it takes for an electrical signal to make it from one end of the segment to another.

This method of accessing a shared medium—waiting some time to ensure it is not in use before transmitting—is called *Carrier Sense Multiple Access*. When multiple hosts try to *access* a single physical wire, they must try to *sense* if the *carrier* is in use before transmitting.

If, as shown in the *Collision* part of the illustration, two different hosts transmit at the same moment, they should receive their signal at the same time they are transmitting it. If a host discovers the transmission on the wire is different than what it is currently sending, there must be two hosts transmitting simultaneously—a collision. According to the Ethernet standard, when a host detects a collision must set a random wait timer, trying again when the timer expires (or wakes up).

Ethernet's method of sharing a single wire is called *Carrier Sense Multiple Access with Collision Detection (CSMA/CD)*.

The single long coaxial wire shared by a group of hosts is called a **bus topology**.

> **NOTE** Real-world deployments no longer use bus topologies.

Ethernet Star Topologies

CSMA/CD can also be used in a **star topology**, as shown in Figure 7-5.

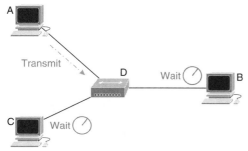

Figure 7-5   *Ethernet Star Topology*

A star topology is formed when every host, or other connected device, connects directly to a central device, like a hub, switch, or router.

The network in Figure 7-5 operates the same way as the networks in Figure 7-4: only one host can transmit at a time. Each host connects via twisted-pair cables to a **repeater** or *hub*, marked as *D* in the illustration.

Repeaters repeat any signal they receive on any port to every other port. When host *A* begins transmitting, its electrical signals are copied or repeated onto every port at hub *D*, so hosts *B* and *C* receive the signals in near real-time (given the amount of time required to carry the signal through the network physically).

Moving from a bus to a star topology might seem to change how network wiring is run and what kinds of cables are in use. In the mid-1980s, the cost and long-term viability of different cabling systems were very much a topic of heated discussion.

NOTE   Real-world deployments no longer use star topologies with Ethernet hubs.

However, moving to a star topology facilitated Ethernet switches' development and deployment, as Figure 7-6 shows.

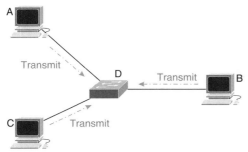

Figure 7-6   *Switched Ethernet Topology*

Replacing the hub in the star's center with either a switch or a router breaks up the electrical circuit. The switch receives and processes the entire packet, holding the packet in memory if two hosts transmit simultaneously.

The switch, however, must still use CSMA/CD to coordinate its transmission with the attached hosts.

Ethernet Twisted Pair

Ethernet twisted-pair cables are rated based on their shielding, the amount of data they can carry, and the maximum length of the cable. Table 7-3 lists common Ethernet cables and their characteristics.

Table 7-3   Common Ethernet Cable Types

Type	Data Rate	Notes
Category 3	10 Mb/s	Introduced in the early 1990s
Category 5	100 Mb/s	Introduced in 1995 100-meter maximum length
Category 5e	1000 Mb/s	Not an official standard
Category 6	1 Gb/s up to 100 meters 10 Gb/S up to 37 meters	Contains a "spline" between each twisted pair to reduce crosstalk
Category 7	Similar to Category 6	Developed by a group of manufacturers; not an official standard
Category 8	40 Gb/s	Generally used for router-to-router connections 30-meter maximum cable length

There is only one twisted-pair Ethernet connector in widespread use: the RJ-45. Figure 7-7 illustrates.

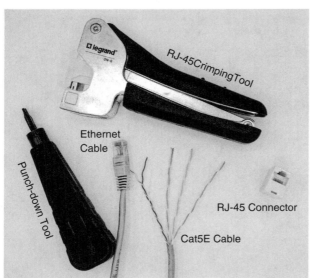

Figure 7-7   *The RJ-45 Connector*

The elements shown in Figure 7-7 are as follows:

- **Punch-down tool**, used for punching individual copper strands into blocks or quick-attach connectors. Punch-down tools are also used to terminate *plain old telephone service (POTS)* and alarm wiring.

- *Ethernet cable*, as built by a factory. You can see the individual wires inside the plastic connector on this version. Note the *strain gage* on where the cable meets the connector; this helps reduce strain on the cable when installed tightly or around sharp bends.

- *Cat 5e cable*, showing the twist in each pair of conductors. The brown/white pair has been untwisted a small amount to show the two separate wires.

- *Crimping tool*, used for crimping wires into a connector when hand-building Ethernet cables.

The RJ-45 connector is an example of a *registered jack*, first standardized by the Bell System in the United States and standardized by the United States *Federal Communications Commission (FCC)* in the 1970s. Technically, the RJ-45 used for Ethernet is a variant, the RJ-45S, but everyone shortens this to RJ-45.

Typically, in phone applications, a jack is used with enough pairs of wire to support the number of circuits:

- Single-line phone: RJ-11 with the two center wires connected

- Two-line phone: RJ-14 with one line connected to the center pair and the second line connected to the two outer pair

- Three-line phone: RJ-25 with three pairs

RJ-45 connections have four pairs, as shown in Figure 7-7. Figure 7-8 shows the wiring for an RJ-45 Ethernet cable.

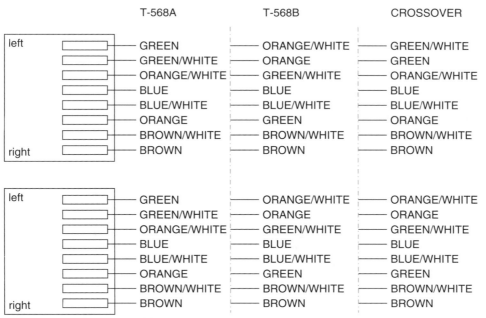

Figure 7-8   *Ethernet Cable Wiring*

When wiring a building or house, you should use either T-568A or T-568B on both ends of *all* the cables. Most network devices will now detect which way the network is wired and adjust accordingly.

If one end of a cable is wired as a T-568A and the other end T-586B, the cable *crosses over* the signals; the transmit connection on one device is connected directly to the receive connector on the other. Crossover cables were once common for connecting two hosts, routers, or switches. Hosts are wired to be connected to switches and switches to hosts; without a **crossover**, these two kinds of devices will not normally communicate.

Most network equipment has a crossover software setting that reverses the wires used for transmitting and receiving, so crossover cables are generally not required when configuring or testing Ethernet networks.

Power Over Ethernet

Because POTS phones draw their power from the phone line, telephone connectors, and cables are designed to carry power and a signal. The computer networking industry uses these original design specifications, modified for computer networks, to support *Power over Ethernet* (**PoE**).

PoE allows a small device to run entirely off the Ethernet cable—without being plugged into a wall outlet or other source of electricity.

PoE is important for IoT, IP-based telephones, wireless access points, and other small devices. So long as PoE is available, these small devices do not need a separate power plug. If you are deploying PoE in a network, you need to pay attention to power draw standards:

- **802.3af/802.3at type 1:** 12.95 watts at 37–57 volts

- **802.at type 2, PoE+:** 25.5 watts at 42–57 volts

- **802.1at type 3, PoE++:** 51 watts at 42–57 volts

- **802.1at type 4, PoE++:** 71.3 watts at 41–57 volts

If you attach a device requiring 50 watts of power to an 802.3af PoE system, for instance, it will not be able to draw enough power to work correctly.

Fiber

Fiber optics are the highest-speed transmission medium for computer networks. Fiber is also the most common long-distance medium and the most widely used in high-density data center networks. Figure 7-9 illustrates the components of a fiber-optic cable.

If the light enters the fiber at the right angle—within the **acceptance cone**—it will bounce off the reflective insides of the cladding until it reaches the other end. The cladding absorbs light entering the core at the wrong angle.

Connectors must be well-designed and matched to prevent light from reflecting off the fiber ends and returning to the sending optical interface.

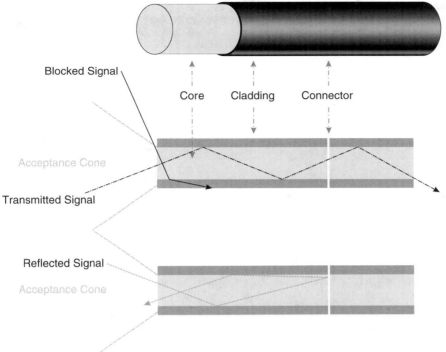

Figure 7-9 *Fiber-Optic Cable Operation*

Transmission by light works in much the same way as transmission through electronic signals—varying the signal frequency to indicate 0s and 1s. Varying the frequency of light changes its color. A light's color is often measured by its **wavelength**, which is directly related to its frequency. Figure 7-10 shows the relationship between frequency and wavelength.

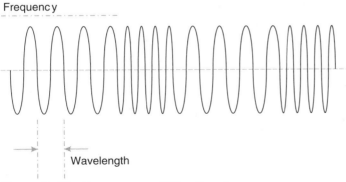

Figure 7-10 *Frequency and Wavelength*

As frequency increases, the length of each wave in the signal (the wavelength) becomes shorter. Each light color has a corresponding wavelength and frequency, as shown in Table 7-4.

Table 7-4   Color Frequencies and Wavelengths

Light Color	Wavelength in Nanometers (nm)	Frequency in Terahertz (THz)
Blue	450–485	620–670
Cyan	485–500	600–620
Green	500–565	530–600
Yellow	565–590	510–530
Orange	590–625	480–510
Red	625–750	400–480

The concept of wavelength is important because fiber-optic cables can carry many different signals using *wave division multiplexing* (**WDM**). Multiple signals using different light colors can be transmitted over the same physical fiber.

Most modern systems use the same Ethernet signaling used over copper wires.

While fiber optics can carry a bidirectional signal, almost all fiber systems use a pair of cables. The device on one end transmits on the first cable and receives on the second, while the device on the other transmits on the second cable and receives on the first.

Fiber Cables

Computer networks use two kinds of fiber-optic cable:

- **Multimode** cable has a larger core, so it can transmit more light, making it ideal for lower power (and less expensive) like *light-emitting diodes (LEDs)*. Multimode fiber can carry data less than 1.5 kilometers.

- **Single-mode** cable has a much smaller core, requiring a higher-power light source—typically a laser. Single-mode fiber can typically carry a signal 80 kilometers. Amplifiers can extend this range to several thousand kilometers.

Small amounts of the light passing through a fiber will be absorbed or dispersed by imperfections in the glass core. This is called **attenuation**. When driven by a transmitter of the same *optical power*, or two light sources of the same brightness, signals passing through a multimode fiber will attenuate more than signals passing through a single-mode fiber.

The attenuation of a fiber-optic cable is measured in **decibels**, or the loss of power from the original light source. The decibel is a logarithmic scale, which measures exponentially rather than linearly. For instance, if a light loses half its brightness when traveling through a fiber-optic cable 1 meter long, it has lost 3 dB of its strength. If every meter of a fiber-optic cable has 3 dB of attenuation, then the signal will have the following:

- 50% of its original strength after traveling through the first meter of fiber-optic cable (3 dB of loss)

- 25% of its original strength after traveling through the second meter of fiber-optic cable (6 dB of loss)

- 12.5% of its original strength after traveling through the third meter of fiber-optic cable (9 dB of loss)

Light will also *disperse* when traveling through a fiber-optic cable, as shown in Figure 7-11.

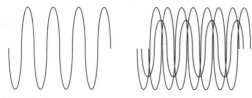

Signal before dispersion   Signal after dispersion

Figure 7-11   *Light Dispersion Through a Fiber-Optic Cable*

Dispersion is worse in multimode fibers because the signal "bounces along the core." Each bounce adds a reflected signal and potential echoes, much like the echo you hear when speaking in a large, empty room.

Fiber Networking Hardware

The four primary pieces of optical network equipment engineers encounter in the field are as follows:

- *Wave* **division multiplexer/demultiplexer (WDM/D):** WDM/Ds are passive filters (they do not require power) and come in pairs, one each for the transmit and receive cables. These devices are often used at the end points of a fiber cable (the *head-end* and *tail-end*) to separate all the channels in the fiber run.

- **Optical add/drop multiplexer (OADM):** OADMs can add or drop a single color in the fiber without disturbing the other colors transmitted through the cable. Figure 7-12 illustrates how an OADM works.

  Conceptually, the OADM splits the single light source from the cable into each color in the spectrum using a prism. Once the light is split, it can be redirected through fiber connectors to other devices (as shown with the orange color in Figure 7-12), or colors can be swapped (as shown with the blue and cyan colors in Figure 7-12).

- **Reconfigurable optical add/drop multiplexer (ROADM):** ROADMs serve the same purposes as OADMs, except operators can dynamically reconfigure which colors are swapped, dropped, or added.

- **Amplifiers:** Amplifiers amplify and clean up the optical signal so operators can extend fiber runs.

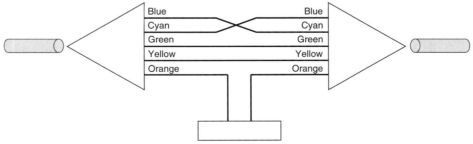

Figure 7-12   *Optical Add/Drop Multiplexer*

Fiber Connectors

Fiber connectors come in many shapes and sizes—in fact, engineers design new connectors almost every year. Some types are common, such as

- **LC connector**, originally called the *Lucent connector*, is often called *Little connector*. The LC is a square plastic latch-in connector for high-density fiber connections. Figure 7-13 contains an LC connector.

- **ST connector**, normally taken to mean *straight tip*, is a round connector with a metal twist-turn-push connection action. These were the most common fiber connectors used in data networks until the widespread use of the LC connector. Figure 7-13 contains an ST connector.

- **SC connector**, normally taken to be *subscriber connector* or *square connector*. The SC is a square latch-in connector.

- **FC connector**, normally taken to mean *ferrule connector*. The FC connector looks similar to an ST but uses a screw-in action to make the physical connection rather than the twist-turn-push.

- **MPO connector**, or *multiple-fiber push-on/pull-off*. As shown in Figure 7-13, MPO connectors are rectangular and can contain multiple pairs of connectors. These connectors are normally used only for indoor cabling.

Figure 7-13   *ST, LC, and MPO Fiber Connectors*

Each connector type comes in either *ultra-physical connect (**UPC**)* or *angled physical connect (**APC**)* configurations. Figure 7-14 illustrates.

When you look across the top of a bowl of water, some light sources reflect off the top, producing glare; however, if the room light is dim enough or the angles are correct, you can also see what is under the water. Optical connectors have the same sort of surface where the two fibers meet.

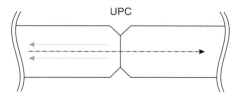

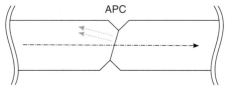

Figure 7-14   *UPC Versus APC*

If the connection is perfectly 90 degrees from the center line of the fiber, less light is reflected to the light source. Because of this, there is less dispersion and attenuation when using UPC connectors.

However, light reflected to the source can overheat or damage the laser or LED. If the fiber run is long enough to require a high-power laser as a source, APC connectors will be used. Angled connections reflect more light, but the cladding absorbs the reflected light.

Looking into a Fiber

Laser warning signs are ubiquitous in computer networking facilities: do not stare directly into the laser. Most—but not all—of these signs are overly cautious. There are several classes of lasers:

- **Class 1:** Less than 10 dBm, completely harmless during normal use

- **Class 1M:** Completely harmless unless viewed through a magnification device

- **Class 2:** Harmless unless you stare into them (but most of the time, you will blink)

- **Class 3:** Less than 27 dBm, should not be viewed directly

- **Class 4:** Greater than 27 dBm, can destroy objects and eyes

A laser's class is determined by the power and wavelength of its output. The human eye can withstand much more power from a light source outside the visible range without damage than within the visible range. Most computer network systems

- Use light outside the visible range.

- Are low enough power to be considered a class 1 laser.

Every laser connected to a router or switch is a class 1 or 1M laser. Optical amplifiers, on the other hand, can easily be rated either class 3 or 4 lasers, so the output from these devices can be dangerous to the human eye.

Since you cannot know what kind of laser is attached to the other end of a fiber-optic cable, here's the general rule: do not look into the end of a fiber-optic cable while it is powered up. The odds are the light there will not harm your eyes, but there are situations where it could.

Developing the habit of looking into a fiber cable to determine if the transmitter is working is just not a good idea.

Of course, you will not see anything even if you look into the end of a fiber-optic cable because the colors of light used in the optical network are in the infrared spectrum. A quick check you can often use is to hold your cellular telephone camera up to the fiber output. Most modern digital cameras can detect and display infrared light sources.

Pluggable Interfaces

Many physical network interfaces are soldered permanently onto a router's or switch's circuit board—especially interfaces up to 10 Gb/s. The popularity and variety of connection types have caused a shift to pluggable interfaces:

- Router and switch vendors do not know whether you need single-mode or multimode fiber connections and which type of connector your network uses.

- Some higher-speed interfaces can be broken down into multiple lower-speed interfaces. You can split a 100 Gb/s interface into ten 10 Gb/s interfaces using a special octopus cable.

Rather than plugging a cable directly into a router or switch, you plug a module with the correct kind of plug into the router or switch, and then you plug the cable (or cables) into the outlet.

Interfaces designed to take many different kinds of optical—or even electrical—interfaces are called **pluggable interfaces**.

There are two basic kinds of pluggable interfaces:

- *Gigabit interface converter* (**GBIC**)

- *Small form-factor pluggable* (**SFP**), shown in Figure 7-15

There are many variations of these pluggable interfaces, such as the XFP shown in Figure 7-15. Most of these variants are restricted to one network interface speed.

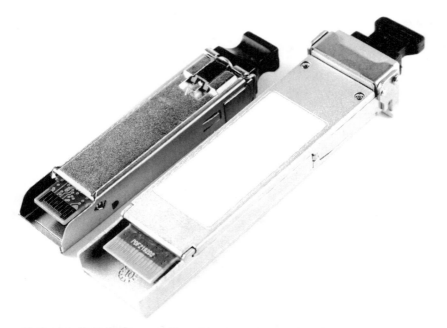

Figure 7-15   *XFP and SFP Pluggable Connectors*

Chapter Review

This chapter took a deep dive into the inner workings of copper and fiber wired transmission methods—from signaling to connectors. The standards and ideas used to transmit data across cables of all kinds change constantly. As a network engineer, you regularly will want to learn more about this one area of research and products.

Learning about all kinds of connectors, interfaces, and cables is a good place to start. This chapter touched on the common kinds of connectors, but there are a lot more connectors and cables used in computer networks than what is covered here.

One key to doing well on the exams is to perform repetitive spaced review sessions. Review this chapter's material using either the tools in the book or interactive tools for the same material found on the book's companion website. Refer to the online Appendix D, "Study Planner," element for more details. Table 7-5 outlines the key review elements and where you can find them. To better track your study progress, record when you completed these activities in the second column.

Table 7-5   Chapter Review Tracking

Review Element	Review Date (s)	Resource Used
Review key topics		Book, website
Review key terms		Book, website
Repeat DIKTA questions		Book, PTP
Review concepts and actions		Book, website

Review All the Key Topics

Table 7-6 lists the key topics for this chapter.

Table 7-6   Key Topics for Chapter 7

Key Topic Element	Description	Page Number
List, paragraph	Electrical signaling terminology	143
Section	Measuring Interference	145
Paragraph	Plenum cable	146
Paragraph	MTU	146
Paragraph	CSMA/CD	148
Paragraph	Bus topology	148
Figure 7-5, Paragraph	Star topology	148
Paragraph	Repeaters	149
Figure 7-7	The RJ-45 Connector	150
Paragraph	Crossover cables	152
Section	Power Over Ethernet	152
Figure 7-9	Fiber-Optic Cable Operation	153
Paragraph, Figure 7-10	Fiber-optic wavelength and frequency	153
Paragraph	WDM	154
List	Fiber-optic cable types	154
Paragraphs	Attenuation and decibels	154
Figure 7-11	Light dispersion through fiber-optic cable	155
List, Figure 7-12	Optical equipment	155
List	Fiber connectors	156
Paragraph, Figure 7-14	Fiber connector configurations	156
Paragraph, list	Pluggable interfaces	158

Key Terms You Should Know

Key terms in this chapter include

voltage, amperage, wattage, frequency, modulation, frequency modulation, carrier frequency, interference, coax, twisted pair, NEXT, FEXT, plenum, MTU, bus topology, CSMA/CD, star topology, repeater, punch-down tool, crossover, PoE, fiber optics, acceptance cone, wavelength, WDM, multimode, single-mode, attenuation, decibels, dispersion, WDM/D, OADM, ROADM, LC connector, ST connector, SC connector, FC connector, MPO connector, UPC, APC, pluggable interface, GBIC, SFP

Concepts and Actions

Review the concepts considered in this chapter using Table 7-7. You can cover the right side of this table and describe each concept or action in your own words to verify your understanding.

Table 7-7   Concepts and Actions for Review

Inductive reactance	The formation of a magnetic field as a signal travels through a wire, and the creation of an electrical signal when a wire is in a changing magnetic field
Two ways to reduce interference	Twisted pairs, shielding
FEXT	Far-end crosstalk; interference measured at the far end of the cable
NEXT	Near-end crosstalk; the amount of interference a cable can reject
Bus topology	All hosts are connected to a single long wire, generally coax
Star topology	Each host has a separate wire connecting to a central point, such as a hub, switch, or router
CSMA/CD	Carrier Sense Multiple Access with Collision Detection; method used by Ethernet to allow multiple hosts to share a single segment
RJ-45	Most common Ethernet twisted-pair connector
Wavelength	Length of a single cycle in a signal; related to the color of light
Single mode	Higher-powered light source and a smaller core
Multimode	Lower-powered light source and a larger core
OADM	Optical add/drop multiplexer, used to drop and add data channels at specific wavelengths or colors of light
LC connector	Little connector, used for high-density fiber-optic installations
ST	Straight tip fiber-optic connector
SC	Square connector, fiber-optic connector
FC	Ferrule connector, fiber-optic connector with a screw-down mechanical connection
UPC	Ultra physical connect, a flat optical connector that optimizes light transmission and reduces reflections
APC	Angled physical connect, an angled optical connector that directs reflected light away from the light source
SFP	Small form-factor pluggable router and switch interface
GBIC	Gigabit interface convertor, a larger form-factor pluggable interface

7

CHAPTER 8

Wireless Networks

This chapter covers the following exam topics:

3. **Endpoints and Media Types**

    3.2 **Differentiate between Wi-Fi, cellular, and wired network technologies.**

    Copper, including sources of interference; fiber; wireless, including 802.11 (unlicensed, 2.4GHz, 5GHz, 6GHz), cellular (licensed), sources of interference

While wired connectivity was the standard in the early years of computer networking, wireless connectivity is now how the majority of individual users connect their devices to the Internet. This chapter begins by exploring wireless transmission concepts. We then consider Wi-Fi, cellular, and satellite communications at a high level.

"Do I Know This Already?" Quiz

Take the quiz (either here or use the PTP software) if you want to use the score to help you decide how much time to spend on this chapter. Appendix A, "Answers to the 'Do I Know This Already?' Quizzes," found at the end of the book, includes both the answers and explanations. You can also find answers in the PTP testing software.

Table 8-1 "Do I Know This Already?" Foundation Topics Section-to-Question Mapping

Section	Questions
Free Space Concepts	1, 2, 3
Wi-Fi	4, 5, 6
Cellular	7, 8
Satellite	9

CAUTION The goal of self-assessment is to gauge your mastery of the topics in this chapter. If you do not know the answer to a question or are only partially sure of the answer, you should mark that question as wrong for purposes of the self-assessment. Giving yourself credit for an answer you incorrectly guess skews your self-assessment results and might provide you with a false sense of security.

1. How does beam forming create a directional signal?

    a. By physically blocking a wireless signal from traveling in some directions

    b. By turning the signal on and off in a specific pattern so the beam goes in only one direction

   c. By combining signals from multiple antennas as they pass through the air

   d. By bouncing signals off solid objects in the room to create a narrow pattern

2. What two characteristics of noise will cause greater interference when mixed with a signal?

   a. Lower power and a frequency close to the signal's frequency

   b. Higher power and a frequency farther away from the signal's frequency

   c. Higher power and a frequency close to the signal's frequency

   d. Lower power and a frequency farther away from the signal's frequency

3. What is the carrier of an electromagnetic signal?

   a. The center frequency, or the frequency onto which the signal is modulated

   b. The physical medium through which the signal is carried

   c. The signaling mechanism carrying the data being pushed through the network

   d. The physical wire carrying the signal

4. What organization defines and supports the Wi-Fi standards?

   a. The Internet Engineering Task Force

   b. The International Telecommunications Union

   c. The World Wide Web Consortium

   d. The Institute of Electrical and Electronics Engineers

5. What Wi-Fi device can extend the range of a Wi-Fi network signal?

   a. Access point

   b. Repeater

   c. Backhaul network

   d. Longer cables

6. What are the primary advantages of Wi-Fi for a network operator? (Select all that apply.)

   a. It does not require configuration of any kind.

   b. It operates in unlicensed spectrum.

   c. It allows for centralized billing based on data usage.

   d. It does not require extensive infrastructure.

7. What is the radio access network (RAN)?

   a. The antenna and transmitter in a Wi-Fi network

   b. The antenna and software on a cellular telephone or other cellular-connected device

   c. A group of cellular towers and the transmitters, and the network connecting those cellular towers

   d. The network connecting a cellular radio tower to the mobile core

8. What is the mobile core?

   a. A set of cellular radio transmitters and towers that can be moved to improve reception when needed

   b. A set of servers and software that authorize users, track user locations, and track cellular network usage

    c. The network connecting the RAN to the Internet

    d. The network connecting multiple MANs

9. What is the key advantage of a low Earth orbit (LEO) satellite system?

    a. Shorter delay because the satellites are closer to the Earth

    b. Shorter delay because the satellites forward traffic more quickly

    c. Each satellite covers a larger part of the Earth than geosynchronous systems

    d. Each satellite can transmit larger amounts of data than geosynchronous systems

Foundation Topics

Free Space Concepts

Transmitting signals through the air uses the same principles as transmitting signals through wires or optical fibers: there is still a carrier, and data is still modulated onto this carrier. The power levels and frequencies differ, but the ideas are the same.

To carry these ideas into the wireless space, we need to look at two additional concepts: wave propagation and wireless interference. The section on wave propagation below also includes a high-level description of a critical technology in the wireless space—beam forming.

Wave Propagation and Beam Forming

In most electrical circuits, we create a path for power to return to the transmitter, as Figure 8-1 shows.

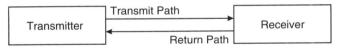

Figure 8-1 *Transmit and Return Paths in a Circuit*

What happens if you remove the return path, increase the power, and remove all the shielding? The wire turns into an antenna. Figure 8-2 illustrates the circuit path with free space radiation.

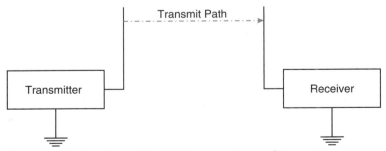

Figure 8-2 *Free Space (Radio) Propagation and Reception*

The signal power now flows from the transmitter through the antenna, into the air (or any other free space, including water and...space), and to the receiver's antenna. The signal causes small currents to flow in the receiver's antenna, which are then translated into the same kind of modulated signal transmitted through wired circuits.

What about the return path? In a way, the Earth itself is the return circuit. Both the transmitter and receiver are connected to the Earth as a ground, which acts like a big "sink," absorbing the return power from the transmission.

Signals dissipate as they pass through the air in various ways. Just traveling through the air uses up energy from the electromagnetic wave, but there are also objects like walls and rain-drops to pass through.

Electromagnetic signals lose roughly half of their power for every wavelength they travel through the air, and more as they travel through various solids. Shorter wavelength, or higher frequency, signals lose power more quickly than longer wavelength, or lower frequency, signals.

The signal transmitted by an antenna is not uniform in space; it forms a wave. Figure 8-3 illustrates.

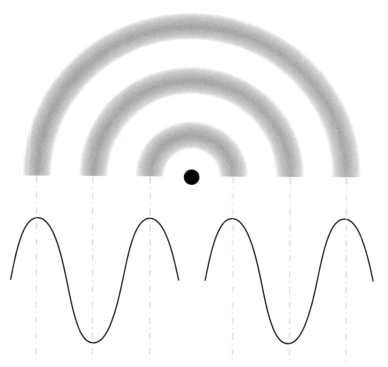

Figure 8-3 *Free Wave Propagation*

Figure 8-3 is what you would see if you

- Look down the antenna wire from the top (the black dot in the center of the image is the antenna wire).

- Cut out half of the signal (to create a space to show the wave). The signal would normally be a complete set of circles.

- Increase the darkness of the color as the signal becomes stronger.

The wave under the propagation illustration shows how the signal strength correlates with the changing power level. The electromagnetic wave is not fixed in space (it is not a *standing wave*), but the signal flows out from the antenna in waves, much like ripples in water. As the signal "washes over" a receiver's antenna, it creates small electrical currents the receiver then cleans up, amplifies, and finally turns into the signal the transmitter originally sent.

The white spaces in the signal are points where there is no power. If you put an antenna in one of the white spaces at just the right moment, it would not pick up any signal—at least until the following wave peak passes.

NOTE   You can shape the signal by bending the wire into more complex shapes, but antenna theory is beyond the scope of this book.

Beam forming works by combining the signal from two (or more) different antennas, called a *phased array*, as shown in Figure 8-4.

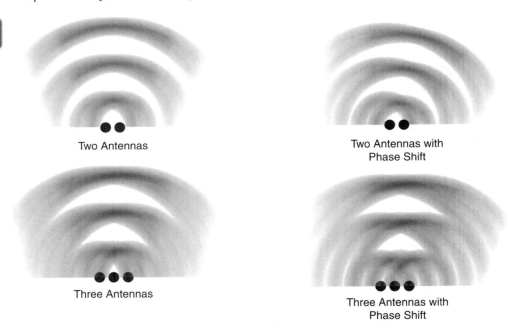

Figure 8-4   *Beam Formation with an Antenna Array*

On the upper left, you can see the darker spots directly above the antennas where the highest power points of the signals are added together, creating a single stronger signal. To either side of the two antennas, the signal is weaker.

Adding more antennas, as shown on the bottom left, increases this effect, allowing the antenna designer to create a narrow range of powerful signals with lower-powered signals on either side. With two antennas in the array, the effect is pronounced. Adding a third antenna increases the strength of the center beam and weakens the strength of the areas outside the beam.

The direction of this beam can be moved by shifting the *phase* of the two signals, as shown by the two wireless propagation patterns on the right side of Figure 8-4. Figure 8-5 illustrates the concept of phase shift.

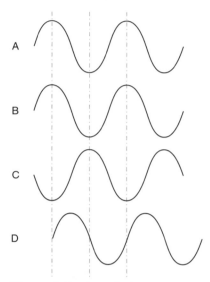

Figure 8-5 *Signal Phase*

In Figure 8-5:

- Combining signals *A* and *B*, which are *in phase*, will double the signal's strength.

- Combining signals *B* and *C*, which are *180 degrees out of phase*, will cancel both out.

- Combining signals *C* and *D*, which are *90 degrees out of phase*, will shift the locations in the propagation where higher power results from the combination of the waves.

When signals of different phases are combined, the direction and strength of the beam formed by two (or more) antennas can be shifted. By feeding different phases of the signal to different antennas in the array, the designer can move the locations the beam reaches without physically moving the antennas.

Wireless Interference

Just as the signals from two antennas will mix intentionally to increase transmission power and form beams, signals from other transmissions and environmental noise will also mix with transmitted signals, degrading the signal's quality.

When other signals or environmental noise mix with a signal, degrading its quality, this is called **interference**.

Noise will have the largest impact when it is either close to the same frequency or is very powerful. More powerful signals might include an electrical wire, an amateur radio set, fluorescent lights, some kinds of LED bulbs, a lightning storm, an automobile engine, a television set, and a generator. Anything using high-power electronics to accomplish a task can emit signals, interfering with wireless data transmission. Wi-Fi, described in the next section, is particularly susceptible to this kind of interference because it operates in an unlicensed frequency range shared by many other kinds of devices.

Microwave ovens are one classic source of interference for Wi-Fi systems because they operate in the same 2.4 GHz frequency range as one band of Wi-Fi. Other devices operating in the 2.4 GHz band include baby monitors, handheld radios, and Bluetooth.

Electromagnetic waves also expend more power when passing through materials other than air. For instance:

- A brick or concrete wall will allow around 20% of a Wi-Fi signal to pass through.

- A sheet of metal will allow around 30% of a Wi-Fi signal through.

- An empty metal rack will allow around 50% of a Wi-Fi signal through.

- A clear window, sheet of drywall, or wooden door will allow around 70% of a Wi-Fi signal through.

These numbers are approximate; a refrigerator, washing machine, or other large appliance largely constructed of metal can block close to 100% of a Wi-Fi signal.

Bandwidth and Signal Strength

Bandwidth is often used to denote the *maximum data-carrying capacity* of a link, whether wired or wireless. The word is taken from the *width* of the frequency **band** the link can use. Figure 8-6 shows a simple example of the concept of bandwidth.

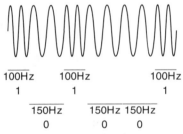

Figure 8-6 *Bandwidth*

In Figure 8-6, a 0 is represented by a 150 Hz signal, and a 1 is represented by a 100 Hz signal. The average of these two frequencies is 125 Hz, so we can call 125 Hz our **carrier** or *center frequency*. For a radio to receive this signal, the receiver would need to be tuned to a center frequency of 125 Hz and have a window of 50 Hz (so it can receive any signal 25 Hz above or below the center frequency).

The bandwidth of this signal is 50 Hz—the maximum frequency subtracted from the minimum frequency. To see how a wider bandwidth would help add more data in each timeframe, imagine if you could use four frequencies rather than two—but there still must be 25 Hz between the frequency representing each *symbol*—in this case a pair of binary digits. You might have something like this:

- 75 Hz represents 00

- 100 Hz represents 01

- 125 Hz represents 10

- 150 Hz represents 11

Now, you could transmit data twice as fast in the same timeframe, but you need 75 Hz of bandwidth (subtract 75 from 150) rather than 50 Hz.

Modern radio systems can send multiple bits of data in each wavelength using more complex modulation, but these systems require much wider bands, or *channels*, of radio frequencies.

For instance, channel 1 of the 2.4 GHz range of Wi-Fi frequencies is from 2401–2423 MHz, with a center frequency of 2412 MHz. The bandwidth of this channel, from a radio frequency perspective, is 22 MHz. Since a single radio signal with a bandwidth of 22 MHz can carry a maximum of 11 Mb/s, this is the specified bandwidth of the link.

However, to reach the optimal data rate, the signal must be strong, and interference must be low. Lower-powered and "dirty" signals cannot carry as many bits of data per wavelength. As signal strength decreases, or interference increases, the data rate decreases.

The Electromagnetic Spectrum

The **spectrum** is the complete set of frequencies available to create a link, and a **channel** or band is a small set of frequencies within the spectrum. Figure 8-7 shows a breakdown of the radio frequency spectrum.

VLF	LF	MF	HF	VHF	UHF	SHF
100km	10km	1km	100m	10m	1m	10cm	1cm
3kHz	30kHz	300kHz	3MHz	30MHz	300MHz	3GHz	30Ghz
Maritime Radio, Navigation	AM Radio, Navigation		FM Radio, Television		Television, Mobile Phones, GPS, Wi-Fi, 4G		Satellite, Wi-Fi

Figure 8-7 *Radio Frequency Spectrum*

Each range of frequencies in the spectrum is used for several different classes of applications, from navigation to satellite communications. Within each band, smaller sets of frequencies are set aside for specific applications.

Wi-Fi

Wi-Fi—alternately *WiFi* or *Wireless LAN*—is ubiquitous in homes, businesses, and offices. This technology is (most likely) the most widely used technology for connecting to a network in the world.

> **NOTE**   Chapter 11, "Basic Network Hardware," considers Wi-Fi configuration in a home network.

Wi-Fi Etymology

Wi-Fi is a marketing takeoff on Hi-Fi, which stands for High Fidelity. Radio systems sporting the Hi-Fi designation reproduce a wider range of the audio spectrum, allowing them to produce more accurate renditions of music regardless of the source. Wi-Fi evokes a highly reliable wireless system.

Wi-Fi is a group of standards ratified and supported by the Institute of Electrical and Electronics Engineers (IEEE) within the **802.11** working group. A letter is added after 802.11 to differentiate between the standards, as shown in Table 8-2.

Table 8-2   802.11 Wi-Fi Standards

Standard	Frequency	Speed	Notes
802.11	2.4 GHz	2 Mb/s	No longer in use
802.11a	5 GHz	1.5–54 Mb/s	
802.11b	2.4 GHz	11 Mb/s	Popularized Wi-Fi
802.11g	2.4 GHz	54 Mb/s	
802.11n	2.4 GHz and 5 GHz	600 Mb/s	
802.11ac	2.4 GHz and 5 GHz	450 Mb/s and 1300 Mb/s	
802.11ax	2.4 GHz and 5 GHz	10–15 Gb/s	Marketing name is *Wi-Fi 6*

There are specific channels within the frequencies given within each country. Table 8-3 shows the channels and their corresponding frequencies used by the 802.11b, g, n, and ax standards in the 2.4 GHz range.

Table 8-3   2.4 GHz Channels and Frequencies for 802.11 Wi-Fi

Channel	Frequency	Notes
1	2412 MHz	
2	2417 MHz	
3	2422 MHz	

Channel	Frequency	Notes
4	2427 MHz	
5	2432 MHz	
6	2437 MHz	
7	2442 MHz	
8	2447 MHz	
9	2452 MHz	
10	2457 MHz	
11	2462 MHz	
12	2467 MHz	Should be avoided in North America
13	2472 MHz	Should be avoided in North America
14	2482 MHz	Only used in Japan

Table 8-4 shows some channels and their corresponding frequencies for the 802.11a, h, j, n, ac, and ax standards in the 5 GHz range. Some countries require *Transmitter Power Control (TPC)* to operate devices on these frequencies.

Table 8-4   5 GHz Channels and Frequencies for 802.11 Wi-Fi

Channel	Frequency	Notes
32	5160 MHz	Indoor use only in Canada
		Indoor use only with TPC in many countries
48	5240 MHz	Indoor use only in Canada
		Indoor use only with TPC in many countries
68	5340 MHz	Indoor or outdoor use with TPC in most countries
		Indoor use with TPC only in the United Kingdom
118	5590 MHz	Indoor or outdoor use with TPC in most countries
		Cannot be used in Canada

Because regulations vary widely, different versions of Wi-Fi devices may be sold in each country.

Table 8-3 and Table 8-4 note some frequencies can be used only if TPC is used. TPC is a method for Wi-Fi transmitters to detect other transmitters in the area and the strength of their connection, and reduce their transmission power to the minimum power necessary to operate correctly.

Wi-Fi Components

Wi-Fi networks are built using wireless adapters, access points, and repeaters. Figure 8-8 illustrates.

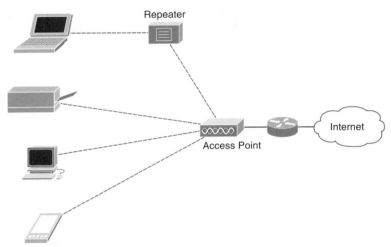

Figure 8-8   *Wi-Fi Network Components*

Figure 8-8 shows the following components:

■ **Wi-Fi connected devices**, such as a laptop computer (host), a printer, a desktop computer (host), and a handheld device—a cellular telephone, tablet, or similar. Each device must have a Wi-Fi *modulator/demodulator (MODEM)*. Most devices have Wi-Fi MODEMS, antennas, and other components built into the device. Desktop computers are the least likely item shown in the figure to have a Wi-Fi interface, but you can generally add one through an interface card or USB port.

■ The **access point**, or AP, bridges between the Wi-Fi and wired networks. Standalone APs act like a switch on a wired network; they copy IP packets from the wireless network to the wired network, replacing the outer physical packet encapsulation from the wireless network with the correct physical encapsulation for the wired network.

■ The **repeater**, which repeats any received wireless signals to Wi-Fi devices too far away to receive the signal from the AP.

In most smaller networks, such as small businesses and residential settings, the AP and router are combined into a single *wireless router*.

Wi-Fi Mesh Systems

Typical Wi-Fi signals will travel around 30 meters or 100 feet in typical indoor settings. This might seem like a lot, but the maximum distance between any points in a large house is longer than what might be immediately obvious. For instance, in a house with three floors:

■ A typical floor in a house will be around 10 feet (or 3 meters), so a three-story house will be around 30 feet (or 10 meters) tall, excluding any attic space.

■ A typical floor in a house can be around 10 meters by 10 meters (or around 30 feet by 30 feet).

■ The distance between opposite corners on the top and bottom floors can be 15 meters (or 50 feet).

Each wall or floor the Wi-Fi signal passes through reduces its strength by 10%–15%. Given these parameters, or intervening kitchen appliances, televisions, and other factors, you do not need to live in a large house to run out of Wi-Fi signal.

One solution to this problem is to install a repeater, as noted previously, but this can be challenging in some situations, and repeaters do not always yield the best Wi-Fi performance.

An alternate solution is installing a Wi-Fi mesh system. Figure 8-9 illustrates such a system.

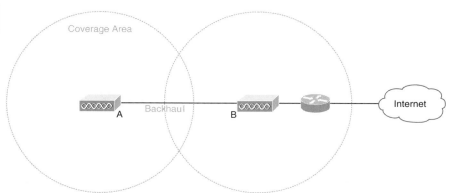

Figure 8-9 *Wireless Mesh System Operation*

In Figure 8-9, two Wi-Fi APs are connected via a **backhaul**, creating a **Wi-Fi mesh**. When a packet is received from the router for some host wirelessly connected to *A*, AP *B* will send this packet along the backhaul to *A* for transmission to the host. From the user's perspective, *A* and *B* combine to create a single Wi-Fi system. Users can roam between the two APs without losing their connection.

The backhaul can be a wired Ethernet if Ethernet cabling is available between the two locations. The backhaul can also be a wireless connection if no physical cabling is available. In the case of a wireless connection, the two APs will choose an otherwise unused channel or use beam forming to create a narrow wireless connection over which they will send packets to one another.

Wi-Fi mesh systems can extend the range of a Wi-Fi system to large distances under the administration of a single network operator.

Advantages and Disadvantages of Wi-Fi

The primary advantages of Wi-Fi are it operates in **unlicensed spectrum**, or *unlicensed frequencies*, and Wi-Fi does not require extensive infrastructure. You do not need to have a license from a local government to set up and run a Wi-Fi transmitter, so long as the transmitter is lower than a specific power level (normally around 250 milliwatts).

Average users or network operators can set up a Wi-Fi system without permission, providing coverage for devices within a house or building. The owner of the system decides which networks Wi-Fi connected users can reach, including

- Devices attached to the internal network only

- Devices attached to the internal network and the global Internet

- Devices attached to the global Internet only (often called a *guest network*)

Operating on unlicensed spectrum is also a disadvantage because Wi-Fi systems must operate with limited transmission power. Some specific problems resulting from the use of unlicensed spectrum include

- Building a Wi-Fi system covering large outdoor spaces, such as a park, is difficult.

- You cannot "roam" between different Wi-Fi networks. Each network is owned and maintained by a different operator, and each operator may have different rules for connecting to the network, what destinations users can reach, etc.

- Many other kinds of devices also operate in these same frequency ranges, such as microwave ovens, IoT devices, and even cellular telephones. Because these frequencies are crowded, other devices are more likely to interfere with the Wi-Fi signal.

- Wi-Fi networks do not limit the amount of data attached devices can send or receive. Network performance will degrade if the network is overloaded.

Sharing the Bandwidth

Another disadvantage of Wi-Fi, when compared to switched wired networks, is all the hosts attached to a single AP through a single channel share the same bandwidth—just like all the hosts being connected to the same physical Ethernet segment. Just like Ethernet, there is a system to share the bandwidth.

Ethernet uses Carrier Sense Multiple Access with Collision Detection (CSMA/CD). Wi-Fi uses *Carrier Sense Multiple Access with Collision Avoidance* (**CSMA/CA**). Rather than detecting collisions and backing off before transmitting again, Wi-Fi avoids collisions using *Request to Send* signaling after hearing another AP send a packet.

Some APs use beam forming to separate transmissions, so each host has separate bandwidth.

Channel Selection

Table 8-3 and Table 8-4 list a lot of channels, each with its frequency. How can you choose which of these frequencies to use?

For large-scale Wi-Fi deployments, engineers use radio receivers to detect the current electromagnetic radiation present in the area and choose a channel with the least amount of existing interference. For smaller installations, operators would try different channels until they find a workable set of frequencies to use.

For small-scale deployments, such as small businesses and residences, most newer APs will survey the electromagnetic radiation and select an optimal set of channels on which to operate. The capability of an AP to automatically select a channel with the least interference is called *Dynamic Frequency Selection (DFS)*.

Cellular

Another kind of almost-ubiquitous wireless network is the cellular network. Cellular networks differ from Wi-Fi networks in many ways, including being designed to

- Operate by large-scale dedicated organizations

- Support global scale, including roaming between wireless connections and networks

- Support end-user billing

- Support defined quality-of-service guarantees

- Control device connection with strong authentication and authorization mechanisms

There are many generations of cellular networks, starting from 2G through the most current, 5G. There are variants within each generation, as well as equipment name changes, etc.—all of which make tracing the history and development of cellular networks complex.

This book focuses on the most recent specification, 5G, for simplicity. Figure 8-10 illustrates the basic components of a 5G cellular network.

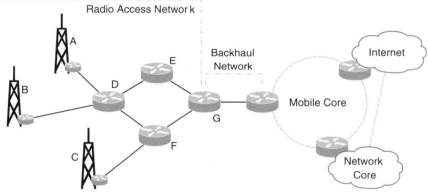

Figure 8-10 *5G Cellular Network Components*

A cellular network is broken into three broad components:

- A *radio access network (**RAN**)*

- A *mobile core*

- A *backhaul network*

The backhaul network carries data from the RAN to and from the mobile core. This network is normally some form of fiber network. Backhaul networks are often leased from other providers or—in some cases—carried over the Internet itself.

The following sections describe the RAN and mobile core in more detail.

Radio Access Network (RAN)

The radio access network is a group of towers and a local network connecting those towers. Each tower has a **base station**, also called a *gNodeB*, that controls the function of the radio and its communication with other network elements. While there are open standards for designing and deploying a RAN, most large-scale cellular providers purchase proprietary systems for this section of the network. The designers of 5G are insisting on more openness in the RAN, including separating the software from the hardware and using as much open-source software as possible.

Connected devices are often called **end users**, or **EU**—a term used throughout this discussion of cellular networks.

The base station is responsible for

- Establishing the wireless channel used to communicate with each EU. This wireless channel is called a *bearer service* because this is the channel used to transfer data to and from the EU.

- Reclaiming channels when an EU has been idle for too long.

- Establishing a *3rd Generation Partner Project (3GPP)* control plane connection to the EU. This control plane signals the kinds of services the EU would like to consume, such as voice, *Simple Message Service (SMS)*, and IP transport. This control plane is also used when an EU moves from one connection point to another to shift wireless channels and handle other administrative tasks.

- Establishing one tunnel per service from the EU to a termination point in the mobile core. These tunnels use *Stream Control Transport Protocol (SCTP)* and *Generic Packet Radio Service Tunneling Protocol (GTP)*, both carried over standard IP networks. **5G** cellular networks convert all voice calls to data packets carried in IP; there is no separate "voice" network in a 5G cellular network, just a tunnel.

- Forwarding packets transmitted by the EU over these tunnels to the mobile core.

A 5G cellular network base station is like a specialized router from an IP networking perspective. Base stations limit the number of UEs attached to the radio network and the number of UEs accessing each available service so the network is not overwhelmed.

 ## Mobile Core

The **mobile core** is a set of servers and software that

- Authenticates users.

- De-encapsulates user data (terminates the tunnels coming from the RAN) and forwards this traffic to the Internet or other service.

- Tracks the user's location and hands off users to other mobile cores when needed.

- Tracks usage and enables billing.

User authentication is based on a *subscriber identity module* **(SIM) card**. Providers (or private network operators) assign each SIM card to a user or device. Each SIM card contains a 64-bit *International Mobile Subscriber Identity (***ISMI***)*, which can be tied to an individual user, and a *private key* for building encrypted tunnels.

The provider must maintain a copy of a directory service of users and ISMIs, be able to connect to every other provider's directory to determine if a UE is authorized, and what levels of service (and what services) the UE should be provided, etc.

NOTE   Chapter 22, "Troubleshooting," explains private keys.

Advantages and Disadvantages of Cellular Networks

The primary advantages of cellular networks are their scale and reach. A provider can build and operate a single cellular network on a global scale, giving users service pretty much everywhere they go (at least in moderately dense population areas). Cellular networks also provide consistent connection quality for connected UEs.

The primary disadvantage of cellular networks is the infrastructure required, such as

- Cellular physical transmitters tend to use specialized hardware and software.

- Base stations tend to be implemented in specialized appliances and specific transmitters or radios.

- The mobile core must support specialized tunneling protocols, complex user authentication, and applications for each service offered (such as voice, gaming, voicemail, etc.).

Organizations deploy private 5G networks for large physical facilities, such as factories and campuses. Private 5G deployments can also supplement local coverage from cellular telephone towers in large office buildings and apartment complexes.

Satellite

Cellular transmitters are placed on towers and Wi-Fi access points are attached to the ceiling because height almost always provides better signal coverage. Satellites take this one step further: antennas in space can reach more of the Earth's surface than a tower of any height. Satellite systems are roughly divided by the distance between the satellites and the surface of the Earth. Figure 8-11 illustrates.

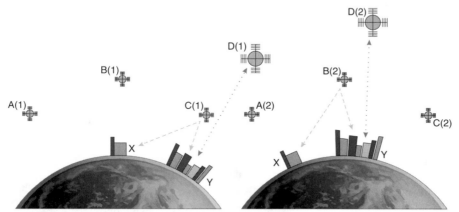

Figure 8-11   *LEO and Geosynchronous Satellites*

Figure 8-11 shows two sets of satellites in two different positions relative to the Earth:

- *A(1)*, *B(1)*, and *C(1)* are LEO satellites in their positions before the Earth rotates.

- *D(1)* is a geosynchronous satellite in its position before the Earth rotates.

- *A(2)*, *B(2)*, and *C(2)* are LEO satellites in their positions after the Earth rotates.

- *D(2)* is a geosynchronous satellite in its position after the Earth rotates.

Satellite *D* is far enough from the Earth to orbit the Earth at the same rate the Earth itself rotates. From X's and Y's perspectives, *D(1)* and *D(2)* are in the same place in the sky. X's and Y's antennas can be tuned for optimal reception from *D* and left in one place.

These are called geosynchronous satellites.

Satellites *A*, *B*, and *C* are closer to the Earth's surface (in a lower orbit), so they appear to move in the sky over time. This means the antennas connecting from X and Y must change positions between *A(1)* and *A(2)*.

These are called *low Earth orbit (**LEO**)* satellites.

Because **geosynchronous** satellites are so far above the Earth, these systems use large dish antennas. These large antennas are generally only installed at ground stations. Traffic is routed through optical cables to the ground station, through the satellite system to a remote ground station, and then back through an optical cable to their final destination.

The advantage of geosynchronous satellites is the antenna on the ground does not need to be constantly adjusted—just when there is some change in the satellite's position. Individual geosynchronous satellites can also reach more of the Earth's surface because they are higher in the atmosphere.

The advantage of LEO satellites is they introduce less delay and jitter into the transmission time. LEO satellites are closer to the Earth, so signals transmitted to and received from these satellites travel a shorter distance. Because the signal travels a shorter distance, a smaller antenna—small enough to mount on a large truck, small boat, or house—can be used to communicate with LEO satellites.

The disadvantage of LEO systems is tracking the satellite. This complex process is taken care of by beam forming antennas (rather than moving the antenna mechanically) and specially developed software.

Chapter Review

Wireless connectivity solutions, like Wi-Fi, cellular 5G, and satellite, are used to expand the Internet into areas impractical to reach using physical cables. These technologies all rely on just a few basic techniques, including transmitting data along electromagnetic waves traveling through free space and beam forming to shape electromagnetic signals for optimal performance.

All free-space wireless transmission systems are more liable to interference than wired systems, and all of these systems vary their data rate (bandwidth) based on the signal strength.

This chapter described bandwidth conceptually. The next chapter will consider the importance of bandwidth in supporting applications, as well as the problems of delay and jitter.

One key to doing well on the exams is to perform repetitive spaced review sessions. Review this chapter's material using either the tools in the book or interactive tools for the same material found on the book's companion website. Refer to the online Appendix D, "Study Planner," element for more details. Table 8-5 outlines the key review elements and where you can find them. To better track your study progress, record when you completed these activities in the second column.

Table 8-5   Chapter Review Tracking

Review Element	Review Date (s)	Resource Used
Review key topics		Book, website
Review key terms		Book, website
Repeat DIKTA questions		Book, PTP
Review concepts and actions		Book, website

Review All the Key Topics

Table 8-6 lists the key topics for this chapter.

Table 8-6   Key Topics for Chapter 8

Key Topic Element	Description	Page Number
Figure 8-4	Beam formation with an antenna array	166
Paragraph	Wireless interference	167
Section	Bandwidth and Signal Strength	168
Section	The Electromagnetic Spectrum	169
Paragraph, Table 8-2	802.11 Wi-Fi standards	170
Section	Wi-Fi Components	171
Figure 8-9, paragraph	Wireless Mesh System Operation	173
Section	Advantages and Disadvantages of Wi-Fi	173
Paragraph	CSMA/CA	174
Paragraph	Dynamic Frequency Selection (DFS)	174
Figure 8-10, paragraph	5G Cellular Network Components	175
Section	Radio Access Network (RAN)	175
Section	Mobile Core	176
Section	Advantages and Disadvantages of Cellular Networks	177
Paragraphs	Geosynchronous and low Earth orbit (LEO) satellites	178

8

Key Terms You Should Know

Key terms in this chapter include

beam forming, interference, bandwidth, band, carrier, spectrum, channel, Wi-Fi, 802.11, Wi-Fi connected device, access point, repeater, backhaul, Wi-Fi mesh, unlicensed spectrum, CSMA/CA, RAN, base station, end user (EU), 5G, mobile core, SIM card, ISMI, LEO (low Earth orbit), geosynchronous

Concepts and Actions

Review the concepts considered in this chapter using Table 8-7. You can cover the right side of this table and describe each concept or action in your own words to verify your understanding.

Table 8-7   Concepts and Actions for Review

Signals travel through the air in …	Waves, rather than uniformly
Amount of power electromagnetic signals lose for each wavelength they travel	About half
Beam form works by …	Combing the signals from multiple antennas, called a phased array
Signals combine because they are …	In phase with one another
Wireless interference is greater from sources …	That are closer and higher power
Some normal household items that block Wi-Fi signals are …	Walls, a sheet of metal, a floor, a television, and a refrigerator
Spectrum	The complete set of frequencies available to create a link (transmit data over wireless signals)
Channel	Small set of frequencies within a spectrum
Bandwidth	The maximum amount of data a signal can carry
802.11	IEEE working group that standardizes Wi-Fi
Usable channels vary by …	Country or governmental authority
Access point	Used to connect a Wi-Fi connected device to an Ethernet network; sometimes combined with a router
Repeater	Repeats a Wi-Fi signal to extend its range
Wi-Fi mesh	Multiple Wi-Fi access points connected through a backhaul to create a mesh
Unlicensed frequency	A frequency that can be used by anyone without coordinating with local authorities or obtaining an operational license
Dynamic frequency selection	The ability of a Wi-Fi access point to select a channel that is either lightly or not used

Radio access network	A collection of towers and transmitters, along with their connecting network, providing cellular service to an area
Mobile core	Software and services that authenticate users, track user location, and manage billing for the cellular network
Low Earth orbit (LEO)	Satellites positioned close to the Earth's surface to reduce delay
Geosynchronous satellite	Satellites positioned further from the Earth's surface so Earth station antennas do not need to be adjusted to track their movements

CHAPTER 9

Bandwidth, Delay, and Jitter

This chapter covers the following exam topics:

1. **Standards and Concepts**

    1.2. **Differentiate between bandwidth and throughput.**

    Latency, delay, speed test vs. iPerf

The preceding two chapters described bandwidth as the capacity of a wired or wireless link. Bandwidth is a fundamental property of computer networks, closely related to delay and jitter—two other fundamental concepts of computer networking. This chapter considers the importance of bandwidth, delay, and jitter and how they are related.

The final section of this chapter discusses how to measure bandwidth and understand bandwidth measurements.

"Do I Know This Already?" Quiz

Take the quiz (either here or use the PTP software) if you want to use the score to help you decide how much time to spend on this chapter. Appendix A, "Answers to the 'Do I Know This Already?' Quizzes," found at the end of the book, includes both the answers and explanations. You can also find answers in the PTP testing software.

Table 9-1 "Do I Know This Already?" Foundation Topics Section-to-Question Mapping

Section	Questions
Bandwidth and Throughput	1, 2, 3
Bandwidth and Delay	4, 5
Jitter	6
Measuring Network Performance	7, 8

CAUTION The goal of self-assessment is to gauge your mastery of the topics in this c hapter. If you do not know the answer to a question or are only partially sure of the answer, you should mark that question as wrong for purposes of the self-assessment. Giving yourself credit for an answer you incorrectly guess skews your self-assessment results and might provide you with a false sense of security.

1. What is bandwidth?

    a. The maximum amount of data a link can carry

    b. Another word for throughput

    c. The amount of data a link delivers under real-world conditions

    d. The amount of data a link delivers without error

2. What is throughput?

    a. Another word for bandwidth

    b. The amount of data a link delivers under real-world conditions

    c. The amount of data a link delivers without error

    d. The projected amount of bandwidth required at some future time

3. What is the relationship between bandwidth and throughput?

    a. Bandwidth will always be lower than throughput.

    b. Bandwidth will always be higher than throughput.

    c. Bandwidth and throughput will always be the same.

    d. There is no relationship between bandwidth and throughput.

4. Bandwidth between two points is the most important measure of network performance.

    a. True, because the available bandwidth is the primary determinant of application performance

    b. True, because bandwidth is directly related to goodput, and goodput determines application performance

    c. False, because delay and jitter can impact application performance as much as available bandwidth

    d. False, because very few applications use all the bandwidth available

5. What are the primary components of delay in a network?

    a. Physical distance and queueing

    b. Transmission delay and queueing

    c. Physical distance, serialization delay, and queueing

    d. Physical distance, bandwidth, and queueing

6. What is jitter?

    a. The amount of time between a packet being transmitted and the same packet being received

    b. Variance in the queue depth on a given interface

    c. Variance in the bandwidth due to link errors

    d. Changes in delay from packet to packet

7. What do web-based speed test tools measure?

    a. The performance of your internal network

    b. The performance of your connection to the Internet

    c. The performance of your connection to the Internet and your provider's local performance

    d. The performance of your web browser

8. What does IPerf (and similar tools) measure?

    a. The performance of your internal network

    b. The performance of your connection to the Internet or your local network performance

    c. The performance of your connection to the Internet

    d. The performance of your web browser

Foundation Topics

Bandwidth and Throughput

Bandwidth is the maximum amount of data you can carry across a link. Bandwidth is often considered the most important measure of a link—for instance:

- Internet service providers almost always rank their services by bandwidth and charge more for higher-bandwidth plans.

- Governments judge the value an Internet service provides to the community by bandwidth.

- Consumers and operators often judge new network technologies by improvements in bandwidth.

While bandwidth is essential when building a network or selecting a service, in operation, *throughput* and *goodput* are more important:

- **Throughput** is the data a link delivers using real sources and under real-world conditions.

- **Goodput** is the amount of data delivered *without error* using real sources and under real-world conditions.

Throughput versus Bandwidth

Why is the throughput always less than the available bandwidth?

First, routing protocols and other network signaling always consume some amount of the available bandwidth. The control plane usually does not take up a lot of bandwidth, but it can during major outages or when routing protocols converge.

Second, there is always some mismatch between the size of the data and the size of frames and packets carried through the network.

Some networking technologies, such as Ethernet, mandate a minimum packet size. Ethernet and Wi-Fi packets must be a minimum size so all the hosts will sense their transmission on the shared medium; otherwise, multiple transmissions will always collide.

Other networking technologies mandate a fixed-size *cell* rather than a frame. For instance, Asynchronous Transfer Mode (ATM) mandates a 5-octet header and a 48-octet payload for a total cell size of 53 octets. If you transmit 50 octets of data on an ATM network, the network must create two cells, so the network uses 106 octets to transmit 50 octets of data.

> **NOTE**   Fixed-cell networks are no longer widely deployed because of this inefficiency.

Third, it is impossible to predict future bandwidth requirements and changes in bandwidth utilization. Figure 9-1 illustrates.

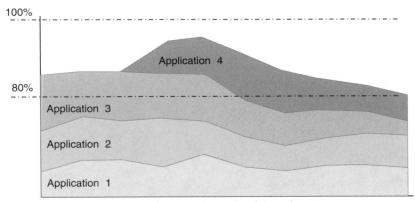

Figure 9-1   *Application Flows and Bandwidth Utilization*

The chart in Figure 9-1 shows the bandwidth utilization of a link across time. The left side of the chart starts with three applications running. These three applications consume around 85% of the available bandwidth.

When *Application 4* starts, the link utilization climbs close to 100% and falls as each application adjusts its bandwidth utilization down.

If there were no available bandwidth when *Application 4* started sending packets, there would be no way for *Application 4* to start, and it would take longer for the four applications to adjust the rate they send data so they can all use the same link efficiently.

There are many other situations where quick increases in bandwidth utilization happen. The network needs some overhead space to absorb these changes and adjust over time. Network designers and engineers *overbuild* networks to carry 50% to 80% more bandwidth than projected requirements.

Most network operators consider 80% bandwidth utilization "full." You will probably not push more than 80% of the stated bandwidth through a link.

Bandwidth versus Goodput

As stated previously, bandwidth is the maximum amount of data you can carry across a link. Throughput is the amount of data being carried through a link.

Goodput is the amount of *user data* successfully carried through a network. While goodput may be closer to throughput than throughput is to bandwidth, goodput will always be less than throughout. There are two primary reasons goodput will always be less than throughput:

- Because of the encapsulation added to move packets around in the network. An IPv6 header is a minimum of 40 octets of data, and the Ethernet frame header is around 20 octets. Out of a 1500-octet maximum-size packet, around 60 octets, or 4%, of the available bandwidth is consumed by headers.

- Because all links fail to deliver packets accurately 100% of the time. There will always be some percentage of errors in moving data across a network.

While throughput is often 50% or less of available bandwidth, goodput is usually a much higher percentage of throughout—90% or higher.

The Bandwidth of a Link versus Bandwidth of a Path

When you purchase a 1 Gb/s link to the Internet from a provider, will you have 1 Gb/s connections to every server and service worldwide? No—because the link between a building and the service provider is not the entire path. Figure 9-2 illustrates.

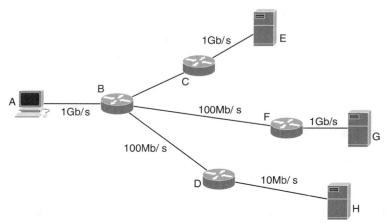

Figure 9-2 *Connection Bandwidth versus Path Bandwidth*

Host *A* has a 1 Gb/s connection to the network but cannot transfer data to servers *E*, *G*, or *H* equally. For each server:

- Host *A* can transfer data to and from server *E* at around 1 Gb/s.

- Host *A* can transfer data to and from server *G* at around 100 Mb/s.

- Host *A* can transfer data to and from server *H* at around 10 Mb/s.

In each case, the maximum transfer speed will be somewhat less than the *minimum* bandwidth of any link between the host and server, minus some percentage for throughput and goodput.

Bandwidth and Delay

If you want the highest bandwidth method to carry data between two cities on opposite coasts of the United States, would you choose a satellite or optical link? The best choice would be neither...because the best choice is a box.

How do you calculate the bandwidth of a box? Start with a large overnight shipping box from any significant carrier. You hand it off to them before 5 p.m., and they will get it to the destination address before 10 a.m. the following day. The price for shipping these boxes varies by size, so we do not want to select the largest possible box. A large box will do.

How much data can you put into a large shipping box? You can generally fit around 1000 Micro-SD cards in a large shipping box (remembering you need to have at least some minimal packaging, and there will be some wasted space). The largest Micro-SD card at the time of this writing is around 2 TB.

To calculate correctly, we need to take note of the difference between bytes—or octets—and bits.

> **NOTE**   The size of a byte changes depending on the computer processor. An 8-bit computer stores 8 bits in a byte; a 16-bit computer stores 16 bits in a byte; a 32-bit computer stores 16 bits in a byte, etc. A byte of data in storage is always 8 bits, and an octet is always 8 bits. In common use, however, a byte is taken to mean an octet. This book uses octets throughout, rather than bytes, for clarity.

Data is stored and processed in octets and transmitted over a network in bits. To calculate the amount of data carried in the box we can do some basic math:

- A 2 TB drive with 8 bits of data per "byte" holds 16,384 Tb of data.

- Then 1,000 of these drives will hold 16,384,000 Tb of data; the box can transport this amount in 24 hours (or less).

- There are 86,400 seconds in 24 hours.

- Dividing 16,384,000 Tb by 86,400 results in about 200 Tb/s.

The box, then, has a bandwidth of 200 Tb/s—much faster than the bandwidth of any available link at any cost. Putting this in different terms: each 2 Tb Micro-SD card can hold around 1000 hours of video so that the box can carry about 1 million hours of video in 24 hours.

Never underestimate the bandwidth of a box.

If boxes have so much bandwidth, why do we build networks? Because people are impatient. There is no lower bound on the impatience of people. Because people are impatient, delay matters.

How long will a person wait for a web page to load? It takes around 3 seconds. A 3-second delay on a voice call is noticeable.

Building a network with a lot of bandwidth will not solve all our problems; we must also pay attention to the amount of delay.

Delay is the time between a sender and receiver receiving a packet.

The first delay element is the physical path between the sender and receiver. Longer paths will have a longer delay because no matter how fast electromagnetic waves travel, longer distances still take longer to traverse than shorter ones. Routing traffic through a satellite will take longer than an optical cable because the signal must travel from the Earth to the satellite and back. Signals also move faster in optical cables than copper ones and through space faster than optical cables.

Clocking Packets onto the Wire

The second delay element is the time required to copy—or *clock*—the signal from computer memory onto the physical cable. The time to copy a packet from memory onto the physical cable is called the *serialization delay*. Figure 9-3 illustrates the serialization of a packet.

9

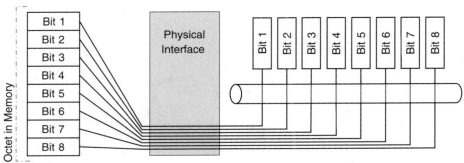

Figure 9-3   *Clocking an Octet of Data onto a Wire*

In Figure 9-3, the physical interface chip takes the first bit of data, modulates it onto the carrier, and sends it. Once the first bit is transmitted, the PHY chip pulls the second bit of data from memory, modulates it onto the signal, etc.

This process takes time, delaying the data being transmitted through the network. Faster links can process data more quickly, so *higher-bandwidth links will have less delay from clocking the signal on and off the wire at each device than lower-bandwidth links.*

Queueing

The third factor in packet delay is queueing. Traffic jams can ensue when traffic from multiple high-speed interfaces is switched to a single outbound interface. Figure 9-4 illustrates queueing.

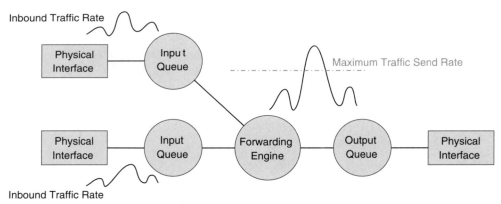

Figure 9-4   *Packet Flow Traffic Jam and Queueing*

The outbound physical interface can transmit packets only as quickly as the link allows. A link of a given bandwidth can accept only a certain number of packets per second. When traffic spikes, as shown in Figure 9-4, packets must be stored in the *output queue* until the outbound physical interface can transmit them all. If the output queue fills up, the router will start dropping the packets it receives.

Packets in the output queue will be delayed while they are waiting. Each router or switch along the packet's path that queues packets, even for a few moments, adds delay.

Suppose the following sequence of events occurs:

- An application sends traffic at a high rate, filling up the output queue on a router along the path.

- The application then slows down to the same rate as the bandwidth available on the router's output interface.

So long as the application sends data fast enough to fill up the router's outbound link, the router's output queue will never empty. The router needs some "quiet time," receiving less traffic than it can transmit to drain its output queue.

When routers along the path cannot drain their output queues, they reach a condition called *buffer bloat*. The additional queueing in the system is not helping manage traffic flows; it is just adding delay.

Adaptive and aggressive queueing mechanisms can resolve a buffer bloat situation.

Jitter

As networks—and the applications depending on networks—become faster, **jitter** often becomes an important measure of computer network performance. Jitter is the difference in delay between packets. Figure 9-5 illustrates jitter.

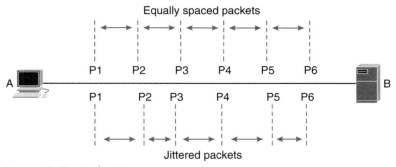

Figure 9-5   *Packet Jitter*

In Figure 9-5, host *A* sends a steady stream of packets toward server *B*, as shown in the *equally spaced packets*. The network, however, is delaying some packets, so they do not arrive at server *B* equally spaced but rather somewhat randomly. The difference in the spacing between the packets in the lower part of the packet is called *jitter*.

Jitter is bad for streaming applications because users expect a constant and consistent stream, but the data needed to produce a constant stream is unavailable. Most streaming applications will buffer data at least some amount to consume packets, remove jitter, and produce a consistent stream. Buffering, however, is another form of queueing, so it resolves jitter by adding delay. Some applications and users can tolerate only small amounts of delay.

Jitter is also bad because applications must tune their timers to react to failures. Figure 9-6 shows a situation where tight timers can improve application performance.

9

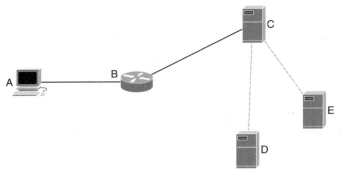

Figure 9-6 *Jitter's Impact on Application Performance*

Suppose server *C* receives a request from *A* that *C* must retrieve from *D* or *E*. If server *C* requests *D* for this information, how long should the application wait before failing over and asking *E* for the information? If the network introduces a lot of jitter, the application at *C* must set its timers longer than it would if the network delivered packets consistently. When applications are divided up on many servers—often called *microservices*—so responses of this kind take multiple round trips over the network, jitter can have a major impact on application performance.

Measuring Network Performance

While there are many tools for testing network performance, three are given as examples in this section: **speed test** websites, **iPerf**, and *Mike's Traceroute (MRT)*.

All these tools test the network's throughput rather than the bandwidth or the goodput. It is impossible, of course, to test the bandwidth of a link for reasons described in previous sections.

Speed Test Websites

Web-based bandwidth tools can directly measure the speed of your connection to the Internet.

We will use *Ookla's Speed Test* web tool as an example of web-based bandwidth testing tools because it is widely used and trusted. Ookla's tool is similar to many other tools of this type. However, you should investigate and use other web-based tools as needed. Figure 9-7 shows the main page of the Ookla tool.

The test is simple: press the **Go** button at the top. There are several interesting points about this tool:

- The tool attempts to find your provider and geographic location based on your public IP address. Geolocation does not always work, so you might need to change your location manually to get accurate results.

- The tool attempts to find a server within your service provider to run the speed test against. Selecting several different servers can help differentiate between server and network performance.

- Selecting *multiple connections* means the speed test will open multiple connections between the host and server, allowing the host to transmit higher traffic levels. Most websites and services open multiple connections by default, so a multiple connection speed test produces results closer to real-world performance.

Figure 9-7   *The Ookla Speed Test Home Page*

Web-based speed tests, such as Ookla's tool, are mostly interested in the performance of your connection to your provider and the performance of your provider rather than the performance of your internal network or the "rest of the Internet." Because of Ookla's focus on your provider's connection and performance, this tool is not generally useful for testing the throughput of your local network.

Ookla also has automatable command-line versions of its tools.

iPerf

iPerf is a different type of network performance tool used to test the performance of your local network and your connection to the Internet.

To test your network's connection to the Internet, you can run iPerf tests between a local host and publicly accessible servers.

You can also run an iPerf server on your local network, allowing you to test your network's performance in isolation from the Internet.

> **NOTE**   iPerf's website is iperf.fr. You can find downloadable servers and clients for various operating systems and a list of public iPerf servers. The source code can be found at https:// github.com/esnet/iperf. iPerf is released under the BSD license, so everyone is free to use it.

You do not need to install iPerf. You download the package, put it in a directory, and run it. If you want to run iPerf locally:

■ Run **iperf3 -s** on one computer you want to use as the server.

■ Run **iperf3 -c x.x.x.x** on each computer where you want to test the network, replacing **x.x.x.x** with the server's IPv4 address.

The result will look something like Figure 9-8.

```
iperf3 homepage at: http://software.es.net/iperf/
Report bugs to:     https://github.com/esnet/iperf
PS C:\data\iperf> .\iperf3 -c 192.168.100.108
Connecting to host 192.168.100.108, port 5201
[  4] local 192.168.100.111 port 64456 connected to 192.168.100.108 port 5201
[ ID] Interval           Transfer     Bandwidth
[  4]   0.00-1.00   sec  43.1 MBytes   362 Mbits/sec
[  4]   1.00-2.00   sec  43.0 MBytes   360 Mbits/sec
[  4]   2.00-3.00   sec  44.9 MBytes   377 Mbits/sec
[  4]   3.00-4.00   sec  43.8 MBytes   366 Mbits/sec      Individual
[  4]   4.00-5.00   sec  43.2 MBytes   362 Mbits/sec      data
[  4]   5.00-6.00   sec  41.4 MBytes   348 Mbits/sec      transfers
[  4]   6.00-7.00   sec  40.9 MBytes   343 Mbits/sec
[  4]   7.00-8.00   sec  41.9 MBytes   350 Mbits/sec
[  4]   8.00-9.00   sec  43.4 MBytes   365 Mbits/sec
[  4]   9.00-10.00  sec  41.9 MBytes   352 Mbits/sec
```

```
                                                    Length of test in seconds
                                                    Total amount of data transferred
                                                    Throughput
[ ID] Interval           Transfer     Bandwidth
[  4]   0.00-10.00  sec  427 MBytes   358 Mbits/sec  sender
[  4]   0.00-10.00  sec  427 MBytes   358 Mbits/sec  receiver
```

Figure 9-8 *iPerf Sample Output*

iPerf begins by showing you the source and destination IP addresses and port numbers. The chart following this shows the size and speed of 10 large data transfers. iPerf sends 10 large data blocks using the Transmission Control Protocol (TCP). The bottom section summarizes the results. The length of the test, the total amount of data transferred, and the throughput (labeled *bandwidth*) are shown for both the sender and receiver.

Each of iPerf's parameters can be changed:

■ **-w** increases or decreases the TCP window size.

■ **-t** changes the duration of the test.

■ **-P** increases the number of threads—or rather, the number of processes iPerf will send data from at the same time. Increasing the number of processes can allow the host to send data faster.

iPerf has a lot of other options you should explore for use in measuring network performance.

NOTE Chapter 14, "Network Transport," considers TCP.

Mike's Traceroute (MTR)

Ookla's (and similar) tools test your connection to the Internet, giving you throughput and delay. iPerf tests your network—either locally or to a publicly accessible server—and gives you throughput. *Mike's Traceroute (MTR)* shows you the delay and jitter across a network.

> **NOTE**   MTR runs only on Linux-like systems, so if you want to run it on Windows, you must install Windows Subsystem for Linux (WSL), available in the Windows Store.
>
> You can find instructions for installing MTR at https://www.bitwizard.nl/mtr/ or https://github.com/traviscross/mtr. MTR is included in many Linux distributions, so you might not need to install it.

You run MTR using a simple command: **mtr x.x.x.x** or **mtr domain.name**. Replace the **x.x.x.x** with a destination IPv4 address or *domain.name* with a destination DNS hostname. The host you test connectivity to does not need to run any special software because MTR works like traceroute.

> **NOTE**   Chapter 15, "Application Transport," discusses DNS.

The result of running MTR against a destination will resemble the output in Figure 9-9.

```
RussPro8 (172.20.251.107) -> rule11.tech (194.1.147.98)
Keys:  Help   Display mode   Restart statistics   Order of fields   quit


                                       Packets       Pings
Host                                   Loss%   Snt   Last  Avg   Best  Wrst StDev
1. host.example                        0.0%    27    0.3   0.4   0.2   0.9   0.2
2. 192.168.100.1                       0.0%    27    0.7   0.8   0.5   1.2   0.2
3. (waiting for reply)
4. lag-63-0.mavltn3901w-dtr1.example.com  0.0%  27  11.6  15.0  10.1  52.1   8.2
5. lag-36.crr01mnchtn.netops.example.com  0.0%  26  21.4  17.8  14.3  24.3   3.0
6. lag-802.prr01chcgil.netops.example.com 0.0%  26  63.3  60.5  53.3  75.4   4.9
7. (waiting for reply)
8. wpx.net
```

Figure 9-9   *MTR Sample Output*

Columns of interest in this output are

- **Packet Loss:** Percentage of packets sent and not answered

- **Snt:** Packets sent to this destination

- **Last:** The delay between sending a ping packet to this destination and receiving the response

- **Avg:** The average delay between sending a ping packet to this destination and receiving the response

- **Best:** The shortest delay between sending a ping packet to this destination and receiving the response

9

- **Wrst:** The longest delay between sending a ping packet to this destination and receiving the response

- **StDev:** Jitter

MTR uses a traceroute to discover the various routers and hosts along the path and then sends a ping packet to each device. The result is a graph of the average delay and jitter to each device along the path.

Chapter Review

Bandwidth, delay, and jitter are three crucial elements of a network's performance; each directly impacts applications running over the network. This chapter described the relationship between bandwidth, throughput, and goodput.

While delay is always longer on lower-bandwidth lengths, other factors—specifically queueing—impact delay. Queueing also impacts jitter.

Finally, we described several tools for measuring and understanding throughput, delay, and jitter.

The next chapter turns to network hardware, cabling, and network diagrams—all important topics for network engineers.

One key to doing well on the exams is to perform repetitive-spaced review sessions. Review this chapter's material using either the tools in the book or interactive tools for the same material found on the book's companion website. Refer to the online Appendix D, "Study Planner," element for more details. Table 9-2 outlines the key review elements and where you can find them. To better track your study progress, record when you completed these activities in the second column.

Table 9-2   Chapter Review Tracking

Review Element	Review Date (s)	Resource Used
Review key topics		Book, website
Review key terms		Book, website
Repeat DIKTA questions		Book, PTP
Review concepts and actions		Book, website

Review All the Key Topics

Table 9-3 lists the key topics for this chapter.

Table 9-3   Key Topics for Chapter 9

Key Topic Element	Description	Page Number
Paragraph, list	Bandwidth, throughput, and goodput	184
Paragraph	Delay: physical path	187
Paragraph, Figure 9-3	Delay: serialization delay	187

Key Topic Element	Description	Page Number
Paragraph, Figure 9-4	Delay: queueing	188
Paragraph, Figure 9-5	Jitter	189
Paragraph	Web tools to measure Internet connection speed	190
Section	iPerf	191
Paragraph	Mike's Traceroute (MTR)	193

Key Terms You Should Know

Key terms in this chapter include:

bandwidth, throughput, goodput, delay, jitter, speed test, iPerf

Concepts and Actions

Review the concepts considered in this chapter using Table 9-4. You can cover the right side of this table and describe each concept or action in your own words to verify your understanding.

Table 9-4   Concepts and Actions

Bandwidth	The maximum amount of data that can be carried through a link
Throughput	The amount of data a link delivers under real-world conditions
Goodput	The amount of error-free data a link delivers under real-world conditions
Path bandwidth	The bandwidth of the minimum bandwidth link along a path
Delay	The time between sending and receiving a packet
Jitter	The variance in delay between packets
Serialization delay	The amount of time required to move a packet from memory onto the physical transmission media
The impact of bandwidth on delay	Higher-bandwidth links have smaller serialization delays, so they tend to introduce smaller amounts of delay
Elements of delay	Physical distance the signal must travel, queueing time, and serialization delay
Speed test website does what?	Tests your connection to the Internet and your local provider's performance
iPerf does what?	Can be used to test local network performance or Internet connection performance
MTR does what?	Can be used to uncover jitter and delay problems in a local network

9

CHAPTER 10

Basic Network Hardware

This chapter covers the following exam topics:

4. **Infrastructure**

    4.1. **Identify the status lights on a Cisco device when given instruction by an engineer.**

    Link light color and status (blinking or solid)

    4.2. **Use a network diagram provided by an engineer to attach the appropriate cables.**

    Patch cables, switches and routers, small topologies

    4.3. **Identify the various ports on network devices.**

    Console port, serial port, fiber port, Ethernet ports, SFPs, USB port, PoE

Routers, switches, and network appliances—*middleboxes*—are the bread and butter of the network world. Creating a network by connecting these things is more than plugging in a few cables and using the network. Laying out the physical and logical design of a network requires a great deal of thought and work.

This chapter begins with the physical form factor of different kinds of middleboxes and then goes into the ports you will encounter in networks. The first section also considers the status lights on many network devices, a common—and quick—network diagnostic tool.

The second section covers the two basic kinds of network diagrams, the kinds of information they contain, and what they are used for. The third section considers the kinds and uses of network wiring and correlating physical layer network diagrams with physical wiring. The final section considers heat and power problems in a network facility.

> **NOTE** Chapter 23, "Configuring a Network," covers configuring Cisco Systems routers and switches in more detail.

"Do I Know This Already?" Quiz

Take the quiz (either here or use the PTP software) if you want to use the score to help you decide how much time to spend on this chapter. Appendix A, "Answers to the 'Do I Know This Already?' Quizzes," found at the end of the book, includes both the answers and explanations. You can also find answers in the PTP testing software.

Table 10-1 "Do I Know This Already?" Foundation Topics Section-to-Question Mapping

Section	Questions
Hardware, Ports, and Lights	1, 2, 3, 4, 5
Network Diagrams	6
Network Wiring	7
Handling the Heat	8

CAUTION   The goal of self-assessment is to gauge your mastery of the topics in this chapter. If you do not know the answer to a question or are only partially sure of the answer, you should mark that question as wrong for purposes of the self-assessment. Giving yourself credit for an answer you incorrectly guess skews your self-assessment results and might provide you with a false sense of security.

1. What is the primary purpose of the management network port?

   a. Provide access to the device's command-line interface

   b. Carry customer traffic within the local network

   c. Connect to a low-speed out-of-band management network

   d. Carry customer traffic to destinations outside the local network

2. What is the primary purpose of the console port?

   a. Provide access to the device's command-line interface

   b. Carry customer traffic within the local network

   c. Connect to a low-speed out-of-band management network

   d. Carry customer traffic to destinations outside the local network

3. How are ports numbered on a router?

   a. Module or slot, kind of port, submodule, and port number on the module

   b. Kind of port, module or slot, submodule, and port number on the module

   c. Port number, kind of port, module or slot, submodule

   d. By the physical location of the port on the device

4. What are the four common light indicators on network devices?

   a. Green, malfunctioned; green flashing, passing traffic; yellow, connecting or malfunctioned; red, operating correctly

   b. Green, passing traffic; green flashing, operating correctly; yellow, connecting or malfunctioned; red, malfunctioned

   c. Green, operating correctly; green flashing, passing traffic; yellow, connecting or malfunctioned; red, malfunctioned

   d. Green, operating correctly; green flashing, malfunctioning; yellow, passing traffic; red, disconnected

5. Do the color and status of lights on all routers and switches indicate the same things?

   a. Every network device uses the same colors and patterns of lights to mean the same thing.

   b. The colors of the lights always mean the same things, but the flashing patterns may vary between vendors.

   c. The colors of the lights may vary between vendors, but the flashing patterns always mean the same thing.

   d. The colors and flashing patterns may vary between individual devices.

6. What diagrams are commonly used in network engineering? (Choose two.)

   a. Topological

   b. Physical

   c. Logical

   d. Overlay

   e. Routing

7. Why is it important to manage cables through management hardware?

   a. Because OSHA regulations require well-organized cables

   b. To prevent cables from hanging off their connectors

   c. Because engineers generally like neatness

   d. To aid in the end-to-end tracing of cables

8. What is the importance of separating hot and cold air in a networking equipment room?

   a. To provide a comfortable environment for technicians

   b. To prevent the mixing of hot and cold air, increasing equipment cooling efficiency

   c. To prevent the mixing of hot and cold air, increasing equipment heating efficiency

   d. To use the heat from the equipment more efficiently in the building

Foundation Topics

Hardware, Ports, and Lights

Racks of equipment, wire running all over the place, lights blinking on and off—when you walk into a large room holding lots of networking gear, you might wonder, "What is all this stuff?" You might feel like the person in Figure 10-1.

The good news is there are only a few classes of equipment in any data processing or networking facility:

- Routers

- Switches

- Patch panels

- Compute servers

- Storage devices

- Optical gear

- Other middleboxes

Figure 10-1 *Racks of Equipment*

The bad news is all these kinds of devices tend to look alike. Figure 10-2 shows a few pieces of computer networking equipment of different kinds (without wiring).

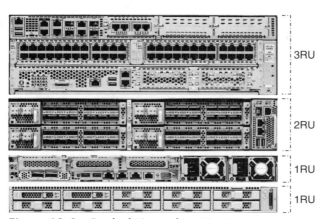

Figure 10-2 *Stacked Networking Equipment*

From top to bottom, Figure 10-2 shows:

- A Cisco 4000 series integrated services router (ISR). You would generally see this kind of router in a small office, where it provides connectivity to the corporate network and Internet as well as voice, security, and other services.

- A Cisco 1004 series optical networking convergence system. You would generally see this type of device in a service provider facility or perhaps used for corporate campus connectivity.

10

- A Cisco UCS C220 rack server. This is a set of hosts attached to the network rather than providing network connectivity.

- A Cisco email security appliance. This specialized appliance is wired into the network so email traffic can pass through rather than providing network connectivity.

In Figure 10-2, each device's height is labeled in **rack units (RUs).** An RU is 1.75 inches or 44.45 mm high. Designers are always trying to make more functionality fit into a single RU. Equipment with more ports or requiring more cooling surface will require more RUs.

Beyond broad generalizations, the only way to know which equipment does what is to read the labels and recognize broad classes of equipment based on their model numbers. Recognizing hardware based on model numbers is not as hard as it might seem because most companies use only a limited range of equipment. For example, they will use only a few models of routers, switches, and other appliances in any individual facility.

Because the ISR router serves many different purposes, it has many kinds of ports. Look at each section of the ISR's back panel, beginning with the upper-left corner in Figure 10-3.

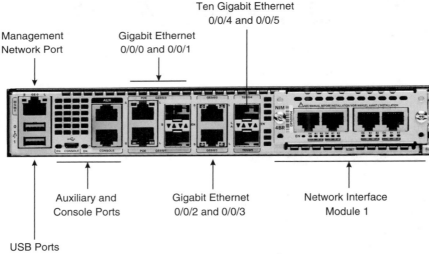

Figure 10-3   *ISR Upper-Left Corner Ports*

The first ports on the left, up to the two 10 Gb/s ports, are *fixed*. You cannot replace fixed ports. Note the lack of screws or a separate plate, unlike the four ports on the left.

The **management network port** connects to a low-speed (normally 1 Gb/s) network to access and manage network equipment. User data is never carried over this network, usually called the *out-of-band management network*. Not all operators build out-of-band management networks. Instead, they manage all their equipment *in-band*, using the same network to carry management and user traffic.

The **auxiliary port** and **console port** provide access to the router's *command-line interface (CLI)* via a terminal application. Console connections come in many forms, including lower-speed Ethernet ports, various kinds of *universal serial bus (USB)*, and multi-pin serial connectors. Most network engineers who spend a lot of time working with physical hardware build a collection of connectors to connect a laptop or tablet computer to network equipment.

Operators typically use console ports to configure a device to connect to the network. Once the device is connected, operators use telnet, *Secure Shell (SSH)*, and other methods to connect to and configure the device. You can think of the console port in most modern networks as a sort of "backup plan"; this is how you connect if all the other ways fail.

NOTE   Chapter 21, "Managing Networks," and Chapter 23, "Configuring a Network," cover accessing routers through Telnet and SSH.

Gigabit Ethernet 0/0/0 and *0/0/1* are the first two network ports in this fixed configuration portion of the router. Each of these ports can be used in one of two ways: as a *Power over Ethernet (POE)* port using an RJ-45 connector or by inserting a pluggable optical connector into the slot next to the RJ-45 port. The single marked-out area over these four ports indicates only one port can be used at a time for each of these interfaces. Inserting a pluggable interface disables the RJ-45 port.

NOTE   Chapter 7, "Wired Networks," covers pluggable and optical connectors.

Gigabit Ethernet 0/0/2 and *0/0/3* are RJ-45-only 1 Gb/s Ethernet ports. These ports do not support POE or pluggable interfaces.

Ten Gigabit 0/0/4 and *0/0/5* are pluggable high-speed interfaces. These are the last two interfaces in the fixed portion of the router configuration.

The first network interface module (**NIM**) is to the right of the two 10 Gb/s ports. Each kind of NIM supports different interface combinations. NIM1 in Figure 10-3 is a *4BR*, which supports voice and *Integrated Services Digital Network (ISDN)* connections. The screws on the left and right sides of the NIM indicate this part of the router is replaceable.

Two more unfilled NIM slots are available to the right of NIM1; Figure 10-3 does not show these slots.

Figure 10-4 shows the center-right module of the ISR.

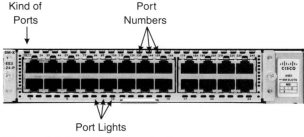

Figure 10-4   *ISR Center-Right Ports*

This set of ports and the one to the left of them are replaceable, as you might expect, because of the screws on either end of the module. Each router with replaceable modules uses different terminology, such as NIM, *5M slot* (as shown here), *VIP*, and many others. These different names describe some significant physical characteristic or capability of the module.

Chassis devices also have **line cards**. There are two differences between a line card and some kind of module:

- A line card normally has a separate forwarding engine, while a module uses the router's forwarding engine.

- A line card usually is larger than a module.

Many line cards or modules indicate the *kind of port* they contain, such as the one shown in the upper left of Figure 10-4. This module contains twenty-four 1 Gb/s ports using RJ-45 connectors. The module's model number, SM-X, is just to the left of the port indicator. You can search for this model number on the Cisco website to discover the capabilities of each port in this module, such as whether they support POE.

In this case, the port numbers are all along the top of the module. A small arrow beside each port number indicates whether the number relates to the upper or lower port. Odd ports are almost always on the top of a row of ports, while even ports are almost always on the bottom.

You might have noticed the ports in Figure 10-3 contained three numbers—TE0/0/4 and TE0/0/5, for instance. Port numbers follow a fairly standard convention across all network equipment manufacturers:

- Two or three letters indicate the speed of the port. *GE* is for *Gigabit Ethernet*, *TE* is for *Ten Gigabit Ethernet*, etc.

- If there is one number, the router has only fixed ports. These ports are numbered starting at 1 and ending at the maximum port count.

- If there are two numbers, the router has slots for modules or line cards. The first number indicates the line card or module slot, and the second indicates the port number on the module or line card.

- If there are three numbers, the router has slots for modules or line cards, and the modules or line cards have slots for submodules. The first number indicates the line card or module slot, the second indicates the submodule slot, and the third indicates the port number on the module or line card.

A small sticker with a table is shown on the right side of Figure 10-4. The table's upper-left cell is marked with a *1*, indicating the upper-left slot contains module 1. The upper-right cell in the table is marked with a *2*, indicating the upper-right slot contains module 2.

Figure 10-4 shows the module in the upper-right slot according to the table, so the interfaces in this module would be GE2/0/1 through GE2/0/24. In this case, the center number is 0 because these ports are connected to the main module itself, not a submodule.

Finally, there is a light for each port along the bottom of the module, shown in Figure 10-4.

Almost every port you encounter in computer networks will have an associated light. These lights, or *light-emitting diodes (LEDs)*, are an important diagnostic tool—if you know what the color and condition of the light mean. Some lights are generally assumed to be common among all networking hardware, such as

- A **solid green status light** means the port is operating correctly.

- A **flashing green status light** means the port is connected and data is being transmitted.

- A **yellow status light** means the port is connecting or has malfunctioned.

- A **red status light** means the port has malfunctioned.

Unfortunately, however, these lights do not always mean the same thing on every piece of networking hardware. For instance, on the Cisco 1120 Connected Grid Router, the pluggable Ethernet 1/1 and 1/2 ports have two lights—one for port speed and another for port status.

- If the port speed light blinks green twice and then pauses, the port is connected at 100 Mb/s.

- If the port speed light blinks green three times and then pauses, the port is connected at 1 Gb/s.

- If the port status light is solid green, the port is connected and active.

- If the port status light is yellow, the port is connected, but there is an error condition.

- If the port status light is flashing green, the pluggable interface can be safely removed.

If you believe a flashing green light means data is being transmitted on a Cisco 1120 Connected Grid, you could be misled.

To add confusion, you can program the lights on many systems to use any color combination you like. Many large-scale operators prefer to use blue rather than green and only solid lights. When you walk into a large data center, the sheer volume of flashing lights can be a bit overwhelming, making it harder to find failed connections rather than easier.

You should always check the equipment manual if you are unsure about the different states of the port lights.

Figure 10-5 shows the lowest of the three sections of the ISR.

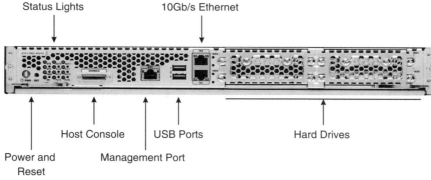

Figure 10-5 *Host (Server) Module in ISR*

The lower section of this ISR contains a host. For some small offices, having a local server installed in a device like this might be useful to support email, web hosting, or other applications. This host module has its own power indicator, reset button, status lights, and console port. There is also a management port for the out-of-band management network described earlier.

This host (server) module has two 10 Gb/s Ethernet ports. These ports would be configured through the host console rather than the router CLI. Four hard drives are also included on this module's right side; each pair has its own cover plate.

Figure 10-6 illustrates the back of another kind of Cisco router—a Cisco 8200 series.

Figure 10-6   *A Cisco Systems 8200 Series Router*

Some routers or other network devices have console, management network, or other ports along the back. The Cisco 8200, however, has only three components. There are two power supplies, one on either side of the router. Each of these power supplies can be removed and replaced. You need to see if you can replace these while the router is powered up and running.

Four fans, often called fan trays, are along the back of the router. These draw air through the router, across the optical ports, electrical ports, and processors. It is critical to cool these components correctly. The fans are replaceable.

Network Diagrams

Networking diagrams are crucial to the documentation required to operate, troubleshoot, and modify a network. Building a good network diagram requires a solid grasp of how the network is built, how it works, and what the diagram itself is supposed to accomplish. There are two broad categories of network diagrams: *physical* and *logical*.

Figure 10-7 illustrates a **physical network diagram**.

In Figure 10-7:

- **CO:** Core router
- **ED:** Edge router
- **FW:** Firewall
- **SV:** Server
- **PP:** Patch panel
- **NET:** Internet connection router

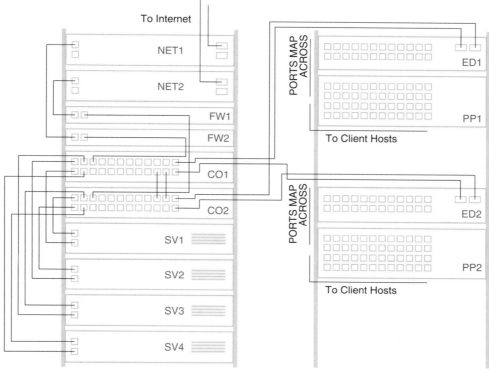

Figure 10-7   *A Physical Network Diagram*

Physical diagrams show where each wire originates and terminates in a network or section. It is common for large-scale networks to require hundreds of physical diagrams to accurately describe how each cable runs, what it connects to, etc.

Physical diagrams are good for understanding a network's physical component, location, and how cables are physically run. For instance, the physical diagram is a good place to start if

- You want to ensure two redundant cables do not run through a single cable tray or conduit—called *circuit grooming*.

- You want to plan out how many cables are needed of a specific length.

- You want to know about the physical size of a piece of equipment—perhaps so you can plan for a replacement.

Physical diagrams do not always contain the following:

- Port numbers, because these can be inferred from where a cable is shown connecting to a piece of equipment. For instance, you can infer the connection from *CO1* port 2 is connected to *CO2* port 3 from this simple diagram.

- Any kind of addresses. You normally will not find IP addresses, physical interface addresses, or any other addresses on a physical network diagram.

10

Figure 10-8 shows a logical diagram of the same network.

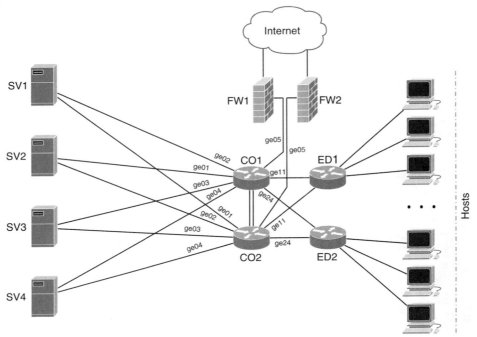

Figure 10-8   *Logical Network Diagram*

Logical network diagrams are abstracted in some ways:

■ Notice the patch panels are not shown in the logical diagram.

■ You can no longer tell which cable runs might be longer or shorter.

■ You can no longer tell what device each rack is in.

Use a logical diagram to follow the traffic flow or understand the control plane configuration and operation. Logical diagrams can also contain the following:

■ Which routing protocol is running between pairs of routers

■ Any policy implemented at a given point in a network, such as packet filtering, route aggregation, etc.

■ Where links are connected (such as the labels given in Figure 10-8)

■ IP addresses

■ Where services are running or located in the network

Many network operators assign device names based on the device's location, bringing more information from the physical world into their logical diagrams.

Two simple rules of thumb are extremely helpful when working with network diagrams:

- Physical diagrams follow the flow of the wires; logical diagrams follow the flow of the packets.

- You should include whatever is helpful without crowding the diagram. You can always have more than one diagram with different pieces of information.

Network Wiring

Every network engineer—at some point in their career, at least—runs network wiring, so it is essential to understand how to perform this fundamental task. Figure 10-9 illustrates cable management.

Figure 10-9   *With and Without Cable Management*

The left side of Figure 10-9 shows a rack cabled without management aids, bundling, or even separation. The result is a tangled mess; seeing and replacing equipment is challenging. In contrast, on the right side of Figure 10-9, the operator cabled the rack neatly and spaced the equipment apart, using horizontal D-ring organizers to hold cables in neat horizontal rows.

As shown on the left side of Figure 10-9, cables hanging off their connectors will strain their connectors. This strain can sometimes cause failures. While most commercially built cables will have *strain gages* (also spelled *strain gauges*) to reduce damage to internal connections, cable management techniques like those shown on the right side of Figure 10-9 can prevent failures of this kind.

10

Other kinds of **rack-mounted cable organizers** include

- Vertical fingerboards
- Vertical lacing bars
- Vertical cable ladders
- Horizontal fingerboards
- Horizontal cable shelves
- Horizontal lacing bars

Cable management systems can take up rack space, so carefully plan the rack layout to include these elements. Raised floors have generally been abandoned in most designs for overhead cable racks, such as the one shown in Figure 10-10.

Figure 10-10   *Overhead Cable Tray*

Engineers must design overhead cable trays to carry the weight of the supported cables. Sometimes, this weight must be calculated into ceiling or rack weight loads.

Copper cables produce heat when power is running through them. Low-power Ethernet cables might not individually produce enough heat to cause damage, but large groups of cables bundled into a tray can. Because of this, heat is also a factor when designing an overhead cable tray system.

Some operators like to include loops in their optical cables, but loops should never be included in copper cables. Copper cables should be cut or commercially built as close to the length needed as possible. Loops add weight to the cable system, act like antennas, or interfere with signal transmission.

You should use patch panels when wiring might frequently change, such as connecting network equipment to network wall jacks in a room or building. Patch panels can also be useful when cable lengths change while replacing equipment.

In summary, wiring to a physical network diagram is easy on the surface but more difficult if the job is to be done correctly.

Handling the Heat

All equipment used in information technology—hosts, routers, switches, and even copper cables—generates heat during operation. However, operating equipment at higher temperatures can reduce its life span or—if the temperature is high enough—cause immediate failures.

Heat is managed in information technology operations by

- Vendors working to reduce the heat their devices produce.

- Vendors designing devices for efficient airflow.

- Liquid cooling.

- Hot air containment.

The first three of these are outside the scope of this book. Hot air containment is common and easily impacted by everyday maintenance tasks. Figure 10-11 illustrates a simple cooling system without hot air containment.

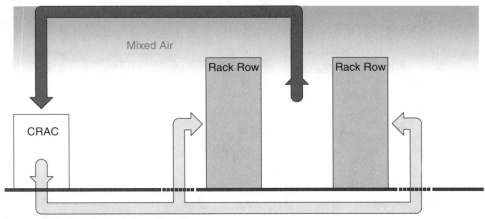

Figure 10-11   *Simple Cooling System*

Figure 10-11 shows a pair of rows of racks from the end. In the figure, a *computer room air conditioner (CRAC)* cools the air and pushes it into the space between the building and a raised floor. Equipment racks sit on this raised floor. This cool air is vented in front of each rack through a floor vent and pulled through the rack, front to back, to cool the equipment.

Hot air expelled from the back of each rack rises toward the ceiling. Fans draw hot air back into the CRAC, cooling it, and the cycle starts again.

10

When pairs of racks are placed back-to-back, a **hot aisle** is created. The more fully sealed off this hot aisle is, the more efficient the cooling process is. In a fully sealed system, there is no mixed air; hot air is directed through ductwork back into the CRAC.

Large-scale data centers may pull air from the outside and cool it through an evaporative process, as shown in Figure 10-12.

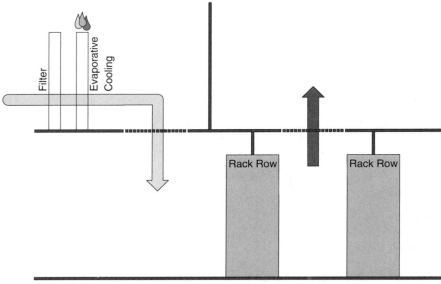

Figure 10-12   *Evaporative Cooling*

Figure 10-12 again shows a pair of data center racks from the end. In this figure, air is drawn directly from the outside by fans, through a filter, and then through a waterfall-like evaporative cooling system. As hotter air flows through the water, the water evaporates, consuming heat from the air and leaving the cooler. This air is then pushed into the data center by fans.

Equipment fans draw this cool air through the rack, cooling the equipment by heating the air. The air is expelled into the hot aisle, wholly isolated from the **cold aisle**, and then pulled by fans back into the outside environment.

Chapter Review

Users tend to think of "the network" as a sort of virtual thing: it exists "out there," but where "there" is, and how bits are translated into signals, signals are carried from place to place, and data is processed are all something of a mystery. Network engineers, however, know that while networks can be described in virtual terms, networks are built out of physical cables, servers, racks, and cooling systems.

Understanding these components and how to use them to build a network is critical to network engineering. This understanding combines wiring diagrams with knowledge of ports, lights, racks, cable management, and cooling to build a physical network.

One key to doing well on the exams is to perform repetitive-spaced review sessions. Review this chapter's material using either the tools in the book or interactive tools for the same material found on the book's companion website. Refer to the online Appendix D, "Study Planner," element for more details. Table 10-2 outlines the key review elements and where you can find them. To better track your study progress, record when you completed these activities in the second column.

Table 10-2   Chapter Review Tracking

Review Element	Review Date (s)	Resource Used
Review key topics		Book, website
Review key terms		Book, website
Repeat DIKTA questions		Book, PTP
Review concepts and actions		Book, website

Review All the Key Topics

Table 10-3 lists the key topics for this chapter.

Table 10-3   Key Topics for Chapter 10

Key Topic Element	Description	Page Number
List	Classes of networking equipment	198
Paragraph	Management network port	200
Paragraph	Auxiliary and console ports	200
List	Port number conventions	202
List, paragraph	LED color meaning	202
Paragraph	Router fan trays	204
Figure 10-7, list, paragraph	Physical network diagrams	205
Figure 10-8, list, paragraph	Logical network diagrams	206
Figure 10-9, paragraphs	Good vs. poor cable management	207
Figure 10-11, paragraph	Cooling system	209
Paragraph	Hot aisles	210

Key Terms You Should Know

Key terms in this chapter include

rack unit (RU), management port, auxiliary port, console port, NIM, chassis device, line card, letters in a port number, numbers in a port number, solid green status light, flashing green status light, yellow status light, red status light, physical network diagram, logical network diagram, rack-mounted cable organizers, CRAC, hot aisle, cold aisle

10

Concepts and Actions

Review the concepts considered in this chapter using Table 10-4. You can cover the right side of this table and describe each concept or action in your own words to verify your understanding.

Table 10-4   Concepts and Actions

Management network port	Connects to a low-speed out-of-band management network
Console port	Provides access to the CLI
Port numbering	Type, module, submodule, port number
Physical network diagram	Good for understanding each physical component of a network, where they are placed, and how they are physically connected
Logical network diagram	Good for understanding traffic flow, control plane configuration, and control plane operation
Physical network diagram follows	The flow of the wires
Logical network diagram follows	The flow of the packets
Strain gage	Helps prevent damage to a connector when the weight of the cable is placed on the connector
Cold aisle	Generally in front of equipment racks, where most equipment is configured to draw air for cooling
Hot aisle	Generally between rows of equipment; may be contained to prevent air mixing

CHAPTER 11

Local Area Networks

This chapter covers the following exam topics:

3. **Endpoints and Media Types**

   3.4. **Demonstrate how to set up and check network connectivity on Windows, Linux, Mac, Android, and Apple mobile OS.**

   Networking utilities on Windows, Linux, Android, and Apple operating systems; how to run troubleshooting commands; wireless client settings (SSID, authentication, WPA mode)6. Endpoints and Media Types

   6.3. **Configure basic wireless security on a home router (WPAx).**

   WPA, WPA2, WPA3; choosing between Personal and Enterprise; wireless security concepts

Network "areas" can be confusing because someone in the computer network space seems to invent a new "area" every few years. Computer networks began with two areas:

- *Local area networks (LANs)* using technologies like token ring, token bus, ARCnet, and Ethernet to carry data over short distances (no more than a few hundred feet).

- *Wide area networks (WANs)* using telephone network technologies, such as T1s and X.25, to carry data over longer distances—throughout a large campus, city, or across the country.

Over the years, we have added the following:

- *Personal area networks (PANs)* use short-distance wireless technologies like Bluetooth to carry data around a single person.

- *Home area networks* (homenets) use short- and medium-distance wireless technologies like Bluetooth and Wi-Fi to carry data around a single home.

- *Car area networks (CANs)* use short-distance wireless and wired technologies to carry data around a single vehicle.

- *Metro area networks (MANs)* use optical and wireless technologies to carry data around a single city or metropolitan area.

Many of these areas were invented in parallel with new data transport technologies. Over time, however, Ethernet, Wi-Fi, and a few other technologies have become common enough—and capable enough—to be used everywhere, causing the distinctions between these areas to blur significantly.

This chapter focuses on networks within the local area. The LAN is considered in the context of a commercial building or campus, while the homenet is considered in the context of a typical home network. This chapter also considers host Wi-Fi-specific configuration as a part of designing, building, and configuring a homenet.

Predicting Technology Changes

Predictions of computer networks are hard to make. I once worked on a project installing telephone technology (telco) based T1s throughout a campus. Because a single T1 did not provide enough bandwidth for the computers and applications being installed along with this new network, 8 to 16 T1 circuits were installed between each pair of buildings throughout the campus. Engineers bundled these circuits together using "inverse multiplexers."

I asked the engineer leading the installation project why they were not using Ethernet or other computer networking technology. The response was: "Computer networking technologies do not have a future. Telco networks will always have higher speeds and longer distances. Eventually, the telco network will reach the host, and computer networks will be abandoned."

Ironically, the next project I worked on was designing and deploying a fiber-optic computer network to interconnect all the buildings on the very same campus. The telco-based T1 network was abandoned within three years.

You do not know what is coming next because you cannot know everything being invented right now, how many companies will try to commercialize a technology, and how many organizations will buy these technologies.

"Do I Know This Already?" Quiz

Take the quiz (either here or use the PTP software) if you want to use the score to help you decide how much time to spend on this chapter. Appendix A, "Answers to the 'Do I Know This Already?' Quizzes," found at the end of the book, includes both the answers and explanations. You can also find answers in the PTP testing software.

Table 11-1 "Do I Know This Already?" Foundation Topics Section-to-Question Mapping

Section	Questions
Building and Campus Networks	1, 2, 3
The Home Network	4, 5, 6, 7
Configuring the Home Network	8

CAUTION The goal of self-assessment is to gauge your mastery of the topics in this chapter. If you do not know the answer to a question or are only partially sure of the answer, you should mark that question as wrong for purposes of the self-assessment. Giving yourself credit for an answer you incorrectly guess skews your self-assessment results and might provide you with a false sense of security.

1. What is an intermediate distribution frame?
    a. A term commonly used to describe any intermediate equipment room or wiring facility
    b. A term commonly used to describe where wiring enters a building and the main equipment, wiring, or wiring facility in the building
    c. A vertical conduit or cable-handling system for pulling cables vertically, between floors, in a building
    d. A form of structured wiring used in data centers

2. What is a building distribution frame?
    a. A term commonly used to describe any intermediate equipment room or wiring facility
    b. A vertical conduit or cable-handling system for pulling cables vertically, between floors, in a building
    c. A term commonly used to describe where wiring enters a building and the main equipment, wiring, or wiring facility in the building
    d. A form of structured wiring used in data centers

3. What is a riser for building wiring?
    a. A term commonly used to describe any intermediate equipment room or wiring facility
    b. A term commonly used to describe where wiring enters a building and the main equipment, wiring, or wiring facility in the building
    c. A vertical conduit or cable-handling system for pulling cables vertically, between floors, in a building
    d. A form of structured wiring used in data centers

4. What components may be separate or combined devices in a home network?
    a. MODEM, router
    b. MODEM, firewall, router, switch, AP
    c. MODEM, firewall, router
    d. Firewall, router, AP

5. What is the MODEM?
    a. Converts telephone signals to computer signals
    b. Converts the long-distance optical or electrical signals to Ethernet in a home network
    c. Converts Wi-Fi signals to Ethernet
    d. Converts computer signals to telephone signals

6. What are the most common connectors for bringing network service to a residential building? (Select all that apply.)
    a. DOCSIS F-connector
    b. Optical LC Connector
    c. Ethernet RJ-45
    d. Optical SC Connector

7. What is a demarc?

    a. Where the provider's network ends and the customer's network begins

    b. A term commonly used to describe where wiring enters a building and the main equipment, wiring, or wiring facility in the building

    c. A vertical conduit or cable-handling system for pulling cables vertically, between floors, in a building

    d. The connector on the MODEM you plug a router into

8. What does the SSID identify?

    a. The Wi-Fi network in a house

    b. A set of services connected to a single Wi-Fi segment or broadcast domain

    c. A non-guest Wi-Fi network

    d. The password you use to connect to a Wi-Fi network

Foundation Topics

Building and Campus Networks

Every commercial building—including retail stores, office buildings, gyms, dorms, and schools—has some form of network connectivity. These networks' complexity varies from "all wireless" access to overhead Category 6A cabling with PoE support for telephone, security, fire detection, and other systems. Figure 11-1 illustrates the basic components of a building network.

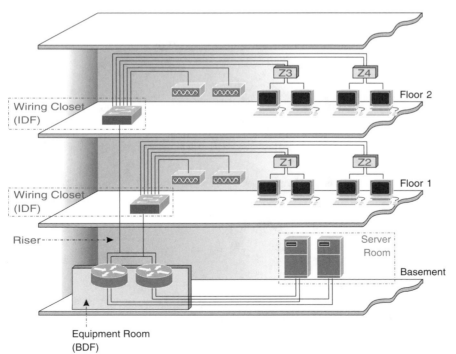

Figure 11-1 *Building a Local Area Network*

11

Outside access to the Internet or a corporate network enters through the equipment room or *building distribution frame (BDF)*.

The following sections describe items of interest in Figure 11-1.

Equipment Closet (Building Distribution Frame)

In physical relay (crossbar and Strowger), telephone networks, wires, and equipment were hung off or tied to large, complex metal frames. Every building had a building entry point (BEP), often a piece of plywood attached to a wall in an equipment room. A small BDF would be constructed in a basement or first-floor room in larger buildings that feed other buildings. Over time, the *BEP* became associated with the *BDF*, and many engineers use the two terms interchangeably.

In some networks, the *main distribution frame (MDF)* overlaps with the BDF. Sometimes, however, a network becomes large enough to have a separate facility to connect all the buildings. This facility is often called the MDF.

Wiring Closet (Intermediate Distribution Frame)

In physical relay (crossbar and Strowger) telephone networks, small frames containing primarily wiring were called *intermediate distribution frames*, or **IDFs**. These IDFs might be on each building floor or between the main switching frame (mainframe) and the BDFs. An IDF is often used for any "intermediate" **wiring closet** or structure.

Server Room

Most buildings, particularly offices not physically located on a corporate campus (*remote locations*), have a few servers for handling local storage and computing requirements. A small office might need to support local voice service or building access control.

The room containing local servers is often called the **server room**.

Routers and servers are often—but not always—located in the same room as the BDF.

Riser

Risers are vertical conduits or spaces designed to hold cables running between floors. Most buildings have only one or two risers. Wiring on each floor runs from a wiring closet horizontally.

Wi-Fi Access Points

Commercial Wi-Fi access points often draw power off a switch in the wiring closet (IDF) through PoE. Large-scale Wi-Fi networks supporting large commercial buildings and campuses often require a *site survey* to uncover interference sources and signal-blocking structures. Engineers use information about the site to select the placement, which channels to use, and the transmission power of each access point.

Zoned Access

Larger buildings often use **zoned access**, shown in Figure 11-1 as *Z1*, *Z2*, *Z3*, and *Z4*. Rather than running cables from every desk—or other location with network equipment—directly to the wiring closet, a series of patch panels or switches are installed throughout the building. Zone access adds some complexity to the original design, but it also adds a lot of flexibility.

The Home Network

Home networks vary from a single unmanaged device providing local Wi-Fi to complex managed networks with multiple virtual networks. Figure 11-2 illustrates a moderately complex home network for discussion.

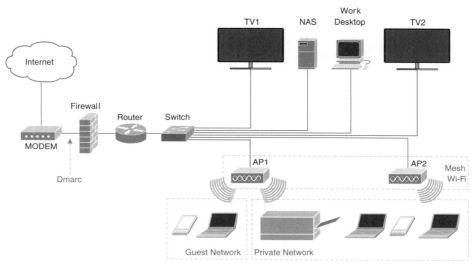

Figure 11-2   *Home Network Example*

A lot is happening in Figure 11-2; the following sections consider parts of the network not considered in previous chapters.

Network Core

The "core" of a home network consists of four devices: the MODEM, the firewall, the router, and the access points. Figure 11-3 shows different ways of combining these devices.

Figure 11-3 shows four of the most common equipment combinations:

- *A* shows the MODulator/DEModulator (MODEM), firewall, and router combined into a single device. At the same time, the switch and AP are separate devices wired into the combined MODEM/firewall/router.

- *B* shows the MODEM as an individual device connected (typically via Ethernet) to a combined firewall/router/switch. One of the switch ports is then used to connect to an AP. Using a separate MODEM is a typical configuration for users with Wi-Fi mesh systems.

- *C* shows a separate MODEM connected to a single device containing the firewall, router, switch, and AP functions. Users with simple networking requirements or who do not have a lot of experience working with networking devices will often use this kind of configuration.

- *D* shows all the functions combined in a single device. Using a single device is a typical configuration for provider-provided networking hardware.

11

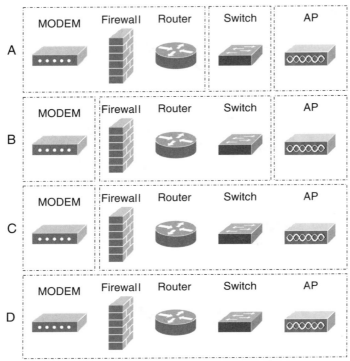

Figure 11-3   *Home Network Core Device Combinations*

Each of these four configurations will be useful for different use cases and different kinds of users.

MODEM

The **MODEM** converts the service provider's longer-distance optical or electrical signals into the typical Ethernet wiring and Wi-Fi connectivity inside the home. Providers generally use one of five methods—forms of *last-mile connectivity*—to connect from a local facility to a home:

- *Gigabyte passive optical network (GPON)* is a standard for carrying network packets over a fiber network. GPON is a *passive* optical network because the home does not require high-powered optics to support high data rates. Wave division multiplexing (WDM) and time-division multiplexing (TDM) are used to support (up to) 64 users on a single fiber run.

- *Data Over Cable Service Interface Specification (**DOCSIS**)* is a set of standards for carrying network packets over a cable television network. DOCSIS essentially "steals" several video channels, splitting them off to carry network data. Version 3.0, which can provide up to 10 Gb/s to the customer (downstream) and 1 Gb/s from the customer to the provider (upstream), is the most commonly deployed version of DOCSIS.

- *Satellite* uses a small satellite dish directly mounted to a home or pole to provide Internet service.

- *Fixed Wi-Fi* uses specialized Wi-Fi antennas and signaling to extend the range of Wi-Fi, making it practical to replace cables between the curb and house with a wireless signal.

- *Fixed cellular wireless* uses 4G and 5G cellular technology to provide Internet connectivity.

The last two kinds of connections are often called *fixed wireless access (FWA)*.

Physical Connections to the Home

Key Topic

There are two kinds of physical connections in most homes:

- GPON, most modern satellite connections, and FWA look like standard Ethernet using an EJ-45 connection in the home.

- Older satellite and DOCSIS connections require a coaxial cable using some variant of the **F connector**, shown in Figure 11-4.

Figure 11-4 *Coaxial F Connector*

One significant difference between these connection methods is how data is carried between the home and provider; Figure 11-5 illustrates.

11

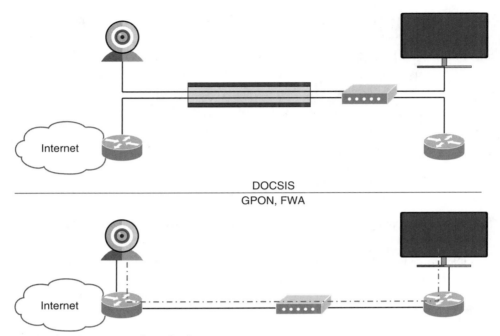

Figure 11-5 *Data and Media Streams*

DOCSIS connections carry data and media streams as separate channels; the MODEM splits these two streams, so

- Televisions and tuners connect to an F connector on the MODEM.
- Phones connect to an RJ-11 phone jack on the MODEM.
- The local router connects to an Ethernet RJ-45 jack on the MODEM.

While a physical failure in the network can cause all three signals to stop working, each stream can stop working independently of the other streams in other failure modes.

GPON, FWA, and other home connections provide only an IP connection. Video, voice (telephone), and other services are converted to IP network streams and carried as data packets over the connection. If IP fails, all the services fail.

Cable Cutting

Many home users no longer use television and video streaming content from cable television providers. Instead, they prefer to draw all their services over a single link running IP. Subscribing to video and other services over an IP-only Internet connection is called **cable cutting** or *cord cutting*. While there is still a physical cable, all in-home services—video, network connectivity, and phone—are provided *Over the Top* (**OtT**) via IP rather than using separate channels for each service.

Cable cutting allows users to use many different OtT streaming services rather than relying on the cable company's video streaming.

Combining the MODEM with Other Devices

Combining the MODEM, router, and firewall, as shown in *A* and *D* in Figure 11-3, means any device can be used with only one of the five kinds of last-mile technology. Combining the MODEM with other devices has some positive attributes, such as

- The user has only one physical device to wire, power, and manage.

- The provider can control the performance of this single device, ensuring a consistent customer experience.

- The provider understands the entire network, all the way to individual user devices connected to the network.

- There is only one physical device to troubleshoot and replace.

- From the provider's perspective, they own the equipment, which is then leased or rented to the user, generating revenue.

Combining the MODEM with other devices also has some negative attributes:

- The user cannot replace their Wi-Fi system or router without replacing the MODEM—or contacting the provider, who then must send a technician out to do the replacement.

- The provider is responsible for the user's internal home network experience, including Wi-Fi dead spots.

- The provider cannot replace the MODEM to upgrade their technology without replacing the user's router and Wi-Fi system. Providers must pay more to upgrade last-mile technology if they combine the MODEM with other devices.

Choosing which to use—using several or one combined device—depends on the situation, the provider, and the user.

Demarcation

Two other terms you will often hear in networking are the *demarcation point* (**demarc**) and *customer premises equipment* (**CPE**).

The demarc is the point at which the provider's network ends and the customer's network begins. Devices and wiring beyond the demarc are the customer's responsibility from the provider's perspective.

The demarc is a physical device in telephone networks like the one shown in Figure 11-6.

The demarc is not a single point when a provider supplies a home network's router, firewall, and Wi-Fi system. The general idea, however, is to divide the part of the network the customer is responsible for from the network the provider is responsible for.

CPE is the provider-supplied equipment physically located in the home (or some other physical space owned by the user).

11

Figure 11-6 *A Telephone System Demarcation Point*

The SSID and Wi-Fi Guest Network

The *service set identifier (**SSID**)* identifies a single set of services or a *wireless local area network (WLAN)*. A single SSID might represent

- A Wi-Fi network on a single AP using a single channel

- A Wi-Fi network on a single AP using multiple channels

- A Wi-Fi network across multiple APs (like a Wi-Fi mesh system) using a single channel

- A Wi-Fi network across multiple APs (like a Wi-Fi mesh system) using multiple channels

- Multiple Wi-Fi networks on one or more AP(s) using a single channel

- Multiple Wi-Fi networks on one or more AP(s) using multiple channels

The SSID is not related to an AP or a Wi-Fi channel; it is a *set of services*. Each SSID represents a different segment or broadcast domain (although the physical channel may—or may not—be shared among multiple SSIDs).

> **NOTE** Devices connected to different SSIDs can only communicate through a router, while all the devices connected to the same SSID may communicate directly.

In a home network, you should choose a single SSID for each set of devices. For instance, you might create separate SSIDs for

- IoT devices like doorbells and thermostats

- Primary hosts, like laptops, tablets, and cell phones

- Guests

Most consumer-grade APs cannot create multiple SSIDs. In this case, you can create two SSIDs:

- The primary SSID for hosts and streaming devices like laptops, tablets, cell phones, and televisions. This SSID has access to the Internet and all internal devices.

- The guest SSID. This SSID has access to the Internet but no access to internal devices.

APs can implement a guest SSID either on a different channel as the primary (internal) SSID or a different channel.

Should you put IoT devices on the primary or guest SSID? The "wisdom of the Internet" is to place IoT devices on the guest SSID, but there are trade-offs (as usual). Some of the reasons to connect IoT devices to the guest SSID include the following:

- If an IoT device comes under the control of an attacker, the attacker cannot reach your internal network devices.

- You do not need to create special rules or policies on your network for IoT devices to communicate with their corresponding cloud services.

- The IoT device has no visibility into the traffic generated by your primary network devices.

Some of the reasons to connect IoT devices to the primary network (internal) SSID include

- The primary network SSID is probably better protected from external attacks.

- Attaching to the **guest network**—generally considered an "open" access point by most users—does not gain access to home control systems.

There is no clear or correct answer to this question; it all depends on the kinds of IoT devices, the security posture of the network, and many other factors.

Which Devices Should Be Wired?

Many users no longer think about wiring network cabling throughout their homes because wireless is common and easy to deploy. What possible disadvantages are there to skipping the cables and just connecting everything to Wi-Fi?

Deciding which devices should be connected through a physical Ethernet cable and which should be connected through Wi-Fi requires a good understanding of Wi-Fi's limits, the likely bandwidth usage of each device, where traffic will flow, and the bandwidth of the upstream connection to the network.

Wi-Fi Limitations

Wi-Fi access points are rated by their maximum speed: a 300 Mb/s Wi-Fi AP can send *or* receive 300 Mb/s. The air through which Wi-Fi signals travel is a shared medium—like a single shared Ethernet cable. Because the air is a shared medium, only one Wi-Fi-connected device can transmit or receive at any moment.

11

One way of seeing this sharing is dividing the available bandwidth among all the connected devices so

- Two devices connected to a 300 Mb/s AP can send *and* receive about 75 Mb/s each.

- Two devices connected to a 300 Mb/s AP can send 100 Mb/s and receive about 50 Mb/s each.

- Four devices connected to a 300 Mb/s AP can send and receive about 32 Mb/s each.

Waiting for open slots to transmit and collisions imposes some overhead, so actual speeds will be lower than simple division indicates.

Further, existing Wi-Fi sessions have priority over new ones. If one user is streaming a movie, and a second user begins downloading a large file through the same AP, the first user's traffic will have priority over the second user's traffic.

Newer technologies, like *Multi-User Multiple Input Multiple Output (MU-MIMO)*, can help the Wi-Fi AP support higher bandwidths for more users. MU-MIMO uses multiple antennas and beamforming to direct signals at different parts of a room, so users in one section of the room do not share the same medium as users in other parts of the room.

Traffic Flows

Most users will send and receive the largest amount of traffic to destinations reachable through the Internet, so their Internet service speed will have as great or greater impact on their connection speed as their local Wi-Fi network. There is little point in getting a 300 Mb/s Wi-Fi router to support two devices, both of which will send and receive traffic from the Internet when your Internet service is 10 Mb/s.

In some cases, users will stream from a device connected to the local network, such as a media or gaming server. In these cases, the Internet connection speed is not as important as the speed of the local network.

Choosing Devices to Wire

You should prefer to wire devices that

- Use a lot of bandwidth for extended periods; these devices will significantly impact Wi-Fi performance.

- Communicate with media or game servers connected to the same local network.

- Act as media or gaming servers.

- Are generally fixed in one place, such as a television or a host normally connected to the network through a docking station.

There are no definite rules around what to connect through Ethernet and what to connect through Wi-Fi. The general rule of thumb, however, is less mobile, higher bandwidth devices will perform better if connected via Ethernet.

Configuring the Home Network

Home network wireless requires several configurations—even if the network has only one device. Each section that follows considers one part of the home network configuration.

Configuring the MODEM

MODEMs are generally "plug and play." The service provider can perform any configuration needed through a remote connection in most modern networks. The biggest questions you need to answer about the MODEM are

- Where should it be located? The MODEM does not need to be close to the router, AP, or other network elements. Any location where the external cable, an internal cable to reach the router, and power are readily available should be fine.

- Are all the lights correct? Like most other networking gear, green lights are generally good, and green blinking lights mean the MODEM is transmitting data. Most MODEMs provide labels describing the meaning of the lights.

Once the MODEM is plugged in and running and the lights look correct, you can configure the router and firewall.

Configuring the Router and Firewall

The router will have at least two interfaces:

- A *wide area network (WAN)* or *outside* interface. This interface should be an RJ-45 cable. The other end of this cable should be plugged into the MODEM.

- A *local area network (LAN)* or *inside* interface. This interface, or set of interfaces, also uses an RJ-45 connector. This is where you connect a switch, AP, or any other device that should have Internet access.

Routers might also have an internal switch supporting four to eight interfaces. It is important to remember these interfaces are *switched* rather than *routed*; the entire set of interfaces is controlled as a single subnet.

Main Configuration Screen

Most routers designed for home use will have a mobile device or web-based configuration application; these devices are not designed for interaction through a command line or automation. Figure 11-7 is a screenshot from the TP-Link Deco configuration app running on a mobile device.

Figure 11-7 shows a straightforward interface with just a few pieces of information and options. You can see the network devices connected in the center of the screen and the number of users connected to each network node. The sample network is a Wi-Fi 6 mesh network, so two network devices are shown.

11

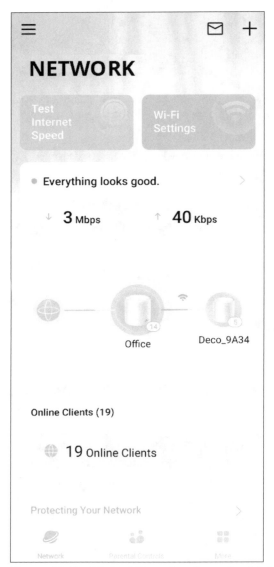

Figure 11-7 *TP-Link Deco Configuration Main Screen*

NOTE The following section considers Wi-Fi settings.

There is also a switch with several connected hosts in this network, but these are not typically shown in the diagrams presented by an app. Figure 11-8 shows the remaining portion of this initial configuration screen.

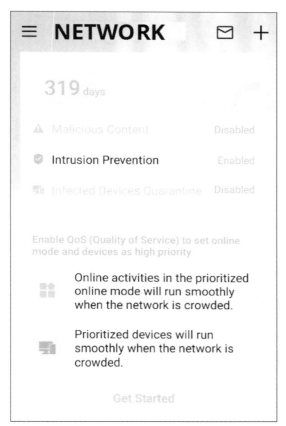

Figure 11-8 *Lower Portion of the Initial Configuration Screen*

The lower portion of this initial configuration screen, shown in Figure 11-8, provides some basic security and quality of service (QoS) settings. These settings do not provide many options—essentially just "on" or "off"—because these devices are designed for users with little training in managing or operating a network.

The *Malicious Content* slider enables a cloud-based system that examines incoming packets for evidence of an attack and outbound packets for evidence of a compromised host or device attached to the network.

The QoS settings prioritize traffic from a small set of hosts over traffic from other hosts. If you have a host used for work, heavy content streaming, or gaming, you can configure the router to prioritize sending packets from these hosts. The QoS settings offer options for streaming, gaming, videoconferencing, and other activities.

The More Settings Screen

Figure 11-9 shows the screen displayed when you select the **More** button on the bottom right of the screen.

11

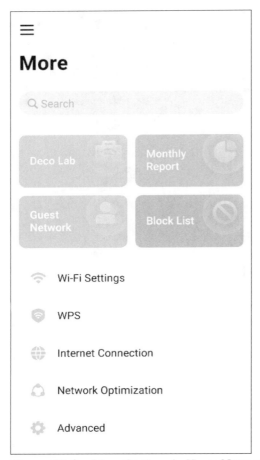

Figure 11-9   *More Options in Home Network Configuration*

The **Guest Network** option allows you to enable a guest network, as discussed previously in this chapter.

The **Block List** option allows you to block specific devices from connecting to the network based on their physical interface (MAC) address. Suppose a neighbor's device often connects to your network. In that case, if you have a local television or other devices you do not want to connect to the network, or an attacker often attempts to access your network, this option can block their access.

NOTE   The section "Configuring the Wireless Access Point" considers Wi-Fi settings in more detail.

The **Internet Connection** option allows you to manually set an IP address for the router or get one from the provider. You normally want to leave this set so the router obtains an address from the provider.

Advanced Options

Choosing the **Advanced** option displays the screen shown in Figure 11-10.

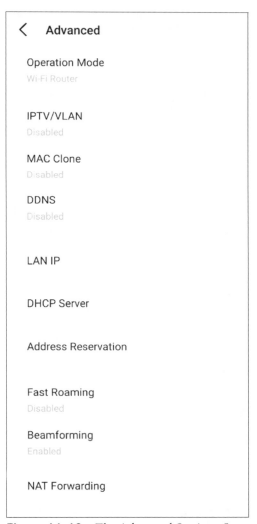

Figure 11-10   *The Advanced Settings Screen for a Home Use Router*

The **Operation Mode** allows you to set the device to act as *only* a Wi-Fi access point—sometimes called *bridge mode*—or as a router and Wi-Fi AP. Choose bridge mode if you have separate routing and Wi-Fi support devices, as shown in Figure 11-3 options, *A* and *B*. Not all routers have built-in Wi-Fi APs like the one shown here, so this option may not be available.

Use the **MAC Clone** option when the provider only connects to a device with a specific physical interface (MAC) address. The MAC clone option allows you to replace a combined router/MODEM device supplied by a provider with a separate router and MODEM.

The **DHCP Server** option allows you to split the home network IP address space into two parts using this option:

- The Dynamic Host Configuration Protocol (DHCP) gives addresses to hosts requesting an address.

- Addresses reserved for manual configuration on devices like network-attached storage (NAS), gaming, and media streaming servers.

For instance, if you know you will never need to connect more than 25 devices to the network, you can set the DHCP pool to 30 addresses (leaving some room for mistakes, overlapping assignments, etc.) and reserve the remaining addresses on the subnet for manually configuring devices.

The **LAN IP** option, in this case, opens a separate screen that allows you to manually configure the router's IP address on the internal interface. Figure 11-11 illustrates the LAN IP screen from the TP-Link application.

Figure 11-11   *LAN IP Configuration*

The default IP address/subnet mask for most routers designed for home use is 192.168.0.1/24, part of the private IPv4 address space. You can set the LAN IP to just about any IPv4 address—although you should stick with one of the private addresses described in Chapter 2, "Addresses." The subnet mask is often not configurable on this class of devices.

NAT Forwarding

The **NAT Forwarding** option allows you to relate a specific port number on the outside (provider-facing) interface to a specific IP address on the internal network. Figure 11-12 illustrates using NAT forwarding to allow external access to a server connected to a home network.

The **NAT Forwarding** option creates a permanent (or static) Network Address Translation (NAT) entry mapping an external address and port number outside the network to a single port number on a host inside the network.

Host *A* might know what IP address to use to reach *B* but cannot know what port number to use to reach a specific service running on *B*. The router translates the addresses and port numbers on traffic traveling between these two hosts using Network Address Translation.

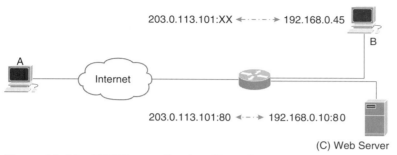

Figure 11-12   *NAT Forwarding in a Home Router*

Host *A* cannot send packets to the web server on server *C*. *C*'s owner, however, might want *A*—or any other host connected to the Internet—to reach this web server. To allow this access, *C*'s owner can configure a permanent NAT mapping from some port on the external IP address—in this case, port 80—to some port on server *C*.

When *A* connects to 203.0.113.101:80, the router translates this to 192.168.0.10:80, so *A* is really connecting to *C*.

Creating this kind of permanent mapping is sometimes called *punching a hole through the firewall*.

Static NAT traversal might not always make a server connected to a home network reachable from the Internet. Many providers now use *Commercial Grade Network Address Translation (cgNAT)* to translate addresses assigned to customers to external, publicly reachable addresses on the Internet. Figure 11-13 illustrates cgNAT.

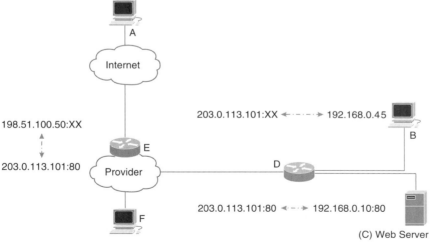

Figure 11-13   *Carrier Grade Network Address Translation*

In Figure 11-13, if host *F* sends packets to 203.0.113.101:80, router *D* translates the address and port number to 192.168.0.10:80 and forwards the packet to host *C*. However, because router *E* translates IP addresses and port numbers using 198.51.100.50, there is again no way for *A* to know what IP address and port number to use when sending packets to host *C*.

11

Configuring the Wireless Access Point

You need to consider three basic options when configuring a Wi-Fi AP for home use: the radio settings, beam forming, and security. Figure 11-14 shows a typical configuration screen for a home Wi-Fi system.

Figure 11-14 *Typical Wi-Fi Network Settings*

The following sections consider each of these three areas of configuration.

SSID and Password

The two most basic settings at the top of the screen are the *network name*, or SSID, and a password.

> **NOTE**   You should always change the SSID and password to local settings; you should never leave them at whatever the factory sets them.

Select a long but easy-to-remember password. The password length matters more than symbols—although you should use symbols if possible.

Security

You should *always* use some form of encryption to protect the data traveling between a host and an AP. If this data is not encrypted, anyone receiving the signal can capture and process your data.

War Driving

War driving is driving around neighborhoods and business areas looking for Wi-Fi systems using common passwords or even open Wi-Fi systems. Once they have accessed the Wi-Fi system, hackers will either steal bandwidth from it or capture data for later use.

Most APs offer Wired Equivalent Privacy (WEP), Wi-Fi Protected Access (WPA), and Wi-Fi Protected Access Pre-Shared Key (WPA-PSK).

WEP was initially ratified in 1999 to provide security equivalent to wired connections for Wi-Fi. Viable attacks against WEP's security were quickly discovered, leading to multiple attempts to make the protocol more secure. These efforts failed; the Wi-Fi Alliance officially retired WEP in 2004.

You should reconfigure any Wi-Fi system using WEP to use some version of WPA. Operators should replace any AP that cannot be configured to support WPA.

WPA was initially ratified in 2003. WPA differs from WEP in three ways:

- WPA uses 256-bit keys rather than the 64- and 128-bit keys used by WEP.

- WPA includes a message integrity code on each packet to ensure hackers cannot tamper with data transmitted on the Wi-Fi network.

- WPA authenticates users and hosts rather than just encrypting traffic passing over the Wi-Fi network.

WPA begins when a session between a device and the AP starts. A public key is selected in one of two ways:

- WPA uses a public key provided by an external server. This form of WPA is often called *enterprise* because of the external server requirements.

- WPA-PSK creates a public key using the SSID and other information. This form of WPA is sometimes called *personal* because it does not require any external servers.

WPA is more secure than WPA-PSK because attackers do not know the information used to create the initial public key.

The AP uses this public key to exchange private keys, which are then used to encrypt data transferred across the Wi-Fi network. Operators should change the private key used to encrypt data regularly.

To snoop on a Wi-Fi data stream secured using WPA, an attacker must discover the current key and find some way to know the next key the AP will use. Attacks of this kind are possible but tend to be challenging to execute.

11

> **NOTE**   Chapter 22, "Troubleshooting," considers encryption in more detail. Chapter 20, "Security Tools," considers authentication in more detail.

WPA2 is a later, more secure version of WPA. The Wi-Fi Alliance is working on WPA3, which is more secure than WPA2.

You should use WPA-PSK for most home networks—unless you want to set up and manage a separate key server.

Configuring a Windows Host for Wi-Fi Connectivity

You can configure Wi-Fi connectivity on a Windows 11 host in two places: the **Quick Settings** section of the taskbar and **Settings**. Figure 11-15 shows the configuration steps using Settings.

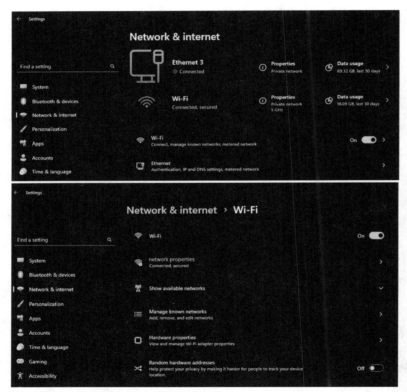

Figure 11-15   *Windows Wi-Fi Configuration*

Selecting **Network & internet** from Settings displays the current network connections. Selecting **Wi-Fi** will then display options related only to Wi-Fi connections. Several options are of interest here:

- **Wi-Fi** is a single selector allowing you to turn Wi-Fi on or off.

- **Network properties** will normally display the SSID of the Wi-Fi network to which this host is connected. This option will open another set of options and information, covered next in this section.

- **Show available networks** causes Windows 11 to search for every network. The complete list of networks might not include Wi-Fi networks that are not advertising their SSID.

- Selecting **Manage known networks** opens a screen listing every network this host has ever connected to. You can configure Windows to auto-connect to specific Wi-Fi networks or forget individual Wi-Fi networks.

- **Hardware properties** provides information about the Wi-Fi adapter connected to this host, including driver and hardware versions.

- Selecting **Random hardware address** causes the host to use a virtual physical (MAC) address when connecting to Wi-Fi APs. This prevents the host from being tracked when roaming between multiple Wi-Fi networks.

To connect to a network, select the SSID from the list of available networks and enter the network password. If the network SSID is not shown, you can enter it manually.

Figure 11-16 illustrates the settings screen for a specific Wi-Fi network.

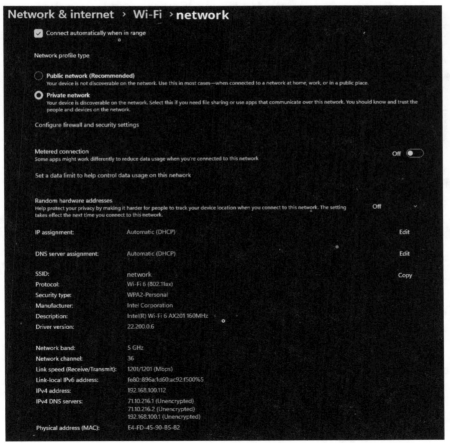

Figure 11-16 *Windows 11 Wi-Fi Network Configuration and Information Screen*

You can select whether the network is *public* or *private* on this screen. If you set a Wi-Fi network to *public*, this host will not advertise its presence to other hosts on the network, and the host will not permit connections from other devices on the same network.

If you set a Wi-Fi network to *private*, the host will advertise its presence on the network, and other devices can connect to the host.

You can also use the Windows 11 taskbar to select a Wi-Fi network quickly. Selecting the network icon (a connected host, as shown in Figure 11-17, or a Wi-Fi icon) brings up a small screen.

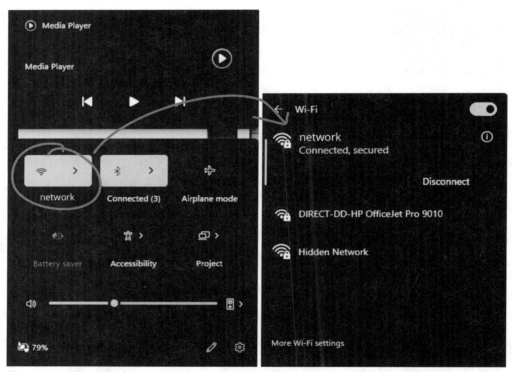

Figure 11-17 *Windows 11 Task Bar Wi-Fi Configuration*

Selecting the arrow on the right side of the Wi-Fi symbol brings up a second screen listing every available network. Select the correct SSID and enter the network's password (configured on the AP) to connect to one of these networks.

The *Hidden Network* is a Wi-Fi network configured not to advertise its SSID. You can only connect to this network if you know the SSID and password.

Configuring Apple's macOS for Wi-Fi Connectivity

Apple's macOS also has two ways to configure Wi-Fi connectivity: through **System Settings** and a quick selection option in the **Apple Menu Bar**. Figure 11-18 shows these two options.

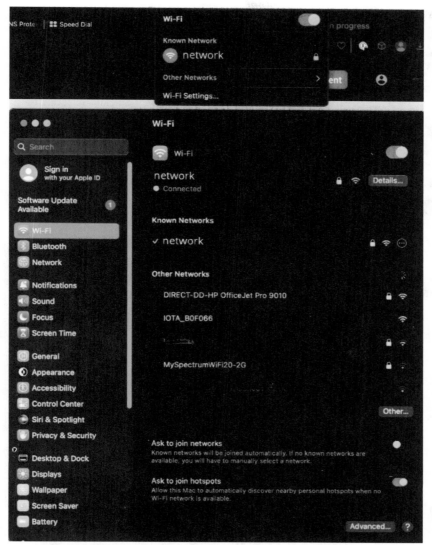

Figure 11-18 *Accessing Wi-Fi Settings in Apple macOS*

You can enable or disable Wi-Fi on both hosts by selecting a slider at the top of the screen. The SSID of the currently connected network is also shown on both screens. The screen in System Settings provides a list of known networks. You can select **Other** to enter an SSID and password manually.

Figure 11-19 shows the detailed information displayed when you select an individual Wi-Fi network.

11

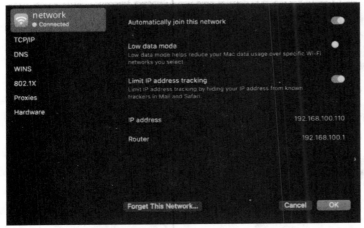

Figure 11-19   *Detailed Wi-Fi Network Information in Apple macOS*

The detailed Wi-Fi information screen allows you to select whether this host should automatically connect to this Wi-Fi network, whether the host should try to reduce the traffic sent across this network, and whether the host should hide your IP address from known trackers.

Configuring Mobile Devices for Wi-Fi Connectivity

Configuring a mobile device is very similar to configuring a Windows 11 or Apple Macintosh macOS host for Wi-Fi connectivity:

- Select a Wi-Fi network to connect to.

- Enter the correct password.

- Connect.

Figure 11-20 illustrates the Wi-Fi connection screens from a mobile phone running the Android operating system.

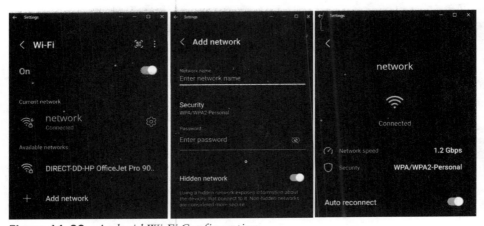

Figure 11-20   *Android Wi-Fi Configuration*

The screen on the far left of Figure 11-20 is the initial Wi-Fi screen. This screen lists the currently connected network and available networks.

If you select **Add network**, the screen in the center of Figure 11-20 appears. This screen allows you to select the SSID, password, and security type of network you would like to use.

The screen on the far right of Figure 11-20 shows the result of selecting the *gear icon* to the right of the network on the far-left screen. This screen shows network details like the connection speed and security type. Using the Auto-reconnect slider, you can configure the device to reconnect to this network whenever it is in range.

Chapter Review

Local area networks, from offices to buildings to homes, are one of the three major classes or types of networks you will encounter in the real world. If you decide to build a career in network engineering, you will probably start by working in an environment with a LAN.

Because LANs are almost universal, you should understand the terms and ideas used in wiring buildings and homes. These include the BDF, IDF, wiring closets, risers, zones used in building wiring, and the demarc, MODEM, firewall, router, switch, and AP used in home networks.

Configuring a wireless home network is also an important skill.

One key to doing well on the exams is to perform repetitive-spaced review sessions. Review this chapter's material using either the tools in the book or interactive tools for the same material found on the book's companion website. Refer to the online Appendix D, "Study Planner," element for more details. Table 11-2 outlines the key review elements and where you can find them. To better track your study progress, record when you completed these activities in the second column.

Table 11-2 Chapter Review Tracking

Review Element	Review Date (s)	Resource Used
Review key topics		Book, website
Review key terms		Book, website
Repeat DIKTA questions		Book, PTP
Review concepts and actions		Book, website

Review All the Key Topics

Table 11-3 lists the key topics for this chapter.

Table 11-3 Key Topics for Chapter 11

Key Topic Element	Description	Page Number
Paragraph	Building distribution frames (BDFs)	218
Paragraph	Risers	218
Paragraph	Zoned access	218

11

Key Topic Element	Description	Page Number
Paragraph	Core network devices	219
Paragraph	MODEM	220
Paragraph	Physical connections in homes	221
Paragraph	Cable/cord cutting	222
Paragraph, Figure 11-6	Demarcation point (demarc)	223
Paragraph	Demarc definition	223
Paragraph	CPE	223
Paragraph	SSID	224
Paragraph, list	Creating two SSIDs	225
Section	Wi-Fi Limitations	225
Paragraph, list	Criteria for wiring devices rather than relying on wireless	226
Paragraph, list	Router interfaces	227
Paragraph, list	Home Use Router Operation Mode, MAC Clone option	231
Paragraph	Home Use Router NAT Forwarding option	232

Key Terms You Should Know

Key terms in this chapter include

BDF, IDF, wiring closet, server room, riser, zoned access, MODEM, DOCSIS, F connector, cable cutting, OtT, demarc, CPE, SSID, guest network

Concepts and Actions

Review the concepts considered in this chapter using Table 11-4. You can cover the right side of this table and describe each concept or action in your own words to verify your understanding.

Table 11-4   Concepts and Actions

BDF	Where outside wiring normally enters a commercial building
IDF	Any wiring closet, equipment room, or wiring structure that handles connectivity between any two other points in the network
Riser	A virtual conduit or facility for carrying cables between floors of a commercial building
Zoned access	Patch panels are installed throughout the floor of a building to increase flexibility
MODEM	Converts long-haul optical and electronic signals into local Ethernet and Wi-Fi signals
DOCSIS	A standard for carrying data across a cable television network
OtT	Carrying voice and video traffic over the data network rather than in parallel with the data network

demarc	The point where the provider's network ends and the customer's network begins
CPE	Customer premises equipment; equipment owned by the provider but installed on the customer's property
SSID	A set of services connected to the same segment or broadcast domain on a Wi-Fi network
Guest network	A network with access to the Internet but not internal devices, such as hosts, printers, etc.

CHAPTER 12

Wide Area Networks

This chapter covers the following exam topics:

1. **Standards and Concepts**
   1.3. **Differentiate between LAN, WAN, MAN, CAN, PAN, and WLAN.**

   Identify and illustrate common physical and logical network topologies

Local area networks (LANs), discussed in the previous chapter, are the first major place or class of networks. Wide area networks (WANs) are the second major place or class of networks. Chapter 13, "Data Centers and Fabrics," considers the third major class of networks—data center fabrics.

Although these three classes of networks use the same basic technologies, these technologies are applied to a unique set of problems. For LANs, the problem is providing service in enclosed spaces—primarily different kinds of buildings. Even the home network faces a unique problem in being easy enough to configure and use for users with little or no training.

The unique challenges of WANs are the sheer geographic distances to cover and the natural terrain and obstacles to carrying digital across these spaces. Engineers face many problems when covering vast geographic distances, including

- Squirrels, groundhogs, mice, and other rodents destroying cables

- Wind, rain, ice, temperature variations, and other weather

- Crossing under water, through (or over) mountains, and other geographic "features"

- Supporting the physical weight of cables carried under the ocean or through the air

- Providing power to long-run network cables and their related facilities

This chapter gives a broad overview of the topologies, challenges, and providers who work to bring digital signals across long distances.

"Do I Know This Already?" Quiz

Take the quiz (either here or use the PTP software) if you want to use the score to help you decide how much time to spend on this chapter. Appendix A, "Answers to the 'Do I Know This Already?' Quizzes," found at the end of the book, includes both the answers and explanations. You can also find answers in the PTP testing software.

Table 12-1 "Do I Know This Already?" Foundation Topics Section-to-Question Mapping

Section	Questions
Common Challenges to Building Wide Area Networks	1, 2, 3
Metro and Last Mile Network Design	4, 5
Transit Provider Design	6, 7
Ring and Hub-and-Spoke Topologies	8

CAUTION The goal of self-assessment is to gauge your mastery of the topics in this chapter. If you do not know the answer to a question or are only partially sure of the answer, you should mark that question as wrong for purposes of the self-assessment. Giving yourself credit for an answer you incorrectly guess skews your self-assessment results and might provide you with a false sense of security.

1. What is a TDR used for?

   a. To measure the delay across a link

   b. To find the location of a cable failure

   c. To measure the jitter across a link

   d. To find the location of a buried cable

2. What is right-of-way?

   a. An owner's grant to some outside party to use a piece of land

   b. A provider's right to bury cables under the ocean

   c. When cars get out of the way of a train

   d. The right to dig up a cable that's already been buried

3. What are two common ways to run cables over long distances? (Choose two.)

   a. Send data through a satellite link

   b. Bury the cables in trenches

   c. Attach the cables to poles

   d. Carry them in large, specially designed ships

4. What are four common last-mile network technologies?

   a. FWA, GPON, DOCSIS, metro fiber

   b. Wi-Fi, GPON, Ethernet, DOCSIS

   c. FWA, Ethernet, DOCSIS, Optical SC

   d. FWA, Optical SC, DOCSIS, metro fiber

5. Why is the last mile often the hardest to provide?

   a. Because physically running cable through the last mile is more difficult than other places

   b. Because the cost of building the infrastructure must be paid for by a small set of users

      c. Because providers cannot use wireless connectivity for the last mile

      d. Because providers cannot use Ethernet for the last mile

6. What is a point of presence?

      a. A provider's local office space for sales and maintenance

      b. A local government office where rights-of-way can be purchased

      c. A local provider facility where circuits are terminated

      d. The customer's property

7. Why would a provider agree to settlement-free peering?

      a. To offer service to a charitable organization

      b. Bidirectional traffic between the providers will be roughly equal

      c. To offer service to another provider

      d. To offer service at an Internet exchange point (IXP)

8. What are the primary advantages of a ring topology? (Choose two.)

      a. You can build a large network using only two ports per router.

      b. Ring topologies converge more quickly than hub-and-spoke topologies.

      c. Rings are two-connected.

      d. Rings can continue forwarding traffic even with two link or node failures.

Foundation Topics

Common Challenges to Building Wide Area Networks

Two primary challenges to building and operating a large network are crossing the legal boundaries to laying and accessing cable runs across personal and public property, called **right-of-way**, and the challenges of physically laying and managing long-distance cables. Each is considered in the following sections.

Right-of-Way

A story passes around the network engineering community of a native tribe in South America that controlled a particular area, including two mountains and a pass between them. A provider buried a cable through the region to connect two moderately sized cities. Within a week of bringing up the new circuit, however, the link failed.

Given this was a brand new fiber, it seemed unlikely there was some physical fault caused by a splice, failed electronics, or some other common problem. There were no reports of construction anywhere along the fiber's path, so it was unlikely a backhoe was responsible.

> **NOTE** *Backhoe fade* happens when a backhoe takes out a communication cable.

Engineers used a *time-domain reflectometer* (**TDR**) to discover the location of the cable break. The operation of a TDR is shown in Figure 12-1.

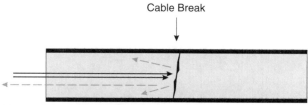

Figure 12-1   *TDR Operation*

The TDR transmits a signal down the cable, whether optical or electrical. If the cable is broken or damaged, some signal will be reflected to the transmitting TDR. The TDR can determine where the break is by measuring the amount of time between transmitting the signal and receiving the reflection.

Following a cable map, technicians can get close enough to the break to find it through visual inspection.

In this particular case, when the technicians arrived at the break, they discovered a member of the local tribe standing over the spot—armed, preventing them from accessing the cable. After some conversation, they determined the local tribe wanted some form of payment for this cable to run across their land.

While a bit humorous, this situation highlights one of the challenges providers face when laying cables across long distances—*right-of-way*.

The idea of right-of-way originates in public paths: members of the public are granted permission to walk across privately owned land to follow paths that existed before the current owner. Courts and governments extended right-of-way, over the years, to an owner granting any use of a piece of land to some other person.

If your driveway crosses someone else's land, you must gain a right-of-way to use it. If you want to place a sign in a farmer's field, you must gain a right-of-way. If you want to bury a cable across someone's land or hang a cable above it from towers, you must gain a right-of-way.

Providers face a singular problem when trying to gain right-of-way to build networks: no one wants a provider digging up their property to cross their land.

Running a cable through hundreds of towns, tens of cities, and a few states requires getting right-of-way from hundreds of governments and private landowners.

Providers often work around this problem by purchasing rights-of-way from existing holders, such as governments, railroads, electrical utilities, and water utilities.

Physical Plant

A provider's *physical plant* is the cables, buildings, and other physical facilities they have built to carry data across long distances. Each kind of physical space presents different challenges to laying and maintaining cables. For instance, Figure 12-2 shows a typical cable installation in Nuuk, Greenland.

Greenland presents many challenges for carrying data over long distances. Cities and villages are separated by hundreds of miles, and there are no roads between them, so the only access is via boat or helicopter. The ground is largely rock, so trenches must be cut by blasting and heavy machinery, or conduits must be affixed to the outside of the rock and cables strung through these conduits.

Another harsh environment for laying cables is under the sea. Figure 12-3 illustrates the undersea cable-laying process.

Figure 12-2 *Cables Attached to Rock in Nuuk, Greenland*

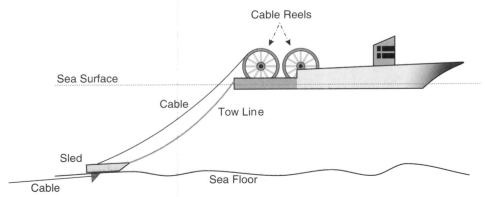

Figure 12-3 *Undersea Cable-Laying Process*

In Figure 12-3, a specially designed ship travels across the ocean surface, using highly accurate positioning technologies to ensure the cable is laid on a specific path. The ship has reels full of special cable for undersea use—shown larger than life. This cable is fed to a sled, which travels across the bottom of the ocean, pulled along by a tow line connected to the ship. The sled pulls the cable from the ship, digs a trench, and buries the cable a few feet under the sea floor.

Hundreds of undersea cables are used to carry traffic across oceans, through seas, and even along coastlines. Figure 12-4 is an undersea cable map.

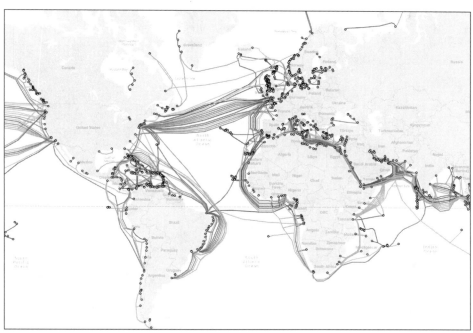

Figure 12-4   *Submarine Cable Map*

The undersea cable map in Figure 12-4 shows the large number of cables now lying on or under the ocean floor. While many of these cables run along continental shelves, some cross oceans, including deep trenches and underwater mountains.

Another common way of installing WAN cables is by attaching them to utility poles. Providers face challenges attaching fiber-optic cables to existing poles because utilities and local telephone companies, which control these poles, often do not want the competition from a new provider in the area. Providers might also need to replace poles if they cannot bear the additional weight of the fiber-optic cables.

Metro and Last-Mile Network Design

Metropolitan area networks (MANs) and last-mile delivery—or *access*—networks are often designed using rings, as shown in Figure 12-5.

Access networks connect end users—organizations and individual users—to the global Internet.

Figure 12-5 shows

- A *fixed wireless access* (**FWA***)* last mile. Connectivity to the towers or transmitters supporting individual homes is normally either a fiber ring or a hub-and-spoke topology.

- A fiber to the neighborhood (FTTN) or fiber to the curb (FTTC) network using **GPON**. Connections to the upstream routers are often a ring or hub-and-spoke topology.

- A **DOCSIS**, or cable television, connection. Cable television may be carried to a neighborhood or curb using fiber technology in either a ring or hub-and-spoke topology.

- A **MAN**. Metropolitan Area Networks are normally built using ROADMs as a ring within a metropolitan area. Each ROADM may connect to a hub-and-spoke network or another ring serving a smaller area like a corporate campus.

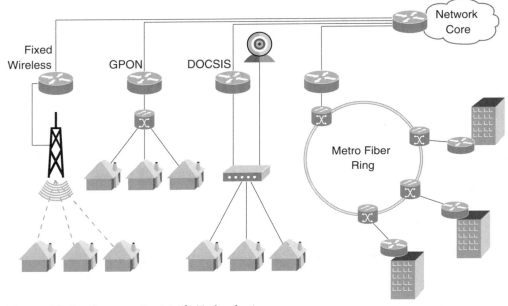

Figure 12-5 *Common Last-Mile Technologies*

The **last mile** is often the hardest for service providers to support because

- The cost of installing cable to individual houses and businesses is generally very high.

- Subscription fees for individual users are generally low.

The cost of installing a cable to an individual might only be recouped after 10 or 15 years of service. Over 15 years, several new generations of networking technology can be invented, designed, and deployed. More sparsely populated areas are more difficult to support financially. Providers often only provide fixed wireless or satellite connectivity in sparsely populated areas.

Transit Provider Design

Transit providers connect last-mile providers, cloud providers, and other large-scale networks to build the core of the global Internet.

12

These are obviously large-scale, complex networks. Most of the time, however, even large-scale providers use interconnected rings to build their networks. There are few specialized topologies used in WANs.

There are several kinds of facilities a large-scale transit provider may operate, including

- **Point of presence (PoP):** This is generally a facility the provider uses to terminate circuits.

- **Colocation facility (CoLo):** A provider's customer can rent space in a CoLo, allowing them to connect hosts directly to the provider's core network. This allows the customer to place servers topologically closer to lots of users and allow the customer to pay the provider for power, space, control over physical access to the hosts, and network connectivity.

- **Peering point:** Providers connect to other providers and customers at peering points. These peering points can either be *public* or *private*. Anyone can rent space in a public peering point, install a router, and connect to the provider's network. Private peering points, on the other hand, can be accessed only by other providers, and are often managed under some form of cost-sharing arrangement between the connecting providers.

Providers connect to other providers for many reasons, but primarily to send traffic from one provider to another. There are three basic kinds of peering in the Internet:

- **Provider-customer peering:** When an organization wants to gain access to the Internet, it can pay a provider for a connection. Last-mile providers often pay global transit providers for **upstream connectivity**.

- **Settlement-free peering:** When two providers would like to connect, and anticipate the amount of traffic to be about the same in both directions, they can build a settlement-free peering connection.

- **Open peering:** Some organizations are given a connection to the Internet without payment (or settlements), even though the traffic levels are mismatched, or the organization would normally be considered a customer of the transit provider. For instance, research organizations are sometimes offered a connection at no cost to support the larger networking community. Social media networks are often also offered service at no cost because the transit provider would prefer the social media network's user traffic stay on their network.

Large-scale transit providers tend to peer with a lot of other organizations.

Ring and Hub-and-Spoke Topologies

The previous sections in this chapter described two basic network topologies: ring and hub-and-spoke. Let's take a closer look at these two topologies. Figure 12-6 illustrates a network with ring and hub-and-spoke topologies.

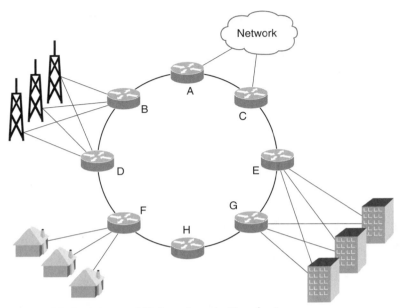

Figure 12-6   *Ring and Hub-and-spoke Topologies*

In Figure 12-6:

- Routers *A* through *H* are configured in a **ring topology**.

- Routers *B* and *D*, along with the three transmitter towers connected to them, are a *dual-homed hub-and-spoke* network topology.

- Routers *E* and *G*, along with the business buildings connected to them, are *a dual-homed hub-and-spoke* network topology.

- Router *F* and the three residences connected to it are a *single-homed hub-and-spoke* network topology.

The advantages of a ring topology are as follows:

- You can build large networks using only a pair of interfaces on each network device.

- The ring is a **two-connected topology**, which means there are at least two paths through the network. If a single router or link fails, the network can still pass traffic to all the remaining destinations.

The primary disadvantage of the ring topology is the available bandwidth to reach any destination decreases for each connected node (router or switch) in the ring. If a new router is added to the ring between *C* and *E*, the *C* to *E* traffic must now compete with traffic entering the ring from this new router. Each additional router adds more traffic without adding more overall bandwidth capacity.

A second disadvantage of ring topologies is each additional node added to the ring causes a bit more delay and potentially adds a bit more jitter.

The primary advantage of the **hub-and-spoke topology** is the ability to support a lot of end locations, such as businesses or homes, with the minimal amount of wiring possible, particularly in densely populated areas. New destinations can be added without reducing the performance of existing destinations.

The primary disadvantage of the single-homed hub-and-spoke topology is the loss of a single device or link disrupts service; every hub and link is a *single point of failure*. Adding a second hub device, and a second set of links, eliminates this single point of failure. Dual-homed hub-and-spoke networks are, however, a lot more complex than single-homed hub-and-spoke networks.

Chapter Review

Wide area networks, whether running under the ocean, across poles, or buried underground, are crucial to building everything from the global Internet to large-scale corporate networks. Operators who build network-spanning large geographic regions face some unique challenges in right-of-way and managing the physical plant.

Two kinds of providers build these long-haul, or wide area, networks: transit and last-mile providers. While transit providers focus on connecting cities to cities or continents to continents, last-mile, or edge providers focus on building networks connecting individual users to the larger global Internet. Last-mile technologies include solutions like GPON, DOCSIS, and FWA.

The primary topologies these providers use are rings and hub-and-spoke.

One key to doing well on the exams is to perform repetitive-spaced review sessions. Review this chapter's material using either the tools in the book or interactive tools for the same material found on the book's companion website. Refer to the online Appendix D, "Study Planner," element for more details. Table 12-2 outlines the key review elements and where you can find them. To better track your study progress, record when you completed these activities in the second column.

Table 12-2 Chapter Review Tracking

Review Element	Review Date (s)	Resource Used
Review key topics		Book, website
Review key terms		Book, website
Repeat DIKTA questions		Book, PTP
Review concepts and actions		Book, website

Review All the Key Topics

Table 12-3 lists the key topics for this chapter.

Table 12-3 Key Topics for Chapter 12

Key Topic Element	Description	Page Number
Paragraph, Figure 12-1	Time-domain reflectometer (TDR) operation	246
Paragraph	Right-of-way	247
Section	Metro and Last-Mile Network Design	249
List	Facilities large-scale transit providers operate	251
List	Types of provider peering	251
List, paragraph	Advantages/disadvantages of ring topologies	252
Paragraphs	Advantages/disadvantages of hub-and-spoke topologies	253

Key Terms You Should Know

Key terms in this chapter include:

right-of-way, TDR, FWA, GPON, DOCSIS, MAN, last mile, PoP, CoLo, peering point, upstream connectivity, settlement-free peering, open peering, ring topology, two-connected topology, metro fiber, hub-and-spoke topology

Concepts and Actions

Review the concepts considered in this chapter using Table 12-4. You can cover the right side of this table and describe each concept or action in your own words to verify your understanding.

Table 12-4 Concepts and Actions

Squirrels	One of the challenges to building long-haul networks is squirrels like to chew on lines hanging from poles
Right-of-way	When a land owner allows an outside entity to use part of their land for some specific purpose, such as burying a cable
TDR	Time-domain reflectometer; used to discover the location of a cable break
Physical plant	The set of cables and facilities built and managed by a provider to support the physical needs of installing and operating cable
Last-mile	The network connecting individual buildings and users to the global Internet
DOCSIS	Carrying IP networking traffic over a cable television network
FWA	Fixed wireless access; using Wi-Fi or cellular telephone technology to carry IP data from a building to the global Internet
GPON	Passive optical networking technology used in last-mile networks

FTTN, FTTC	Fiber to the neighborhood, fiber to the curb
MAN	Metro-area network; normally a ring
Point of presence	A provider facility where long-haul circuits are terminated and a geographical area is served
CoLo	Colocation facility, where providers and customers colocate networking and information technology hardware
Peering point	A facility where providers and their customers interconnect
Provider-customer peering	When an organization purchases access to the global Internet from a provider
Upstream provider	A provider from which an organization is purchasing access to the global Internet
Open peering	Provider-customer peering in which the provider does not charge for access to the global Internet
Settlement-free peering	Two providers peer without charging one another settlement
Ring topology	Simple two-connected topology using two ports on each device
Hub-and-spoke topology	A topology with a small number (usually two or less) hub devices providing connectivity to a larger number of remote sites

Part III

Services

As exciting as addressing, formatting, and carrying data around in packets, the purpose of a computer network is to provide and enable real-world services. Networks use addressing, routing, cables, and wireless signals to carry four kinds of services through the local and wide areas.

Packet transport is the most basic service that networks provide. Transmitters need to format data so the network can carry it and receivers can understand it. Chapter 6, "Network Models," noted formatting data is called *marshaling* in the Recursive InterNetwork Architecture (RINA) model.

Networks transport packets from host to host, so this is a "middle layer" construction.

Application transport services are built on packet transport systems. At the application layer, information is again formatted by a transmitter so the receiver can understand it, but network devices do not, in general, need to understand application transport formatting deeply.

Names and *time* are two more network services crucial to the way applications and humans use a network. Two complex systems, including specialized protocols and servers, provide these services: the *Domain Name System (DNS)* and *Network Time Protocol (NTP)*.

Applications run on servers, but there is no reason they must run directly on physical servers owned, managed, and controlled by the organization using the application. Selling compute, storage, and networking capacity as a service is called *cloud computing*.

Each chapter in this part of the book considers one of these kinds of services.

The chapters in this part of the book are as follows:

Chapter 13: Data Centers and Fabrics

Chapter 14: Network Transport

Chapter 15: Application Transport

Chapter 16: Names and Time

Chapter 17: Cloud Computing

Data Centers and Fabrics

This chapter covers the following exam topics:

1. **Standards and Concepts**

    1.3. **Differentiate between LAN, WAN, MAN, CAN, PAN, and WLAN.**

    Identify and illustrate common physical and logical network topologies

Chapter 11, "Local Area Networks," introduced the idea of local area networks (LANs), designed and built for short distances. Chapter 11 used building and home networks as two examples of LANs. Chapter 12, "Wide Area Networks," introduced wide area networks (WANs). This chapter introduces the third class, or "place," in modern networks, the *data center (DC)*. As they do with LANs and WANs, engineers often build DCs to support specialized requirements using two or three common topologies.

The chapter begins by considering the kinds of applications engineers design DCs to support, like large-scale retail sites, social media sites, cellular telephone networks, and large-scale Internet interconnection points. The second part of this chapter describes the most common type of topology used to support these applications, the *spine-and-leaf* fabric. The *Clos* and *butterfly* fabrics are both commonly used kinds of spine-and-leaf fabrics.

"Do I Know This Already?" Quiz

Take the quiz (either here or use the PTP software) if you want to use the score to help you decide how much time to spend on this chapter. Appendix A, "Answers to the 'Do I Know This Already?' Quizzes," found at the end of the book, includes both the answers and explanations. You can also find answers in the PTP testing software.

Table 13-1 "Do I Know This Already?" Foundation Topics Section-to-Question Mapping

Section	Questions
Web Applications	1, 2
Internet Exchange Points	3
Spine-and-Leaf Fabrics	4, 5, 6, 7, 8, 9

CAUTION   The goal of self-assessment is to gauge your mastery of the topics in this chapter. If you do not know the answer to a question or are only partially sure of the answer, you should mark that question as wrong for purposes of the self-assessment. Giving yourself credit for an answer you incorrectly guess skews your self-assessment results and might provide you with a false sense of security.

1. What kinds of servers or services are often components of a web service?

   a. Front-end or web server, back-end server

   b. Front-end or web server, back-end server, database service

   c. Back-end server, database service

   d. Web application firewall, front-end server, database service

2. Why must DC fabrics have very low latency and jitter?

   a. Responding to a single user request may require traffic to pass through the network multiple times.

   b. Faster networks are less expensive to design, manage, and maintain.

   c. Typical web services have too many user requests to handle if the network is too slow.

   d. Low latency and jitter networks require less power.

3. What does an Internet exchange provider use a route server for?

   a. To carry routes between transit providers

   b. To carry routes between content providers

   c. To carry routes between cloud providers

   d. To carry routes between all the operators connected to the IXP fabric

4. What four things differentiate a network from a fabric?

   a. Fabrics are regular, fabrics are planar, fabrics rely on high-bandwidth links, and fabrics have predictable performance.

   b. Fabrics are not regular, fabrics are planar, fabrics rely on high fan-outs, and fabrics have predictable performance.

   c. Fabrics are regular, fabrics are nonplanar, fabrics rely on high-bandwidth links, and fabrics have unpredictable performance.

   d. Fabrics are regular, fabrics are nonplanar, fabrics rely on high fan-outs, and fabrics have predictable performance.

5. Why is a spine-and-leaf fabric called a spine-and-leaf fabric?

   a. Because they have three stages

   b. Because these fabrics have spines and leaves

   c. Because they look like spiny fish

   d. Because they have two layers

6. Why is a three-stage spine-and-leaf fabric called a Clos fabric?

   a. After the inventor's name, Charlie Clos

   b. CLOS is an abbreviation for Combined Low-delay Open Speed

   c. After the name of the research lab in which it was invented

   d. Because the inventor's wife was named Clorice

7. Are spine-and-leaf fabrics used for computer networks nonblocking or noncontending, and why?

   a. Nonblocking, because every host connected to the fabric can send traffic to any other host connected to the fabric at full speed

   b. Nonblocking, because the network will prevent traffic from entering the network when all the links are too full

   c. Noncontending, because the network does not prevent traffic from entering the network

   d. Noncontending, because no two connected workloads ever share the same bandwidth

8. Why might a network designer choose a butterfly over Clos fabric design? (Choose two.)

   a. Larger scale

   b. Easier to cable and build

   c. Lifecycle management

   d. More power efficient

   e. Smaller scale

9. How many ports can a butterfly fabric be designed to support?

   a. Hundreds

   b. Thousands

   c. Hundreds of thousands

   d. Millions

Foundation Topics

Web Applications

Much of the data people use the modern Internet to access resides in data centers, and users access the data through the *Hypertext Markup Language (HTML)*.

> **NOTE** Chapter 15, "Application Transport," discusses HTML and the Hypertext Transfer Protocol (HTTP).

Content providers, such as search engines and social media networks, develop and manage some of the largest web applications on the global Internet. Banks, retail websites, and many other businesses also develop and manage large-scale web applications.

Figure 13-1 illustrates the relationship between users, web applications, and user accessed data.

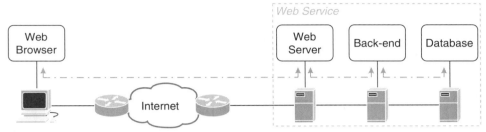

Figure 13-1   *Web Application Architecture*

Figure 13-1 shows a single host communicating with a **web service**. There are three kinds of servers used to build the web service:

- The **web server** or **front-end server** takes data from the back-end server and formats it for different browsers.

- The **back-end server** takes information from many different data sources, including other applications and databases, to build a page.

- The *database service* stores information about users, services, events, etc., and feeds it to the back-end server.

While the illustration shows one of each kind of server or application within the web service, there are potentially thousands of each:

- The service might need thousands of web servers to support millions of concurrent users. When users connect to the service, they must be routed to a server with low utilization and access to the correct information.

- The service might need thousands of back-end services to supply the various sections of a single page in a web service. For instance, a retail site might have one back-end server to build a list of items on sale, a second to build a list of popular items, a third to build a list of recommended items based on previous purchases, and a fourth to show the status of current orders. Social media services often have thousands of back-end services building and supplying information to the front-end servers.

- The service will need thousands of databases to store, sort, and analyze data.

All these applications must communicate within one or more data centers over a network. Web applications encounter network scale, accumulated jitter, and accumulated delay challenges.

Web-application network scale can be described with one word: *huge*. Many web-based applications require hundreds of thousands of servers. To support huge numbers of hosts and services, DC networks must sometimes be designed to support hundreds of thousands of servers, and DC fabrics must be connected through *data center interconnect* (**DCI**).

Figure 13-2 illustrates the accumulation of delay and jitter across a network.

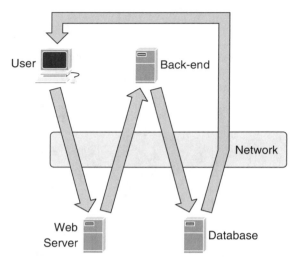

Figure 13-2 *Delay Accumulation Across a Network*

In Figure 13-2, each user's request for data from a web-based service causes four separate connections, each of which must travel across the same network. If it takes even a tenth of a second for a packet to cross the network, the user will not receive the information for about half a second.

The example shown in Figure 13-2 is simpler than the real world. For every byte of data a typical web-based application receives, it will send about 10 bytes of traffic across the data center network.

Because user experience directly results from the time required for the web-based service to respond to a request, engineers must design DC fabrics to reduce delay and jitter.

Internet Exchange Points

*Internet exchange points (**IXPs**)* are critical in the global Internet. IXPs provide

- Connectivity for regional providers
- Colocation facilities
- Regional access to users for content providers, edge security, etc.

NOTE   Chapter 5, "What's in a Network?" describes the role of IXPs in the global Internet.

Figure 13-3 illustrates global connectivity from an IXP's perspective.

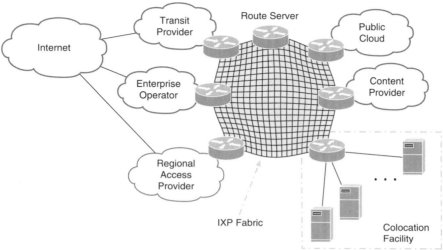

Figure 13-3 *IXP Connectivity*

Figure 13-3 contains several points of interest:

- A regional access provider, enterprise operator, and transit provider connect along the left side of the IXP fabric. The enterprise operator and regional access provider may connect to the transit provider through the IXP fabric separately. Connecting to a transit provider through the IXP fabric and separately at some other peering point with a second transit provider offers redundant connections and resilience.

- The **route server** at the top carries routing information between the routers connected to the IXP fabric. Rather than exchanging routes (*peering*) directly with the transit provider, they can peer with the route server. If every organization connected to the IXP fabric peers with the route server, they can receive every reachable destination over a single connection. However, traffic does not flow through the route server; it flows across the IXP fabric directly between the various organizations.

- The IXP's customers can install servers, routers, and other devices in the *colocation facility*, connecting them directly to the IXP fabric. Servers in this colocation facility have much higher-speed access to destinations on the global Internet than a server located within a corporate data center.

There is no direct connection between the IXP fabric and the global Internet. IXPs do not provide access to the Internet, just a place to connect between all the various kinds of providers and organizations on the global Internet.

Spine-and-Leaf Fabrics

Web applications and IXPs require large-scale networks to connect thousands—or even millions—of devices. Public and private clouds also need to build these large-scale networks to connect large numbers of servers.

NOTE Chapter 17, "Cloud Computing," covers public and private clouds.

These operators do not use traditional network designs to connect large numbers of servers and devices. Instead, they use network **fabrics**. A network fabric differs from a traditional network in four important ways:

- Fabrics are *repeatable* and *regular*. Almost any section of a fabric can be moved to another place in the fabric without change or with only minor changes.

- Fabrics are **nonplanar**. A fabric cannot be described or drawn without pairs of connections crossing one another in the diagram.

- Fabrics rely on high **fan-out** to carry high traffic volumes rather than high link speeds.

- The characteristics of a fabric can be described in mathematical terms, making it (somewhat) easy to predict performance. For instance, the likelihood of a fabric dropping a packet is related to the *oversubscription rate*, which you can calculate directly by examining the fabric's design.

Fabrics can also appear to be a single device from the "outside" or the connected devices. There are no "magical ports" on a fabric when sending traffic between two connected devices; every port provides (largely) identical service.

There are many kinds of fabrics, including toroid and hypercube. Designers rely on **spine-and-leaf fabrics** for most large-scale designs, however. There are two common kinds of spine-and-leaf fabrics: the Clos and the butterfly.

Clos Fabrics

By the early 1900s, telephone companies were building large networks. The size of these networks made them difficult to build, manage, and troubleshoot. Operators had to manually connect circuits using *switchboards*, as shown in Figure 13-4.

Figure 13-4   *A Switchboard*

These switchboards were replaced with mechanical relay *crossbars* and *Strowger fabrics*, which were large, heavy, and hard to wire, and required a lot of electricity. In 1938, Edson Erwin started working out an alternative: the *spine-and-leaf* fabric. Charlie Clos formalized the concept in a paper in 1952, and telephone companies started replacing their large crossbar and Strowger fabrics soon after. Figure 13-5 illustrates a **Clos fabric**.

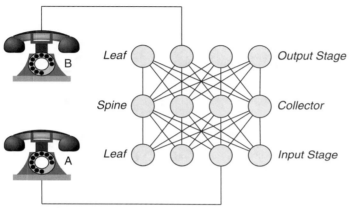

Figure 13-5 *A Telephone Clos Fabric*

In Figure 13-5, telephone A calls telephone B. As the user at A dials B's number, the various stages of the fabric open and close switches to build a complete electrical path between the two telephones. There are three stages in a Clos fabric:

- The input stage accepts connections from attached devices (telephones).

- The collector stage collects connections from the input stage and distributes them to the output stage.

- The output stage connects the fabric to the receiving device (telephone).

Building the circuit from A to B is called *making the circuit*, or simply a *make*. When A's user hangs up, the circuit is *broken*; this action is called a *break*.

If telephone B's line is already in use, the collector rejects the call, and A's user will receive a busy signal. Rather than delivering part of the information, the fabric rejects the make. Because the network will never drop any data, it is called **nonblocking**.

The switches in the input and output stages are also called *leaves*, and the collector is called a *spine*—hence the name *spine-and-leaf fabric*.

Figure 13-6 shows a small three-stage Clos fabric used to build a computer, rather than a telephone, network.

The three-stage Clos is illustrated "flat" on the left side of Figure 13-6, much like a Clos fabric used in a telephone network. Servers, or *workloads*, can be attached to any leaf, also called *top-of-rack switches (ToRs)*. The same network is illustrated on the right side of Figure 13-6, only with the spine routers (or switches) at the top of the diagram.

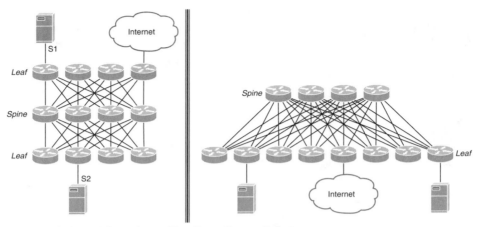

Figure 13-6 *A Three-Stage Clos Data Center Fabric*

You should note two interesting points about this design:

■ There are links between ToRs or spine routers. All links are between a leaf and spine switches.

■ External connectivity is always attached in the same place as a server. The Internet or other external connection into a fabric should always be treated like any other workload.

Using the right routers or switches, you can build Cos fabrics with tens of thousands of ports.

NOTE There are exceptions to the second point—where external connectivity attaches to the DC fabric. These exceptions are outside the scope of this book.

NOTE This book will always illustrate spine-and-leaf fabrics using a format like the illustration on the left of Figure 13-6.

In a telephone network, the sender always initiates the process of connecting (circuit) to the receiver. The make process is, therefore, unidirectional: circuits always flow from the sender to the receiver. In computer networks, however, any connected device can send traffic to any other connected device without making a circuit, so the flow is *bidirectional*.

Because traffic in computer networks can flow in either direction, they are called *folded fabrics*.

A final point of interest is when Clos fabrics are used to build a computer network—they are **noncontending** rather than nonblocking. There is no circuit setup process in a computer network, so the network itself cannot reject incoming traffic at the edge; a host cannot get a busy signal when it tries to send a packet through a network to another host.

In most cases, this is not a problem; every pair of hosts connected to a Clos fabric can send traffic to one another at the full bandwidth of their connection. However, if two hosts try to send traffic at their full bandwidth to a third host, the network will drop some of the traffic.

> **NOTE** This description of nonblocking assumes the fabric is not oversubscribed. Oversubscription is beyond the scope of this book.

Butterfly Fabrics

A **butterfly fabric** is like a Clos fabric but has five stages instead of three. Figure 13-7 illustrates a small butterfly fabric.

> **NOTE** Some network engineers called a butterfly a five-stage Clos. For clarity, this book always calls a three-stage spine-and-leaf a *Clos* and a five-stage the design described in this section a *butterfly*.

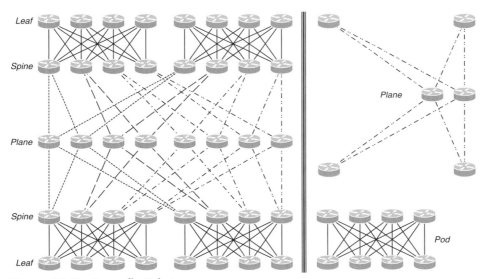

Figure 13-7 *Butterfly Fabric*

The left side of Figure 13-7 illustrates a butterfly fabric laid out "flat" so you can see all the connections. There are five hops, or stages, between any two ports in different pods, so this is a five-stage fabric.

The right side of Figure 13-7 illustrates the two parts of a butterfly fabric: the plane and the pod. The spine routers are in a pod and a fabric, which sometimes makes it hard to see the two parts on the drawing of a large-scale butterfly. These two pieces can be treated as separate modules for network design and lifecycle management:

- Once a packet enters a specific plane, it will travel along the plane to the destination. Designers can separate different kinds of traffic onto different planes to simplify quality of service (QoS) and other traffic management problems.

- There is only one path from any plane router to any destination on the fabric. Designers can use this property to steer packets through the fabric.

- A single pod can be removed, repaired or rebuilt, and re-added back to the fabric— without impacting the rest of the network. Operators can use this to build, test, and replace entire pods while the fabric remains in production.

- An entire plane can be removed and replaced with minimal impact on the network's operation.

Figure 13-8 illustrates another way butterfly fabrics are sometimes drawn.

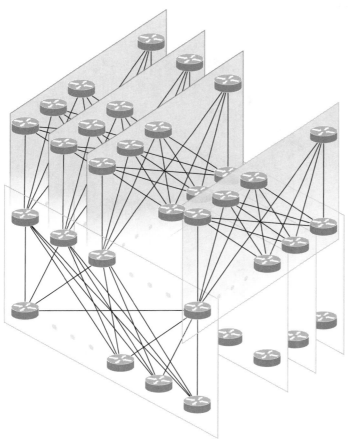

Figure 13-8   *A Three-Dimensional Illustration of a Butterfly Fabric*

Figure 13-8 is harder to decipher but more compact.

Butterfly fabrics can support hundreds of thousands of servers.

Chapter Review

Data center fabrics are a critical part of the Internet's infrastructure. Most of the shopping, playing, watching, searching, and anything else you do on an Internet-connected app happens on a data center fabric. Most of the traffic passing through the Internet also passes through data center fabrics, as do almost all telephone calls.

Designers almost universally choose three-stage spine-and-leaf fabrics for small- to large-scale fabrics and five-stage butterfly spine-and-leaf fabrics for large- to really large–scale fabrics. Spine-and-leaf fabrics have unique qualities: they are regular, nonplanar, and use large numbers of parallel links (high fan-out) to support vast amounts of traffic.

One key to doing well on the exams is to perform repetitive-spaced review sessions. Review this chapter's material using either the tools in the book or interactive tools for the same material found on the book's companion website. Refer to the online Appendix D, "Study Planner," element for more details. Table 13-2 outlines the key review elements and where you can find them. To better track your study progress, record when you completed these activities in the second column.

Table 13-2   Chapter Review Tracking

Review Element	Review Date (s)	Resource Used
Review key topics		Book, website
Review key terms		Book, website
Repeat DIKTA questions		Book, PTP
Review concepts and actions		Book, website

Review All the Key Topics

Table 13-3 lists the key topics for this chapter.

Table 13-3   Key Topics for Chapter 13

Key Topic Element	Description	Page Number
List	Three kinds of servers to build the web service	261
Paragraph	Data Center Interconnect (DCI)	261
Figure 13-2, Paragraph	Delay accumulation across a network	261
Bullet	Route server	263
List	How a network fabric differs from a traditional network	264
Paragraph	Folded fabrics	266

Key Terms You Should Know

Key terms in this chapter include

web service, web server, front-end server, back-end server, DCI, IXP, route server, fabric, nonplanar, fan-out, spine-and-leaf fabric, Clos fabric, nonblocking, noncontending, butterfly fabric

Concepts and Actions

Review the concepts considered in this chapter using Table 13-4. You can cover the right side of this table and describe each concept or action in your own words to verify your understanding.

Table 13-4   Concepts and Actions

Front-end server	Web server; formats data for a user to consume
Back-end server	Combines information from many sources to fulfill a user's request
Database service	Stores information about users, services, events, etc.
DCI	Data center interconnect; connects multiple DC fabrics
Delay accumulation	Impact of an application requiring multiple trips across the network to fulfill each user request
IXP	Internet exchange point (or provider); provides regional connectivity and colocation facilities
Route server	Carries routing information between routers connected to an IXP fabric
Nonplanar	A network that cannot be drawn without links crossing
High fan-out	Relying on large numbers of parallel links to provide the bandwidth required to support applications
Clos	Three-stage fabric design based on the work of Charlie Clos
Butterfly	Five-stage fabric design
Spine-and-leaf	A fabric design with spine and leaf nodes
ToR	Leaf node in a spine-and-leaf network; top of rack
Noncontending	A network that will not drop traffic as long as the link to no single attached device is overloaded
Nonblocking	A network that will refuse traffic at the edge if the traffic cannot be carried to the destination

CHAPTER 14

Network Transport

This chapter covers the following exam topics:

1. **Standards and Concepts**

   1.5. **Describe common network applications and protocols.**

   TCP vs. UDP (connection-oriented vs. connectionless), FTP, SFTP, TFTP, HTTP, HTTPS, DHCP, DNS, ICMP, NTP

The first part of this book covered the basics of addressing, routing, and network models. The second part covered the physical aspects of building networks and transporting data. Figure 14-1 illustrates these chapters compared to the Open Systems Interconnect (OSI) and Recursive Internet Architecture (RINA) models.

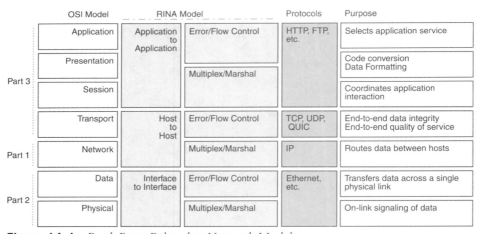

Figure 14-1 *Book Parts Related to Network Models*

This chapter returns to the beginning to consider the shipping boxes used to carry data through a network. The early chapters called this packaging *encapsulation*. What does this encapsulation look like? How does a transmitter package data so the receiver will understand it?

This chapter covers five protocols, their operation, and encapsulation:

- Internet Protocol version 4 (IPv4)

- Internet Protocol version 6 (IPv6)

- User Datagram Protocol (UDP)

- Transmission Control Protocol (TCP)

- QUIC

This chapter also touches on identifying flows, fragmentation, and *path maximum transmission unit (PMTU)* discovery.

"Do I Know This Already?" Quiz

Take the quiz (either here or use the PTP software) if you want to use the score to help you decide how much time to spend on this chapter. Appendix A, "Answers to the 'Do I Know This Already?' Quizzes," found at the end of the book, includes both the answers and explanations. You can also find answers in the PTP testing software.

Table 14-1 "Do I Know This Already?" Foundation Topics Section-to-Question Mapping

Section	Questions
Internet Protocol Version 4	1, 2, 3
Internet Protocol Version 6	4, 5
User Datagram Protocol	6
Transmission Control Protocol	7
Quick UDP Internet Connections (QUIC)	8
Identifying Flows	9
Path MTU Discovery	10

CAUTION The goal of self-assessment is to gauge your mastery of the topics in this chapter. If you do not know the answer to a question or are only partially sure of the answer, you should mark that question as wrong for purposes of the self-assessment. Giving yourself credit for an answer you incorrectly guess skews your self-assessment results and might provide you with a false sense of security.

1. What is the primary purpose of the Internet Protocol?

   a. Carry web pages across the Internet

   b. Provide a consistent set of network abstractions across different kinds of physical links

   c. Provide addressing for Internet-connected devices

   d. Support a lot of different kinds of hosts

2. What must a receiver do to use the data contained in a fragmented packet?

   a. Nothing; the data is usable the way it is received

   b. Reassemble the original packet as it was transmitted

   c. Request the sender retransmit the data in a smaller packet

   d. Reconstruct the packet based on Forward Error Correction (FEC) data

3. What is TTL used for in IP networks?

    a. Discard packets that have been forwarded too many times

    b. Determine the age of data being carried through the network

    c. Limit the number of encapsulations a router can place on a piece of data

    d. Aid in the correct ordering of packets carried through the network

4. What is PA address space?

    a. Address space that can be used independently of a single provider

    b. IP address space a registry assigns to a customer

    c. IP address space a provider assigns to a customer

    d. IP address space publicly usable by anyone to connect to the Internet

5. Why do many network engineers consider NAT harmful?

    a. NAT increases the size of packets being carried through the network.

    b. Embedded IP addresses will not match the source and destination addresses in the header.

    c. NAT breaks PMTUD.

    d. NAT makes it too hard to find the actual host that transmitted a packet.

6. What does a connection-oriented transport service provide?

    a. Flow control, error control, and limited-time delivery

    b. Services for applications that can operate even if small amounts of data are dropped

    c. Flow control, error control, and in-order data delivery

    d. Services for transmitting data to multiple destinations

7. What process do TCP and QUIC both use to set up a session?

    a. A nonce to identify the session

    b. Three-way handshake

    c. Two-way handshake

    d. Cryptographic key exchange

8. How does QUIC speed up the second connection between two applications?

    a. Skipping the three-way handshake

    b. Using previously stored encrypted session information to skip the three-way handshake and key exchange

    c. Skipping encryption key exchange

    d. Using faster UDP packets to carry the handshake

9. What five things (tuples) are used to identify a flow uniquely?

    a. Source address, destination address, protocol number, source port, destination port

    b. Source address, destination address, flow label, source port, destination port

    c. Source address, destination host identifier, protocol number, source port, destination port

    d. Source host identifier, destination address, flow label, source port, destination port

10. Why is path maximum transmission unit discovery important?

    a. To prevent IPv6 routers from fragmenting packets as they are carried through the network

    b. To prevent IPv4 packets from being dropped because they take too long to transmit

    c. To prevent IPv4 routers from fragmenting packets as they are carried through the network

    d. To prevent dropping packets when a link with a smaller MTU than the packet is encountered

Foundation Topics

Internet Protocol Version 4

In the early 1970s, scientists and engineers began working on a new computer networking technology. They designed this technology around a basic three-layer model:

- The *physical layer* would handle the physical process of carrying data between two interfaces.

- The *network layer* would provide an interface between physical transports (there were many at the time) and applications.

- The *application layer* would handle carrying data between applications using the network layer.

This initial set of protocols was called the *Transmission Control Protocol* or *Transmission Control Program*, both shortened to **TCP**.

In 1977, Jon Postel split TCP into two protocols—one providing the interface between physical and network transports and the second providing the actual transport of data, including **flow control** and **error control**. Postel's split significantly simplified both protocols.

The upper layer protocol was still called TCP, and the new lower layer protocol was called the *Internet Protocol (IP)*. Postel published a *Request for Comment (RFC)*, a format all researchers used to propose protocols, calling it TCPv3.

The research community worked on and with TCPv3 for two years, publishing *Internet Protocol version 4* (**IPv4**) in 1980. The United States Department of Defense (US DoD) adopted IPv4 for all its computer systems, and the *Internet Engineering Task Force (IETF)* adopted IPv4 as a standard in 1981.

IPv4's primary job is to provide a consistent set of networking abstractions across different physical links. Figure 14-2 illustrates the role of IPv4.

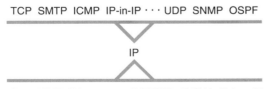

Figure 14-2 *The Role of IP*

All the protocols above IP in Figure 14-2 can run on any physical network topology without modification. The designers of each protocol below IP ensure the IP protocol can run their medium. Splitting IP from TCP allowed IP to focus on addressing and ensuring consistent formatting across different kinds of physical media.

IPv4 carries data through encapsulation—forming a packet by adding a header to a data block. Figure 14-3 illustrates the IPv4 header.

Version	IHL	Type of Service	Total Length	
Identification			Flags	Fragment Offset
TTL		Protocol	Header Checksum	
Source Address				
Destination Address				

Figure 14-3   *The IPv4 Header*

The IPv4 header carries a lot of information about where the packet of information is going, where it came from, and how it should be handled:

- *Version* is always 4.

- *Internet Header Length (IHL)* gives the total length of the header in octets.

- *Type of Service* describes how routers should queue this packet. Should this packet be given priority, can the packet be discarded, etc.?

- *Total Length* is the total length of the IPv4 packet in octets.

- *Identification* is used to control and identify fragments.

- *Flags* are used to control and identify fragments.

- *Fragment Offset* is used to identify fragment order for **reassembly**.

- *Time to Live (TTL)* notes how many routers may process this packet before it should be discarded.

- *Protocol* indicates the kind of protocol carried in this packet (UDP, TCP, etc.).

- *Header Checksum* provides a basic check for packet corruption in transmission.

> **NOTE**   Other fields, such as options, are outside the scope of this book.

Two fields are particularly interesting to network engineers—those used for **fragmentation** and the TTL.

Fragmentation

In Figure 14-4, Host *A* sends a packet toward server *D*.

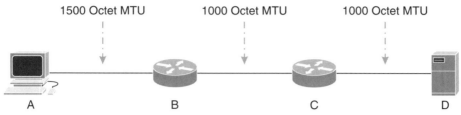

Figure 14-4   *Packet Fragmentation*

Because *A* only knows its local link, it builds a 1500-octet packet. Router *B* needs to forward this packet toward *C*, but the link between *B* and *C* can only support 1000 octets or smaller packets. Router *B* has two choices:

- Drop or discard the packet.
- Break the packet into smaller pieces, or *fragment* it.

Router *B* might break the packet into two smaller packets or *fragment* the packet. To fragment the packet, router *B*

- Copies the packet into memory.
- Splits the data the packet is carrying (called the *payload*).
- Copies the original header onto the newly created packet.
- Sets the *identifier* field in both packets to some number so the receiver knows these are part of a set of packets created from a single packet.
- Sets the *offset* field in the second header to where it splits the data.

Router *B* then forwards these two packets to router *C*, which then forwards them to server *D*. Server *D reassembles* the two packets into one and passes the data to the upper layer protocol for processing.

Fragmentation is no longer widely used in computer networks. Fragmenting packets requires a lot of processing power and memory. Most routers no longer support IPv4 fragmentation, and many hosts will discard fragmented packets.

Instead of fragmentation, most hosts now support *Path MTU Discovery*, considered in a later section.

Time to Live

In Figure 14-5, what if

- *B*'s best path to *F* is through *C*?
- *C*'s best path to *F* is through *E*?
- *E*'s best path to *F* is through *D*?
- *D*'s best path to *F* is through *B*?

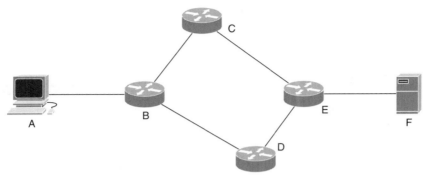

Figure 14-5   *Control Plane Routing Loop*

Why would router *E* point toward *D* to reach server *F* rather than to *F* itself? When a network runs two different routing protocols—each protocol serving a different purpose—this kind of *control plane routing loop* is possible because neither protocol might completely understand the topology. Humans also make mistakes.

If host *A* sends a packet to server *F*, the packet will be forwarded to *C* by *B*, then to *E* by *C*, then to *D* by *E*, then back to *B* by *D*, then to *C* by *B*, etc. Any packets *A* sends to *F* will be passed along this *forwarding loop* seemingly forever.

The job of *time to live* **(TTL)** is to prevent routers from eternally forwarding packets in a loop like this.

When host *A* sends a packet, it includes a TTL in the packet header. Each router forwarding the packet subtracts 1 from (or *decrements*) the TTL. If a router reduces the TTL to 0, it will discard the packet rather than forward it.

If, for instance, host *A* sends a packet with a TTL of 5 toward server *F*:

1. Router *B* would decrement the TTL by 1 while processing the packet and forward it to *C*.

2. Router *C* would decrement the TTL by 1 while processing the packet and forward it to *E*.

3. Assuming router *E*'s routing table is incorrectly using router *D* for the next hop toward *F*, router *E* will decrement the TTL by 1, so it is now 2, and forward the packet to *D*.

4. Assuming router *D*'s routing table uses *E* as its next hop toward server *F*, router *D* will decrement the TTL by 1, so it is now 1, and forward the packet to *E*.

5. Router *E* will receive the packet, decrement the TTL by 1 so it is now 0, and discard it.

Internet Protocol Version 6

The engineers and scientists working on RFC 971, the first standardized version of IPv4, concluded a 32-bit address space would be enough. At the time, there were 4.5 billion people worldwide, and a 32-bit address space can support up to 4.3 billion addresses. The folks working on specifying IPv4 could not anticipate several things, however, including

■ The commoditization of computer hardware and the accompanying explosion of smaller computers individual businesses and users could afford.

- The introduction of portable devices, such as cellular telephones and tables, which connect to the Internet.

- The connection of millions of "things" to the Internet, such as appliances and control systems.

- The amount of IP address space wasted through aggregation.

The IETF made several attempts to use existing IPv4 address space more efficiently, such as *Network Address Translation (NAT)*. In January 2011, IANA allocated the last two address blocks to registries.

The only real solution was to design a new protocol with a larger address space.

IPv6 Goals

*Internet Protocol version 6 (**IPv6**)* was designed with a variety of goals, including

- Increasing the address space from 32 bits to 128 bits.

- Building autoconfiguration of devices into the protocol.

- Allowing extensions to the IP header.

- Eliminating NAT.

- Eliminating packet fragmentation.

Two of these goals are worth examining in a little more detail.

Autoconfiguration

Chapter 2 described how IPv6's *Stateless Address Autoconfiguration (SLAAC)* works, but not why IPv6's designers included autoconfiguration in the base protocol.

Renumbering entire networks full of thousands of devices is challenging. Even when using DHCP to configure devices, it can take months of planning, testing, and work to move from one set of IP addresses to another. Because renumbering is hard, network operators prefer not to renumber.

The difficulty of renumbering, however, must be balanced against the efficient use of the IPv6 address space.

Smaller organizations need smaller blocks of address space, which

- Are harder to aggregate, increasing the number of routes carried by routers in the Internet core.

- Are difficult to recover when a smaller organization fails or no longer needs the address space.

It is more efficient for registries to allocate IP addresses to network providers, and for network providers to assign address space to their customers. However, if smaller organizations are assigned addresses by their provider, they must renumber their networks every time they change providers.

In other words, *provider-assigned (**PA**)* addresses are more efficient for the global Internet, while *provider-independent (**PI**)* addresses are more efficient for organizations building and operating networks.

Operators can resolve this tension using NAT. If an operator translates private internal addresses to external public addresses, they can change providers by changing the configuration on a few edge devices.

One of IPv6's original goals was to eliminate NAT, so IPv6's designers included autoconfiguration in the base protocol specification.

Autoconfiguration has not proven ideal in every situation, however. For instance:

- Autoconfiguration is still difficult to deploy in very large networks.

- Some organizations must legally be able to tie a specific IP address to a specific user.

- NAT arguably has some utility in network security.

- Tying a host's IPv6 address to its physical address can have bad security side effects.

An IPv6 version of *Dynamic Host Configuration Protocol (DHCPv6)* was developed and deployed to resolve some of these problems for large organizations, and NAT is still in widespread use.

Eliminating NAT

Figure 14-6 illustrates one reason IPv6's designers wanted to eliminate NAT.

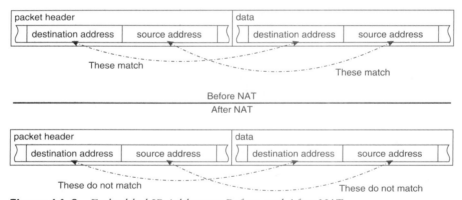

Figure 14-6   *Embedded IP Addresses Before and After NAT*

Some applications embed the source and destination addresses *within* the data portion of the packet. If the source and destination addresses are translated, the addresses in the header and the data portion of the packet no longer work, and the application will not work correctly.

NAT implementors have largely learned how to mitigate these changes, but NAT deployments can still sometimes be messy.

IPv6's designers also wanted to eliminate NAT to increase path visibility through the entire Internet. Translating the source and destination addresses makes it more difficult for network operators to trace the path of a packet from source to destination.

As with autoconfiguration, NAT has proven more challenging to eliminate than IPv6's designers anticipated. A stateless NAT form, NAT66, is still widely available for IPv6 networks.

IPv6 Packet Format

The IPv6 packet header is simpler than the IPv4 packet header. Figure 14-7 illustrates.

Version	Traffic Class	Flow Label	
Payload Length		Next Header	Hop Limit
Source Address			
Destination Address			

Figure 14-7 *The IPv6 Header*

The most apparent difference between the IPv6 and IPv4 headers is all the fragmentation fields, including identification, flags, and fragment offset, are missing. Routers cannot fragment IPv6 packets, so removing these fields from the header makes sense.

A host can use the *flow label* to identify a group or stream of related packets.

IPv6 uses the *hop limit* to limit the number of times a packet can be forwarded—just like the IPv4 TTL.

The *next header* field indicates either the type of protocol data carried in this packet—UDP, TCP, etc.—or the kind of *extension header* following this header. IPv6 extension headers extend the protocol's capabilities, as shown in Figure 14-8.

IPv4 Header

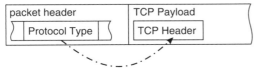

IPv6 Header

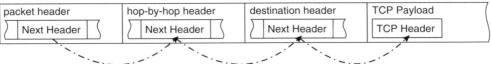

Figure 14-8 *IPv6 Extension Headers*

IPv4's *protocol type* field can contain only a protocol. Because of this, there is no easy way to extend IPv4 headers to include tunneling information, processing instructions to routers, etc.

On the other hand, IPv6's *next header* can describe an extension header or a protocol type. Hosts can chain multiple extension headers onto the IPv6 header. Routers process information in the *hop-by-hop header*, and hosts process information in the *destination header*.

Routers process *only* the hop-by-hop header.

User Datagram Protocol

User Datagram Protocol (UDP) provides a connectionless transport service for carrying data across an IP network.

Connectionless versus Connection-Oriented Transport Protocols

Table 14–2 describes the differences between **connectionless transport** and **connection-oriented transport**.

Table 14-2   Connectionless versus Connection-oriented Transport Protocols

Characteristic	Connectionless	Connection-oriented
Basic Description	Simple "send-and-forget" protocol	Looks like a circuit, or a direct connection between two devices
Connection Process	None; source just sends packets to the destination	Uses some form of *handshake* to verify devices on either end of the circuit can communicate
Reaction to Dropped Packets, Segments, or Data	None	Tracks transmitted data and requests retransmission if anything is missing
Reaction to Transmission Errors	If detected, data is dropped	Requests retransmission if detected
Flow Control	None; transmitter sends at its own pace	Transmitter and receiver communicate to ensure data is being transmitted at a rate both can support
Data Reordering	Not detected	Reorders data correctly if detected

As a connectionless protocol, UDP offers very few services; the transmitter puts data into UDP-encapsulated segments, puts these segments into IP packets, and sends them.

Connectionless protocols are useful for

- Short, single-packet transmissions, like the *Domain Name Service (DNS)*.

- Streaming applications, like voice or video, where a single lost or corrupted packet of information can easily be ignored, and by the time missed information is retransmitted, it would not be valuable.

- When a transmitter wants more than one host to receive the packet (such as multicast and broadcast).

NOTE   Chapter 2, "Addresses," describes multicast and broadcast.

NOTE   Chapter 16, "Names and Time," describes DNS.

The UDP Header

UDP has a simple header, shown in Figure 14-9.

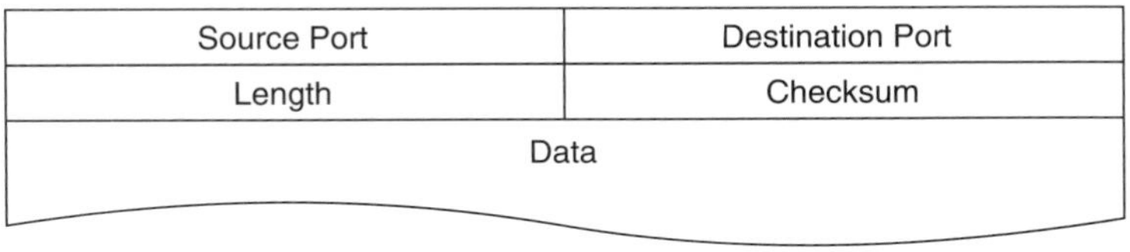

Source Port	Destination Port
Length	Checksum
Data	

Figure 14-9   *The UDP Segment Header*

UDP uses the *source* and *destination* ports to determine which application or service should receive this data. The *length* describes the amount of data this segment carries in octets.

Checksums

Many computer network protocols use a *checksum* to determine whether data has been changed in transit. Transmitters use a formula or process to calculate a checksum when sending a packet, placing the result into a field in the packet.

Receivers also use the same formula or process to calculate a checksum. If the receiver's calculated result matches the one the transmitter stored in the packet, the data has not been changed. If these two calculations do not match, the data has been changed.

Transmission Control Protocol

The *Transmission Control Protocol (TCP)* is a connection-oriented transport protocol. Connection-oriented protocols are useful for

- Transmitting large amounts of data, such as large files.

- Transmitting continuing streams where losing information cannot be tolerated, such as stock market information.

For instance, TCP is used for carrying emails and websites because these kinds of data are large and sensitive to data loss.

Building a TCP Connection

TCP builds a *connection* to:

- Make certain transmitted data is received

- Make certain data is transmitted and received in the same order

- Control the transmitter's speed so neither the network nor the receiver is overwhelmed

Unlike early physically switched telephone networks—like the ones Chapter 13 describes—TCP runs over a packet-based IP network. TCP builds a virtual connection, or *session*, rather than a physical one, to support streaming over underlying less-than-reliable networks.

TCP uses a **three-way handshake** to build the initial connection. Figure 14-10 illustrates the three-way handshake process.

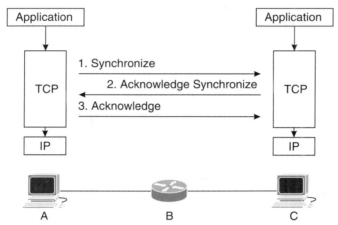

Figure 14-10   *TCP Three-way Handshake*

The three steps shown in Figure 14-10 are

1.   Host *A* sends a packet to *C* indicating it would like to open a new TCP connection. This packet contains an opening *sequence number*, used to track transmitted and received data, and a port number indicating which application running on *C* should receive data carried over this session. This packet is often called an *SYN*.

2.   Host *C* determines if the application indicated by the port number is running. If the application exists, host *C* will set aside memory for this connection, build the data structures needed to track the connection state, and send an *acknowledgment* packet back to *A*. This packet will also contain a SYN from *C* so the connection's parameters can be set correctly. This packet is often called a *SYN-ACK*, and the connection is *half-open*.

3.   Host *A* learns *C* is reachable through the network and the correct application is running on *C* by receiving *C*'s acknowledgment. To complete the circuit setup, *A* acknowledges *C*'s SYN. This packet is often called an *SYN-ACK ACK* or just an *ACK*.

Host *A* uses a port number to indicate which application on *C* should receive the data carried on in this session. Chapter 2 described port numbers as the address of an application running on a host.

It is not uncommon for hosts to have multiple TCP sessions, as shown in Figure 14-11.

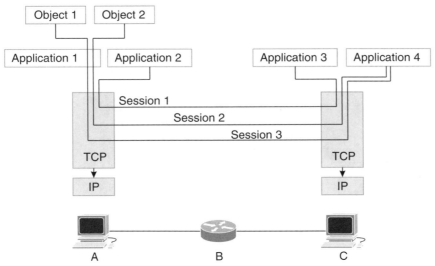

Figure 14-11 *Multiple TCP Sessions Between Hosts*

In Figure 14-11:

- Application 1, running on host *A*, has two objects—images, text files, etc.—to send to application 4, running on host *C*. Rather than sending these two objects in a single TCP session, *A* opens two sessions to *C*.

- Application 3, running on host *A*, opens a separate TCP session to host *C* to send data to application 4.

TCP will open one session per application. Applications may also open more than one TCP session. Two TCP sessions running in parallel will transfer data faster than a single session until the network, or one of the two hosts, runs out of resources.

There are two ways TCP on host *A* can terminate the session:

- Stop sending data. If *A* doesn't send data for a while, *B* will terminate the session.

- Send a *reset*, or *RST*, packet.

TCP Flow and Error Control

Applications rely on TCP to deliver packets without errors and without overwhelming the network or receiver. TCP uses *sliding window flow control* to accomplish these goals. Figure 14-12 illustrates **windowed flow control**.

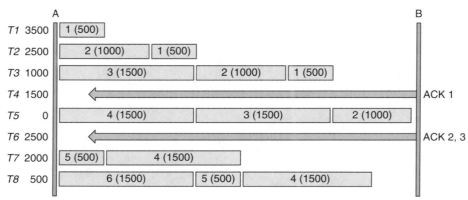

Figure 14-12   *Windowed Flow Control*

Let's look at the labels in Figure 14-12 before looking at how windowed flow control works:

- On the far left, *T1* through *T8* indicate periods of time. Whether these are seconds, milliseconds, or something in between does not matter.

- The next column, starting with *3500* at the top, is how many octets of data *A* can transmit at this moment in time.

- The center portion of the illustration shows packets *A* has transmitted and *B* has not acknowledged. Each packet has a label (*1 through* 6) and a size. Each packet also has a *sequence number*, which is not shown in the illustration.

- The arrows from *B* to *A* represent acknowledgments for data transmitted from *B* to *A*.

- The far-right column tells you which packets of data *B* is acknowledging.

The *window size* in Figure 14-12 is 4000 octets, which means *A* may send a total of 4000 octets of data to *B* before waiting for *B* to acknowledge receiving some data. In Figure 14-12:

- **T1:** *A* transmits a single 500-octet packet of data toward *B*, labeled *packet 1*. Packet 1 will have a sequence number of 1. The *window size* is 4000 octets, so *A* can still transmit another 3500 octets of data before waiting for an acknowledgment.

- **T2:** As far as *A* can tell, packet 1 is still "in flight," either carried through the network or processed at *B*. *A* transmits packet 2, which has a length of 1000 octets. Packet 2's sequence number will be 501; packet 1's sequence number will be added to packet 1's length. *A* can still transmit another 2500 octets of data before waiting for *B* to acknowledge receiving any data.

- **T3:** Packets 1 and 2 are in flight, but *A* can still send up to 2500 octets of data. *A* sends packet 3, which is 1500 octets long. *A* can only send another 1000 octets of data before being forced to wait for *B* to acknowledge receiving some packets it has already transmitted. Packet 3's sequence number is set to 1501, and packet 2's sequence number is added to packet 2's length.

- **T4:** *B* receives packet 1 and sends an acknowledgment (shown as *ACK 1* in Figure 14-12). *A* can now send 1500 more octets of data—the 1000 octets it could send at *T3* plus the 500 octets *B* just acknowledged receiving.

- **T5:** Packets 2 and 3 are still in flight, but *A* can send another 1500 octets of data without waiting on *B*. *A* transmits packet 4, which is 1500 octets. *A* cannot send more data until *B* acknowledges receiving some packets, so its window is now set to 0. Packet 4's sequence number is set to 3001, packet 3's sequence number plus packet 3's length.

- **T6:** *B* acknowledges receiving packets 2 and 3. *A* can now send up to 2500 octets of data before being forced to wait on *B*.

- **T7:** Packet 4 is still in flight. *A* transmits packet 5, leaving it with 2000 octets it can send before being forced to wait on *B*. Packet 5's sequence number is 4501, and packet 4's sequence number is added to packet 4's length.

- **T8:** *A* sends packet 6, so it can only send 500 octets before being forced to wait on *B*. Packet 6's sequence number is 5001, and packet 5's sequence number is added to packet 5's length.

By examining the sequence numbers, *B* can tell the network has dropped a packet. For instance, if packet 5 were dropped when *B* receives packet 6, it will notice the 500-octet "gap" in the sequence numbers:

- Packet 4's sequence number is 3001, and its length is 1500 octets.

- Packet 6's sequence number is 5001, and its length is 1500 octets.

Subtracting packet 4's length from packet 6's sequence number leaves a gap of 500 octets, so a 500-octet packet must have been dropped someplace. A gap in the sequence numbers can be caused by *A* sending *B* data too fast or because a router's queue fills up, forcing the router to drop the packet.

B can also verify each packet has been transmitted without error using the included checksum. Corrupted packets are intentionally dropped at *B*.

If *B* detects a dropped packet, it will send *A* a retransmit request. Missing packets—no matter the reason—always mean the transmitter needs to slow down.

This example uses 4000 octets as a window size. In actual TCP implementations, the window size varies over time.

When a transmitter receives a retransmit request, it closes the window and enters *slow start*. Closing the window means the transmitter will wait for the receiver to acknowledge receiving data more often; less data will be in flight at any given time.

As data is successfully transmitted (each time the receiver acknowledges receiving data), the window size is opened or grows larger.

> **NOTE** Algorithms used to calculate the correct window size based on network conditions are complex and outside the scope of this book.

Quick UDP Internet Connections (QUIC)

TCP has several significant limitations, including

- A three-way handshake is required for all connections, even between previously connected hosts.

- Multiple TCP sessions, each requiring a three-way handshake, are required to carry multiple data streams, as shown in Figure 14-11.

- TCP does not automatically encrypt data. A second protocol, such as *Transport Layer Security (TLS)*, must encrypt data with TCP.

- Because the TCP header is not encrypted, the inner workings of TCP are transparent to middleboxes. Some network devices modify TCP header fields while processing packets, making it hard to modify the TCP specifications.

> **NOTE**   Chapter 20, "Security Tools," considers data encryption in more detail.

Google initially deployed *Quick UDP Internet Connections (**QUIC**)* through its web browser and across their servers in 2012. The IETF began working on Internet standards for QUIC in 2013. Some key points about QUIC include

- QUIC uses the same sliding window flow control mechanism as TCP.

- QUIC sessions can carry multiple streams of data rather than just one.

- The entire QUIC header and data are carried inside a UDP packet. Routers, switches, and other network middleboxes do not "see" QUIC packets, only UDP packets.

The unique part of QUIC is the session connection process. Figure 14-13 compares TCP's session connection process with TLS encryption to QUIC's session connection process.

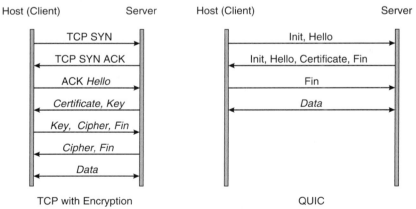

Figure 14-13   *TCP, Encryption, and QUIC Session Connection Processes*

From top to bottom of the diagram, the arrows show which direction each kind of data is sent (client to server or server to client). The previous section on TCP session setup discussed the SYN, SYN-ACK, and ACK used by TCP. QUIC's *Init* is similar to TCP's SYN, and QUIC's *Fin* is similar to TCP's ACK.

The remaining information relates to encryption, including

- The *certificate* contains information about the host.

- The *key* contains a key used to encrypt data carried over this session.

- The *cipher* describes or sets the algorithm used to encrypt data carried over this session.

QUIC initializes a session in fewer steps by combining some steps and eliminating overlapping steps.

QUIC assigns a nonce, or a unique identifier, to the session during session setup. If a client connects to a server using TCP to retrieve some information, disconnects, and reconnects a few minutes later, the entire TCP three-way handshake must be repeated. If the client connects using QUIC, it can supply the nonce from a previous session and pick up where it left off.

Identifying Flows

Figure 14-14 shows a packet with both IP and TCP headers.

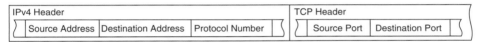

Figure 14-14 *A Packet with IP and TCP Headers*

There are five identifiers in Figure 14-14:

- Source address

- Destination address

- Protocol number

- Source port

- Destination port

This set of five identifiers is unique for any session between two hosts on a network. This set of identifiers, often called the **five tuples**, is used to identify, log, and track sessions.

Path MTU Discovery

In Figure 14-15, host *A* would like to send a packet to server *E*.

If *A* sends a packet 4000 octets long, router *B* must fragment the packet (as described earlier in this chapter) or drop the packet. Even if router *B* decides to fragment the packet, *C* will receive a packet too large to transmit to *D*, so *D* will either need to fragment the packet again or drop the packet.

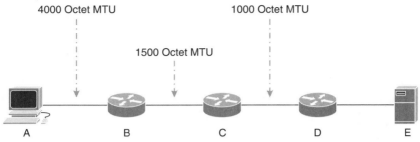

Figure 14-15   *Path MTU Discovery*

As noted in the previous discussion of fragmentation in this chapter, few routers support fragmentation, and IPv6 does not even provide the fields needed for routers to fragment packets. Even if fragmentation is available, it would be better for host *A* to send packets that can be forwarded through the entire network without modification.

Host *A* can discover the largest packet it can send to *E* if

- Each device that discards a packet sends an ICMP *Fragmentation Needed* error for IPv4 packets or an ICMP *Packet Too Big* error for IPv6 packets.

- Host *A* receives these ICMP error message packets and reduces the size of the packets it sends.

The process of routers sending ICMP messages when a packet cannot be forwarded because it is too large and the source host adjusting the size of the packets it sends is called *Path MTU Discovery (***PMTUD***)*.

Some routers—and other middleboxes—are configured so they do not send ICMP errors when a packet is dropped, so PMTUD does not always work.

Chapter Review

This chapter considered the five most common transport services provided by IP networks:

- IPv4

- IPv6

- UDP

- TCP

- QUIC

IPv4 and IPv6 separate the physical and logical data transmission so IP networks can work across many physical networks. UDP provides a simple data transport method ideal for situations where small amounts of data can be dropped without causing an application to fail. TCP and QUIC provide a more complex data transport mechanism with flow control, error control, and encryption.

Along the way, this chapter explored fragmentation, connectionless data transmission, connection-oriented data transmission, identifying flows, and PMTUD.

In the next chapter, we move up a layer to discuss application transport, including protocols designed to transfer files, remotely access a system, and carry web pages across the Internet.

One key to doing well on the exams is to perform repetitive-spaced review sessions. Review this chapter's material using either the tools in the book or interactive tools for the same material found on the book's companion website. Refer to the online Appendix D, "Study Planner," element for more details. Table 14-3 outlines the key review elements and where you can find them. To better track your study progress, record when you completed these activities in the second column.

Table 14-3 Chapter Review Tracking

Review Element	Review Date (s)	Resource Used
Review key topics		Book, website
Review key terms		Book, website
Repeat DIKTA questions		Book, PTP
Review concepts and actions		Book, website

Review All the Key Topics

Table 14-4 lists the key topics for this chapter.

Table 14-4 Key Topics for Chapter 14

Key Topic Element	Description	Page Number
Paragraph	Primary job of IPv4	275
Paragraph	IPv4 data encapsulation	276
Paragraph, list	Packet fragmentation	277
Paragraph	Difference between PA and PI addresses	280
Section	IPv6 Packet Format	281
Table 14-2	Characteristics of connectionless and connection-oriented transport protocols	282
List	Usefulness of connectionless protocols	282
Figure 14-10, list	TCP three-way handshake	284
Paragraph	TCP sessions and relationships to applications	285
Figure 14-12, list	Windowed flow control	285
Paragraph	Window size in TCP implementations	287
Paragraph	Slow start	287

Key Topic Element	Description	Page Number
Paragraph	QUIC and nonces	289
Section	Identifying Flows	289
Paragraph	Path MTU Discovery (PMTUD)	290

Key Terms You Should Know

Key terms in this chapter include

TCP, flow control, error control, IPv4, reassembly, fragmentation, TTL, IPv6, PA address space, PI address space, connectionless transport, connection-oriented transport, three-way handshake, windowed flow control, QUIC, five-tuple, PMTUD

Concepts and Actions

Review the concepts considered in this chapter using Table 14-5. You can cover the right side of this table and describe each concept or action in your own words to verify your understanding.

Table 14-5   Concepts and Actions

IP's primary role	Provide a consistent set of networking abstractions across different kinds of physical links
IPv4 fragment offset	Used to identify fragment order for reassembly
Checksum	Provides a basic check for packet corruption
Fragmentation	Breaking a packet into multiple smaller packets so it can be carried across a smaller MTU link
TTL	Time to live; used to prevent a packet from being forwarded eternally in a forwarding loop
IPv6 goals	Increase address space, autoconfiguration, header extensions, eliminate NAT, eliminate fragmentation
NAT application impact	Mismatched embedded and header addresses
IPv6 Next Header	Either indicates which upper layer protocol is being carried in the packet or the type of header following this header
Connectionless	A simple service to transmit data across a network
Connection-oriented	A more complex transport service providing retransmission in the case of dropped packets or errors, and provides flow control
UDP	Connectionless IP-based transport protocol
Best for streaming applications	Connectionless transport
Best for sending data to multiple destinations	Connectionless transport
Three-way handshake	Used by TCP and WUIC to build a session
Multiple TCP sessions	Two hosts may build multiple TCP sessions to support multiple applications or for a single application to carry multiple objects

CHAPTER 15

Application Transport

This chapter covers the following exam topics:

1. **Standards and Concepts**

    1.5. **Describe common network applications and protocols.**

    TCP vs. UDP (connection-oriented vs. connectionless), FTP, SFTP, TFTP, HTTP, HTTPS, DHCP, DNS, ICMP, NTP

This chapter continues moving further from the physical transport elements, beyond network transport services, to look at application transport services. It might seem as though between the physical transport protocols, like Ethernet, and the network transport protocols, like the *Internet Protocol (IP)* and *Transport Control Protocol (TCP)*, computer networks would not need any more transport protocols. Why keep adding layers once the four fundamental problems—multiplexing, marshaling, error control, and flow control—are solved?

There are two reasons: address context and fitting the protocol to the transferred data.

Chapter 2, "Addresses," first introduced *address scope*: an address has meaning only within a given scope. IP addresses have meaning within the scope of the network, and port numbers have meaning within the scope of a single host. There are, at times, addresses below these, such as a specific window within a web browser. Higher-level protocols provide these kinds of addresses.

Chapter 14, "Network Transport," introduced *connectionless* and *connection-oriented* network transports, and yet, TCP does not understand the *kind* of data it carries. Application designers can increase efficiency by transferring some of the complexity of application communications from the application into the protocols. Application-level transport protocols help applications by absorbing some complexity, making applications more straightforward to develop and deploy.

This chapter often strays into applications these services are tied to. Specifically, this chapter considers *Secure Shell (SSH)*, *Secure Hypertext Transfer Protocol (HTTPs)*, and *Secure File Transfer Protocol (SFTP)*.

Before jumping into these protocols, this chapter describes one final protocol concept: *Type-Length-Value (**TLV**)* and *Fixed-Length* data formatting. These two formatting, or *marshaling*, methods are used in every network protocol, from physical to application transport.

"Do I Know This Already?" Quiz

Take the quiz (either here or use the PTP software) if you want to use the score to help you decide how much time to spend on this chapter. Appendix A, "Answers to the 'Do I Know This Already?' Quizzes," found at the end of the book, includes both the answers and explanations. You can also find answers in the PTP testing software.

Table 15-1 "Do I Know This Already?" Foundation Topics Section-to-Question Mapping

Section	Questions
Marshaling Systems	1, 2, 3, 4, 5
Secure Shell	6, 7
Hypertext Transfer Protocol	8
File Transfer Protocol	9

CAUTION The goal of self-assessment is to gauge your mastery of the topics in this chapter. If you do not know the answer to a question or are only partially sure of the answer, you should mark that question as wrong for purposes of the self-assessment. Giving yourself credit for an answer you incorrectly guess skews your self-assessment results and might provide you with a false sense of security.

1. What are the two primary ways protocols encode data? (Choose two.)
   a. Type-length value encoding
   b. Compressed bit encoding
   c. Fixed-length encoding
   d. Binary

2. What two context items does a protocol provide for interpreting bits on a wire? (Choose two.)
   a. Bit pattern
   b. Grammar
   c. Dictionary
   d. Command codes

3. What is the difference between a type-value and a type-length value?
   a. Type-value encoding assumes the length of the value is fixed.
   b. Type-length value encoding assumes the length of the value is fixed.
   c. Type-length value encoding indicates the length and type of information carried.
   d. Type-length encoding assumes the kind of information is fixed.

4. Why can fixed-length encoding be considered more efficient than TLVs?
   a. Fixed-length fields can be encrypted more easily.
   b. The type and length fields must be carried along with the data itself.
   c. Fixed-length fields will always be carried, regardless of whether they are needed.
   d. Fixed-length fields can be compressed more easily.

5. Why can TLVs be considered more efficient than fixed-length encoding?
   a. More TLVs will fit into a packet than fixed-length fields.
   b. TLVs can be encrypted more easily.
   c. Fixed-length fields will always be carried, regardless of whether they are needed.
   d. If the TLV is properly defined, you need only one per packet to carry every kind of information.

6. Secure Shell (SSH) is used for

    a. Transporting HTML files from a server to a client.

    b. Accessing the command line of a remote system through a terminal.

    c. Transporting large media files from a server to a client.

    d. Securely observing the screen of another computer.

7. Why should you set up an SSH key rather than using a username and password?

    a. You never need to enter a password again if you use an SSH key.

    b. SSH connections are not encrypted unless you use an SSH key.

    c. You can use the same SSH key on multiple servers.

    d. The username and password are only used to create a key in SSH.

8. What kinds of information can the Hypertext Transfer Protocol (HTTP) carry?

    a. Hypertext

    b. Video, images, hypertext, and many others

    c. Video, images, and hypertext

    d. Hypertext and images

9. How many TCP sessions does an FTP session require?

    a. One

    b. Two

    c. Three

    d. Four

Foundation Topics

Marshaling Systems

There are two common ways to format data in a computer network: the *fixed-length field* and *type-length-value*. The following sections consider each of these.

Fixed-Length Fields

How should a host interpret the bits shown in Figure 15-1?

```
0110 0000 0000 0000 0000 0000 0000 0000
0000 0101 1101 1100 0000 0110 0001 0000
0010 0000 0000 0001 0000 1101 1011 1000
0000 0011 1110 1000 0000 0000 0000 0000
0000 0000 0000 0000 0000 0000 0000 0000
0000 0001 0000 0000 0000 0001 0000 0001
```

Figure 15-1 *A Series of Bits Received*

What the host needs is

  ■ Context describing what these bits contain, or a **grammar**.

  ■ Translations from sets of bits to data, or a **dictionary**.

For instance, applying the IPv6 header specific to the string of bits shown in Figure 15-1 results in Figure 15-2.

Ver	Class		Flow Label			
0110	0000	0000	0000	0000	0000 0000 0000	

Payload Length		Next Hdr	Hop Limit
0000 0101 1101 1100		0000 0110	0001 0000

Source (1)	Source (2)
0010 0000 0000 0001	0000 1101 1011 1000

Source (3)	Source (4)
0000 0011 1110 1000	0000 0000 0000 0000

Source (5)	Source (6)
0000 0000 0000 0000	0000 0000 0000 0000

Source (7)	Source (8)
0000 0001 0000 0000	0000 0001 0000 0001

Figure 15-2 *Using Fixed-Length Fields to Interpret Bit Received*

Overlaying the IPv6 header fields, the host can interpret these bits as

- Version: 6

- Class: 0

- Flow label: 0

- Payload length: 1500

- Next header (type): 6

- Hope limit: 16

- Source (1): 2001

- Source (2): db8

- Source (3): 3e8

- Source (4): 0

- Source (5): 0

- Source (6): 100

- Source (7): 101

This IPv6 packet, containing a TCP segment, can be forwarded through 16 more routers, sourced from 2001:db8:3e8::100:101.

The host knows where each field is in this string of bits because the contents and length of each field are described in a standard **protocol specification**. Each field in the protocol is described with a *fixed length*, so this kind of encoding is called **fixed-length encoding**, or *fixed-length fields*.

If the transmitter and receiver use the same standard to encode or marshal the data into a stream of bits, they can transfer data across the network. Figure 15-3 illustrates the relationship between the sender, receiver, and specification.

15

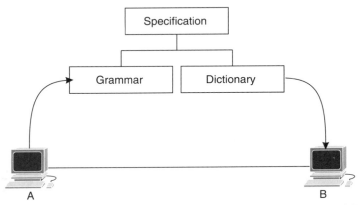

Figure 15-3 *Relationship Between Transmitter, Receiver, and Specification*

In Figure 15-3:

- An external organization, developer, etc., creates a specification for a protocol.

- A coder develops an application that encodes and decodes data using the specification.

- This software is installed on host *A*, where it is used to encode data using the specification.

- This software is installed on host *B*, where it is used to decode data using the specification.

The protocol specification provides the grammar and dictionary required to build the application that encodes and decodes data carried across the network.

Type-Length Values

Fixed-length fields place all the interpretative elements in the protocol specification outside the communications channel. Because of this, fixed-length encoding often uses network resources efficiently; the network does not need to carry any additional information to describe transmitted data.

There are, however, two situations where fixed-length encoding is suboptimal:

- Carrying a field of rarely used information in every packet to make fixed-length encoding work can be wasteful. For instance, the IPv6 header has several rarely used extension headers. If they were included in the base header, the network would carry around a lot of 0s for no reason.

- Carrying variable-length information in a fixed-length field is nearly impossible. For instance, a protocol may support either a 32-bit IPv4 address or a 128-bit IPv6 address, but not both simultaneously.

Figure 15-4 illustrates three ways to encode either an IPv4 or IPv6 address.

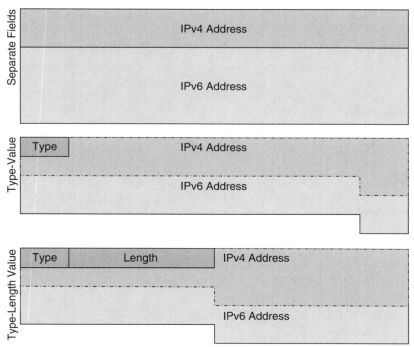

Figure 15-4 *Variable-Length Field Encoding Options*

The top of Figure 15-4 illustrates encoding IPv4 and IPv6 addresses in separate fields. If the protocol can support only one or the other, the space for the alternate address will be filled with 0s, being carried through the network and consuming space in the *maximum transmission unit (MTU)* for no reason.

The center of Figure 15-4 illustrates the same information but using a *type* field. The protocol's specification can use this field to carry either an IPv4 or IPv6 address in the single address field:

- If type is set to 4, the field is 32 bits long and contains an IPv4 address.

- If type is set to 6, the field is 128 bits long and contains an IPv6 address.

Including just a type, making the field a *type-value*, is useful when the field can contain one of several possible values, each of which has a specific length.

The bottom of Figure 15-4 illustrates including both *type* and *length* fields. The protocol's specification can use these two fields to carry either an IPv4 or IPv6 address in the single address field:

- If type is set to 4, the field's length is set to 32 bits, and the address field carries an IPv4 address.

- If type is set to 6, the field's length is set to 128 bits, and the address field carries an IPv6 address.

TLVs contain both a *type* and *length*. TLVs are often used when the data type does not imply or specify its length. For instance, imagine carrying a digital music file—the kind of data is "music," but the length will depend on the individual song, so you need to specify both.

TLVs are also useful when you want to carry one or more items. For instance, suppose you want to be able to encode anywhere from 1 to 30 IPv4 addresses in a single packet. In this case, you could have a type indicating the field carries IPv4 addresses and a length indicating how many IPv4 addresses are included.

TLVs are used in virtually every protocol, including routing protocols like BGP and application layer transport protocols like HTTPs.

Secure Shell

Network engineers rely on the *command-line interface (CLI)*, accessed via a *command prompt*. The most reliable way to access the command prompt is by physically connecting a computer to the device's console port.

But in large-scale networks, routers, switches, and other network devices can be scattered all over the world. Even if you are in the same building with a network device, why would you want to get up from your desk and go into a particular (and perhaps cramped) room so you can plug your computer into a physical device?

Network engineers rely on remote access to the command prompt through a *terminal application*.

*Secure Shell (**SSH**)*, designed as a secure replacement for *Telnet*, is one of the most widely used terminal applications, so it is worth knowing.

Because SSH is an application, it must be installed on both the client—the host you will be accessing the server from—and the server. Most devices you connect to, including routers, switches, and Linux hosts, will already have an SSH application installed.

Linux and macOS hosts also already have SSH installed. Windows does not have SSH installed, but many different SSH programs are available. The most widely used Windows SSH program is called *PuTTY*. Because PuTTY is an open-source application developed and maintained by volunteers, it is free to download and use.

Figure 15-5 illustrates SSH's connection setup.

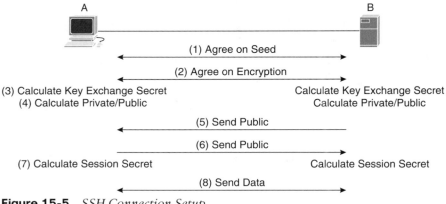

Figure 15-5   *SSH Connection Setup*

Host *A* begins the connection by starting a *Transmission Control Protocol (TCP)* session on port 22 with server *B*. Once the TCP three-way handshake is complete, *A* and *B* negotiate a *seed (1)* and the session encryption method (2). Once *A* and *B* have agreed on these parameters, they use the seed value to generate a secret key, or *key exchange secret (3)*, and a *private/public key pair (4)*.

NOTE   Chapter 20, "Security Tools," describes asymmetric encryption using private/public key pairs and symmetric encryption using secret keys.

Server *B* sends its newly generated public key to host *A (5)*, and host *A* sends it to server *B (6)*.

Host *A* and server *B* calculate a secret key to encrypt the data using the encryption method negotiated at (2). This key is used to encrypt transmitted data and unencrypt received data.

This process might seem overly complex, but it results from engineers, developers, and cryptographers working together to build a very secure system. SSH is designed so attackers will find breaking into, or listening in on, an SSH session challenging. Each point where a key might be compromised is protected using the results of a prior step.

Connecting to a host or network device using SSH is simple:

- On Apple macOS or Linux computers, open a terminal window. At the prompt, type **ssh**, followed by the IP address or hostname of the device you would like to connect to.

- On Windows computers, install and run the PuTTY terminal emulator. Type in the name or IP address of the host you would like to connect to and instruct PuTTY to connect.

- Type in your username when requested. Use your username on the remote system, not the one you use to access your local computer, for this prompt.

- Type in your password when requested. Use your password on the remote system, not the one you use to access your local computer, for this prompt.

NOTE   If you want to connect using a hostname, there must be some way to map the server's name to an IP address. Organizations can create DNS name entries for this purpose, or you can use a local **hosts** file to map from names to IP addresses.

Once the session is created, the user is presented with a terminal screen like the one shown in Figure 15-6.

15

```
● ● ●                    🖳 rwhite — rwhite@bos-lhvru0: ~ — ssh bos-lhvru0.bos01.corp.akamai.com — 118×38
rwhite@bos-mpsll ~ % ssh ▭▭▭▭▭▭▭▭▭▭▭▭▭                                                                      ▣

****************************************************************
                        NOTICE TO USERS

This computer system is for authorized use only. Users (authorized or
unauthorized) have no explicit or implicit expectation of privacy.

****************************************************************
Welcome to Ubuntu 20.04.5 LTS (GNU/Linux 5.15.0-60-generic x86_64)

 * Introducing Expanded Security Maintenance for Applications.
   Receive updates to over 25,000 software packages with your
   Ubuntu Pro subscription. Free for personal use.

     https://ubuntu.com/pro
Last login: Thu Apr  6 15:43:43 2023 from 172.27.118.187
rwhite▭▭▭▭▭▭▭:~$
rwhite▭▭▭▭▭▭▭:~$
rwhite▭▭▭▭▭▭▭:~$
rwhite▭▭▭▭▭▭▭:~$ ls -al
total 44
drwx------ 5 rwhite rwhite 4096 Mar 23 12:44 .
drwxr-xr-x 5 root   root   4096 Mar  2 10:24 ..
-rw------- 1 rwhite rwhite 1181 Apr  6 15:44 .bash_history
-rwx------ 1 rwhite rwhite  220 Mar  2 10:24 .bash_logout
-rwx------ 1 rwhite rwhite 3839 Mar  2 10:26 .bashrc
drwx------ 2 rwhite rwhite 4096 Mar 21 17:40 .cache
drwxr-xr-x 2 rwhite staff  4096 Mar 21 17:43 .certs
-rwx------ 1 rwhite rwhite  807 Mar  2 10:24 .profile
-rw------- 1 rwhite rwhite   12 Mar 23 12:44 .python_history
drwx------ 2 rwhite root   4096 Mar 23 12:23 .ssh
-rw-r--r-- 1 rwhite rwhite    0 Mar 23 11:18 .sudo_as_admin_successful
-rw------- 1 rwhite rwhite  802 Mar 22 08:03 .viminfo
rwhite▭▭▭▭▭▭▭:~$
rwhite▭▭▭▭▭▭▭:~$
rwhite▭▭▭▭▭▭▭:~$ █
```

Figure 15-6 *SSH Terminal Window*

Some systems allow you to create a public and private key pair called an **SSH key** *pair* to log in to the system without using a password; for instance, there are no username or password prompts in Figure 15-6. To create and use an SSH key pair:

1. From a terminal, enter the command **ssh-keygen -t rsa**.

2. SSH will ask you for a filename. You can press Enter here unless you have a specific reason to name the SSH key something other than the default.

3. SSH will ask you for a passphrase. This passphrase protects the **SSH key**, not the connection between the local host and the SSH server. If you enter a passphrase here, the SSH key itself will be encrypted, and programs must ask you for the passphrase to unencrypt the key before using it. If you do not enter a passphrase here, SSH (and other programs) can access and use this SSH key without asking for permission.

4. SSH will print a *fingerprint* to the screen, create a file containing a public key, or create a private one.

Once you have the public and private keys, you need to copy the public key to the server. You can do this using the command **ssh-copy-id username@ip_address**, replacing the *username* with your username on the server and *ip_address* with the server's IP address.

You can copy the public SSH key to multiple servers or network devices, allowing you to connect to all these devices using a single passphrase (to unlock the key).

Figure 15-7 illustrates the relationship between an SSH connection's private key, public key, and passphrase.

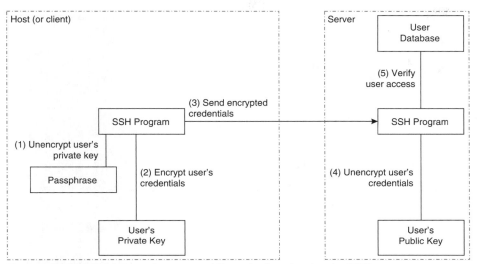

Figure 15-7   *Keys, Passphrases, and User Authentication in SSH*

In Figure 15-7:

1.   The host's SSH program asks for the user's passphrase to unencrypt their private key.

2.   The host's SSH program encrypts the user's stored login credentials with the user's private key.

3.   The host's SSH sends the user's encrypted login credentials over the network to the server.

4.   The server's SSH program unencrypts the user's login credentials using the user's public key.

5.   The server's SSH program checks a user database to determine if this user can access the server's resources.

Hypertext Transfer Protocol

Opening a web page almost seems like magic—typing in a single *Uniform Resource Locator (URL)* results in images, videos, text, and other graphic elements combined into a page within a web browser. The magic under the hood includes

■   The *Hypertext Markup Language (**HTML**)* and *Cascading Style Sheets (CSS)*. These elements describe the content and styling of a web page. HTML provides most of the content in modern websites, while CSS provides most of the styling. The web browser *renders* this information into web pages. A group of web pages is often called a *website*.

■   Images, videos, and other files.

■   Apps written in JavaScript and other languages run within the web browser.

While users tend to think of a web browser as an application, it is a virtual machine—able to download information, resize and render images, and run applications.

The *Hypertext Transfer Protocol (**HTTP**)* carries all the different kinds of information needed to build a web page.

> **NOTE** HTTPs adds encryption to HTTP. This book uses *HTTP* and *HTTPs* interchangeably; readers should assume all HTTP sessions are encrypted and, therefore, HTTPs.

For instance, if a web browser encounters this snippet of HTML in a file:

```
<t>Hello, World!</t>
```

it will print out "Hello, World!" in the current position on the web page. If it encounters

```
<a href="https://orange.example.com/image-01.png">Download image
1</a>
```

the browser will print out "Download image 1" and create a link from *Download image 1* to the file *image-01.png* at the location shown in the *href* tag. If the browser encounters

```
<a href="https://banana.example.com/page2.html">Go to page 2</a>
```

it will print out "Go to page 2" and create a link from *Download image 1* to the file indicated within the *href* tag. If the user clicks on a link, the browser must resolve the name (using the *Domain Name Service* or *DNS*), open a connection with the server, and download the file. If the browser encounters

```
<img src="image-02.png" alt="The second image" width="500"
height="500">
```

the browser will fetch the file *image-02.png* from the server where it fetched the HTML file and render the image on the screen with a width and height of 500 pixels. If the screen is less than 500 pixels wide, the browser must *resample* the image, creating a smaller version to display on the user's screen.

HTML relies on HTTP to transport all this data; HTTP runs over TCP or QUIC.

TCP and QUIC are network transport services. Why build another protocol on top of these to carry HTML packets specifically? Because HTTP implements a *client/server architecture* on top of TCP or QUIC. The web browser acts as a client to the web server, requesting and pushing information based on the user's actions. The web browser controls the flow of information across the network.

The three most important HTTP requests are

- **GET**, which requests data of some kind from the server.

- **HEAD**, which requests information about data. Every data in HTML has a description, such as the length of an audio file, the resolution of a video file, the size of an image, or the language of a piece of text. A HEAD request allows the browser to determine whether this is the correct information (is this in the right language?) and to preplan a page layout.

- **POST**, which pushes information to the server. For instance, when a user selects the **Submit** button on a website, the browser uses an HTTP POST to send any information in a form to the server for processing.

HTTP adds application-specific capabilities to TCP's or QUIC's transport service.

File Transfer Protocol

Transferring data organized into files is a big part of what the Internet does. While many protocols, like HTTP, include file transfer to support a specific application, users often want to transfer a file outside any other application's context.

The *File Transfer Protocol* (**FTP**) is designed to transfer large files between hosts. The FTP protocol is often implemented as a separate program or daemon called FTP.

Figure 15-8 illustrates FTP's connection process.

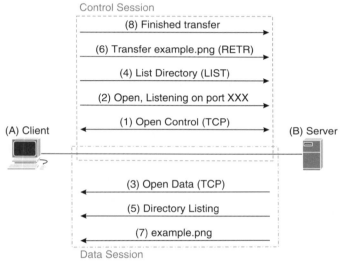

Figure 15-8   *FTP Connection Operation*

FTP is unique because it builds two different connections between the client and server:

■ FTP sends and receives commands over the *control* session.

■ FTP transfers data over the *data* session.

Using a separate control channel allows FTP to terminate a file transfer immediately, rather than waiting for a "terminate" signal embedded in a large file transfer to reach the server. Figure 15-8 illustrates an *active* FTP session:

1. The client opens a control session using TCP with the server.

2. In the initial opening messages, the client tells the server which IP address and port number the server should use to open a data session with the client.

3. The server opens a second TCP session using the IP address and port number indicated by the client.

4. The client requests a listing of the files in the local directory using the **LIST** command. The client can send commands to change the server's directory (or folder), etc.

5. The server returns a text listing of the current directory.

6. The client asks the server to send a copy of the *example.png* file using the **RETR** (retrieve) command.

7. The server sends a copy of the file over the data session.

8. The server notifies the client it has finished transferring the file using the control session.

FTP can also operate in *passive mode*, which means the client opens both the control and data sessions. In this case, step 2 in Figure 15-8 is a message from the server to the client, telling the client which IP and port numbers to use to open a data session. The arrow on the line in step 3 of Figure 15-8 is reversed in a passive connection; the client opens the data session instead of the server.

Clients use passive FTP behind a *Network Address Translator (NAT)*. Because the client opens both sessions, the server does not need to know about the address translator modifying the source and destination addresses on packets transmitted from the client to the server.

FTP is no longer widely used because the protocol is not private; neither the control nor data sessions are encrypted to protect transferred information. FTP was extended to create FTPS, allowing clients to request a *Transport Layer Security (TLS)* encrypted data session. Encrypting the data session, however, protects only the transferred data—not the information, like passwords, transmitted across the control session.

*Secure File Transfer Protocol (**SFTP**)* has primarily replaced FTP. SFTP is similar to SSH but includes FTP-like file transfer capabilities.

Two other file transfer protocols worth knowing are

■ Trivial File Transfer Protocol (TFTP), which does not support authentication or encryption, and does not detect or correct errors. TFTP is sometimes used to load a network device's configuration from a remote server.

■ Secure Copy Protocol (SCP), which uses the same methods as SFTP to securely transfer files between two hosts. SCP is often considered more efficient for file transfers between hosts connected to the same network, while SFTP is considered more efficient for transferring files between hosts connected far apart (in network terms).

Chapter Review

Application services differ from network services in several key ways, including

■ Network services provide generic transport mechanisms usable by any application.

■ Application services provide specific transport services optimized for a specific application or purpose.

■ Network services run on top of IP, which abstracts different kinds of physical transport.

■ Application services run on top of network services.

This chapter considered three network services: remote terminal access, file transfer, and web-specific transport. Each has unique points designed for solving a specific set of problems. This chapter also considered the different ways of encoding information—fixed length versus TLVs.

The next chapter considers two more widely used network systems and their transport protocols: the *Domain Name System (DNS)* and *Network Time Protocol (NTP)*. Neither of these protocols is immediately visible to end users, yet both are critical to the operation of the global Internet.

One key to doing well on the exams is to perform repetitive spaced review sessions. Review this chapter's material using either the tools in the book or interactive tools for the same material found on the book's companion website. Refer to the online Appendix D, "Study Planner," element for more details. Table 15-2 outlines the key review elements and where you can find them. To better track your study progress, record when you completed these activities in the second column.

Table 15-2   Chapter Review Tracking

Review Element	Review Date (s)	Resource Used
Review key topics		Book, website
Review key terms		Book, website
Repeat DIKTA questions		Book, PTP
Review concepts and actions		Book, website

Review All the Key Topics

Table 15-3 lists the key topics for this chapter.

Table 15-3   Key Topics for Chapter 15

Key Topic Element	Description	Page Number
Paragraph	Protocol fixed-length fields/encoding	297
Figure 15-3, list	Protocol specification, grammar, and dictionary	297
Paragraph	Fixed-length encoding efficiency	298
List	Suboptimal scenarios for fixed-length encoding	298
Paragraph	Secure Shell (SSH)	300
Paragraph	SSH key pair	302
Paragraph	How a web browser acts	303
Paragraph	Hypertext Transfer Protocol (HTTP)	304
Paragraph	File Transfer Protocol (FTP)	305
List	FTP connections/sessions	305
Paragraph	Secure FTP (SFTP)	306

Key Terms You Should Know

Key terms in this chapter include

TLV, grammar, dictionary, protocol specification, fixed-length encoding, SSH, SSH key, HTML, HTTP, GET, HEAD, POST, FTP, SFTP

Concepts and Actions

Review the concepts considered in this chapter using Table 15-4. You can cover the right side of this table and describe each concept or action in your own words to verify your understanding.

Table 15-4   Concepts and Actions

Fixed-length fields	An encoding system using fields with fixed lengths and meaning
Dictionary and grammar	Context provided by a protocol specification for interpreting data on the wire
Type-length value	An encoding system that includes the type and length of data carried in a field along with the data itself
SSH	Secure replacement for Telnet; provides secure terminal access to a remote system like a server, router, or switch
SSH key	A pre-shared public/private key pair used to establish SSH sessions
HTTP	Protocol designed to build a client/server relationship between a web server and web browser; used to carry all the data needed to build a web page
HTTPs	A version of HTTP with encrypted sessions
FTP	Protocol designed to transfer large files between hosts
SFTP	File transfer system similar to FTP within SSH; provides encrypted file transfer between hosts
FTP control session	One of two TCP sessions built by FTP; used to send commands starting or ending a file transfer, etc.
FTP active mode	An FTP session where the client starts the control session, and the server starts the data session
FTP passive mode	An FTP session where the client starts both the control and data sessions

CHAPTER 16

Names and Time

This chapter covers the following exam topics:

1. **Standards and Concepts**

   1.5. Describe common network applications and protocols.

   TCP vs. UDP (connection-oriented vs. connectionless), FTP, SFTP, TFTP, HTTP, HTTPS, DHCP, DNS, ICMP, NTP

You could type in a service's IP address to reach a website or SSH to a server if you know it. Most users type in a **domain name** containing short words and dots instead. Networks do not know how to route packets to names. Networks only know how to route packets to IP addresses.

The *Domain Name System (DNS)* translates names users identify services with to the IP addresses networks know how to use to carry packets.

This chapter begins with the structure of a domain name and how domain names are converted into IP addresses. With these basics in place, this chapter then moves into common DNS records, DNS security, how to work with DNS on hosts, and how to diagnose problems with DNS.

The second part of this chapter considers another important—yet often ignored—network service, the *Network Time Protocol (NTP)*. Time might not seem like a significant problem, but almost everything financial relies on accurate time to function.

"Do I Know This Already?" Quiz

Take the quiz (either here or use the PTP software) if you want to use the score to help you decide how much time to spend on this chapter. Appendix A, "Answers to the 'Do I Know This Already?' Quizzes," found at the end of the book, includes both the answers and explanations. You can also find answers in the PTP testing software.

Table 16-1 "Do I Know This Already?" Foundation Topics Section-to-Question Mapping

Section	Questions
The Domain Name Space	1, 2, 3
The Life of a DNS Query	4, 5, 6, 7
DNS Architecture and Operations	8
DNS Security and Privacy	9
Diagnosing DNS	10
The Network Time Protocol	11

1. A recursive server processes domain names
   a. From the left to the right because sections to the left contain sections to the right.
   b. From the right to the left because more specific information is on the right.
   c. From the right to the left because sections to the right contain sections to the left.
   d. From the left to the right because less specific information is on the left.

2. What can domain names represent? (Select all that apply.)
   a. An organization
   b. A topological location on the Internet
   c. A service
   d. A piece of information
   e. A physical server

3. Domain names can be translated to which of the following?
   a. IP addresses
   b. IP addresses or services
   c. IP addresses, services, or topological network locations
   d. IP addresses, services, or other pieces of network naming information

4. What kind of DNS server does a host query to resolve a domain name?
   a. Root
   b. Recursive
   c. TLD
   d. Authoritative

5. A root DNS server will return the following:
   a. The correct TLD server to ask about a domain name
   b. The correct authoritative server to ask about a domain name
   c. The IP address of the host with the requested server
   d. The physical location of the requested server

6. How long will information about a domain name be cached once resolved?
   a. Until the responding server indicates the information has changed
   b. Until the recursive server has responded and the information is no longer needed
   c. Until the time-to-live times out
   d. Until a timer local to the server expires

7. What are *A* and *AAAA* DNS records?

   a. IPv4 addresses

   b. IPv6 addresses

   c. IPv4 and IPv6 addresses

   d. The geographic location of the server

8. What information does a DNS root server provide?

   a. It accepts the initial query and recurses through the domain to find the corresponding IP address.

   b. It indicates which top-level domain (TLD) server to ask about a given domain.

   c. It provides the correct authoritative server to ask about a domain.

   d. It authoritatively maps a domain name to an IP address.

9. What is the primary objective of a DNS cache poisoning attack?

   a. To prevent a user from reaching a service

   b. To observe a user's browsing habits

   c. To misdirect a user to the attacker's web server

   d. To uncover an organization's internal DNS structure

10. What is the difference between tracing and resolving a domain name?

    a. These are two names for the same thing.

    b. Tracing the domain name shows every query, while resolving the domain name shows only the results.

    c. Tracing the domain name shows only the results, while resolving the domain name shows every query.

    d. Servers can trace domain names, while hosts can only resolve domain names.

11. What is a stratum 0 device in Network Time Protocol?

    a. A server with a specialized clock module

    b. A device with physical access to a highly accurate clock

    c. A service getting time from a higher-stratum device

    d. A server farthest away from a highly accurate clock

Foundation Topics

The Domain Name Space

Figure 16-1 illustrates the *dotted decimal* format of domain names.

The DNS *namespace* is *hierarchical*. Moving from the right to the left:

- The name becomes more specific.

- Names on the left are *contained within* or are a *part of* the name to the right.

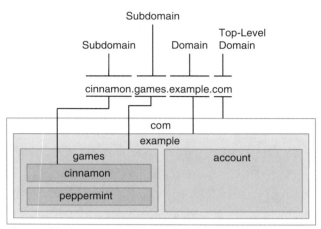

Figure 16-1 *DNS Name Format*

For example, the *example* domain is part of the *.com top-level domain (TLD)*. The *example* domain is also more specific than *.com* by itself, just as a street name is more specific than a city, and a street number is more specific than a street name.

Multiple *example* domains may exist—one within *.com* (*example.com*), another within *.net* (*example.net*), another within *.org* (*example.org*), etc. Each of these *example* domains is unique *because each is contained in a different TLD*—just like there can be different (and unique) "Elm Streets" in different cities.

The names to the left, *games* and *cinnamon*, are **subdomains**. There can be, in theory, an infinite number of levels in DNS, but most domains have only three or four levels, including the TLD, domain, subdomains, and service.

Domain names can be confusing because they represent one of three different things.

Domain Names Can Represent an Organization

Almost every company worldwide has a domain name it uses for its website and email addresses. Hence, a domain name can represent an organization. Subdomains, likewise, can represent a part of an organization.

Domain Names Can Represent a Service

A domain name can represent a service; for instance:

■ Google.com is a search engine; books.google.com is a search engine specializing in books.

■ Amazon.com began by specializing in books; read.amazon.com is a subdomain for reading digital books supplied by Amazon.

Sometimes the farthest left part of a domain explicitly calls out a service, such as

■ www.example.com is a web service.

■ mail.example.com is a mail service.

■ ftp.example.com is an FTP service.

The three services in the preceding example might run on the same host, or they might each run on a completely different host. When no service is included in the domain name, a host can assume each service should be contacted on their *well-known port numbers*.

> **NOTE**   Chapter 2, "Addresses," explains well-known port numbers.

Domain Names Can Represent a Piece of Information

A domain name can represent a piece of information, like

- A cryptographic key
- Where to get a cryptographic key
- An IP address to domain name mapping (the reverse of the domain name to IP address mapping)
- An alias, or *CNAME*, pointing to another domain name

Domain Names and Addresses from a Computer Networking Perspective

It is easy to be confused about what domain names and IP addresses represent; a little review might be helpful.

From a computer networking perspective, an IP address might represent

- An IP address can be assigned to an interface.
- An IP address can represent a host, a service (in the case of anycast), or a group of receivers.

Unlike an IP address, a domain name might represent

- A single host.
- A service, like a web server.
- A group of hosts.
- A group of hosts running a given service, like a web server.
- A piece of information.
- A pointer to some other domain name (an alias or *CNAME*).

There is some overlap in what an IP address and a domain name can represent, but domain names and IP addresses are not equivalent. Even though domain names can (often) be translated to IP addresses, and IP addresses can (sometimes) be translated to domain names, they do not always represent the same thing.

The Life of a DNS Query

A domain name is often used in a Uniform Resource Locator (URL) context. A URL normally has two parts:

- A service, like *https://* and *ftp://*

- A domain name where the service can be reached

When a user types a URL, how is the domain name part of the URL translated to an IP address? An email address, likewise, consists of two parts:

- A *mailbox* or the recipient's name

- A domain name where email can be delivered to the recipient

The domain name must be translated to an IP address to reach the web page or send the email.

 DNS servers *resolve* a domain name by finding the correct IP address or some other information represented by the domain name.

Figure 16-2 illustrates a web browser running on a host, trying to reach the service at *www.example.com*.

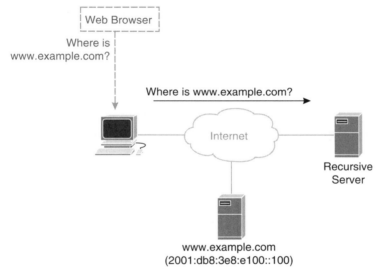

Figure 16-2 *DNS Query from Host to Recursive DNS Server*

When the user types *www.example.com* into the address bar on the web browser, the browser does not have an IP address to retrieve the files needed to build a website. The browser—an application running on a host—asks the network stack on the host operating system to resolve www.example.com into an IP address.

NOTE   Chapter 4, "Wired Host Networking Configuration," discusses how to view and configure the recursive DNS server used by a host.

The host networking stack will build a DNS *query* and send it to a server. This first-level DNS server is often called

- A *resolving server* because it resolves DNS queries.

- A *caching server* because it caches the results of previous queries.

- A **recursive server** because it recurses through the domain name, asking different servers to help resolve the domain name.

> **NOTE**   This book calls this first-level DNS server a *recursive server*.

The entire DNS database, a *zone file*, is too large for a single server to store and process every query efficiently. Because of this, different parts of the DNS database are broken up and stored on different servers throughout the Internet. Each server type has information about one part of the domain name—the TLD, the domain, and the subdomains.

How does the host know the recursive server's address? The host learns the recursive server's address through manual configuration or a protocol like the *Dynamic Host Configuration Protocol (DHCP)*.

> **NOTE**   Chapter 2 and Chapter 4 consider DHCP.

The recursive server begins at the far right on the domain name, the TLD. The recursive server needs to know where to find information about the domains within this TLD. The recursive server sends a query to one of the **root servers** to discover the address of the correct **TLD server**. The TLD server knows about every domain in the TLD. Figure 16-3 illustrates the recursive service querying of a root server to find out about the *.com* root server.

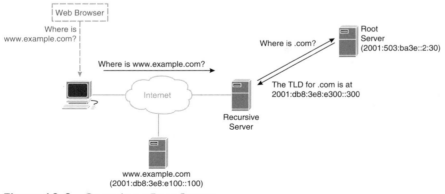

Figure 16-3   *Querying a Root Server*

How does the recursive server know where to send DNS query packets to a root server? There are only 13 root server addresses in the world. Each *root instance* is given a letter. Instance A's address is used in Figure 16-3.

The root server answers the recursive server's query with an IP address where it can reach the TLD server for the correct domain—in this case, *.com*.

The recursive server will now ask the *.com* TLD server where to find out about domains within *example.com*. Figure 16-4 illustrates this query.

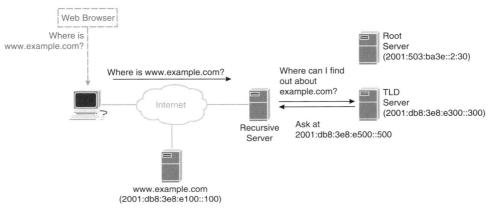

Figure 16-4 *The TLD Query*

The TLD server responds to the query with the IP address of an **authoritative server**. Note the recursive query only asked for information about *.com* in the first query to the root server, but it asks about *example.com* in the second query. As the recursive server discovers more information about the destination, it moves left to more specific information in the domain name. Asking different servers for more specific information is the recursion process.

The recursive server queries the authoritative server, asking for the full domain name. Figure 16-5 illustrates this final query.

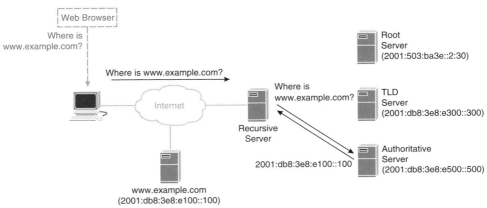

Figure 16-5 *The Authoritative Query*

The authoritative server will, finally, give the recursive server an IP address for the service. Once the recursive server receives this information, it will

- Send a DNS response to the host so it knows to send IP packets to 2001:db8:3e8:e100::100 to reach the service at www.example.com.

- Cache the response to this query if other hosts ask for the same information.

Host operating systems also cache DNS responses. If another application on the same host (such as a different web browser) asks about this domain name, the operating system can provide information from the local cache.

How long will the host and recursive server hold on to the answer? Each DNS response contains a *time to live (TTL)*, telling the recursive server and host how long the server thinks this response will be valid. Recursive servers and hosts can time out a cache entry more quickly than the TTL indicates, but they should never hold a DNS cache entry for longer than the TTL.

Negative DNS Responses

What happens when a user types in a non-existent domain name? The host will still build a query and send the query to the recursive server. How the recursive server handles the query depends on whether the domain does not exist or the domain exists, but the requested service does not.

For instance, if a user tries to access *doesnotexist.example.com*:

- The recursive server queries the root server to discover where to ask about *.com*.

- The recursive server queries the TLD server to discover where to ask about *example.com*.

- The recursive server queries the authoritative server to discover how to reach *doesnotexist.example.com*.

- Because this domain does not exist, the authoritative server will respond with *NXDOMAIN*. This domain does not exist.

DNS servers can respond with NXDOMAIN—the root, the TLD, or the authoritative. Recursive servers will cache NXDOMAIN responses in the same way they cache other responses, based on the TTL in the response.

If a user tries to access *www.example.com*, and *example.com* exists but the *www* service does not exist:

- The recursive server queries the root server to discover where to ask about *.com*.

- The recursive server queries the TLD server to discover where to ask about *example.com*.

- The recursive server queries the authoritative server to discover how to reach *www.example.com*.

- The authoritative server will respond by stating the domain exists, but there is *no record for the request type*.

Only the authoritative server will respond with this *no-record* response because only the authoritative server will know about individual services available at a given domain or subdomain. Recursive servers will also cache this kind of negative response. Since no TTL is given with this kind of negative response, the recursive server relies on a local configuration to set the TTL.

Common DNS Records

DNS contains far more information than mappings between domain names and IP addresses. Table 16-2 lists a few of these record types and what they are used for.

Table 16-2   DNS Record Types

Record Type	Usage
A	Domain name to IPv4 address
AAAA	Domain name for IPv6 address
CAA	Certificate authority; where to get a cryptographic certificate for this domain
CNAME	Alias; if a recursive server encounters a CNAME, it will look up the name listed in the CNAME and respond with the resulting IP address
HTTPS	Provides information about a domain, such as the set of services supported and aliases, to improve web server connections
LOC	Geographical location associated with a domain name
MX	Mail server
PTR	Translates an IP address to a domain name
RRSIG	Provides information required to protect DNS responses
TXT	Originally designed to carry human-readable text

Some of these record types have been extended far beyond their original purpose. For instance, the TXT record can carry *glue records*, encryption information, policy, etc.

DNS Architecture and Operations

There are four kinds of DNS servers:

- Recursive servers accept the initial query, recursing through the domain name to resolve the query to an IP address
- Root servers know which server to ask about each TLD
- TLD servers know which authoritative server to ask about each domain name
- Authoritative servers map a domain name to an IP address

Each of these kinds of servers must be purchased and operated. All DNS servers must access the Internet, which means they use bandwidth. Who pays for all of this?

Recursive Servers

Recursive servers are often operated by

- Large-scale cloud providers, like Google, Microsoft, LinkedIn, IBM, Microsoft, etc. Almost every large-scale provider has a publicly accessible recursive server, although they do not always advertise the existence of these servers.
- DNS security service companies. For instance, OpenDNS operates commercial recursive DNS servers with additional security services.

- Equipment manufacturers, like Apple. These manufacturers often operate recursive servers with additional features to support their ecosystem.

- Access providers. They operate recursive servers as a part of their access services.

- Large companies. They operate recursive servers as part of their network operations. These servers are generally not public; they cannot be accessed outside the company's network.

Recursive servers are the most common kind of DNS server. Some widely used recursive servers include

- 8.8.8.8 & 2001:4860:4860::8888, operated by Google.

- 77.88.8.8 & 2a02:6b8::feed:0ff, operated by Yandex.

- 1.1.1.1 & 2606:4700:4700::1111, operated by Cloudflare.

- 9.9.9.9 & 2620:fe::fe, operated by Quad9.

- 208.67.222.222 & 2620:119:35::35, operated by OpenDNS.

Using a global recursive server (like those in the preceding list) rather than your local access provider's DNS server could improve your DNS performance, give you a different "view" of the global Internet, or provide privacy or filtering services unavailable on your access provider's recursive DNS server.

Root Servers

DNS was initially deployed on four physical root servers, running on PDP-10 mainframe computers, in the mid-1980s. Three different organizations ran these four servers:

- SRI International managed one DNS root server using JEEVES.

- Information Sciences Institute managed two DNS servers using JEEVES.

- The Ballistic Research Laboratory of the U.S. Army managed one server using Bind.

JEEVES was the first DNS server developed; Bind was developed quickly afterward. Bind is still available as an open-source application. In the early 2000s, management of the root domain was transferred to the *Internet Assigned Numbers Authority (IANA)*, and the number of root servers expanded to 13, as shown in Table 16-3.

Table 16-3   Root Server Operators

Root Zone	Organization	Location
a	Verisign	United States
b	Information Sciences Institute of the University of Southern California	United States
c	Cogent Communications	United States
d	University of Maryland	United States
e	Ames Research Center of the United States Civil Space and Aeronautics Agency (NASA)	United States

Root Zone	Organization	Location
f	Internet Systems Consortium	United States
g	United States Department of Defense	United States
h	U.S. Army Research Lab	United States
i	Netnod AB	Sweden
j	Verisign	United States
k	RIPE NCC	Netherlands
l	ICANN	United States
m	WIDE	Japan

NOTE   The j root was initially operated by a company called Network Solutions. Verisign acquired Network Solutions in 2000, taking on responsibility for the j root in addition to the a root.

Since the 2000s, the DNS ecosystem has expanded to meet the seemingly ever-expanding Internet, but there are still only 13 root servers. How do these 13 servers support the millions of DNS queries sent to root servers daily?

Root servers are no longer single servers; each root server address represents a service, with thousands of servers supporting each service. Figure 16-6 shows a map of the root server instances in Singapore.

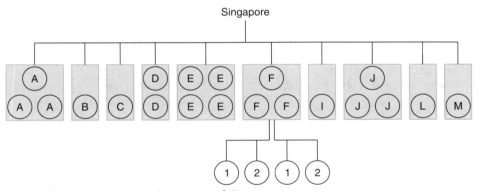

Figure 16-6   *Root Server Sites Around Singapore*

In Figure 16-6, there are

- Three sites with instances of *A*.

- One site with an instance of *B*.

- One site with an instance of *C*.

- Two sites with instances of *D*.

- Four sites with instances of *E*.

- Three sites with instances of *F*.

- One site with an instance of *I*.

- Three sites with instances of *J*.

- One site with an instance of *L*.

- One site with an instance of *M*.

Not every zone runs a site in every city, but the zones are represented worldwide. Each site also might have more than one instance; one of the *f* sites in Singapore has two instances. Each instance is physically located in a different facility, with different power sources, connections to the Internet, etc.

DNS's root zone is a highly distributed and resilient system, which is good because it is one of the principal foundations of the global Internet.

TLD Servers

A background in how domain names are distributed and managed is required to understand who operates TLD servers.

IANA does not manage individual domain names. Do not look on IANA's website for a domain name. Instead:

- IANA allocates the management of a TLD to an organization.

- TLD owners allocate management of the domain names within the TLD to one or more registrars.

- Registrars sell individual domain names to hosting companies and domain name management companies, who then resell individual domain names to users.

This complex chain of interactions allows for each organization to control their part of the DNS system independently of the others, with the following implications:

- IANA has no control over how domain names are assigned and managed beyond some basic rules required to acquire a TLD.

- Each TLD owner manages how domains are registered while not directly controlling the assignment of individual domain names.

- Resellers, like hosting companies and domain name management companies, offer registration services for many different TLDs.

TLD servers are operated and managed by TLD owners.

Authoritative Servers

Authoritative DNS servers are maintained by any organization that assigns and manages domain names, including

- Large organizations like colleges and companies that have a domain name.

- Domain name resellers

- Hosting companies

Hosting companies, for instance, will sell individual users or organizations website hosting. Many hosting companies bundle a domain name with the website and run an authoritative server to answer queries about the IP address of each site they host.

DNS Security and Privacy

Using DNS exposes a lot of user information. Consider the situation shown in Figure 16-7.

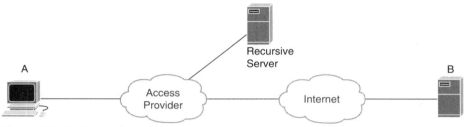

Figure 16-7 *Typical DNS Query Path*

Host *A*'s DNS queries to the recursive server are not encrypted or otherwise protected. The *access provider*—or an attacker positioned in the access provider network—can, if they would like to, capture every DNS query sent by every host attached to (or behind) their network. An outside observer who can capture and analyze every DNS query from a user, or even a group of users, can better understand their browsing habits, interests, concerns, etc.

Imagine the following situation, for instance:

- A person checks out of their doctor's office, generating DNS queries to a payment service.

- A person meets with a friend at a local restaurant, generating DNS queries to social media and payment processing sites.

- The friend searches for a particular disease while at the restaurant, generating DNS queries for a website specializing in this medical condition.

Anyone observing these DNS queries can infer the person has just been informed they have the medical condition—a significant breach of their privacy.

Encrypted DNS Queries

Encrypting the DNS queries between host *A* and the recursive server would block the access provider—and any attacker within the access provider network.

DNS over HTTPs (**DoH**) and *DNS over Transport Layer Security (DoT)* are designed to encrypt data between the host and the recursive DNS server. There are some significant differences between these two technologies, however:

- DoH is implemented in the web browser. The host operating system's network stack no longer participates in DNS queries if DoH is used. DoH is widely implemented and supported by DNS recursive servers and web browsers.

- DoT is implemented in the operating system network stack. DNS recursive servers or host operating systems do not widely implement DoT.

There are several downsides to implementing DoH, including

- The operating system's DNS cache is no longer aware of previous responses; each web browser or other application must send a query for each domain name.

- Local network operators no longer have access to the contents of DNS queries for administrative purposes. For instance, if an organization or user uses a firewall that blocks DNS queries to limit access to specific websites, those filters will no longer work.

Oblivious Encrypted DNS Queries

Encrypting DNS queries prevents access providers and attackers in the access provider's network from observing a user's data, but the recursive server can still observe this information. *Oblivious DNS over HTTPs (**oDoH**)* aims to resolve this problem. Figure 16-8 illustrates the operation of oDoH.

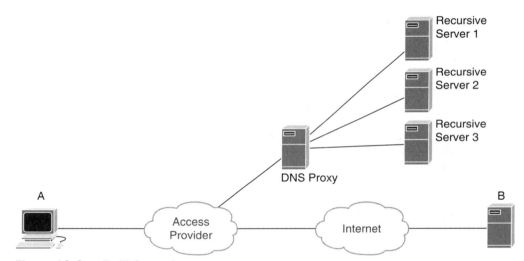

Figure 16-8 *oDoH Operation*

In oDoH, the recursive server is replaced by a DNS proxy. From the perspective of the host or web browser, this proxy server acts precisely like a recursive DNS server.

When host *A* sends an encrypted query, the proxy unencrypts the query and randomly selects a recursive DNS server to send the query to. Since there are thousands of recursive servers, the user's DNS queries are scattered over the Internet. There is no way for a single DNS recursive server to gain a complete understanding of a user's queries.

Users still need to trust the proxy not to record their queries. However, because there are open-source implementations of oDoH, organizations and individuals can build their own oDoH servers, pointing their web browsers at these servers rather than recursive DNS servers. Some companies, like Apple, run private, non-recording oDoH servers as part of their customer privacy protection systems.

Encrypted DNS Records

DNS responses are also important for security; consider the network shown in Figure 16-9.

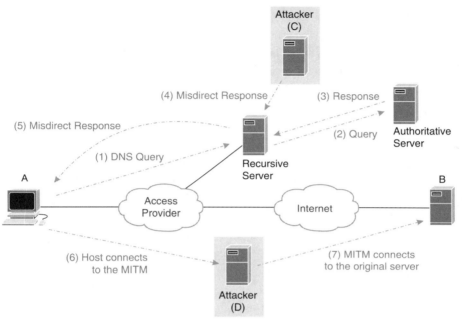

Figure 16-9 *DNS Man-in-the-Middle Attacks*

In Figure 16-9:

1. Host *A* sends a query to the recursive server.
2. The recursive server sends a query to the authoritative server.
3. The authoritative server responds with the correct answer, pointing the user to server *B*.
4. An attacker, observing this transaction, sends a response to the recursive server just a few moments later. This response points the user to the attacker's server, *D*, rather than the correct server. The recursive server's cache is now *poisoned*; it will give incorrect answers to other hosts asking how to reach this domain name.
5. The recursive server sends the misdirected response, pointing at server *D* rather than *B*, to host *A*.
6. Host *A* connects to the IP address supplied by the recursive server; there is no way for host *A* to know this is not the correct server.
7. The attacker's server, *D*, connects to the correct server, *B*, so it passes the user's transactions back to the correct server. The user believes their transactions are processing normally.

The attacker can now see the transactions between the user and the server. Session encryption cannot solve this problem because host *A* will build an encrypted session with *D* just as easily as with *B*.

16

One way to solve this problem is for the host to find another source for the server's encryption certificate than the server itself. CAA DNS records provide an independent source of certificates for a given server. If the attacker is astute, however, they can also poison the cached version of the CAA records.

Another option is to *sign* DNS records using a set of extensions to DNS called **DNSSEC**.

A *signature* is created using cryptographic algorithms. Each DNS owner can sign their DNS records using a *private key*, and hosts can check the signature using a *public key*. There is no way an attacker can re-create the signature on the DNS response they send to poison the recursive server's cache.

Diagnosing DNS

As with all services on a network, DNS does not always work correctly. If you cannot reach a website—or some other service—because the name does not resolve, how can you track down and correct the problem? You can use several tools and techniques, including **nslookup**, **dig**, and web-based tools.

Name Server Lookup

*Name Server Lookup (**nslookup**)* is available on Windows, Apple macOS, and Linux. This ubiquitous tool can be used to manually resolve a domain name.

While these examples use nslookup in interactive mode, you can also enter these same commands on the command line.

Let's begin by entering interactive mode and setting the recursive name server to 9.9.9.9:

```
PS C:\Windows\System32> nslookup

Default Server:  rns01.charter.com

Address:  71.10.216.1


> server 9.9.9.9

Default Server:  dns9.quad9.net

Address:  9.9.9.9
```

DNS queries will now be sent to 9.9.9.9. Now let's do a simple lookup:

```
> rule11.tech

Server:  dns9.quad9.net

Address:  9.9.9.9


Non-authoritative answer:

Name: rule11.tech

Addresses: 192.0.2.1

          192.0.2.2
```

There are two addresses because the server, in this case, has two different public-facing interfaces. The service *rule11.tech* can be reached using either of these addresses.

The response shown for rule11.tech is a **non-authoritative answer** because the DNS server responded using cached information; it did not ask the authoritative server for this information. A non-authoritative response is not incorrect, invalid, or "stale."

The nslookup utility can do much more than resolve domain names, such as resolving DNS aliases or *CNAMEs*:

```
> set type=CNAME
> www.rule11.tech
Server:   dns9.quad9.net
Address:  9.9.9.9

Non-authoritative answer:

www.rule11.tech canonical name = rule11.tech
```

To query for a CNAME, use **set type=CNAME**. The response is again non-authoritative; *www.rule11.tech* points to *rule11.tech*. Whenever someone tries to reach *www.rule11.tech*, the DNS server will answer with *rule11.tech*'s IP address instead.

If a mail server needs to know the IP address of *rule11.tech*'s email service, it would look up the *MX record* for this domain:

```
> set type=MX
> www.rule11.tech
Server:   dns9.quad9.net
Address:  9.9.9.9


Non-authoritative answer:
www.rule11.tech canonical name = rule11.tech
rule11.tech MX preference = 10, mail exchanger = in1-smtp.
messagingengine.com
rule11.tech MX preference = 20, mail exchanger = in2-smtp.
messagingengine.com
```

The answer indicates the mail server needs to send any mail to a server in *messagingengine. com*, an email hosting service. The mail server needs to look up the MX record for one of these servers to find their IP address.

nslookup can also tell you the domain name of the authoritative server for a domain name:

```
> set type=NS
> www.rule11.tech
```

```
Server:   dns9.quad9.net

Address:   9.9.9.9


Non-authoritative answer:

www.rule11.tech canonical name = rule11.tech

rule11.tech      nameserver = pdns1.registrar-servers.com

rule11.tech      nameserver = pdns2.registrar-servers.com
```

TLD servers will answer with this information when telling a recursive server where to ask about *rule11.tech*. You can also use nslookup to discover the TTL for a domain name:

```
> set type=SOA

> www.rule11.tech

Server:   dns9.quad9.net

Address:   9.9.9.9


Non-authoritative answer:

www.rule11.tech canonical name = rule11.tech

rule11.tech

        primary name server = pdns1.registrar-servers.com

        responsible mail addr = hostmaster.registrar-servers.com

        serial   = 1613507444

        refresh = 43200 (12 hours)

        retry    = 3600 (1 hour)

        expire   = 604800 (7 days)

        default TTL = 3601 (1 hour 1 sec)
```

The DNS *start of authority (SOA)* record contains information like the domain administrator's email address and the TTL.

Finally, you can also discover what domain name an IP address is associated with by using nslookup:

```
> set type=PTR

> 192.0.2.1

Server:   dns9.quad9.net

Address:   9.9.9.9
```

```
Non-authoritative answer:

1.2.0.192.in-addr.arpa          name = wpx.net
```

Mail servers use this kind of *reverse lookup* to verify a sender's domain is the same as their mail server's domain.

Domain Information Groper

*Domain Information Groper (***DIG***)* is another helpful tool. You can use DIG to discover everything nslookup can supply. However, DIG has one more option not available in nslookup: the ability to trace all the queries sent to DNS servers to resolve a request.

For instance, using the **+trace** option of DIG to examine the domain name *rule11.tech*:

```
Pro8:~$ dig @9.9.9.9 rule11.tech +trace
```

```
; <<>> DiG 9.18.12-0ubuntu0.22.04.1-Ubuntu <<>> @9.9.9.9 rule11.
tech +trace
; (1 server found)
;; global options: +cmd
.                         3285    IN      NS      l.root-servers.
                                                  net.

. . .

.                         3285    IN      NS      j.root-servers.
                                                  net.
.                         3285    IN      NS      k.root-servers.
                                                  net.

;; Received 687 bytes from 192.5.5.241#53(f.root-servers.net) in
29 ms


. . .


tech.                     172800  IN      NS      b.nic.tech.
tech.                     172800  IN      NS      e.nic.tech.
tech.                     172800  IN      NS      f.nic.tech.
tech.                     172800  IN      NS      a.nic.tech.
```

```
;; Received 616 bytes from 212.18.249.60#53(f.nic.tech) in 49 ms


    . . .


rule11.tech.              3600      IN       NS        pdns1.registrar-
                                                       servers.com.

rule11.tech.              3600      IN       NS        pdns2.registrar-
                                                       servers.com.


    . . .


rule11.tech.              1799      IN       A         192.0.2.1
rule11.tech.              1799      IN       A         192.0.2.2
rule11.tech.              1800      IN       NS        pdns1.registrar-
                                                       servers.com.

rule11.tech.              1800      IN       NS        pdns2.registrar-
                                                       servers.com.


;; Received 133 bytes from 156.154.133.100#53(pdns2.registrar-
servers.com) in 49 ms
```

This (truncated) output has three sections.

The first section shows the root server query result and the first response from a root server for the *.tech* TLD. The second section is the query to the TLD server and the TLD server's response. The third section is the query to the authoritative server and the authoritative server's response.

DIG uncovers the entire DNS query chain.

Web-Based DNS Tools

Many command-line tools for diagnosing DNS have web-based alternatives. Figure 16-10 illustrates one, **nslookup.io**.

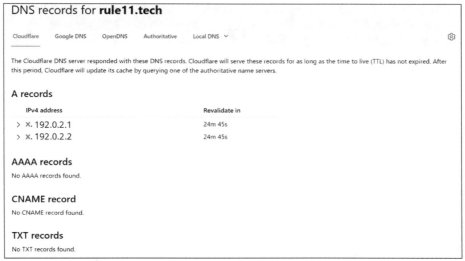

Figure 16-10 *A DNS Lookup Using nslookup.io*

nslookup.io allows you to choose from five different DNS servers and returns:

- Any IPv4 addresses associated with DNS A records

- Any IPv6 addresses associated with DNS AAAA records

- How long the cached item is valid, or how much of the TTL remains

- Any CNAME record (alias) associated with this domain name

- Any TXT records associated with this domain name

The web interface contains information not contained in Figure 16-10:

- The list of authoritative DNS servers for this domain name (the NS records)

- The mail servers for this domain name (the MX records)

- The TTL and administrative contact (the SOA record)

There are positive and negative aspects to using a web-based tool or a command-line tool:

- Web-based interfaces tend to be more user-friendly.

- Command-line interfaces have a "cool factor" that web-based interfaces do not.

- Command-line interfaces can be automated through scripts.

- Web browsers are not available on all servers or network devices.

- Command-line interfaces work in private networks (networks not connected to the global Internet).

- Command-line interfaces show what "this" host knows about domain names rather than what other hosts on the global Internet might know.

Using a command-line interface, like DIG or nslookup, to discover what a local host knows about a given domain name, and comparing this information to a global view from a web-based interface, is often a helpful troubleshooting technique.

The Network Time Protocol

When users think of time, they think about the clock on their host, tablet, phone, or some other mobile device showing the correct time, but there is much more to time in a network than display. For instance:

- Two users have an item in their carts, but only one is available. Both users check out at about the same time. Which one should be allowed to check out, and which one should be notified the item has already been sold?

- Two users place orders to sell stock at about the same time. Which sell order should be completed first, and what is the final price for the second sale?

- Someone deposits some money into your account. A few moments later, you withdraw the same amount. Should the deposit or withdrawal be counted first?

In thousands of situations, the relative timing of two events can impact. Since the computer network is often the only connection between two users or hosts, the network's time is often used to "judge" event ordering.

*Network Time Protocol (**NTP**)* is the standard protocol for synchronizing network devices and hosts within a few milliseconds of one another across a global network. Figure 16-11 illustrates NTP's operation.

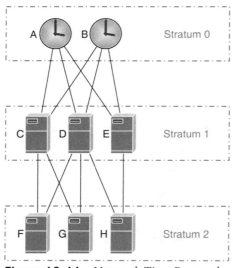

Figure 16-11   *Network Time Protocol*

Stratums, as shown in Figure 16-11, are the distance between trusted sources of time and the local server. Stratum 1 servers directly query trusted sources of time, while stratum 2 servers query stratum 1 servers, etc.

Stratum 0 devices are atomic clocks, the *Global Positioning System (GPS)* radio clocks, or devices using *Precision Time Protocol (PTP)* to obtain sub-microsecond time from some other stratum 0 devices. Stratum 0 devices must be accurate to less than a micro-second and generate a hardware signal every second to connected stratum 1 servers.

Stratum 1 servers may be connected to several stratum 0 devices and other stratum 1 servers.

NTP is a *client/server* protocol; the client queries a server for the current time. A server can act as a client to other NTP servers and as a server to other servers, hosts, and devices.

To compute the precise local time an NTP client:

- Queries one or more servers for the current time.

- Computes the *round-trip time (RTT)* to each queried server.

- Removes the RTT from each server's response and discards all but the three closest responses.

- Calculates the correct time from the three closest responses.

NOTE   The precise math used to compute the correct local time is outside the scope of this book.

Once the client computes the correct time, it adjusts the speed of the local clock to either catch up or slow down to the correct time.

Chapter Review

Names and time are two important services in the global Internet—in fact, in any network. Domain names are resolved using DNS, a global, distributed, disaggregated system. DNS separates responsibilities and roles, enabling an entire ecosystem of organizations, and preventing any single organization from dominating the Internet's name space.

While network engineers do not always support the DNS infrastructure, it is important for network engineers to understand the process of DNS resolution and to know how to troubleshoot and fix **domain name resolution** problems.

From a user's perspective, there is no real difference between naming and reachability; it is all just a "part of the network."

Time is even less obvious to users than names. Network time is hidden behind applications, and does not, at first glance, appear to be very important. Network time, however, is crucial to the proper operation of many services, and the time ecosystem is complex.

The next chapter considers cloud computing—what it is and why it is important. Many engineers seem to think the cloud will eliminate the need for computer networking expertise, but the opposite is true. Connecting to a cloud, and connecting resources within a cloud, is still an important part of a network engineer's role.

One key to doing well on the exams is to perform repetitive spaced review sessions. Review this chapter's material using either the tools in the book or interactive tools for the same material found on the book's companion website. Refer to the online Appendix D, "Study Planner," element for more details. Table 16-4 outlines the key review elements and where you can find them. To better track your study progress, record when you completed these activities in the second column.

Table 16-4   Chapter Review Tracking

Review Element	Review Date (s)	Resource Used
Review key topics		Book, website
Review key terms		Book, website
Repeat DIKTA questions		Book, PTP
Review concepts and actions		Book, website

Review All the Key Topics

Table 16-5 lists the key topics for this chapter.

Table 16-5   Key Topics for Chapter 16

Key Topic Element	Description	Page Number
Paragraph	DNS name format, domains, and subdomains	312
Section	Domain Names Can Represent an Organization	313
Section	Domain Names Can Represent a Service	313
Paragraph	Relationship of domain names and IP addresses	314
Paragraph	How DNS servers resolve domain names	315
List	Different names for first-level DNS servers	316
Paragraph	Role of the recursive server	317
List	The recursion process	317
Paragraph	TTL in DNS responses	318
List	Global recursive servers	320
Paragraph, Figure 16-6, list	Root servers	321
Figure 16-7, paragraph	Vulnerability of DNS queries	323
Paragraph	Role of DNS over HTTP (DoH) and DNS over Transport Layer Security (DoT)	323
Paragraph	Role of Oblivious DNS over HTTPS (oDoH)	324
Paragraph	Non-authoritative responses to a lookup	326
Paragraph	Role of Network Time Protocol (NTP)	332
Paragraph	Stratum devices, GPS, and PTP	333

Key Terms You Should Know

Key terms in this chapter include

domain name, subdomain, recursive server, root server, TLD server, authoritative server, DoH, oDoH, DNSSEC, nslookup, non-authoritative answer, DIG, NTP, stratum, domain name resolution

Concepts and Actions

Review the concepts considered in this chapter using Table 16-6. You can cover the right side of this table and describe each concept or action in your own words to verify your understanding.

Table 16-6   Concepts and Actions

Order of domain name processing by recursive server	Right to left; more specific information is on the left
Three things a domain name can represent	An organization, a service, a piece of information
Resolving a domain name	Finding the IP address or other information related to a domain name
Alternate names for a recursive server	Resolver, caching server
DNS server that a host queries to resolve a domain name	Recursive server
Recursive server query order	Root, TLD, authoritative
A DNS record	IPv4 address
AAAA DNS record	IPv6 address
TLD	Top-level domain; on the far right side of the domain name
Root server	Knows which server to ask for information about each TLD
TLD server	Knows which server to ask for information about each domain name
Authoritative server	Resolves a domain name to an IP address, service, etc.
DoH	DNS over HTTPS; designed to protect DNS queries sent from hosts to recursive servers
DNSSEC	A method of signing DNS records so recursive servers and hosts can verify the information in the record is correct
nslookup	A utility available on almost every host for manually resolving domain names

16

CHAPTER 17

Cloud Computing

This chapter covers the following exam topics:

1. **Standards and Concepts**

   1.4. Compare and contrast cloud and on-premises applications and services.

   Public, private, hybrid, SaaS, PaaS, IaaS, remote work/hybrid work

The "cloud" began as the space between the user and the provider, a new "computing paradigm, where the boundaries of computing will be determined by economic rationale, rather than technical limits alone," according to Ramnath K. Chellappa. In other words, cloud computing promised to make computing power a commodity, replacing the paradigm of custom-built computing, storage, and network solutions common at the time.

Software as a Service (SaaS) providers led the way into cloud computing by selling a service, including the computing, storage, and networking capacity needed to run the service, rather than software companies installed on their on-premises hardware. The first widely available cloud computing service was Salesforce. This single application changed the conversation in information technology from how to build internal systems to using the most effective solution for a problem and built corporate trust in the idea of using a public-facing application rather than internal resources.

In the early 2000s, Amazon moved to a cloud computing architecture, eventually creating *Amazon Web Services (AWS)* in 2006. AWS widened the field of cloud computing by replacing infrastructure rather than individual software applications.

Cloud computing has changed the conversation around information technology—even for companies that do not use large-scale cloud providers. Cloud computing has moved information technology's perception from arcane, technologically advanced, hard-to-build systems to user- and task-focused systems.

This chapter begins by looking at the many different models of cloud computing—all the variations of *as a Service (aaS)*. After laying this basic groundwork, this chapter looks at hybrid- and multi-cloud computing and the current directions in using cloud computing.

After these broader technology-focused topics, two shorter sections address choosing when to use public versus on-premises resources and the impact of cloud computing on network engineering.

"Do I Know This Already?" Quiz

Take the quiz (either here or use the PTP software) if you want to use the score to help you decide how much time to spend on this chapter. Appendix A, "Answers to the 'Do I Know This Already?' Quizzes," found at the end of the book, includes both the answers and explanations. You can also find answers in the PTP testing software.

Table 17-1 "Do I Know This Already?" Foundation Topics Section-to-Question Mapping

Section	Questions
Cloud Computing	1, 2, 3, 4, 5
Private versus Public Cloud	6, 7, 8
The Impact of Cloud Computing on Network Engineering	9

CAUTION The goal of self-assessment is to gauge your mastery of the topics in this chapter. If you do not know the answer to a question or are only partially sure of the answer, you should mark that question as wrong for purposes of the self-assessment. Giving yourself credit for an answer you incorrectly guess skews your self-assessment results and might provide you with a false sense of security.

1. Who owns the physical resources in an off-premises public cloud deployment?

   a. The organization using the resources

   b. The colocation facility owner

   c. The public cloud provider

   d. The Internet Exchange Point

2. Who owns the resources in an off-premises private cloud deployment?

   a. The organization using the resources

   b. The colocation facility owner

   c. The public cloud provider

   d. The Internet Exchange Point

3. What is the difference between PaaS and SaaS?

   a. PaaS provides an application; SaaS provides a set of services used to build applications.

   b. SaaS provides storage; PaaS provides storage, compute, and network connectivity.

   c. SaaS provides an application; PaaS provides a set of services used to build applications.

   d. PaaS is never connected to the global Internet; SaaS is always connected to the global Internet.

4. What is the difference between a cloud region and an availability zone?

   a. An availability zone is a collection of regions sharing a common fate (if one goes down, they all go down).

   b. A region is a geographic area; an availability zone is an independent fabric within a region.

   c. An availability zone is a set of resources with completely different sources of power and connectivity; a region is a continent.

   d. A region is a city; an availability zone is a section of the city.

5. What are common ways to connect to a public cloud? (Choose three.)

  a. Through an Internet exchange point

  b. Through a VPN

  c. Through a regional hub

  d. Through public peering

  e. Through a transit provider

  f. Through a direct connection

6. What is a hybrid cloud model?

  a. Spreading an application between two different public clouds

  b. Using both on- and off-premises hardware to build a private cloud

  c. Using both on- and off-premises public cloud deployments

  d. Spreading an application across private and public clouds

7. What is a multi-cloud model?

  a. Spreading an application between two different public clouds

  b. Using both on- and off-premises hardware to build a private cloud

  c. Using both on- and off-premises public cloud deployments

  d. Spreading an application across private and public clouds

8. What is *not* a common driver for deciding between public and private clouds?

  a. Access pattern

  b. Internet connectivity

  c. Data ownership

  d. Corporate culture

9. Should network equipment be treated as cattle or pets, and why?

  a. Pets, because each network is unique

  b. Pets, because each router or switch adds unique capabilities to the network

  c. Cattle, because this enables automated network management

  d. Cattle, because the network is just a commodity

Foundation Topics

Cloud Computing

Cloud computing can be roughly divided into *who owns the resources* and the *kind of service*. The following sections discuss these two aspects of cloud computing and the components of a typical large-scale public cloud service.

Who Owns the Resources

Engineers and users typically think of the cloud as renting resources in a large-scale provider's data center: "cloud is just someone else's computer." This view of cloud computing was accurate for the first few years of the technology.

Public cloud means resources owned, operated by, and located in the data centers of a large-scale cloud provider.

Private cloud meant networks designed and operated like a cloud owned and operated by a company or organization (not a large-scale cloud provider). Engineers often use the terms *private cloud* and *on-premises* interchangeably.

Over time, however, companies created many new models for consuming cloud computing, including

- **Off-premises public cloud:** Renting resources in a large-scale provider's data center.

- **Distributed public cloud:** Renting resources distributed throughout colocation facilities operated by a large-scale provider.

- **On-premises public cloud:** Renting resources on the customer's premises, operated by a large-scale provider.

- **Off-premises private cloud:** Resources located in colocation facilities operated by the organization.

- **On-premises private cloud:** Resources located on the organization's premises, operated by the organization.

Public cloud broadly means someone else owns and operates the infrastructure.

Private cloud broadly means the organization using the resources owns and operates the resources.

On-premises broadly means the equipment is physically located on the user's property.

Colocated means the equipment is in a facility not owned by the user or a cloud provider.

17

You can combine these terms to describe different cloud computing deployments. For instance, some cloud providers will install hardware in a customer's facilities—so the physical equipment is on-premises—but the customer accesses these local resources through the provider's interfaces. The result is an on-premises public cloud service.

Cloud Computing Service Models

The second way to classify cloud computing is the kind of service offered. However, this classification is more malleable than public, private, and colocated cloud because corporate marketing departments are always searching for ways to differentiate their product, and companies are constantly inventing new services to sell. Some of the kinds of cloud services include

- *Platform as a Service (**PaaS**):* The cloud service includes servers, network connectivity between the servers, Internet (or external) connectivity, database services, a library of installable software, etc. PaaS replicates everything an organization provides to internal developers by building and operating a data center.

- *Software as a Service (**SaaS**):* The cloud service is a complete software package used directly by end users. SaaS runs the service entirely in a specialized cloud, so users do not need to install software; the application is accessed entirely through a web interface.

- *Infrastructure as a Service (**IaaS**)*: The cloud service includes servers, network connectivity between the servers, and Internet (external) connectivity. The user is responsible for installing applications, building virtual topologies, etc.

- *Application Programming Interface as a Service (APIaaS)*: The cloud service is a set of APIs developers can use when building an application. For instance, programmatic interfaces into chatbots, social media services, and data analytics services are APIaaS. These APIs are typically accessed through the global Internet, so the network engineering team does not interact with this cloud service.

- *Storage as a Service (STaaS)*: The cloud service provides remote storage—like a hard drive accessed remotely over the network. STaaS is usually distributed across colocation facilities rather than deployed in centralized large-scale data centers.

- *Network as a Service (NaaS)*: The cloud service connects remote sites, workers, and the global Internet. An organization might run its own data center and campus networks but purchase NaaS to connect all its devices into a single network. NaaS services often include user authentication and authorization services.

As you can see from this list, just about anything in information technology can be sold "as a service."

Typical Public Cloud Service Mix

Large-scale public cloud services provide hundreds of different services. For instance, one cloud provider offers more than 15 kinds of computing services, including

- Virtual servers with varying numbers of processors and amounts of memory.

- Spot instances, which are the same servers but for very limited amounts of time. Spot instances are typically used to support "background" processing.

- Server management and orchestration systems like Kubernetes.

- Serverless computing services.

- Application programming interfaces (another form of serverless computing).

- Services to create ultra-low applications for 5G cellular networks.

- The ability to scale each compute resource dynamically based on demand.

Computing resources are just the beginning of the services available through a large-scale public cloud provider. Other services include

- Relational databases

- Document databases

- NoSQL databases

- Caching services

- Data warehousing

- Time-series databases

- IoT services

- Neural networks and artificial intelligence services

- Content delivery

- Real-time recommendation engines for applications

- Virtual desktop services

Cloud Resilience

Large-scale public cloud services can provide good resilience if application developers take advantage of the service's resilience features. Most cloud services deploy data centers into **cloud regions** and split each region into several **availability zones**. Figure 17-1 illustrates the relationship between regions and availability zones.

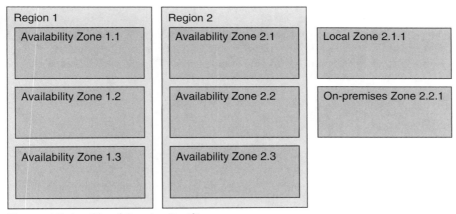

Figure 17-1   *Cloud Service Resilience*

Figure 17-1 shows

- *Region 1* and *Region 2*. These two regions represent one or more physical data centers connected by a metropolitan area network (a fiber ring or similar). Regions are independently connected to the provider's network core and can operate without any connection to the provider. Because these regions are connected to different power grids and use independent network access, one region failing should not impact the operation of any other region.

- Several *availability zones* within each region. Each availability zone is connected to a separate power source (although generally on the same power grid) and has separate network connectivity. One availability zone failing should not impact other availability zones within the same region.

  Providers usually build separate data center fabrics for each availability zone. These fabrics may be in the same building, on the same campus, in separate buildings within the same geographic region—or a combination of all three. In every case, availability zones are always built-in provider-owned facilities.

- *Local and on-premises* zones are not considered resilient and are not built-in provider-owned data centers.

  - Local zones usually are built in co-colocation facilities operated by access and exchange providers but managed using the cloud provider's software. These zones can be considered extensions to an availability zone within a region. Like a content distribution network, local zones bring data closer to users.

  - On-premises zones are built on the cloud provider customer's property. This physical hardware is owned and operated by the cloud provider for the exclusive use of a single customer. These are on-premises public cloud services.

Cloud service users need to consider regional and global resilience, how close they need their application to be to their users, and whether an on-premises solution might be better than a provider-owned physical facility.

Connecting to the Cloud

Once you have deployed a service in a public cloud, you need to send data to the service, retrieve data from the service, and allow users to connect. Network engineers will often be responsible for setting up these different kinds of connections. Figure 17-2 illustrates different kinds of cloud connectivity.

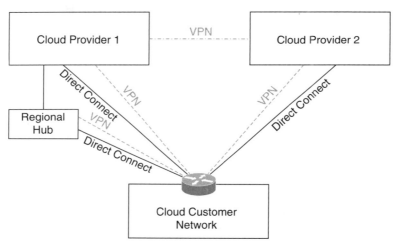

Figure 17-2   *Common Cloud Connectivity Options*

Cloud providers typically provide *virtual private network (VPN)* and direct connections to their service.

A **direct connection** is a purpose-built circuit leased from a transit or access provider, connecting the customer's and cloud provider's network.

A VPN connection is a virtual link, normally built using IPsec, over the global Internet.

> **NOTE**   Some vendors also offer connectivity to a public cloud through a software-defined wide area network (SD-WAN). SD-WAN is outside the scope of this book.

Table 17–2 summarizes the differences between these options.

Table 17-2   Cloud Connectivity Summary

VPN Connection	Direct Connection
Less expensive service	More expensive service
Traffic to and from the cloud will be included in existing Internet connections (could increase Internet connectivity costs)	Has no impact on existing Internet traffic (will not impact current Internet connectivity costs)
Uses existing hardware, software, and physical connections	Requires new hardware, software, and physical connections
Connection quality varies based on Internet connection quality	Connection quality is managed and supported by the cloud provider
(Generally) higher latency	(Generally) lower latency

Connectivity to a cloud service can also be directed at a regional data center or a separate **regional hub**. Cloud providers often locate regional hubs at colocation points like regional access providers and IXPs. Connecting to a regional provider has advantages, including

- Circuit runs might be shorter and less expensive.

- Suppose the customer can connect to a regional hub within the access provider they already use, or a local IXP with good connectivity to the access provider they already use. In that case, they will likely get a higher-quality connection.

The primary disadvantage to connecting through a regional hub is that they are usually built in some form of colocation facility, so the resilience of the regional hub might not be as good as the cloud provider's data center.

Public versus Private Cloud

With all the cloud options available, network engineers—and business leaders—often have trouble deciding whether to deploy applications in a public or private cloud. There is no single answer to this question; as with all trade-offs in information technology broadly and network engineering specifically, the answer will always be some variant of "How many balloons fit in a bag?"

How big is the bag? Are the balloons inflated or not? What are the balloons inflated with— water or air? There are too many variables to give an answer beyond more questions to ask and guidelines to follow.

This section considers three applications as "case studies." These case studies assume

- Public and private cloud options have similar capabilities. For successful and well-managed private cloud deployments, developers and application owners will experience similar private and public cloud options, and the positive and negative aspects of the two options are balanced.

- While a private cloud will always require more planning and operations than public cloud operations, these are often offset by lower costs than a public cloud.

- Business leaders are more interested in solving actual problems in information technology than in following the latest trend.

- Commercial applications and services available only as a pure cloud-based SaaS solution are not considered here.

Insurance Estimation Application

Suppose a large insurance company wants to build a new application to streamline estimates and approval for natural events like floods and tornados. The company often employs contractors and part-time adjusters during significant events. This means

- Company representatives will use their devices, preferably tablets, to run this application.

- The application must be accessible over low-bandwidth links, including cellular networks, guest Wi-Fi, etc.

- Corporate security is concerned with protecting the network from infiltration through privately owned devices.

- Corporate leadership is very concerned about exposing internal information about customers, risk management, risk aversion, and other aspects of the business. Company leadership believes that turning crucial data over to a public cloud provider risks the company's continued profitability.

The company's information technology leaders are especially concerned about *data gravity*, illustrated in Figure 17-3.

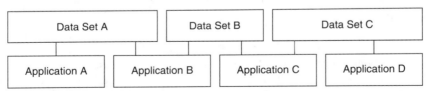

Figure 17-3 *Data Gravity*

In Figure 17-3:

- Application *A* is moved from a private, on-premises cloud (or a traditional data center network) to a public cloud provider. Data set *A* is moved to the public cloud to support application *A*.

- Application *B*, still on-premises, suffers a significant performance loss because part of the data *B* uses is now only accessible through a VPN between the on-premises data center and the public cloud instance. To resolve this situation, the IT team moves application *B* to the cloud, along with data set *B*.

- Application *C*, still on-premises, suffers a significant performance loss because part of the data it uses is accessed over a VPN. To resolve this, application *C* is moved to the public cloud.

Data gravity can be summarized in three rules:

- It is harder to move data around than people think.

- Applications tend to follow existing data.

- New data tends to follow existing applications.

Many public cloud providers are open about using data gravity in their favor. Public cloud providers often allow customers to move data into their cloud service for free. Some providers will bring a specially designed truck on-site to pull data out of existing data centers to transfer it to the cloud without using the network. However, removing data is not easy; public cloud providers often charge to pull data from the cloud, and no "data transfer trucks" are available to pull data from a public cloud and transfer it to an on-premises private cloud.

There are several points of tension in these requirements:

- Any information representatives collect must be pulled off the device as quickly as possible to protect the data. Individually owned devices tend to be more easily compromised, potentially causing a breach of private data.

- Any interface between representative-owned devices and the corporate network must be heavily guarded against infiltration.

- Data must be pulled from cloud services into company-owned and operated private cloud resources as much as possible.

These tensions suggest the best solution would be a hybrid-cloud deployment. Figure 17-4 illustrates a possible model for this application.

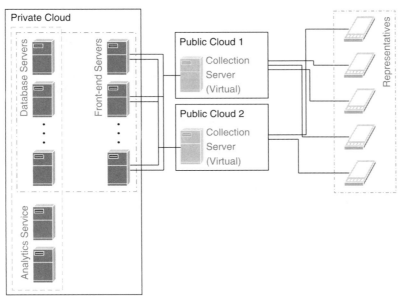

Figure 17-4   *Remote Worker Insurance Claim Application*

The application has four distinct parts:

■ Collection servers running in the public cloud. Representatives connect to this application through a web browser to record information through handwritten notes, forms, photographs, etc. Each collection server has access to only a single case file at a time, as requested by the representative. This reduces the scope of data released if one of these collection servers is breached.

■ The data collected in the public cloud application is then transferred to a set of front-end servers. These servers are accessible only by the collection servers, protecting them from data breaches and other attacks.

■ The front-end servers do the initial data cleanup, sending alerts to internal employees, managers, etc., when specific conditions are met (such as a claim over a given dollar amount). The data is then transferred to a database server. Access to the data stored on the front-end servers is tightly controlled by the user and role in the company.

■ The database servers store the data for other applications, like the analytics service in the illustration. Access to this data is tightly controlled on a per-application basis.

This application follows a *hybrid multi-cloud* deployment model, taking advantage of widely available cloud services while preserving corporate data ownership by storing and processing the data in a private cloud.

Multi-cloud models use more than one cloud provider.

Hybrid cloud models use a mixture of public and private cloud services.

Manufacturing IOT Deployment

For the second example, consider a manufacturing company deploying quality control sensors along its assembly line. Instead of trying to inspect a completed item—a set of high-end headphones—at the end of the manufacturing process, they will use robotic measuring systems to catch out-of-specification parts and assemblies at several points in the manufacturing process.

Some of the quality control inspectors who currently run a complete suite of tests over each completed set of headphones will move into positions where they receive alerts about a failed test on a tablet. Once notified, these "roving inspectors" will examine the failed part, determine if a pattern of failures is emerging (with the help of a data analytics system), and decide whether to move production off the affected workstation. These inspectors will also be trained to perform some repairs locally or open tickets for a trained technician to come in and repair the impacted equipment.

Corporate leadership is very protective of information about the production line's efficiency, failure rate, and failure modes. The *chief information security officer (CISO)*, an expert in industrial espionage, is concerned that access to this information would give competitors a good overview of the company's proprietary manufacturing process.

Figure 17-5 illustrates an application design that would work for these requirements.

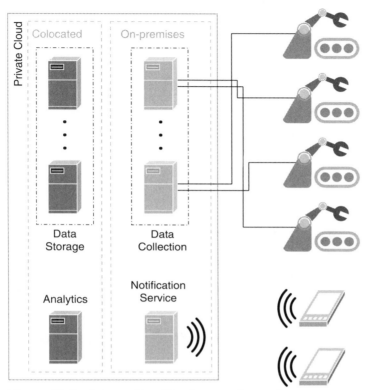

Figure 17-5 *Private Cloud Deployment Example*

Figure 17-5 shows another multi-stage application:

- Factory floor equipment has wired network access to a set of on-premises data collection servers.

- These virtual servers do some initial processing, sending the data to an off-site colocation facility for storage.

- Analytics servers in the colocation facility look for patterns, failures, etc., and send raw notification streams to the on-premises notification servers. These servers are **off-premises** but still part of the private cloud.

- The on-premises notification servers filter and schedule notifications to quality control inspectors.

Even though some of the servers in this example are physically located at a colocation facility, they are owned and managed by the company. Therefore, this example follows a *private cloud* deployment model.

Private cloud deployments supply cloud-like services using hardware and software owned and managed by the organization.

Customer Analytics

Figure 17-6 shows one final example of deploying cloud services.

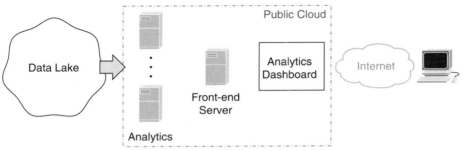

Figure 17-6   *Public Cloud Analytics Example*

In this case, a company has decided to build an analytics dashboard showing sales information. This dashboard should be accessible to anyone with the correct security credentials (username and password) through the global Internet. The company's CISO has reviewed the shared data and determined the risk of breaching the data available through the dashboard is manageable.

The application shown in Figure 17-6 contains the following:

- A *data lake* collects all of a company's available information into a single unstructured database. This data lake may be implemented in a public or private cloud; the data source is unimportant.

- Information is drawn from the data lake into an analytics engine running on public cloud resources.

- Analysis results are transferred to a front-end server, and the data is deleted.

- The front-end server presents the data through a web interface.

- Users can reach the web interface through the global Internet.

Because large quantities of data are transferred *into* the cloud service, and small amounts of data are accessible through a web-based dashboard, this solution works with how cloud providers structure their service. Deleting the transferred data once the analysis is completed reduces the amount of data an attacker might access if they breach the cloud service.

This scenario is an example of a *public cloud-native application*. A public **cloud-native** application is designed to run entirely in the cloud, where data enters the cloud but does not leave and is accessed through some web interface.

Choosing Public or Private Cloud

These three examples highlight some decision factors for using a public, private, or hybrid cloud deployment. Table 17-3 summarizes some of these decision factors.

Table 17-3   Public versus Private Cloud

Factor	Public Cloud	Private Cloud
Access Pattern	Widespread, including remote or hybrid users	Users connected physically or virtually to the corporate network
Information Control	Provider controls physical information	Organization controls physical information
	Easier to get data into the cloud than out of it	Equal cost for getting information into and out of the cloud
Cost	Operations and management costs are less expensive	Operations and management costs are more expensive
	Computing and storage costs are (generally) more expensive	Computing and storage costs are (generally) less expensive

Most decisions about whether to use a public or private cloud will be heavily influenced by culture rather than costs and data ownership.

The Impact of Cloud Computing on Network Engineering

Some network engineers believe cloud computing will eventually end the practice of network engineering. While cloud computing impacts the scale and scope of network engineering, the real-world results are more nuanced than destroying or displacing an entire career field.

Pets versus Cattle

Early cloud services emphasized turning information processing into an easily accessed commodity. For instance, you might hear statements like: "The network should be like water: it should deliver packets with no muss or fuss...it should just work." Cloud has indeed helped commodify networks, but this has not been, and will probably not be the disaster many pundits prophesy.

Commodification has occurred in forwarding engines (FEs or ASICs), and hardware has become less important in networking. Network hardware design is mainly well-understood: routers and switches are sold based on their port speeds, overall bandwidth, buffer depth, and the balance between processing speed and features.

While individual routers and switches may move closer to being commodities, *the network itself is not*. If a router, switch, or another network middlebox is like an individual rail car, the entire network is closer to a complete transportation system. Networks are becoming more complex, and moving data is becoming more critical to businesses daily.

Individual network devices are treated less like pets and more like cattle...but this is not bad. Instead of focusing on individual devices, network engineers can think about how businesses and applications use the network. Moving up the stack adds value.

Automation

Moving from pets to cattle also enables network automation. Automation (done correctly) can reduce network outages, increase security, and make the network more consumable for developers and application owners.

There is a second-order effect from the large-scale environments built by cloud providers. These large-scale networks *require* automation to operate efficiently. The skills and lessons created by developing these tools inevitably "leak down" into smaller networks over time, improving every organization's ability to build and deploy private clouds efficiently.

Cloud-Based Network Management

Public cloud solutions are also being directly adapted to managing and troubleshooting networks. Many private cloud systems rely on a public cloud component to monitor the network, predict outages, and optimize resources.

For instance, Cisco Systems offers the *Cisco Cloud Network Controller* for managing on-premises networks. These tools allow network engineers to shift their focus to design and application support rather than monitoring and managing the network.

Remote and Hybrid Work

Before cloud computing, accessing corporate resources while traveling to a conference, taking a cruise, going to a coffee shop, or even working in your backyard was—at its easiest—difficult. In the early days of network engineering, accessing the corporate network involved racks full of computers acting as hosts for dial-in clients, wired to racks of MODEMs. Remote access was slow, clunky, and error-prone.

Cloud computing caused a complete revolution in remote access.

Any applications requiring widespread remote access can use the *public cloud native* or *hybrid* deployment models to reach tens of thousands of users no matter where they are. Access to applications in the private cloud is still easier because of *Security as a Service* options and the *zero trust* models created in the cloud computing world.

In the cloud era, it is much easier to work from anywhere all the time (fully remote) or part of the time (hybrid work) and to support users who prefer fully remote or hybrid work.

Employment Shifts

Even if the worst possible predictions were accurate, and every company moved their data into some public cloud, the world would still need network engineering skills.

First, vendors and public cloud operators need people with network engineering expertise to build their products.

Second, every modern application developed runs over a network. Application developers who understand how networks work and how to make an application run effectively and efficiently over a network are not very common. Security engineers with network engineering skills will always be more successful.

Even in the worst-case scenario, network engineering skills translate to many other kinds of work in information technology.

Information Technology Cycles

Finally, remember the information technology field has always gone through cycles. Movements toward decentralization have always followed mass movements toward centralization. While most business leaders focus on "best common practices" or "doing what everyone else is doing," there is always room for innovation in the real world, and innovation often means at least a little bit different.

Chapter Review

This chapter was all about cloud computing, beginning with differentiating between public and private cloud, on-premises, off-premises, and the different kinds of services offered by public clouds. While new *as a Service* offerings are invented every day (it seems), so you cannot know every cloud model, network engineers should be at least familiar with SaaS, PaaS, and IaaS.

Cloud resilience and connectivity were covered next. Connecting to cloud services will always fall to network engineers.

Three case studies then illustrated different cloud deployment models: hybrid, multi-cloud, public cloud-native, and private cloud. These examples showed how network engineers and application developers must work together to create the best possible user experience. Choosing between public and private clouds is a matter of correctly assessing the strengths and weaknesses of each option for each application or use case—combined with a strong dose of the corporate culture.

Finally, this chapter considered the real-world implications of cloud computing on network engineers.

The book's next part moves from services to security, beginning with a taxonomy of security concepts related to network engineering. The security section also considers privacy—one of the least thought about and yet important topics in information technology.

One key to doing well on the exams is to perform repetitive spaced review sessions. Review this chapter's material using either the tools in the book or interactive tools for the same material found on the book's companion website. Refer to the online Appendix D, "Study Planner," element for more details. Table 17-4 outlines the key review elements and where you can find them. To better track your study progress, record when you completed these activities in the second column.

Table 17-4   Chapter Review Tracking

Review Element	Review Date (s)	Resource Used
Review key topics		Book, website
Review key terms		Book, website
Repeat DIKTA questions		Book, PTP
Review concepts and actions		Book, website

Review All the Key Topics

Table 17-5 lists the key topics for this chapter.

Table 17-5   Key Topics for Chapter 17

Key Topic Element	Description	Page Number
Paragraphs	Public cloud, private cloud, on-premises, and colocated cloud terminology	339
List	PaaS, SaaS, and IaaS cloud computing service models	339

Key Topic Element	Description	Page Number
Figure 17-1, list	Cloud service regions and zones	341
Paragraphs, Table 17-2	Direct vs. VPN connections	342
Paragraphs	Multi-cloud vs. hybrid cloud models	346
Paragraph	Private cloud deployments	347
Figure 17-6, paragraphs	Public cloud-native application	348

Key Terms You Should Know

Key terms in this chapter include

public cloud, private cloud, on-premises, PaaS, SaaS, IaaS, cloud region, availability zone, cloud direct connect, regional cloud hub, multi-cloud, hybrid cloud, off-premises, cloud-native

Concepts and Actions

Review the concepts considered in this chapter using Table 17-6. You can cover the right side of this table and describe each concept or action in your own words to verify your understanding.

Table 17-6 Concepts and Actions

On-premises	Network, computing, and storage are physically located on the user's site
Off-premises	Network, computing, and storage are physically located someplace other than the user's site, such as in a public cloud provider's data center or a colocation facility
Public cloud	A cloud service operated by a public service provider
Private cloud	A cloud service operated by the organization/user
PaaS	Platform as a Service; replicates everything an organization would provide through Internal IT systems
SaaS	Application as a Service; an application provided as a service
IaaS	Infrastructure as a Service; compute, memory, and network connectivity provided as a service (does not include databases, applications, etc.)
Cloud region	Group of data center fabrics connected by high-speed links, generally within a single geographic region
Availability zone	A set of resources within a cloud that should fail separately from (not share fate with) other availability zones within the same region
Hybrid cloud model	Spreading an application between private and public clouds
Cloud-native	An application designed and developed to be deployed in a cloud environment
Cattle, not pets	Looking at networking hardware as replaceable units of work or commodities

Part IV

Security

Network engineers who believe their network will never be attacked or breached are wrong.

"But my network is too small for anyone to care!" No, it is not. Every network carries private information. There is an attacker out there who is interested in the data on your network.

Rather than assuming nothing can or will go wrong, assume

- Your network will be attacked at some point in the future, causing services to be unreachable or unusable.

- Your network will be breached at some point, and the attacker will threaten to either destroy critical data or release it publicly.

Against these threats, you can

- Reduce the impact of attacks through planning. It is much easier to execute an existing plan (no matter how imperfect) than it is to create a plan on the fly in the middle of an attack.

- Reduce the odds your network will be attacked (or at least reduce the frequency at which your network is attacked) by presenting a harder target to the rest of the world.

Beyond believing "my network will never be attacked," many network engineers do not take security seriously because *security is hard*. Engineers often feel as if they are playing one of those "whack-a-mole" arcade games. Attackers always seem to have an advantage.

Furthermore, security uses a completely different vocabulary. The concepts are often foreign to network engineers.

The situation is not as dire as it might seem.

Security *is* hard, but taking even basic steps can prevent a lot of problems. Security is one of those realms where 80% of all attacks can be solved by closing 20% of the holes in your security "shields."

Security *is* hard, but you can learn the lingo. Resist the urge to reduce security to a set of real or virtual devices to install and configure. Resist the urge to "install a firewall and call it done."

This part of the book will give you a helpful introduction to security concepts, lingo, and tools.

Chapter 18 considers basic security and privacy concepts. When you are done with Chapter 18, you should have a solid mental map of the security space. Chapter 19 discusses how attackers work, and Chapter 20 considers some of the security tools engineers use. Chapter 20 covers configuring some security tools.

The chapters in this part of the book are as follows:

Chapter 18: Security and Privacy Concepts

Chapter 19: Attacks and Threats

Chapter 20: Security Tools

Security and Privacy Concepts

This chapter covers the following exam topics:

6.   Security

    6.2.   Describe foundational security concepts.

        Confidentiality, integrity, and availability (CIA); authentication, authorization, and accounting (AAA); Multifactor Authentication (MFA); encryption, certificates, and password complexity; identity stores/databases (Active Directory); threats and vulnerabilities; spam, phishing, malware, and denial of service

Perhaps the most challenging part of learning security is building a mental map of the space. What are security's significant divisions? How do all the parts fit together? These answers are not as easy to find as they should be because security professionals often write (and speak) to a narrow set of security issues in detail.

This chapter is different. We begin with a *taxonomy* of security, or—more simply—by looking at the major divisions and areas of security. The section following this mental map looks at privacy in some detail, and the final section looks at the concept of *authentication, authorization, and accounting (AAA)*.

"Do I Know This Already?" Quiz

Take the quiz (either here or use the PTP software) if you want to use the score to help you decide how much time to spend on this chapter. Appendix A, "Answers to the 'Do I Know This Already?' Quizzes," found at the end of the book, includes both the answers and explanations. You can also find answers in the PTP testing software.

Table 18-1   "Do I Know This Already?" Foundation Topics Section-to-Question Mapping

Section	Questions
A Security Taxonomy	1, 2, 3, 4
Privacy Concepts	5, 6, 7
Authentication, Authorization, and Accounting	8

CAUTION   The goal of self-assessment is to gauge your mastery of the topics in this chapter. If you do not know the answer to a question or are only partially sure of the answer, you should mark that question as wrong for purposes of the self-assessment. Giving yourself credit for an answer you incorrectly guess skews your self-assessment results and might provide you with a false sense of security.

1. How are security and privacy related?
   a. Security primarily relates to controlling access to a network, while privacy relates to preventing unauthorized users from accessing data.
   b. The tools used to ensure privacy and provide security largely overlap.
   c. Security is not related to privacy; these are entirely different fields of work and study.
   d. Security primarily relates to individuals, while privacy primarily relates to organizations.
2. Confidentiality is concerned with
   a. Preventing unauthorized users from accessing data.
   b. Encrypting data while it is being carried over the network.
   c. Making certain it is not changed while being stored or transmitted.
   d. Deleting data once you are done with it.
3. How does resilience play a role in data integrity?
   a. Resilience does not play a role in data integrity.
   b. Having multiple copies of data prevents an attacker from taking the only copy.
   c. Having multiple copies of data allows an operator to detect and correct changes in the data.
   d. Resilience prevents an attacker from blocking access to an application or data store.
4. What does *shift left* mean?
   a. Designing security into systems, rather than waiting until a system is deployed to "bolt-on" security
   b. Moving equipment as far left in the rack as possible
   c. Shifting access controls as close to the user as possible
   d. Moving troubleshooting as close to design as possible
5. Are IP addresses considered PII?
   a. Yes, but it does not matter because the network uses IP addresses for their original design.
   b. No, an IP address cannot identify an individual user.
   c. No, IP addresses are not legally classified as PII.
   d. Yes, and they should be handled as PII in logging systems.
6. What is deidentification?
   a. Removing information from a data set to prevent the identification of individual users
   b. Suppressing, injecting noise, aggregating, and segmenting data to decrease the possibility an individual user can be identified
   c. Removing data from packets so the transmitting application can no longer be identified
   d. Encrypting data so an unauthorized party cannot examine an individual user's data

7. How can operators use aggregation to protect user privacy in network logging?

    a. Aggregation is a control plane concept; it is not related to user privacy.

    b. Host information can be removed from source and destination IP addresses, leaving just the subnet.

    c. Sets of packets can be stored in a single store, separate from other stores, to prevent unauthorized access to an entire flow.

    d. Moving all private data onto a single host helps prevent attackers from accessing it.

8. How do identity stores relate to AAA servers?

    a. AAA servers contain separate lists of users than a centralized identity store.

    b. AAA servers store authentication information, while identity stores store only directory information.

    c. AAA servers often rely on identity stores for user credentials and authorizations.

    d. AAA servers do not rely on identity stores.

Foundation Topics

A Security Taxonomy

Security can be roughly divided into two broad domains:

- **Organizational security:** Protecting the assets and operations of organizations of all sizes and shapes.

- **Personal security:** Protecting the dignity of individual users of technology.

Sometimes there is tension between these two domains. What is best for the organization is not always best for the person, and what is sometimes best for individuals is not always what is best for the organization. Engineers who deal with data of any kind must learn to understand both sets of requirements, when to balance desires and requirements in these domains, and when one domain should override the other.

Figure 18-1 illustrates three primary personal and organizational security goals.

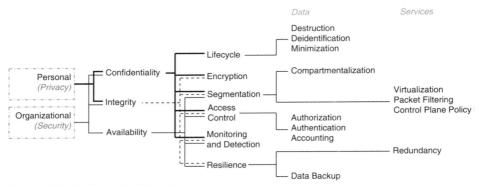

Figure 18-1 *Security Domains*

The left side of Figure 18-1 shows the two large domains and three security goals.

Confidentiality describes protecting information from access by unauthorized parties. A *party* is not just a person but also a thing or process; even processes need permission to access information. Data confidentiality is supported by the following:

- **Lifecycle controls:** Destroyed data is much less likely to be compromised than existing data. Data that has been minimized in some way damages people and organizations more than raw data.

- **Encryption:** Only authorized users and processes should have access to the keys and processes required to unencrypt data.

- **Segmentation:** It is more challenging to take, unencrypt, and combine data stored in multiple locations or files than in a single, large file.

- **Access Control:** Only authorized users should be able to access data.

- **Monitoring** and **Detection:** Monitoring systems are sometimes too late to prevent data's unauthorized taking or use. On the other hand, monitoring systems can raise alerts against suspicious activity, preventing a breach. Monitoring systems can also raise an alert when a breach first occurs so defenders can quickly close the breach, minimizing the damage.

Each of these security methods can improve information confidentiality.

Integrity describes an operator's confidence that data has not been intentionally or unintentionally changed while stored and processed. The following methods support integrity:

- *Encryption*: Changes in encrypted data will prevent the data from being unencrypted or producing errors for the modified portions.

- *Segmentation*: Attackers can change only those parts of the data they can access. If multiple segmented copies of data have overlapping information, you can detect and rebuild altered data.

- *Access Control*: Attackers can change only the data they can access.

- *Monitoring and Detection*: Monitoring cannot *prevent* an unauthorized person or process from changing data. Monitoring can *alert* administrators to unexpected data changes.

- **Resilience:** If data has been unintentionally or unexpectedly changed, resilience methods can help restore data to its original state.

Finally, **availability** describes a user's ability to use network-based resources and data to get something done. Availability is often the primary focus of network security because of *distributed denial of service (DDoS)* and similar attacks.

NOTE   Chapter 19, "Attacks and Threats," discusses specific attacks like DDoS.

18

Availability relies on the following security methods:

- **Segmentation:** When a single system is broken down into smaller, replaceable subsystems, attacking—and even shutting down—one of those subsystems will have a smaller impact on the larger system. Further, breaking one large system into subsystems enables faster troubleshooting and isolation of compromised subsystems.

- **Access Control:** The more access an attacker has to a system, the more damage they can do.

- **Monitoring and Detection:** Good monitoring reduces the *dwell time*, or the amount of time an attacker has to compromise a network or system.

- **Resilience:** More resilient systems can survive in the face of various denial-of-service attacks.

Security tools, like data deidentification, compartmentalization, virtualization, and packet filtering, support these methods.

> **NOTE**   Chapter 20, "Security Tools," discusses general security tools. The "Privacy Concepts" section later in this chapter discusses privacy-focused tools.

Shift Left

Shift left is a common term in the network engineering and security communities, but what does it mean? Figure 18-2 gives this term context.

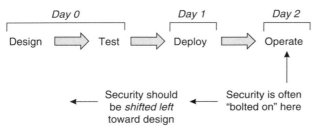

Figure 18-2   *Shift Left*

Figure 18-2 shows a standard design/deploy/operate cycle. Most network engineers do not think about security in the design or testing phases because they do not see how security can be designed or effectively tested before deployment.

Shift left means bringing security and privacy into the design, testing, and deployment phases of network engineering.

There are many ways security can be designed into a network. For instance:

- **Encryption:** A network's design can encrypt all carried traffic. Pervasive encryption requires rethinking monitoring and management systems because it can impact network design and operations in many ways.

- **Segmentation:** Network engineers often break networks into segments, modules, or virtual topologies to increase scale. Security is another good reason to create multiple segments, even when one will support the required scale.

- **Access Control:** Access control is often relegated to the network edge. Designers often assume users who pass through the network edge are authorized to access any network resources. Building a network with security segmentation supports access control and helps stop an attacker's lateral movement.

- **Monitoring and Detection:** Monitoring should be used for more than ensuring network operation. Users and data passing through specific barriers in the network should raise alarms, for instance.

- **Resilience:** A highly resilient network design is one of the primary tools network engineers can use to prevent or counter denial-of-service attacks.

Testing is another good place to bundle in security. Penetration testing, the proper operation of security systems, and many other security issues can be included in design testing.

In short, shifting security left is always a good idea in network design and operations.

Privacy Concepts

Most engineers—especially network engineers—are happy to leave user privacy to security and privacy professionals. At first glance, it does not seem as though network engineers should worry too much about users' privacy.

The larger information technology context does not help this situation. Privacy is a distant second compared to allowing the organization to operate more efficiently or profitably. Common privacy tropes include

- If you have done nothing wrong, you have nothing to hide.

- If people want my (or my user's) data, there is not much I can do about it.

- The privacy statement users agree to when they use our service protects us (as an organization).

- Large providers and vendors say they care about my (and their) users' privacy; this is enough.

These lines of argument are no longer valid. *If you touch or transport a user's data, you are responsible, at least in part, for keeping their data private.* Privacy drops to the lowest level of legal compliance rather than risk and harm reduction far too often.

This section considers various aspects of user privacy, where user privacy intersects with network engineering, and the tools network engineers can use to support privacy.

Personally Identifiable Information

One of the most critical concepts in privacy is *personally identifiable information* (**PII**). PII is any piece of information, or collection of information, that can identify an individual user. This definition might seem broad; maybe some examples will help, such as

- A government-issued personal identification number, such as the *Social Security number* in the United States or a driver's license number

- Location history gathered from a cellular telephone, or any other tracking device or service

18

- Financial account numbers, such as those issued by banks and investment firms

- Medical history

These examples are, perhaps, obvious. You should be cautious with sharp or simple definitions of PII. Many not-so-obvious combinations of data can still identify an individual user.

Network operators also collect PII. For instance, the IP address assigned to a user's host or mobile device can be used to identify an individual user. Randomized IP addresses, regular renumbering, and *Network Address Translation (NAT)* might make connecting an IP address with an individual user more difficult. Still, individual users can be identified using the logs most operators keep, given a time and IP address. Many law enforcement agencies require operators to maintain logs that can be used to correlate an IP address to an individual user.

The *history of locations from which a user has accessed a network* is often also considered PII. People are generally creatures of habit, accessing the network from just a few places, all likely close to their homes.

The *domain names, websites, and services users access across time* can often be used to identify an individual user. Even if these sites or services do not include financial or medical institutions, people tend to share a lot of personal information with online services and interact with online services in easily identifiable patterns.

It is always better to be a little cautious about data about users.

Data Lifecycle

Many of the privacy protection tools available to network engineers will make sense only within the context of a data lifecycle. Figure 18-3 illustrates a data lifecycle from a privacy perspective.

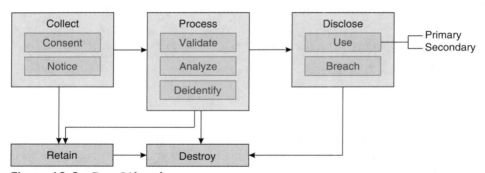

Figure 18-3   *Data Lifecycle*

There are many different paths through the five data lifecycle steps shown in Figure 18-3. For instance:

- Data might be collected, processed, used, and destroyed without being stored.

- Data might be collected, validated, and stored for later analysis and use.

- Existing data might be analyzed, generating new data to retain.

Regardless of the path, each step has privacy risks and tools.

Collection requires **consent** and **notice.** Users should know what data will be used for, how easy it will be to identify them from the data, who it may be shared with, and when it will be destroyed.

Consent is problematic in information technology. Notices about how data is used, stored, and destroyed must contain much information.

Processing can mean validating data and searching for patterns in data through analysis. Processing can also mean removing, adding, or altering data to make identifying individuals more challenging (or impossible), called **deidentification.**

Disclosing data means using the data in some way, such as modifying a web page shown to a user. A data **breach** is, essentially, unauthorized consumption or use of data. Breaches are normally associated with external people or organizations, but insiders can also cause a data breach.

Primary data use is why it was collected or how the operator told the user they would use the data. Any other use of data is *secondary*. **Secondary data use** can be difficult to justify from a privacy perspective.

Retaining data is storing it, and *destroying* data is erasing it in a non-recoverable way.

The Law and Privacy

Privacy has become a rich area of legislation and legal action over the last decade. Many nations and regions (such as the European Union), following broad public concern, have enacted privacy regulations, including

- **Data sovereignty:** These regulations cover where data collected about citizens or residents may be stored and tightly control where information can be transferred to another area. Data storage and transfer are negotiated between countries.

- **Consent and notification:** Many countries require companies to notify users when collecting data and tell users how their data will be used.

- **Restrictions on data collection about minors:** Some governments require a parent or legal guardian to consent for a minor. A minor cannot, in other words, consent to **data collection.**

- **Breach reporting:** Almost every government now has regulations about reporting breaches. How long after a breach occurs, who is impacted, who the breach must be reported to, and what kinds of information were taken in a breach are all often covered by these regulations.

Engineers cannot ever hope to become legal privacy experts, but engineers should be aware of these laws and who to talk to in their organization about complying with these regulations.

18

Privacy Tools

Many clever ways exist to improve user privacy; Figure 18-4 illustrates some options.

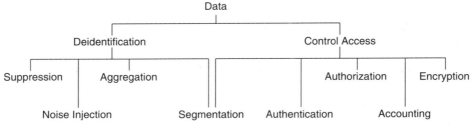

Figure 18-4 *Privacy Tools*

Short of destroying data, you can either *deidentify* or *hide* it to preserve privacy. Figure 18-4 is not exhaustive; every available privacy tool is not shown. The following sections explain the deidentification tools shown in Figure 18-4.

> **NOTE**   Chapter 20 discusses encryption in detail, so it is not considered here.

> **NOTE**   The final section of this chapter discusses authentication, authorization, and accounting (AAA).

Deidentification tools can be applied

- After data is collected and before it is processed or stored.
- When data is pulled from storage for processing or use.

Negative aspects of deidentification tools include

- Reducing the data's usefulness.
- Not entirely hiding an individual user's identity.

Data analysts and data scientists use mathematical models to control the change introduced into a data set to achieve the maximum deidentification level while preserving the data set's usefulness.

Suppression

Suppression removes data that can be used—alone or in combination with other pieces of data—to identify a person. Figure 18-5 shows how data suppression works.

In Figure 18-5, the city and last name fields have been removed from the data set, making it more difficult to relate each record to a specific individual. Many people with the first name of Sneezy might live in Kentucky.

First Name	Last Name	Number	Street Name	City	State
Sneezy	Smith	123	Flowstone Way	Mammoth Caves	KY
Sleepy	Sanders	456	Stalactite Rd	Tuckaleechee Caverns	TN
Grumpy	Ghosh	789	Drill Place	Carlsbad Caverns	NM

First Name
Sneezy
Sleepy
Grumpy

Number	Street Name
123	Flowstone Way
456	Stalactite Rd
789	Drill Place

State
KY
TN
NM

Figure 18-5 *Data Suppression*

Suppression is always used on already-collected data. In many cases, it is better to *minimize* data collection—or to collect only what is needed to solve a specific problem—and then discard the information once used.

Noise Injection

Rather than stripping out or suppressing data, *noise injection* inserts or replaces existing information with false data. Figure 18-6 illustrates noise injection.

First Name	Last Name	Number	Street Name	City	State
Sneezy	Smith	123	Flowstone Way	Mammoth Caves	KY
Sleepy	Sanders	456	Stalactite Rd	Tuckaleechee Caverns	TN
Grumpy	Ghosh	789	Drill Place	Carlsbad Caverns	NM

First Name	Last Name	Number	Street Name	City	State
Sneezy	Smith	456	Flowstone Way	Mammoth Caves	KY
Sleepy	Sanders	123	Stalactite Rd	Tuckaleechee Caverns	TN
Grumpy	Goranga	789	Drill Place	Carlsbad Caverns	NM
Silly	Snoozer	678	Dull Mews	Ruby Falls	NJ

Figure 18-6 *Noise Injection*

Figure 18-6 shows two tables—the upper before noise injection and the lower after. Two pieces of false data are highlighted:

- Swapping the number portion of the street address for the first two entries
- Changing the last name on the third entry

A fourth entry is also added.

Aggregation

Data aggregation replaces more specific information with less specific information. Figure 18-7 illustrates data aggregation.

First Name	Last Name	Number	Street Name	City	State
Sneezy	Smith	123	Flowstone Way	Mammoth Caves	KY
Sleepy	Sanders	456	Stalactite Rd	Tuckaleechee Caverns	TN
Grumpy	Ghosh	789	Drill Place	Carlsbad Caverns	NM

First Name	Last Name	Number	Street Name	Region
Sneezy	Smith	123	Flowstone Way	Southeastern U.S.
Sleepy	Sanders	456	Stalactite Rd	Southeastern U.S.
Grumpy	Ghosh	789	Drill Place	Southwestern U.S.

Figure 18-7   *Data Aggregation*

Figure 18-7 shows replacing the city and state fields with a new region field. Placing users in a larger pool of potential duplicates reduces the identifiability of individual users.

Segmentation

Every user or process does not need access to all available information about a set of users to do their work. In these cases, a single piece of information can be segmented or partitioned.

Segmenting, or **partitioning**, breaks data into several sets, each of which must be accessed separately. Figure 18-8 illustrates data segmentation.

First Name	Last Name	Number	Street Name	City	State
Sneezy	Smith	123	Flowstone Way	Mammoth Caves	KY
Sleepy	Sanders	456	Stalactite Rd	Tuckaleechee Caverns	TN
Grumpy	Ghosh	789	Drill Place	Carlsbad Caverns	NM

First Name	Last Name
Sneezy	Smith
Sleepy	Sanders
Grumpy	Ghosh

Number	Street Name
123	Flowstone Way
456	Stalactite Rd
789	Drill Place

City	State
Mammoth Caves	KY
Tuckaleechee Caverns	TN
Carlsbad Caverns	NM

Figure 18-8   *Data Segmentation*

In Figure 18-8, the table containing names and complete addresses is broken into three separate tables. Segmented data must contain a *key* showing which data in one table relates to another to recombine the information.

If a user wants to discover

- The most common last name among the organization's customers, they need only the first of the three tables.

- The city with the highest density or number of customers, they need only the third of the three tables.

- The correlation between users' names and their regions, they need only the first and third of the three tables.

The fewer tables a user or process is given access to, the less likely the user or process is to identify any individual.

Privacy and Network Operations

Privacy applies in different ways to many areas of information technology, including network engineering. Network engineers need to be careful of privacy in two distinct areas:

- Packets traveling through the network

- Information logged to understand and improve network operations

The following sections consider each of these areas of concern.

Forwarded Packets

Packets traveling through a network contain many kinds of private information, including DNS queries, passwords, and medical information—essentially, anything within a packet or flow can be private. Network engineers cannot do much to protect this data beyond encrypting it where it makes sense.

The packet's source and destination IP addresses are also considered private. IP addresses, however, are both necessary for the network to work correctly and used by the network for their primary purpose.

Overall, packet forwarding does not raise many privacy concerns for network engineers.

Logged Information

Network operators capture a lot of information, including

- The source address, destination address, source port, destination port, and protocol number of packets forwarded through the network.

- The contents of packets, which can include passwords, usernames, and other private information.

- Each DNS query.

- When users are connected to the network and for how long.

- Where users connect to the network (home, the office, a coffee shop, etc.).

This information is either directly personally identifiable or can be combined with other information to identify an individual user. An attacker could use this information to reconstruct an individual's daily life and interests. Information about users can also be used to form other attacks.

Most network operators do not spend a lot of time thinking about how to protect this private information from attack because

- They are not aware this information is private and, therefore, legally protected in many areas.

- They do not believe logged information is valuable enough to be a target.

Protecting Logged User Information

How can network engineers use privacy tools to protect users?

Suppression is not as helpful as minimization in network operations. Network operations should record the minimal information possible to maintain and optimize the network.

Noise injection might not seem to have a place in network monitoring at first glance. Consider captured packets, however. There is no reason to keep the data *inside* the packet. Instead, the packet's contents could be replaced with generated data with characteristics close to the original.

Aggregation will (obviously) apply to the source and destination IP addresses. Subnet-to-subnet traffic information will often be "good enough" in understanding long-term network performance trends as host-to-host traffic information.

Segmentation might be used in network operations by keeping DNS query information separate from packet forwarding logs and enforcing individual access rights for the two kinds of information.

These tools can also apply *over time*. For instance, a network operator might implement the policies described in Table 18-2 to protect user privacy.

Table 18-2   Network Logging Retention Policy Example

	On Collection	After 5 Days	After 30 Days
User IP Address	Keep intact	Keep intact	Aggregate IPv4 to /24 Aggregate IPv6 to /60
Server IP Address	Keep intact	Keep intact	Keep intact
DNS Query	Keep intact	Remove external subdomains from query	Remove all subdomains from query
Packet Contents	Keep intact	Replace with randomized data	Destroy

Information can be removed in various ways throughout the life of logging data, reducing the risk of PII leaking in the case of a data breach.

Authentication, Authorization, and Accounting

The phrase *authentication, authorization, and accounting (**AAA**)* describes the steps a user must pass through to access resources. Figure 18-9 illustrates the typical login process using a centralized AAA server.

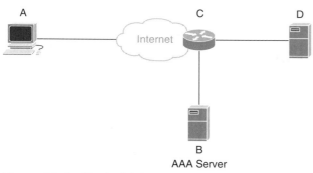

Figure 18-9 *Typical AAA Process*

A user at host *A* attempts to connect to server *D*. Router *C* intercepts this request, sending it to an AAA server, *B*. The AAA server will *challenge* the user for one or two kinds of authentication:

- Something you have, such as an authentication code from an app, an authentication device, or a badge

- Something you know, such as a password or passphrase

- Something you are, such as being in a specific location, a fingerprint, or face recognition

Passwords and passphrases are considered the weakest form of authentication. Most systems require *two-factor authentication (2FA)* or *multifactor authentication (MFA)* when using a password or passphrase to log in. The AAA server returns a *token* to router *C*.

Router *C* matches this token to a set of policies. This set of policies describes whether the user is *authorized* to access server *D*. If the user is authorized, *C* will forward the user's traffic to the server.

Finally, router *C* will record, or log, traffic flowing between *A* and *D*. This allows the operator to track what the user sends, receives, etc. This step is *accounting*, which is keeping track of who accesses what data and what data moves where in the network.

The three steps are, then,

- *Authentication* verifies the user's identity.

- *Authorization* verifies the user's ability to use a resource or access a data source.

- *Accounting* tracks what the user is doing.

While Figure 18-9 illustrates the AAA process between a router, user, and AAA server, operators configure AAA in other ways, including

- Locally configured username and password files are often used on individual hosts.

- AAA services run locally on each host or service rather than on a network device through which users access the service.

- Large organizations often operate separate AAA services for internal and external users.

Identity Stores

AAA servers rarely have a list of every user, their credentials, and the services they are authorized to use. Instead, AAA servers rely on information from an **identity store**, a specialized application used to support

- Information technology AAA services.

- Internal and external user directories.

- Building entrance control.

- Internal mail and telephone systems.

Administrators can control many aspects of employee access within a single identity store rather than using many different applications. Some typical identity stores include

- *Active Directory* is a directory service developed by Microsoft for Windows domain networks. A server running the *Active Directory Domain Service (AS DS)* provides AAA, a lightweight directory, and other services.

- *OpenLDAP* is an open-source directory service. Configuring and managing OpenLDAP is (generally) more complex than many commercial identity stores.

- *JumpCloud* is a SaaS, or cloud-based, identity store.

While Active Directory is the most widely deployed identity store, other options exist for organizations that desire an alternative.

Chapter Review

Because forming a mental map of the terms and ideas in a domain is an important place to start your learning journey, this chapter began with an overview of the entire security space. The "core chart" of this chapter's taxonomy is Figure 18-1, which illustrates the essential security domains and methods and a few of the many tools professionals use to secure networks and data.

All security can be classified into

- Confidentiality, or keeping private things private.

- Integrity, or making sure data is not unintentionally or intentionally changed.

- Availability, or maintaining systems so users can access the data and applications they need to get things done.

The section part of this chapter considered the importance of security and some of the many tools available for keeping user information private. Network engineers often skip over privacy for various reasons. This is a mistake. We should all take privacy seriously.

Finally, this chapter considered how AAA systems work.

The next chapter focuses on attacks. Once again, we start by building a mental map of the space.

One key to doing well on the exams is to perform repetitive spaced review sessions. Review this chapter's material using either the tools in the book or interactive tools for the same material found on the book's companion website. Refer to the online Appendix D, "Study Planner," element for more details. Table 18-3 outlines the key review elements and where you can find them. To better track your study progress, record when you completed these activities in the second column.

Table 18-3   Chapter Review Tracking

Review Element	Review Date (s)	Resource Used
Review key topics		Book, website
Review key terms		Book, website
Repeat DIKTA questions		Book, PTP
Review concepts and actions		Book, website

Review All the Key Topics

Table 18-4 lists the key topics for this chapter.

Table 18-4   Key Topics for Chapter 18

Key Topic Element	Description	Page Number
Paragraph	Confidentiality	361
Paragraph	Integrity	361
Paragraph	Availability	361
Paragraph	Shift left	362
Section	Personally Identifiable Information (PII)	363
Section	Data Lifecycle	364
Section	Suppression	366
Section	Noise Injection	367
Section	Aggregation	368
Section	Segmentation	368
Section	Authentication, Authorization, and Accounting	370
List	Function of the three steps of AAA	371
List	What identity stores support	372

Key Terms You Should Know

Key terms in this chapter include

confidentiality, lifecycle controls, encryption, segmentation, access control, monitoring, detection, integrity, resilience, availability, shift left, PII, privacy consent, privacy notice, deidentification, disclosure, breach, primary data use, secondary data use, data collection, partitioning, AAA, identity store

Concepts and Actions

Review the concepts considered in this chapter using Table 18-5. You can cover the right side of this table and describe each concept or action in your own words to verify your understanding.

Table 18-5   Concepts and Actions

Confidentiality	Protecting information from access by unauthorized parties
Lifecycle control	Defining how data will be stored, used, deidentified, and destroyed once collected
Segmentation	Also called partitioning, splitting data into multiple stores to prevent a single user or process from accessing all of it
Access control	Using AAA systems to control access to a data store or application
Resilience's role in data integrity	Operators can use multiple copies of a data store to verify data has not been changed
Integrity	An operator's confidence that data has not been intentionally or unintentionally changed while being stored or processed
Shift left	Moving security and privacy as close to the design phase as possible
PII	Personally identifiable information; handling and use of PII is often regulated
Kinds of PII that networks log	IP addresses, packet contents, DNS queries, user locations, user access patterns
Consent and notice	Notifying users of what data a system collects, how it will be used, how it will be stored, and how it will be destroyed
Deidentification	Suppression, noise injection, aggregation, and segmentation; reduces the chance of an individual user being identified in a data set
Primary data use	Using data for the purpose given in the privacy consent and notice

CHAPTER 19

Attacks and Threats

This chapter covers the following exam topics:

6. **Security**

  6.2. **Describe foundational security concepts.**

  Confidentiality, integrity, and availability (CIA); authentication, authorization, and accounting (AAA); Multifactor Authentication (MFA); encryption, certificates, and password complexity; identity stores/databases (Active Directory); threats and vulnerabilities; spam, phishing, malware, and denial of service

When it comes to security, most people believe two things:

I am not a target. I do not have anything of real value or enough influence to be a target of cybercrime. My organization does not have enough value to be a target of cybercrime.

I am smart enough not to be taken in.

The truth is more complex.

Everyone has something of value, and everyone is a target. Scamming one million people out of one dollar is just as effective as scamming one person out of a million dollars. People do not pay much attention to risk when the price is low.

Even the "least important" (if there is such a thing) employee has access to some computer, data, or system of value.

Everyone can be taken in. Criminals might not be the most intelligent among humans, but it does not take a lot of intelligence to compromise a network. All it takes is a bit of determination, a soft target, and some good tools.

Furthermore, although most criminals might not be brilliant, some highly intelligent criminals exist. As Sherlock Holmes remarked, "It's a wicked world, and when a clever man turns his brain to crime, it is the worst of all."

Engineers can go a long way toward successfully defending their networks by understanding standard terms, common attacks, and common defenses against those attacks. The first section of this chapter explains common terms.

The following three sections of this chapter consider the process of breaching and attacking a network: gaining access, lateral movement, and attack actions.

The final section describes denial-of-service attacks.

NOTE Chapter 20, "Security Tools," considers common defenses.

"Do I Know This Already?" Quiz

Take the quiz (either here or use the PTP software) if you want to use the score to help you decide how much time to spend on this chapter. Appendix A, "Answers to the 'Do I Know This Already?' Quizzes," found at the end of the book, includes both the answers and explanations. You can also find answers in the PTP testing software.

Table 19-1 "Do I Know This Already?" Foundation Topics Section-to-Question Mapping

Section	Questions
Defining Attacks and Threats	1, 2, 3
Gaining Access	4, 5, 6
Lateral Movement	7
Attack Actions	8
Denial of Service	9

CAUTION The goal of self-assessment is to gauge your mastery of the topics in this chapter. If you do not know the answer to a question or are only partially sure of the answer, you should mark that question as wrong for purposes of the self-assessment. Giving yourself credit for an answer you incorrectly guess skews your self-assessment results and might provide you with a false sense of security.

1. What is a network's attack surface?
   a. The set of walls, doors, gates, etc., along the perimeter of the network
   b. Every point where the network connects to the outside world
   c. A possible point of attack against a defensive system
   d. A potential violation of security

2. What is a vulnerability?
   a. The set of walls, doors, gates, etc., along the perimeter of the network
   b. Every point where the network connects to the outside world
   c. A possible point of attack against a defensive system
   d. A potential violation of security

3. What is an exploit?
   a. Every point where the network connects to the outside world
   b. A possible point of attack against a defensive system
   c. A potential violation of security
   d. A tool designed to allow a threat actor to take advantage of a vulnerability

4. What are the two differences between spam and phishing? (Choose two.)

   a. Spam is sent to a large audience; phishing targets one person.

   b. Phishing is sent to a large audience; spam targets one person.

   c. Spam does not require a lot of research time; phishing requires research about the target.

   d. Phishing does not require a lot of research time; spam requires research about the target.

5. Which of the following is an objective of malware?

   a. Prevent other malware from being installed on the host

   b. Translate everything the user sees into another language

   c. Leak private information to the attacker

   d. Make people sick so they cannot work

6. What kinds of information can an attacker access using an MITM?

   a. Only information transmitted "in the clear" or without encryption

   b. Anything transmitted using session encryption

   c. Anything in either the transmitter's or receiver's memory

   d. Anything displayed on the transmitter's computer screen

7. What is the importance of lateral movement to an attacker?

   a. To install a virus on as many computers as possible

   b. To discover who works at the organization

   c. To discover printers so the attacker can print things

   d. To discover hosts and services containing the organization's critical information

8. What is a C2 system?

   a. A system used to find and remove malware from a host or other device

   b. A system used to manage DDoS attacks

   c. A system used by attackers to maintain access to the network

   d. A system used to launch a DoS attack

9. From where can an attacker launch a DDoS attack?

   a. From within the network

   b. From within the same city as the network

   c. From within the same country as the network

   d. From anywhere in the world

Foundation Topics

Defining Attacks and Threats

Figure 19-1, a fortified wall, will be used as a reference in this discussion of security terms.

Engineers often use the metaphor of a fortified wall, a walled city, or a castle to describe information technology security. Even though metaphors are rarely perfect, they are often helpful in describing concepts in an easy-to-understand way.

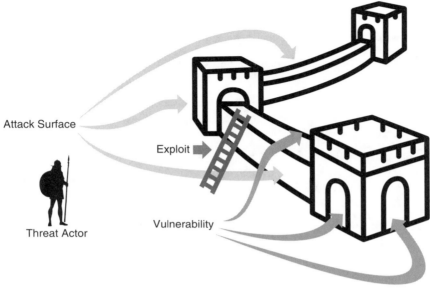

Figure 19-1 *Security Terminology*

Attack Surface

In a fortified position, the **attack surface** is the entire set of walls, gates, etc., making up a defensive position. In a network, the attack surface is at every point where the network connects to the Internet, any external system, and any place where the network connects to users. Attack surfaces do more than divide the "inside"—behind the walls or inside the network—from the "outside." Every access control and every segment boundary is an attack surface, including

- The set of devices connecting the Internet to the internal network.

- The division between the user and kernel spaces in an operating system.

- Interfaces between humans and computers, like web pages and applications.

Every piece of software, hardware, and every point where your network connects to the "outside world," and any place where people and computers interact, is an attack surface.

Examining a system to find and describe the attack surface is often helpful, especially if you intentionally try to find unexpected holes in your existing defenses. Many walled castles have fallen to enemy forces because of a rough-cut shepherd's path or an attacker's ability to attack a city's water supply.

Vulnerability

A **vulnerability** is a possible point of attack against a defensive system. In Figure 19-1:

- Doors are vulnerable to being broken down or breached.

- Walls can be climbed or topped; objects can even be vaulted over.

19

Vulnerabilities in information technology are classified using the *Common Vulnerabilities and Exposures (CVE)* system developed by MITRE. Each publicly disclosed vulnerability in hardware or software is given a number and then classified by

- The **exploitability** of the vulnerability, or how easy it is for an attacker to gain control of a system using this vulnerability.

- What kind of access an attacker must have to take advantage of this vulnerability. Does the attacker need to be able to access a piece of hardware (local execution), or can an attacker take advantage of a vulnerability across a network (remote execution)?

- What kind of access an attacker gains by taking advantage of the vulnerability. Does the attacker gain complete control over an entire system? Or do they gain access only to a single piece of software?

- How widely the impacted hardware or software is used. A widely used open-source software vulnerability is much worse than in a custom-built hardware system.

- Whether a patch or easy-to-use workaround is available that would prevent attackers from using this vulnerability.

Each CVE is given a number and rating and published in several online places. Information security professionals spend a lot of time examining new CVEs and evaluating whether they should deploy some defensive mechanism or patch their software.

Zero day was initially used to describe vulnerabilities "built into" an application, especially if the defect resulted from an attacker gaining access to the application's source code. As with most terms in information technology, the meaning of this term has expanded over time to mean any previously unknown vulnerability for which there is no mitigation.

NOTE Chapter 20 describes mitigation in more detail.

Threat

A **threat** is a potential violation of security. Threats are sometimes immediate and real; for example, there is some information, such as a notice from a government agency, about plans to attack an organization or kind of organization. Threat notifications often describe the attacker's goals and may include the vulnerability an attacker plans to exploit.

A **threat actor** is a person or organization behind a threat or attack. Figure 19-1 includes a threat actor armed with a shield and spear. Whether or not this person attacks the wall, it is a good idea to have someone (or something) watching this person.

Exploit

An **exploit** is a tool allowing a threat actor to exploit a vulnerability. In Figure 19-1, a ladder is an exploit used against the wall, taking advantage of a wall's vulnerability.

Hackers often build libraries of exploits and sell them on the open Internet. Threat actors can purchase one of these libraries and build an attack without understanding the underlying system or vulnerability.

Risk

A **risk** is any potential event, such as an attack, that can disrupt an organization's operations. Risks include the existence, motivation, and skills of a threat actor; exploits available to the threat actor; vulnerabilities in the attack surface; and an assessment of the damage the event could cause to the organization.

Gaining Access

Attackers always begin the attack by gaining access to a host, server, middlebox, or other device the operator trusts. Access to this initial device provides a "home base," or **beachhead**, from which to work. Attacks focused on gaining unauthorized access inside a network are often called *intrusion attacks*.

There are almost infinite ways an attacker can gain access to a beachhead inside your network; some are considered in the following sections.

Social Engineering

Attackers use **social engineering** to convince users to turn over their internal access credentials, allow someone into a secured area (such as a corporate office), or access some resource. For instance:

- Tailgating another person walking into a corporate office

- Claiming the user's computer has a problem, and you are going to fix it for them

- Claiming someone the user cares about is kidnapped, in financial trouble, etc.

Social engineers often rely on overloading a victim with too much information or convincing someone they can be trusted, and they use many ways to contact the victim.

The Ingenuity of Social Engineering Attacks

Social engineering attacks can be unexpectedly creative. For instance, I have seen attackers claim to be newly married to the victim while playing the sound of a crying baby in the background to convince a support person to add her to the victim's account. This attack is especially insidious, as you must close some accounts to remove users.

In other cases, attackers have posed as fire or building inspectors to gain access to restricted areas. Attackers sometimes work in pairs, such as when one person acts like a frustrated employee pressuring a security guard to give them access to a building quickly. At the same time, another acts like a flower delivery person who needs immediate access.

Email and *messenger-based* (text messages, private messaging, and voice) social engineering attacks are the most common, including **spam** and **phishing**. While *spam* and *phishing* are often used interchangeably, they are distinctly different.

Spam is unsolicited advertisements, mailing lists, etc. Spam is usually directed at large numbers of people; it is not customized for one specific person. Spam might be an advertisement from a company you did not ask for, contain an infected attachment, or ask you to click on a link.

19

Phishing is like spam, but it is customized to the receiver. Attackers may spend a few minutes to hours researching an individual victim and customizing an email the victim is more likely to act on. The attacker might try to emulate an email from an organization the victim already trusts, such as Google, Microsoft, an email provider, or a bank.

> **NOTE** Chapter 20 discusses strategies for countering spam, phishing, and other social engineering attacks.

Attackers quickly take advantage of new technologies, such as deepfakes and large language model artificial intelligence (LLM/AI) systems.

Threat actors use deepfakes to mimic the voice, physical characteristics, or writing style of someone the victim trusts. The deepfake is used to convince the victim to take some action. If the voice on the other end of the phone sounds like your manager, you are likely to give them your password; if it does not, you are likely to be more suspicious. As deepfakes become more realistic, they become more dangerous.

Deepfakes and Social Engineering Attacks

When this book was written, security professionals reported a case where a woman received a phone call from her daughter. The daughter stated she had been kidnapped, and her mother needed to send a large sum of money to a bank account in the next hour, or she would be harmed. The woman found a way to contact her daughter and discovered she was still safe. The attacker used a deepfake of her daughter's voice.

LLMs are used to research a victim and write a convincing email quickly. LLMs can assemble an authentic-looking email from a large, trusted organization with little effort from the attacker.

Malware

While viruses, worms, spyware, and keyloggers are technically different computer programs, they are all kinds of a broader class of software called malware.

Malware is a *self-replicating* application designed to disrupt a computer system. Malware generally tries to do one of three things:

- Prevent the user from accessing data, either by encrypting it (ransomware) or deleting it (wiper)

- Log interactions between users and the system to steal passwords, discover private information, etc.

- Leak private information to the attacker

These actions will be considered in more detail later in this chapter.

Malware self-replicates by

- Finding other vulnerable computers through the host's network connection.

- Installing itself on vulnerable websites so visitors' computers can be infected.

- Infecting portable media like USB thumb drives.

Hackers can also spread malware through software during a supply chain attack.

Supply Chain Attack

Supply chain attacks gain access to a network through some element of their supply chain. Here are some famous supply chain attacks:

- In late 2013, an attacker accessed Target's data center, ultimately breaching the company's network and installing malware on its *point of sale (PoS)* systems. The malware, in turn, took millions of customers' data. Security experts believe Target's data center was breached via a relationship with its heating, ventilation, and air conditioning (HVAC) contractor.

- In 2020, the security vendor SolarWinds was breached, and backdoor access was inserted into its code. The infected code was installed by hundreds of SolarWinds customers, allowing attackers to breach their networks easily. Several of SolarWinds' customers were breached using this entry point.

- In 2021, Microsoft's Exchange Server code was breached, and a back door was added.

Supply chain attacks are some of the most difficult to detect and counter. For commercial vendor (*closed source*) products, users must place their trust entirely in the vendor's security. For open-source packages, users must either trust the community or have engineers on staff who can examine the package's code for potential security threats.

Poor Configuration

Poor configuration, including poor passwords, is the primary cause of breaches. Basic rules in this area include

- Make certain attack surfaces are well understood and each apparent vulnerability is blocked through configuration.

- Eliminate default configurations and passwords.

- Enforce good passwords.

- Use tools to find and replace compromised passwords.

In general, network engineers should always reduce risk by making every entry point into the network secure.

Man-in-the-Middle Attacks

*Man-in-the-middle (**MITM**)* attacks force traffic through a third party, unencrypting and re-encrypting traffic transparently. Figure 19-2 illustrates an MITM.

19

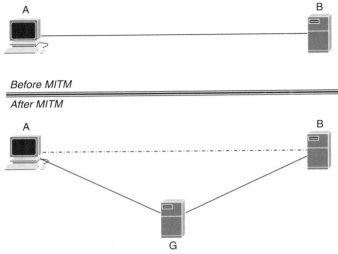

Figure 19-2   *Man-in-the-Middle Attack*

Before the MITM in Figure 19-2, host *A* and server *B* are encrypted using a shared private key. This connection is secure; outside parties cannot see the data transmitted between *A* and *B*.

After the MITM in Figure 19-2:

- Host *A* believes it has a secure session with server *B*, but it has a secure session with the attacker's server, *G*.

- Server *B* believes it has a secure session with host *A*, but it has a secure session with the attacker's server, *G*.

Because *G* is unencrypting data from *A* and then re-encrypting it to transmit it to *B*, the attacker can see the transmitted data in the clear. The attacker can access credentials, account numbers, usernames, and any other information transmitted from host *A* to server *B*. The attacker can use all this information to breach *B*'s or *A*'s networks.

The attacker can also inject new information into the secured session. In particular, the attacker could bundle malware in a website or even replace an executable file with malware.

NOTE   Chapter 16, "Names and Time," describes MITM in relation to the Domain Name System (DNS).

 Lateral Movement

Access to a single device in a network is not necessarily very useful for an attacker. Once the attacker has gained access to a single device, they must find and gain access to either a lot of systems or a small set of systems with critical data.

Lateral movement is moving from the initial beachhead further into the network by compromising additional devices in the network.

Figure 19-3 illustrates an example of the lateral movement process.

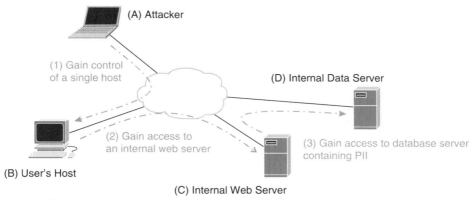

Figure 19-3 *Lateral Movement*

In Figure 19-3:

1. The attacker uses a zero-day exploit, phishing campaign, physical access, or attack against a single user. Once the attacker has gained access to this first beachhead in the network, they will explore the network using internal tools like local DNS caches, DNS queries, local IPv4 Address Resolution Protocol (ARP) caches, and IPv6 Neighbor Discovery (ND) caches. The attacker can then explore local username and password stores, such as the credentials stored in a web browser.

2. By exploring the network, the attacker discovers an internal web server. The attacker assumes this server is essential because the user regularly connects. Attempting to connect to the server through a command line reveals information about the web server installed on the server and the server's operating system. This information leads the attacker to a prebuilt exploit for the version of a web server or operating system installed on the server. Using this exploit, the attacker gains access to the web server.

3. Because the web server does not store data locally, it must connect to a database server to build user web pages. To connect to this database server, some processes on the web server must have an account on the server, which must be stored in some file. Once the attacker finds this information, they can log in to the database server as a trusted process. The web server draws on an identity store to provide internal directory services in this case. Hence, the attacker has access to the personal information of every user in the network. If there are known vulnerabilities for this identity store or some exploit available, the attacker can access the entire identity store, including usernames and passwords.

Lateral movement through the network is critical for attackers who want to maximize the disruption they cause or the information they gather.

Attack Actions

What options does an attacker have who has breached a network and moved laterally through at least a few systems? The following sections describe a few alternatives.

Command and Control

The first thing any attacker does is build a *Command and Control (C2)* system, which will allow them to re-access the network if the operator discovers them, tracks down how they breached the network, and attempts to block future access.

Most **C2 systems** configure the compromised system to contact an external server periodically for instructions, such as creating a secure tunnel between the compromised system and the attacker's server. Security systems seldom inspect traffic from inside a network as thoroughly as from *outside* the network.

Sometimes attackers will leave a back door, often in the form of an innocuous-sounding username and password.

Once the network is breached, the attacker aims to increase their *dwell time*—the amount of time they can stay inside the network without detection. Some attackers have dwelled in networks for years without discovery.

Data Exfiltration

An attacker's second goal is often to *exfiltrate data*, or copy it from internal sources to a place where the attacker can examine and analyze it. Once data has been exfiltrated, it can be

- Held for ransom. If the organization does not pay the attacker some money, the attacker will release the data "into the wild." Holding data for ransom normally means posting the data on some publicly available server. The organization will be highly motivated to pay the ransom if the stolen data includes private information, such as bank or medical records, or source code for a popular product. Of course, like all kidnapping situations, there is no reason to believe an attacker will keep their end of the bargain, even once any ransom has been paid.

- Sold off to people who will use it to scam legitimate users, use the information to breach other systems, or even use the exfiltrated usernames and passwords to break into users' other accounts.

Data exfiltration can occur in many ways, including

- Through a custom-built VPN tunnel

- Through physical USB thumb drives via an accomplice

- Through DNS queries (very slow, but it still works)

Clever attackers can often exfiltrate data without the operator noticing.

Ransomware

Suppose the attacker is concerned about building the C2 system needed to dwell in a breached network for a long while, or perhaps they are concerned the process of exfiltrating data can expose the attacker. What kinds of actions can an attacker take in this case? The most common attack in these cases is ransomware.

Ransomware encrypts the user's data using a key and system the user does not know, so the user cannot access or use the system.

Once the attacker installs ransomware, the system displays a message stating the operator should send money to an anonymous account. Once the attacker receives the ransom, they will send a key and software to the user to unencrypt their data.

Denial of Service

Attackers launching a *denial-of-service* (**DoS**) or *distributed denial-of-service* (**DDoS**) attack are (funny enough) trying to deny the use of some service by exhausting some fixed or finite resource. DoS attacks can be launched from a few devices and attempt to exhaust some system resources. DDoS attacks are launched from hundreds or thousands of devices distributed throughout the Internet and typically attempt to exhaust an external resource, like consuming an entire link's or interface's capacity.

Attackers might use DoS or DDoS attacks to

- Slow down a competing gamer's server to cheat.

- Distract a security team from an intrusion attack occurring at the same time.

- Take down a company's website during a critical period to damage the company's reputation or business.

- Cause a server to fail, exposing vulnerabilities when the server reboots or recovers.

The reasons for launching a DoS attack are as varied as attackers.

DoS attacks differ from intrusion attacks because the attacker does not (necessarily) need to gain access to the network to launch a DoS attack. Servers (or IP addresses) can be directly attacked remotely. Not all DoS attacks are external, either. Once an attacker has breached a network, they can use devices they control to launch an *internal* DoS attack.

In many cases, intrusion attacks require some skill to execute. DoS attacks, however, are available as a *service*—an instance of cloud computing "gone bad."

The following sections explain several different kinds of DoS attacks.

Direct (or Burner) Attack

Figure 19-4 illustrates a direct, or burner, DDoS attack.

In a **direct DDoS attack**, the attacker begins by compromising hundreds or thousands or even millions of devices. These devices can be servers, IoT devices like printers and cameras, network devices like routers and switches, and hosts. After compromising these devices, the attacker (or DDoS service) installs C2 software to generate packets on demand, creating a botnet.

A *botnet* is a collection of devices under the control of an attacker used to launch DDoS attacks.

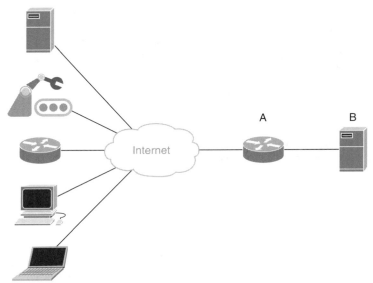

Figure 19-4 *A Direct DDoS Attack*

Launching a DDoS attack uses the C2 system to instruct many hosts to send the largest packets they can, at the highest rate, toward the target's IP address. The target in Figure 19-4 is server *B*.

A direct DDoS attack uses many hosts sending traffic directly to a victim to consume bandwidth-related resources.

If the attacker can send enough traffic:

- Router *A*'s link to the Internet will be overwhelmed.

- The router *A* to server *B* link will be overwhelmed.

- Server *B*'s interface will be overwhelmed.

In all three cases, the attacker exhausts some resources and blocks server *B* from accepting traffic through sheer traffic volume.

Direct DDoS attacks are sometimes called *burner attacks* because devices controlled by the botnet are exposed. Once these devices are exposed, operators can track down and fix or block them, *burning* the attacker's ability to use them.

Because compromised devices use their actual IP addresses, direct DDoS attacks do not use source address spoofing. **Source address spoofing** occurs when a device or host transmits packets using some other address than the one its interfaces are configured to use.

Reflection Attack

Reflection attacks use well-connected servers to reflect and amplify a DDoS attack. Figure 19-5 illustrates a reflection attack.

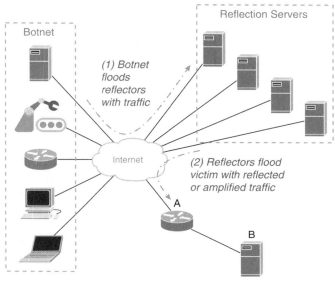

Figure 19-5 *DDoS Reflection Attack*

A **DDoS reflection attack** proceeds in two steps, as shown in Figure 19-5.

In the first step, shown as (1), the attacker instructs the members of the botnet to send large volumes of traffic to well-known servers on the Internet (for external DDoS attacks) or within an organization's network (for internal DDoS attacks). DNS servers are a favorite reflection target because they are almost always connected using high-speed links. DNS servers generally run on high-performance hardware and will almost always answer requests from any IP address connected anywhere on the network.

Attackers configure the botnet members to send

- Packets sourced from the victim's IP address (the source address is spoofed).

- Small DNS queries resulting in multipart responses.

In the second step, shown as (2), the DNS server will respond to these queries by sending large packets of information to the victim's address, consuming link bandwidth.

Reflection attacks do not burn the botnet because the attack uses spoofed source addresses. It is nearly impossible to track down the actual source of a packet with a spoofed source address.

Attackers can use smaller botnets for reflection attacks because the attack is amplified in the reflection process. Even if part of their botnet is discovered and corrected, the odds of losing a significant portion are much lower in a reflection attack.

Resource Exhaustion

Attackers can also exhaust resources other than bandwidth. Some examples include

- The DNS cache on a recursive server. While many servers will time cache DNS query responses out more quickly as the cache fills up, clever attackers can build a series of queries just fast enough to fill the recursive server's cache but not so fast as to trigger cache reduction processes.

■ The *Transmission Control Protocol (TCP)* cache of half-open sessions. A server must keep track of every TCP open message it acknowledges. Once the client acknowledges the server's initial acknowledgment, the server can move the session into the open state and transmit data. If an attacker sends enough TCP open messages to a server quickly enough, the server can run out of room to store half-open session information and stop accepting new sessions.

■ The *Network Address Translation (NAT)* cache on smaller routers and switches. Each NAT translation must be stored in memory; forcing a router or switch to add thousands (or even millions) of new translations quickly can overflow the NAT cache. Once a router or switch runs out of NAT translation storage, it stops accepting new connections or randomly drops old ones.

An attacker can exhaust multiple resources on hosts, servers, and middleboxes. There is always some new way of attacking network-connected devices no one has thought of before.

Chapter Review

This chapter began with a taxonomy of terms: What are attack surfaces, vulnerabilities, threats, exploits, and risks? Understanding these terms gives you a good grounding in the world of security.

The next section explained how an attacker can gain access to your network. In all its many forms, social engineering is the most common way attackers gain access to a beachhead within a network. Poor configuration is the second; it is amazing how many news reports of data breaches say "an unprotected database was left on a cloud service instance" or "the attacker gained access through a network device configured with the manufacturer's default passwords."

We then moved to three things attackers do once they have gained access to a network, including installing C2, data exfiltration, and ransomware. The last topic of discussion was denial-of-service attacks.

This chapter has largely been "bad news"—all the different ways an attacker can access your network and what they can do once they have gained access. The next chapter discusses "good news"—how network engineers and security professionals deploy to counter many of these vulnerabilities.

One key to doing well on the exams is to perform repetitive spaced review sessions. Review this chapter's material using either the tools in the book or interactive tools for the same material found on the book's companion website. Refer to the online Appendix D, "Study Planner," element for more details. Table 19-2 outlines the key review elements and where you can find them. To better track your study progress, record when you completed these activities in the second column.

Table 19-2   Chapter Review Tracking

Review Element	Review Date (s)	Resource Used
Review key topics		Book, website
Review key terms		Book, website
Repeat DIKTA questions		Book, PTP
Review concepts and actions		Book, website

Review All the Key Topics

Table 19-3 lists the key topics for this chapter.

Table 19-3   Key Topics for Chapter 19

Key Topic Element	Description	Page Number
Paragraph	Everyone has something of value/is a target	376
Paragraph	Attack surface	379
Section	Vulnerability	379
Section	Threat	380
Section	Exploit	380
Section	Risk	381
Section	Gaining Access	381
Paragraph	Social engineering	381
Paragraph	Spam	381
Paragraph	Phishing	382
Paragraph	Malware	382
Section	Supply Chain Attack	383
Section	Man-in-the-Middle Attack	383
Section	Lateral Movement	384
Paragraph	Command and Control (C2) system	386
Paragraph, list	Data exfiltration	386
Paragraph	Ransomware	387
Paragraph	Denial of service (DoS)/distributed denial of service (DDoS)	387
Paragraph	DoS versus intrusion attacks	387
Paragraphs	Direct DDoS aka burner attacks	388
Paragraph	Source address spoofing	388
Paragraph, Figure 19-5	Reflection attack	388

19

Key Terms You Should Know

Key terms in this chapter include

attack surface, vulnerability, exploitability, threat, threat actor, exploit, risk, beachhead, social engineering, spam, phishing, malware, supply chain attack, MITM, lateral movement, C2 system, data exfiltration, ransomware, DoS, DDoS, direct DDoS attack, source address spoofing, DDoS reflection attack

Concepts and Actions

Review the concepts considered in this chapter using Table 19-4. You can cover the right side of this table and describe each concept or action in your own words to verify your understanding.

Table 19-4   Concepts and Actions

I am not a target	A myth many people believe about security
Attack surface	Every point where the network connects to the outside world
Vulnerability	A possible point of attack against a defensive system
Exploitability	The ease with which a vulnerability can be exploited
Threat	A potential violation of security
Exploit	A tool designed to allow a threat actor to take advantage of a vulnerability
Threat actor	A person or organization behind a threat or attack
Risk	Any potential event, such as an attack, that can disrupt an organization's operations
Beachhead	The initial point at which an attacker gains access to the network; the place from where the attacker expands their control and access
Social engineering	Tricking a user into giving an attacker access to a protected resource
Spam	A form of electronically based social engineering sent to a large number of users
Phishing	A form of electronically based social engineering sent to a well-researched individual user

CHAPTER 20

Security Tools

This chapter covers the following exam topics:

6. Security

6.1. Describe how firewalls operate to filter traffic.

Firewalls (blocked ports and protocols); rules deny or permit access

6.2. Describe foundational security concepts.

Confidentiality, integrity, and availability (CIA); authentication, authorization, and accounting (AAA); Multifactor Authentication (MFA); encryption, certificates, and password complexity; identity stores/databases (Active Directory); threats and vulnerabilities; spam, phishing, malware, and denial of service

Chapter 19, "Attacks and Threats," introduced a lot of terminology and attacks but did not describe how engineers can defend their networks against those attacks. In other words, Chapter 19 described a lot of *problems*. This chapter describes many *solutions* to the problems described in Chapter 19.

This chapter begins by examining authentication tools: How do you control who is allowed to access resources and when they are allowed to do so? What makes a password good or poor? The second section of this chapter considers a broad range of defensive tools, including firewalls and defense in depth. "Countering Spam and Phishing" considers specific techniques to reduce and detect spam and phishing emails.

The final two sections of this chapter are more technical. The fifth section discusses encryption, focusing on public and private key encryption. The last section examines *virtual private networks (VPNs)*, what they do well and poorly, and Tor networks.

Just as there are many different attacks, there are many different defenses. Each defense described here deserves its own book or video series, but you will know the basic concepts and ideas by the end of this chapter.

"Do I Know This Already?" Quiz

Take the quiz (either here or use the PTP software) if you want to use the score to help you decide how much time to spend on this chapter. Appendix A, "Answers to the 'Do I Know This Already?' Quizzes," found at the end of the book, includes both the answers and explanations. You can also find answers in the PTP testing software.

Table 20-1 "Do I Know This Already?" Foundation Topics Section-to-Question Mapping

Section	Questions
Authentication Tools	1, 2, 3, 4, 5, 6
Defensive Tools and Design	7
Countering Spam and Phishing	8, 9
Encryption	10
Virtual Private Networks	11

CAUTION The goal of self-assessment is to gauge your mastery of the topics in this chapter. If you do not know the answer to a question or are only partially sure of the answer, you should mark that question as wrong for purposes of the self-assessment. Giving yourself credit for an answer you incorrectly guess skews your self-assessment results and might provide you with a false sense of security.

1. Why can you trust a website with your SSO credentials?

    a. Because your user credentials are transferred and stored securely

    b. Because your user credentials are not transferred to the website

    c. Because your user credentials are transferred securely, the receiving site does not store them

    d. Because your connection to the website is encrypted

2. What is one negative aspect of SSO?

    a. Your credentials are shared with multiple websites or systems.

    b. Most SSO systems do not support 2FA and other advanced authentication methods.

    c. An attacker who gains access to one password gains access to many of a user's accounts.

    d. Websites that use SSO do not encrypt their traffic.

3. What does password strength refer to?

    a. The length of the password

    b. The password's entropy bits

    c. The number of different kinds of characters used in a password

    d. The number of words in a passphrase

4. After adding some symbols, lowercase letters, and uppercase characters to make guessing a password more difficult, what will add more strength to a password?

    a. Making the password longer

    b. Adding more variation by replacing letters with numbers

    c. Adding more variation by mixing up the case more

    d. Making the password shorter in length so it is easier to remember

5. What is one vulnerability of text message–based 2FA systems an attacker might be able to exploit?

    a. You could lose your phone, so you can no longer access your account.

    b. Text message–based 2FA systems still require a password or passphrase.

    c. An attacker could clone or swap your phone's SIM so they receive the 2FA text messages.

    d. The attacker could make a copy of your fingerprint and use it without you being present.

6. What do biometric systems store a copy of on your device for verification?

    a. Your personal identification number

    b. A picture of your face, finger, etc.

    c. Your telephone number

    d. A digital hash of your face, fingerprint, etc.

7. What does stateful packet filtering use to determine which packets to forward or drop?

    a. The source and destination IP addresses

    b. The contents of the packet in the context of an upper-layer protocol

    c. The state of the session between the transmitter and receiver

    d. A hash of the source and destination addresses divided by a hash of the packet's contents

8. What email fields does a DKIM header sign?

    a. The sender's email address, the receiver's email address, the body of the message, the message's subject, and other fields

    b. Only the sender's and receiver's addresses

    c. The source and destination IP addresses

    d. The sender's telephone number

9. Is it always safe to click on links in emails you receive?

    a. Yes, because of the many layers of security built into email systems

    b. Yes, because no one is likely to send you a link to a password stealing website

    c. No, because the security systems in email do not validate links

    d. No, because email is easy to intercept and read

10. What is nonrepudiation?

    a. Keeping communications and information confidential

    b. Proving data has not changed since it was transmitted

    c. Proving a sender sent a piece of information

    d. Proving a person is who they say they are

11. What is the security justification for using a VPN?

    a. To make it look like you are in a different location

    b. To protect your data from being read by attackers who intercept your traffic

    c. To ensure your data is protected all the way to the server you are communicating with

    d. To make certain you know the identity of the server you are communicating with

Foundation Topics

Authentication Tools

Chapter 19 began the authentication discussion with *authentication, authorization, and accounting (AAA)* tools. This section extends the authentication discussion with important concepts like *single sign-on (***SSO***)* and **zero trust**. None of these authentication systems are foolproof, however; they all require strong passwords or passwordless authentication. Creating and enforcing strong passwords is important enough to merit a separate discussion.

Single Sign-On

When you first choose to log in to a website, you might encounter several options, such as *log in with Google*, *log in with Facebook*, etc.

Single sign-on (SSO) systems allow a user to provide authentication for one system through another system where they already have credentials. Many organizations—companies, colleges, governments, etc.—use SSO systems. You probably have several questions about SSO, like

- How does this work?

- Can I trust a website with access to my Google or Facebook credentials?

- Why do organizations implement these kinds of systems?

Figure 20-1 shows how an SSO system works.

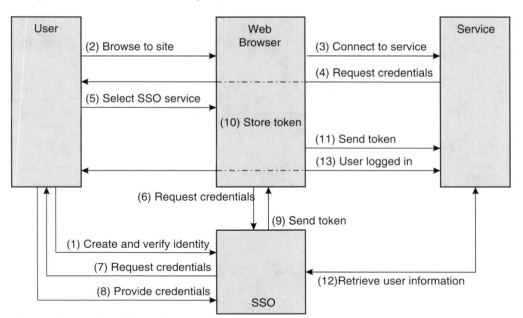

Figure 20-1   *How Single Sign-On Works*

In Figure 20-1:

1. The user creates an identity with a service offering SSO. This service might be a social media site, a *Software as a Service (SaaS)* provider, or another *federated identity* service.

2. The user browses a website.

3. The user's browser connects to the service.

4. The service requests credentials. This credential request often includes several options, such as *log in using email*, *log in using Google*, *log in via Facebook*, etc.

5. The user selects the provider with their identity—the provider they used in step 1.

6. The browser sends an authentication request to the SSO service.

7. The SSO service requests the user's credentials. The browser usually opens a new tab or redirects to the SSO provider's page for this step.

8. The user provides their credentials to the SSO service. The SSO service verifies the user's credentials and creates a token. This step often includes some form of *two-factor authentication* (**2FA**), like a token from an authentication application or a number texted to the user's phone. The SSO service could also use some form of passwordless authentication.

9. The SSO service provides the token to the web browser, verifying the user's identity.

10. The browser stores, or caches, the token. If the user browses to another website that uses the same SSO service, the browser can provide this stored token rather than asking the SSO service for authentication again.

11. The browser sends this token to the service.

12. The service verifies the token with the SSO service and then retrieves any information allowed by the service.

13. The user is logged in to the service.

This process might seem complex, but there is no simpler way to solve the problems an SSO system sets out to solve. SSO has several advantages over each service holding its information about each user.

First, the user needs to manage only one password to log in to multiple services. Because people are generally bad at creating and remembering passwords, reducing the number of passwords individual users must remember is a significant positive aspect of SSO services.

Second, augmenting passwords and passphrases with a 2FA system, or replacing passwords with a passwordless system, is often easier when using SSO. These might increase security, protecting the user and the service.

Third, SSO systems help preserve user privacy. The service can retrieve only information about the user the SSO system allows. If the SSO system has privacy controls, and the user takes advantage of them, SSO systems can prevent services from knowing much more than "this user is who they say they are."

For example, most SSO systems do not use your email address as an identifying token, so the service might not even get your email address when you log in to your account.

The SSO service does not know what kind of business you transact with a service, either. Dividing your identity and transactions into two services is a basic form of privacy-preserving information partitioning.

SSO systems also have negative aspects. One common criticism of SSO systems is an attacker gaining access to your SSO credentials gains access to all your accounts. Some organizations or countries may also block access to SSO systems, so users who rely on SSO can no longer access any of their accounts.

Some countries control the SSO services their citizens can use to impose social controls. In some cases, countries restrict what individuals can purchase or do by not allowing them to use their SSO credentials to interact with some services.

Zero Trust

Chapter 19 illustrated the network edge as a walled fortification—how engineers once built networks. There was the inside of the network, where all the trusted users and traffic lived, and the outside of the network, where all the untrusted users and traffic lived, a fortified exterior defense system, and then a *demilitarized zone (DMZ)* where devices that need access to both inside and outside resources lived.

As noted in Chapter 19, this view of the network is still useful for explaining security terms. Still, it is no longer a useful model for building real-life network security because

- Cloud connectivity and the digitization of business means networks no longer have an "inside" and an "outside."

- There are no trusted users any longer. Employees, contractors, and other "trusted users" might present a smaller threat than an "outsider," but they present a threat network operators must mitigate.

You might wonder about the second point: Why are insiders a threat? The primary reason insiders are considered a threat in modern systems is social engineering attacks. A user with the best intentions can still be tricked into allowing an attacker to access business-critical systems.

How should engineers design systems in a world with lowered levels of trust? Engineers can use zero trust principles.

20

Zero trust is a security framework requiring users to authenticate each time they access a service or data. It assumes there is no network edge.

Figure 20-2 illustrates the components and terminology of a zero trust system.

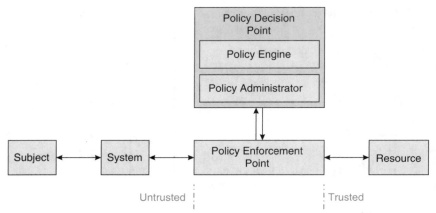

Figure 20-2 *Components and Terminology of a Zero Trust System*

The terminology differs slightly from a traditional security system, but many concepts are the same. In Figure 20-2:

- The **subject** is the user, a process, or even software running on a device (such as your refrigerator).

- The *system* is the hardware, such as a host, network middlebox, or thing (such as your refrigerator).

- The *policy enforcement point* (**PEP**) is the device blocking or allowing traffic flows. The PEP includes the configuration or other rules the device follows to enforce policies.

- The *resource* is a database, application, or anything else you normally access from a host or device.

- The **policy administrator** is the person or organization making the rules about accessing resources.

- The **policy engine** is the security plan.

Zero trust systems rely on continuous authentication, authorization, and accounting to protect resources against threats inside and outside the network.

Strong Passwords

Security systems can rely on three things to prove a user is who they say they are: something they know, something they have, and something they are. Passwords and passphrases are something you know.

A *password* is a set of characters. A *passphrase* is a (longer) set of characters pronounceable as a phrase or sentence.

Password strength measures how easily a password can be guessed or discovered using a brute-force attack. A *brute-force attack* uses software to quickly guess thousands—or even millions—of possible passwords. Password strength is measured by calculating the number of

entropy bits, or how many attempts a brute-force attack would need to try before discovering the password. Table 20-2 gives the entropy bits for several common password patterns.

Table 20-2   Password Strength

Length	Character Set	Entropy Bits
10	Numbers only (1–9)	33
10	Case-insensitive letters (a–z where *a* is treated the same as *A*)	40
10	Case-insensitive letters and numbers (a–z where *a* is treated the same as *A*, 1–9)	52
10	All ASCII characters (treating *a* as different than *A*, all symbols, etc.)	77
20	All ASCII characters (treating *a* as different than *A*, all symbols, etc.)	144
30	All ASCII characters (treating *a* as different than *A*, all symbols, etc.)	221

Once you get past easy-to-guess passwords, according to Table 20-2, adding more symbols, uppercase, lowercase, and other randomness to a password does not make any difference in its strength. The possibility of symbols forces a brute-force attacker to try every possible symbol in every possible character of the password, making the entire password harder to discover.

Suppose you have a 10-character password with the following:

- One-third of the characters are set to uppercase letters.

- One-third of the characters are set to lowercase letters.

- One-third of the characters are set to numbers or symbols.

Compare this password to a 15-character password with the following:

- One character is an uppercase letter.

- One character is either a number or a symbol.

- The remaining 13 characters are lowercase letters.

Which password is more secure? The 15-character password. Adding more symbols or variations will make the password harder to guess. Still, after a minimal number of additional randomness, more variation will not make a password more challenging to discover through a brute-force attack.

How secure should passwords be? This is not a good question to ask! Users should use the strongest password they can work with (there are human limits) and the system allows.

20

But, seriously, how secure should a password be? This depends on

- How many times within a period can an attacker try a password?

- How many times can an attacker try a password before the account is locked?

The faster an attacker can attempt a different solution, and the more times an attacker can try, the stronger the password needs to be. For systems that lock out users after three or four tries and can be accessed only via some application interface, a complexity of around 40–60 is probably currently sufficient.

If an attacker might take an entire password file to try guesses as quickly as possible, and there is no limit on the number of tries, the strength must be much higher—at least above 100. Operators should consider any passwords stored in a file an attacker can take during a breach in this latter category.

Again, however, users should always use their strongest password, within human limitations. Some general guidelines include the following:

- Passwords should be at least eight characters long; longer is better.

- Avoid using the same for two different systems.

- Avoid character repetition.

- Avoid using easy-to-guess information, even if you replace characters with numbers, symbols, etc.

Should users be forced to change their password periodically? The primary reason for these requirements is to limit the damage an attacker can do with a compromised password. Attackers using current attack methods can build back doors into most systems in just a few days, so the utility of short-lived passwords is widely questioned.

However, it is important to force users to change their passwords if a file of passwords— even encrypted ones—is taken in a data breach. Once an attacker has a copy of a user's password in digital format, it is only a matter of time before they discover the password.

Human capacity has been mentioned several times. What does this mean? Humans are

- Poor at creating passwords with a complexity greater than about 40 entropy bits.

- Poor at remembering passwords with a complexity greater than about 40 entropy bits.

One way to counter these limitations is using an SSO system. Using an SSO system is not possible in all situations.

Using a password manager is the primary way to counter human password limitations. Each system a user accesses can be assigned a different password, randomly generated to have the highest strength possible. A user can have hundreds of passwords, one for each system they access, all high strength, and none repeated.

What about creating a password to unlock the password manager? One common technique is to use a long passphrase. Nonsense phrases are often perfect. The process might look something like this:

- Choose three or four words, creating a phrase that makes no sense but is still easy to remember.

- Separate the words with a symbol, character, or number.

- Add in a couple of capital letters at easy-to-remember places in the phrase.

This process often results in a very hard-to-guess and strong passphrase. The longer the phrase, the stronger the passphrase will be.

A second method people often use is

- Write down a sentence of 10 to 15 words. Make certain this sentence is easy to remember.

- Take a pattern of letters from each word, such as the first letter, the first two letters (for shorter sentences), the second letter of each word, etc.

- Capitalize one or two of these letters.

- Add some numbers someplace within the letters or replace one or two of the letters with numbers or symbols.

This process creates an easier-to-remember password of around 15 characters.

Two-Factor Authentication (2FA)

As mentioned earlier, three factors are used to authenticate a user:

- Something you know

- Something you have

- Something you are

Passwords and passphrases are something you know. Because people often create easy-to-guess passwords or are sometimes compromised, security experts recommend adding a second factor—specifically, something you have.

Two-factor authentication (2FA) adds a second factor, usually something you have, to the first form of authentication, normally a password or passphrase.

20

The first common form of 2FA is texting a code to a cellular telephone. The advantage of this system is most users have a cellular telephone, and cellular providers are good at assigning only a single number to a single phone or account. There are ways to attack this kind of 2FA, however. For instance:

- Attackers can replicate SIM cards so two devices have the same phone number.

- An attacker can steal your phone or even use your phone for 2FA to break into an account while you are asleep or otherwise unaware of what is happening.

- Some phone systems allow you to share your account so other users see your text messages.

- If you lose your phone, you lose access to your account; there must be some backup for the 2FA system.

Despite these limitations, text messaging is one of the most widely used 2FA systems.

A second common form of 2FA is a rotating security code—often called *tokens*—tied to a device or application. To use this form of 2FA, the user installs an app on one of their devices, like a cellular telephone, or purchases a hardware security token device. The 2FA app or device generates a new code periodically—usually every 60 seconds.

This timing of token generation is synchronized with a token generator used by the service. Users log in to their account using their password or passphrase *and* a token from the token generator. The server can verify the two tokens match to authenticate the user.

A third common form of 2FA is push notifications. In this case, the user installs an app on a mobile device such as a cellular telephone. When a user attempts to log in to a service, the service will push a notification to the user's device. The user must authenticate by approving the login request.

Passwordless Systems

Many security experts believe **passwordless** systems are the future of authentication. Passwordless systems eliminate *what you know* from the authentication process, relying on some combination of *what you have* and *what you are*.

Passwordless systems use something you have and something you are to authenticate users.

Typical passwordless systems use two forms of authentication:

- Physical possession of a device like a USB key, host, or mobile device

- A biometric sensor of some type

Figure 20-3 illustrates a passwordless authentication system using a facial recognition camera.

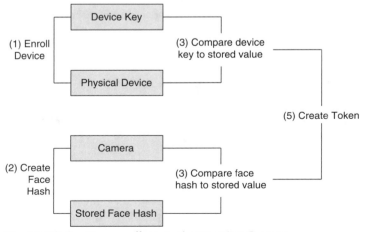

Figure 20-3   *Passwordless Authentication System*

In Figure 20-3:

1. The user, manufacturer, dealer, or operator enrolls the device on activation. Enrollment includes using a hardware-based identifier like a physical interface address or *embedded identification document (EID)* to create a device key. The device is stored in secure device memory.

2. The user uses the camera to create a cryptographic hash of their face. The device does not store a picture of the user's face but uses their picture as the basis for a hash, which is then encrypted or signed using the key created in step 1.

3. When the user attempts to log in to the device—or any service requiring a token—the device key is retrieved from secure memory and compared to a key created using the same information and algorithm. If these match, the first stage of authentication passes.

4. A token is created and handed off to the requesting app. This token might unlock the phone, log in to a password manager or a secure system, etc.

One of the most common misconceptions about biometric systems is they store a copy of your fingerprint or your face on the device. If an attacker breaks into your device's secure storage, they will not see any images but rather just a long string of numbers. This number describes the user's face, fingerprint, etc.

One of the risks of biometric systems is you cannot get a new fingerprint or face if an attacker somehow steals enough information about your face to re-create the local cryptographic hash of your body part. Short of getting plastic surgery, it is difficult to change your face.

Facial and fingerprint recognition systems also are notoriously fickle. Users often struggle to be recognized, and these systems are prone to accepting faces and fingerprints that do not match the authenticated user's.

NOTE The "Encryption" section later in this chapter explains encryption and cryptographic hashes.

Defensive Tools and Design

The network often provides the *first*—and sometimes the only—*layer of defense* for network-connected devices. This section explains stateful packet filtering, contextual packet filtering, the firewall, source address validation, and defensive layering.

Stateful and Contextual Packet Filtering

Network security's "pointy end" is stateful and contextual packet filtering—the primary defensive network tool.

Stateful packet filtering forwards or drops packets based on the state of a connection. Figure 20-4 illustrates stateful packet filtering.

20

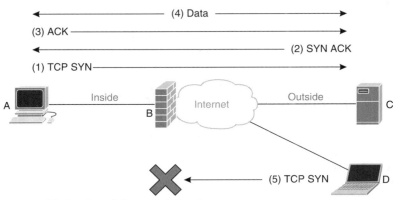

Figure 20-4 *Stateful Packet Filtering*

Firewall *B* allows only TCP packets for sessions with existing state from the outside to the inside network.

In Figure 20-4:

1. Host *A* sends a TCP SYN to open a session with server *C*. Firewall *B* notes this TCP SYN and opens a temporary "hole" in its local filters to allow the anticipated SYN-ACK from server *C*.

2. Server *C* receives *A*'s TCP SYN and responds with a SYN ACK. Firewall *B* allows this packet through because of the previously opened hole in its filters.

3. Host *A* sends an ACK to server *C*. This ACK completes the TCP connection setup. Firewall *B* configures its filters to allow TCP packets with the correct port number from server *C* to host *A*.

4. Host *A* and server *B* can now transmit and receive data through the firewall.

If host *D* attempts to start a TCP session with *A*, it will begin by sending a TCP SYN (step 5 in the figure). Because the firewall does not have an existing TCP connection, Firewall *B* will drop the packets from host *D*, blocking *D*'s ability to connect to *A*.

A stateful packet filter is a sort of "one-way mirror," allowing traffic flows originating from the inside network and blocking traffic flows originating from the outside network.

Contextual packet filtering forwards or drops packets based on their content. Figure 20-5 will be used to explain contextual packet filtering.

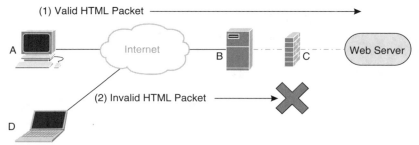

Figure 20-5 *Contextual Packet Filtering*

In Figure 20-5, hosts *A* and *D* communicate with the web server on server *B*. A *web application firewall (WAF)* is running on the server. Every packet transmitted to the web server must pass through the WAF after being received by server *B* before being forwarded (internally) to the web server.

Application firewalls (AFs) filter packets based on a deep knowledge of an application's state. Each kind of application, including web servers, Domain Name System (DNS) servers, database servers, etc., can have a custom application firewall.

In Figure 20-5, host *A* sends a *Hypertext Markup Language (HTML)* to server *B* at (1). The WAF will check the packet format for errors, including

- The resource exists on the web server.

- The HTML packet does not contain an *injection attack*.

- The host is either sending a session initiation packet, or the packet is within an existing flow.

- The sequence numbers are correct.

WAF *C* will not forward the packet to the web server if these checks fail. For instance, if host *D* attempts to send a packet with a poorly constructed HTML command could potentially cause the web server to crash at (2), WAF *C* will drop the packet.

A second kind of contextual packet filter is an *intrusion detection system (**IDS**)*. Figure 20-6 illustrates an IDS.

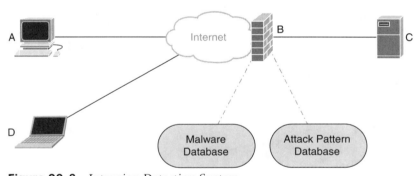

Figure 20-6   *Intrusion Detection System*

In Figure 20-6, IDS *B* has two databases:

- Malware database containing bit-level patterns of known malware apps

- Attack pattern database containing packet-level patterns of known and learned attacks

The IDS examines traffic forwarded from hosts *A* and *D* toward server *C* for any packets containing bits matching known malware or a pattern of packets indicating *C* is being attacked (such as some form of resource exhaustion attack). If *B* detects any of these conditions, it drops the relevant packets.

Intrusion detection systems (IDSs) filter packets based on knowledge of common attacks.

While stateful packet filtering, contextual packet filtering, and intrusion detection can be standalone services, they are often combined with other services in a firewall.

A firewall is a collection of network security services in a single appliance or virtual services. Firewalls often include stateful packet filtering and intrusion detection services. Firewalls may include *Network Address Translation (NAT)*, contextual packet filtering, address- and port-based packet filtering, and other security-related functions.

Encryption and Filtering

Stateful and contextual packet filtering rely on information within packets to protect servers and applications, but what if the packets in a stream are encrypted? Encryption prevents middleboxes, including firewalls, from effectively seeing the information needed to filter based on state.

One solution to this problem is to include a proxy function on the firewall. Suppose the firewall acts as a man-in-the middle, unencrypting and encrypting traffic as it travels between the client and server. If the firewall acts as a man-in-the-middle, the firewall will have enough information to filter traffic effectively.

Another solution is to place the firewall between the end of the encrypted tunnel and the application. Application firewalls generally receive traffic after the host's network stack has unencrypted it but before the application.

As operators and users encrypt larger amounts of traffic, engineers must move toward proxies and application firewalls to continue providing effective security.

Source Address Validation

Chapter 19 describes *reflection attacks*, where attackers reflect traffic off servers toward a victim. Figure 20-7 illustrates.

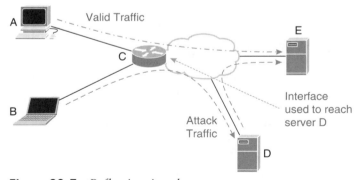

Figure 20-7 *Reflection Attack*

In Figure 20-7, router *C* receives a valid traffic flow from host *A*, trying to get to a web server on *E*. However, an attacker uses host B to reflect traffic through server *D* as part of a reflection attack against *E*.

Ideally, router *C* would be able to block the attack traffic while allowing the valid traffic, but how can *C* tell the difference between the two?

One difference is *A sends packets from its actual IP address, while B sends packets from server E's source address.* In fact, the source of *B*'s attack traffic is not even in the same subnet as router *C*'s connection to *B*. In other words, *C*'s path to the packet's source—the *reverse path*—is not through the interface where it received the packet.

Unicast reverse-path forwarding (uRPF) discards any packet where the reverse path, or the path to the source address, does not match the forwarding interface—the interface through which the router would forward a packet to reach the source address.

Defense in Depth

Systems, including networks, should never have one line of defense. Attackers should always pass through multiple lines of defense to reach their objective. Figure 20-8 illustrates the concept of **defense in depth**.

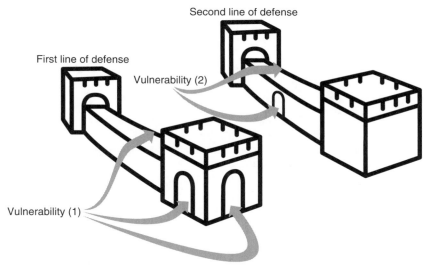

Figure 20-8 *Defense in Depth*

Key Topic

Defense in depth forces an attacker to move through multiple defensive lines or systems to reach their objective.

20

Figure 20-8 shows these multiple lines of defense as multiple fortified walls. Each line of defense should have a different set of vulnerabilities, if possible.

As an example, imagine an organization has an application with access to sensitive information about its employees. The defenses around this application might include the following:

■ The application's servers are on a separate virtual network topology.

■ Users must log in to the organization's network using 2FA before accessing the application's website (the website is available only to internal users).

- Users do not get an application account unless they need to.

- Users must log in to the application separately using 2FA.

- Users' actions are logged while they are using the service.

These layers of defenses, each with vulnerabilities and controls, make it much harder for an attacker to access sensitive information.

Countering Spam and Phishing

Social engineering through email, texts, and private messages is the most common information technology attack.

Spam is any unwanted mail, including advertising, newsletters you did not ask for, and scams sent to thousands (or even millions) of users.

A **phish** is a targeted attack against an individual user, using information about the user to craft an email the user is more likely to respond to or act on.

Attackers often want you to

- Open an attachment that installs malware.

- Visit a website that installs malware.

- Give them account numbers (or other private information).

- Give someone access to your computer.

Each of these can have disastrous consequences for you and your organization. Learning to guard against phishing attacks is a critical engineering skill and an important life skill. This section explains how you can defend yourself against phishing attacks.

Each of these approaches is something you can also show family members, friends, and users to help them.

System-Level Defenses

Many elements of the email ecosystem work to block spam and phishing emails before they even arrive in your inbox. Figure 20-9 illustrates the many checks involved in sending and receiving email in a system supporting *Domain-based Message Authentication, Reporting, and Conformance (***DMARC***)*.

Figure 20-9 begins with a user composing a mail in a *client*, usually an application running on a mobile device, host, or web page on a server running in the cloud. This client sends the mail to the sending server using Simple Mail Transfer Protocol. This server may also be called a mail transfer agent.

*Simple Mail Transfer Protocol (***SMTP***)* is designed to transfer mail between two servers. The *Internet Engineering Task Force (IETF)* has extended SMTP to carry text, images, HTML, encrypted mail, etc., through *Multipurpose Internet Mail Extensions (MIME)*.

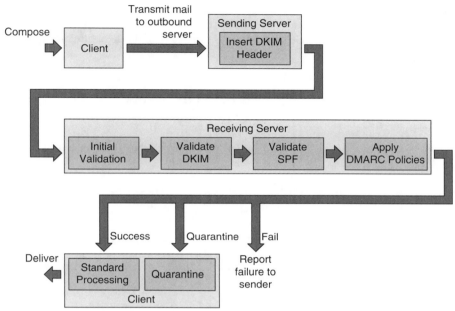

Figure 20-9   *Security in the Email Ecosystem*

A *mail transfer agent (***MTA**) transfers email using SMTP.

Sending servers will almost always require the sender to log in to email. Forcing senders to log in prevents attackers from using a random email server to send a phishing email and makes most emails traceable to their originator. While requiring senders to log in to an email server blocked large amounts of spam, attackers have adapted their techniques by building and managing email servers and abusing free email systems.

The sending server creates a *DomainKeys Identified Mail (***DKIM**) header and attaches it to the mail. This DKIM header signs the sender's email address, the receiver's email address, the body of the message, the message's subject, and other fields. This signature is encrypted using the sender's private key.

The sending server looks up the receiver's domain name, the part after the @ symbol in the email address, to discover the receiving server's IP address. The sending server opens a connection to this IP address and uses SMTP to send the mail to the receiving server.

Most receiving servers will perform several initial checks before processing the mail, including

- Checking local IP blocklists for this sender.

- Checking the reputation of the sender's domain name.

- Rate limiting mail from this sender.

- Searching for the sender's IP address using a reverse DNS *inaddr.arpa* lookup; verifying the sender's IP address is in the same domain as the sender's address.

Once these basic checks are completed, the receiving server retrieves the sender's public key using DNS. The receiving server calculates a signature, encrypts it using the sender's public key, and compares this newly calculated encrypted signature with the signature included by the sender.

If these signatures do not match, the mail has been modified and should be discarded.

Another policy called the *Sender Policy Framework (**SPF**)* uses DNS. The SPF contains a list of valid email addresses in a domain. The mail should be discarded if the sender's address is not on this list.

The receiving server then retrieves the sending domain's policies, called the DMARC, and checks the email against these policies.

If the email passes these tests, the receiving server stores the mail for a client to retrieve later. The mail might also be marked as spam by the receiving server, in which case it will be quarantined. Users can normally release quarantined mail through a web interface.

Receiving mail servers will process local filters at this point. These filters may include blocked senders, sorting mail into folders, etc. Most receiving servers will also process mail through a spam filter.

A **spam filter** searches mail for keywords, key phrases, attachments, suspicious links, suspicious Hypertext Markup Language (HTML), etc. Based on this search, a spam filter sets a spam score for each mail. If the spam score is high enough, the mail will be marked as spam and sorted into a special folder.

The next time the receiver's mail client connects to the receiving server, it will retrieve any new mail. Mail clients use two protocols to retrieve email:

- *Post Office Protocol v3 (POP3)* physically copies mail from the server to the client. Mail retrieved by POP no longer exists on the server.

- *Internet Message Access Protocol (IMAP)* synchronizes the server's folders with the client's. Mail accessed through IMAP remains on the server so multiple clients can access and manage it.

Internet mail is a complex system with many security mechanisms built into every stage of transmitting mail from a sender to a receiver.

How to Detect a Phish

Even though Internet mail systems contain many different checks, a large amount of spam and phishing email—especially well-researched spear phishing—is still delivered. You still need to know how to detect spam and phishing emails.

Begin by checking the destination email addresses. If the destination email address is not your actual address, the mail is addressed to many people you do not know, or you are "blind copied" on the email, the email is probably spam or phishing.

Next, look at the source email address. A good technique is to copy the source email address to your clipboard and paste it into a text editor (like Notepad on Windows or Text Editor on macOS). Look at the sender's domain—the part after the @ symbol. If the sender's domain does not match the domain of links in the mail, and the mail is not a newsletter, the mail is probably spam or a phish.

If you have an account with the sender's organization, open their website and log in manu-ally; do not click any links. Once you are in your account, check the information in the mail using menus, searching, etc. You should *never* click on the link in an email unless you are *certain* the mail is valid and the link is good.

Even if the mail looks legitimate, *do not click on the links*. Instead, right-click or Ctrl-click on any linked text, copy the link location, and paste it into a text editor. Once you paste the link, check the domain name; if the mail is spam or phishing, the domain name will be buried among text strings and random characters. Ensure you find the *actual* domain, not a string that looks like a domain in the middle of the link.

Once you find the domain, check it against the sender's domain. You can also enter the *domain* without anything else in the link to see where it leads.

Finally, *do not download and open attachments* unless you know the sender. Even if you know the sender, be careful with attachments, as attackers can take over or hijack a user's mail account.

If you find the email is spam or phishing, you can use a *Whois* tool on the Internet to look up the domain name. Whois will give you an "abuse contact" email address. Forward the spam or phishing email to the abuse address in the Whois record. You can often report spam and phishing emails to your provider.

Encryption

Previous sections have discussed many ways encryption is used in information security. We rely on encryption for

- *Confidentiality*, or keeping our communications and information confidential.

- *Integrity*, or proving no one has changed a piece of data between the sender and receiver.

- *Nonrepudiation*, or proving a sender sent a piece of information.

- *Authentication*, or proving a person is who they say they are.

Up to this point, however, we have not explored how encryption works. Encryption essen-tially performs a complex mathematical operation that combines data with a key, resulting in unreadable data. The process can be reversed to retrieve the original text. Figure 20-10 illus-trates how basic encryption works.

20

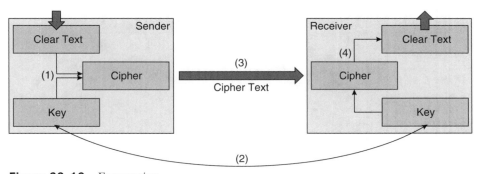

Figure 20-10 *Encryption*

In Figure 20-10:

1. A **cipher** mathematically combines a key and **clear text** to create **cipher text**.

2. The **key** used to create the cipher text is transferred to the receiver.

3. The cipher text is transmitted to the receiver across a network (or in some other way).

4. The receiver mathematically combines the key and the cipher text to recover the clear text.

Figure 20-10 illustrates *symmetric* or *shared key cryptography* because the sender and receiver use the same key to encrypt and unencrypt the data. Protocols like *Secure Hypertext Transfer Protocol (HTTPS)*, QUIC, and *Transport Layer Security (TLS)* all use symmetric cryptography to protect information traveling between the sender and receiver.

The primary advantages of symmetric cryptography are

- It is simpler to implement than other forms of cryptography.

- Converting from plain text to cipher text and back is relatively fast and inexpensive. Symmetric encryption can be performed in specialized hardware, while asymmetric encryption cannot.

The primary disadvantage of symmetric encryption is *anyone who has the key can encrypt or unencrypt the data.* If an attacker somehow gets the key you use for symmetric cryptography, they can send information that looks like it came from you and read your encrypted messages.

Symmetric cryptography is often called *secret key cryptography* because the key must be protected to keep the communication channel secure.

Is there some way to encrypt data without using a key both sides of the conversation must keep secret? Yes—*public key encryption*. Figure 20-11 illustrates public key encryption.

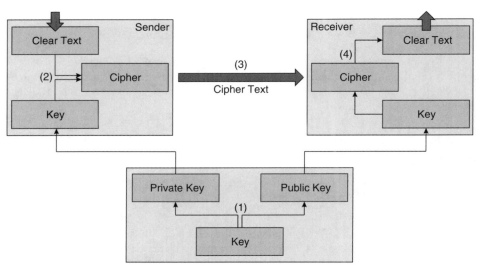

Figure 20-11 *Public Key Encryption*

In public key encryption, as with private key or symmetric encryption, a key is combined with data to create cipher text. The receiver then reverses the process to recover the original clear text. However, public key encryption uses two different keys rather than a single shared key. In Figure 20-11:

1. The user creates a single, long key. This key is split in half, creating a **private key** and **public key**. Either half of the original key can become either key. The keys are different and used for different purposes, but there is no mathematical difference between them. The public key is published on a website, through DNS, in a directory service, etc. The private key is held privately by the sender.

2. The sender combines the private key with the clear text to create the cipher text.

3. The cipher text is transmitted across a network to the receiver.

4. The receiver combines the sender's public key with the cipher text (unencrypts cipher text) to recover the original clear text.

Public key cryptography systems have two keys, one of which can be published, while the other must be kept secret.

Public key or **asymmetric cryptography** has one advantage over private key cryptography: the sender and receiver do not need to share a **secret key**. Because of this, public key cryptography systems can be used over open networks, like the Internet, to create secure communication channels and cryptographic signatures.

The disadvantages of public key cryptography are as follows:

- Public key cryptography is more complex to implement, leading to more bugs, etc.

- Public key cryptography requires more processing power, so it is more expensive and slower than private key cryptography

Because asymmetrical cryptography is computationally expensive, it is not generally suited to encrypting large amounts of data, such as a video or audio stream. Public key cryptography is almost always used as a *block cipher* for small data blocks and rarely as a *stream cipher*.

A *block cipher* is an encryption system used for fixed-length data sets—a single file. A *stream cipher* is an encryption system for streaming data, such as video or audio. The difference is not the kind of data but how the data is presented—as a single object or a stream.

Public key cryptography is, however, widely used for exchanging private keys and creating cryptographic signatures.

Exchanging Private Keys

Protocol designers combine the best aspects of public and private key cryptography to create secure transport protocols. Figure 20-12 illustrates how these protocols use these two forms of cryptography.

20

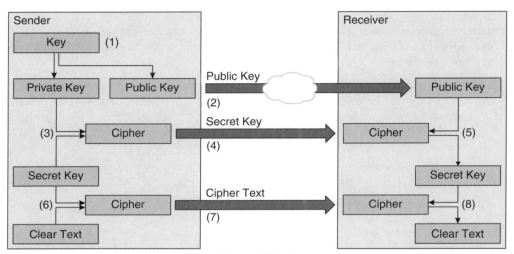

Figure 20-12   *Combining Public and Private Key Cryptography*

In Figure 20-12:

1. The sender creates a key for a public key cipher, split into public and private keys. The sender stores the private key securely.

2. The sender publishes the public key to a server on the Internet, through DNS, etc. The receiver finds this public key and stores it locally.

3. The sender creates a secret key, stores it securely, and uses the private key to encrypt the secret key.

4. The sender transmits the encrypted secret key as cipher text to the receiver.

5. The receiver uses the sender's public key and a cipher to recover the private key. The receiver securely stores this secret key, often called a **session key**.

6. The sender uses the secret key and cipher to convert clear text to cipher text.

7. The sender transmits the cipher text over the network to the receiver.

8. The receiver uses the secret key and cipher to recover the original clear text.

Secure transports often include *anti-replay* protections in this kind of key exchange.

Replay attacks are when an attacker captures and replays packets off the network. These attacks can be used to access a protected system or cause an action (such as a bank transfer) to happen more than once.

Cryptographic Signatures

Public key cryptography is also widely used to create **cryptographic signatures** or **cryptographic hashes**. Figure 20-13 illustrates.

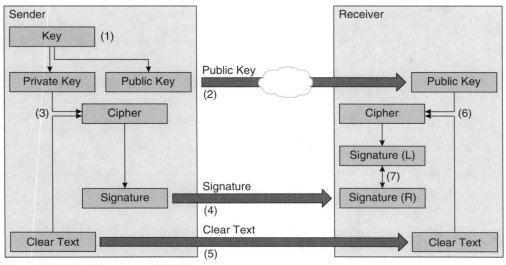

Figure 20-13 *Cryptographic Signatures*

In Figure 20-13:

1. The sender creates a key, which is divided into public and private keys.

2. The sender publishes the public key through a website, DNS, etc. The receiver retrieves this key.

3. The sender uses the private key and cipher to create a cryptographic hash.

4. The sender transmits this signature across the network to the receiver. The receiver stores this as *Signature (R)*.

5. The sender transmits the original data, in clear text (not encrypted), across the network to the receiver.

6. The receiver uses the public key and cipher to create a signature for the clear text, calling it *Signature (L)*.

7. The receiver compares the local and remote cryptographic hashes. If they match, the signature is valid.

This process might seem like a lot of work to carry data across a network. If you are going to build a hash of the data, why not just encrypt the data? Because:

■ Public key cryptography is computationally expensive for large volumes of data.

■ Sometimes you want anyone to be able to read or see data, but you want those who are interested to be able to verify the data they receive is what you sent. For instance, you want anyone to be able to read your emails, but you also want the recipient to know—for certain—the email they are reading is what you sent.

■ Sometimes you want anyone to be able to read or see data, but you want everyone to be able to verify you sent it. For instance, anyone should be able to read a legal document, but signers should not be able to claim they did not sign it.

20

- Sometimes you do not want to store the original data, but you do want to verify the data you have is the same as some future copy of the same data. For instance, you do not want to store users' passwords. Instead, you want to store cryptographic hashes of each user's password, which you can compare to passwords they enter later.

Cryptographic hashes are repeatable signatures across a piece of data. These hashes are repeatable, but they cannot be unencrypted.

These use cases are critical in real-world uses of cryptography, specifically:

- *Authentication* is ensuring a person is who they claim to be.

- *Validation* is ensuring data has not changed from what the sender transmitted.

- **Nonrepudiation** is ensuring someone cannot claim they did not sign or send something.

Virtual Private Networks

You often do not want network devices between your host and some destination to be able to see the information you are sending. *Virtual private networks (VPNs)* use cryptography to hide traffic passing across the Internet. Figure 20-14 illustrates a VPN.

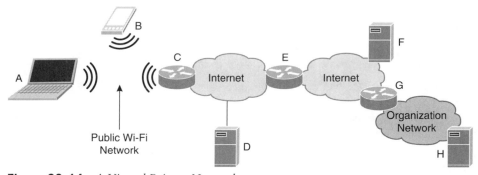

Figure 20-14   *A Virtual Private Network*

Assume host *A* wants to communicate with server *F* without any other hosts connected to the public Wi-Fi network—like mobile device *B*—being able to see the information it sends. Host *A* can accomplish this by building an encrypted tunnel using IPsec to some intermediate device, such as server *D*. In this case:

- Host *A* creates a packet with *A* as its source and *F* as its destination address.

- Host *A* places this packet in an encrypted tunnel and forwards it to router *C*. Server *D* is the destination of the tunneled packet.

- Host *A* sends this packet to router *C*.

- Router *C* forwards the packet to server *D*.

- Server *D* unencrypts the packet's outer header and finds a packet destined for *F*.

- Server *D* forwards the inner packet—the packet *A* created—to *F*.

From *F*'s perspective, the packet's source is still host *A*, so traffic from *F* to *A* will travel directly back through the network. Since the packets are unencrypted at *D*, devices like *E* can still see the plain text data.

It might not seem like encrypting just the packets host *A* sends to *F* is very useful, but it does make the *A* to *F* connection more secure. Consider what happens when *A* starts an encrypted connection with *F*.

Host *A* must start this encrypted session with a three-way handshake and exchange a session key with *F*. If device *C* observes this initial session startup, it may be able to execute a man-in-the-middle (MITM) attack. Observing the key exchange may allow *C* to observe all the data traveling between *A* and *F*. Protecting the public Wi-Fi portion of the path increases the overall session security.

If more security is desired, host *A* can build a *Secure Sockets Layer (SSL)* tunnel to server *D* instead of an IPsec tunnel. In this case, server *D* is a **proxy**, terminating the IP connection. The IP connection between host *A* and server *D* is now separate from those between servers *D* and *F*.

From *F*'s perspective, the source IP address is server *D*. In this case:

- Host *A* builds a packet with *D* as the destination address. The data inside this packet is encrypted using a session key negotiated by *A* and *D*.

- Host *A* sends this packet to router *C*. Device *B* cannot read the contents of this packet because it is encrypted.

- Router *C* forwards this traffic to *D*.

- Server *D* unencrypts the data and sends it to server *F* in packets using *D*'s source address.

- Server *F* responds to these packets by sending them to *D*.

- Server *D* encrypts *F*'s responses into its encrypted tunnel with host *A* and sends them back over the network to *A*. Device *C* cannot read these packets because they are encrypted.

If *A* and *F* build an encrypted session, the traffic from *A* to *D* will be "double encrypted," and the traffic from *D* to *F* will still be encrypted. Router *E* will still be able to see the traffic without its first layer of encryption.

Proxies encrypt traffic in both directions *and* hide the origin's IP address. Tunnels on the open Internet protect traffic in only one direction and do not hide the origin's IP address.

Organizational VPNs, however, can protect traffic in both directions. Assume server *H* is within an organization's network—like a company or college. Router *G* acts as a VPN server for this network. In this case:

- Host *A* builds a packet with *H*'s destination address.

- The host encapsulates this packet in an encrypted IPsec packet with *G*'s destination and forwards it to router *C*. Device *B* cannot read the contents of this packet because it is encrypted.

20

- Router *C* forwards this packet toward *G*. Router *E* cannot read the contents of this packet because it is encrypted.

- Router *G* receives the packet, unencrypts it, and finds a packet destined for server *H*. Router *G* forwards it to *H* over the internal organizational network.

- Server *H* responds, sending a packet with *A*'s IP address. The only route *H* has to *A* is through router *G*; it cannot reach *A* through the global Internet.

- Router *G* receives this packet and finds its path to *A* is through a *tunnel interface*. This is an IPsec encrypted tunnel, so *G* encrypts the packet and sends it toward *A*.

- Host *A* receives the packet and unencrypts it.

Because organizations can control the path traffic takes through their network and ensure both sides of a flow are encrypted, tunneled VPNs are a common solution for organizational VPNs.

Many commercially available VPN products will act in tunneled or proxy mode, depending on the traffic sent over the secured connection.

Chapter Review

The previous chapter considered all the various attacks—or rather, problems in network security. This chapter showed how each of these threats can be countered. The chapter began with an overview of authentication tools and concepts, including SSO, zero trust, 2FA, and passwordless. While many future-looking members of the information technology community hold that passwordless solutions are the obvious choice, passwordless still faces many challenges.

One of the most important topics considered in this chapter is password complexity. Every information technology professional should be able to build strong passwords and know how to manage passwords. Another important topic this chapter considered is detecting and countering spam and phishing attacks. Social engineering attacks through electronic media— email, text messages, and private messages—are the most common way attackers gain access to a network.

This chapter could scratch the surface of encryption, a complex topic. Some engineers and researchers spend their entire careers working in and around encryption. Finally, this chapter outlined various VPN options, including their positive and negative aspects.

The next part of the book moves into network troubleshooting, management, and configuration. Chapter 21 kicks off the next section by explaining basic troubleshooting concepts.

One key to doing well on the exams is to perform repetitive spaced review sessions. Review this chapter's material using either the tools in the book or interactive tools for the same material found on the book's companion website. Refer to the online Appendix D, "Study Planner," element for more details. Table 20-3 outlines the key review elements and where you can find them. To better track your study progress, record when you completed these activities in the second column.

Table 20-3   Chapter Review Tracking

Review Element	Review Date (s)	Resource Used
Review key topics		Book, website
Review key terms		Book, website
Repeat DIKTA questions		Book, PTP
Review concepts and actions		Book, website

Review All the Key Topics

Table 20-4 lists the key topics for this chapter.

Table 20-4   Key Topics for Chapter 20

Key Topic Element	Description	Page Number
Paragraph	Single sign-on (SSO)	397
Paragraph, Figure 20-2, list	Zero trust system	399
Paragraph, Table 20-2	Password strength, entropy bits, and brute-force attacks	400
List	Three factors for authenticating a user	403
Paragraph	Two-factor authentication	403
Paragraph, list	Passwordless systems	404
Paragraph, Figure 20-4, list	Stateful packet filtering	405
Paragraph, Figure 20-5	Contextual packet filtering	406
Paragraph	Application firewalls (AFs)	407
Paragraph	Intrusion detection systems (IDSs)	408
Paragraph	Defense in depth	409
Section	Countering Spam and Phishing	410
Paragraph	Simple Mail Transfer Protocol (SMTP)	410
Paragraph	Mail transfer agent (MTA)	411
Paragraph	DomainKeys Identified Mail (DKIM)	411
Paragraph	Sender policy framework	412
Paragraph	Spam filter	412
Paragraph, Figure 20-10, list	Encryption	413
Paragraphs, list	Advantages and disadvantages of symmetric/secret key cryptography	414
Paragraphs, list	Advantages and disadvantages of asymmetric cryptography	415
Paragraph	Cryptographic hashes	418

20

Key Terms You Should Know

Key terms in this chapter include

SSO, zero trust, 2FA, subject, PEP, policy administrator, policy engine, entropy bits, passwordless, stateful packet filtering, contextual packet filtering, application firewall, IDS, defense in depth, phish, DMARC, SMTP, MTA, DKIM, SPF, spam filter, cipher, clear text, cipher text, key, symmetric cryptography, private key, public key, asymmetric cryptography, secret key, session key, cryptographic signature, cryptographic hash, nonrepudiation, proxy

Concepts and Actions

Review the concepts considered in this chapter using Table 20-5. You can cover the right side of this table and describe each concept or action in your own words to verify your understanding.

Table 20-5 Concepts and Actions

SSO	Single sign-on
SSO advantages	Users need to memorize only one password, easier to augment with 2FA, SSO helps preserve user privacy
SSO disadvantages	An attacker who gains access to one password gains access to multiple accounts
Zero trust	Security system requiring users to authenticate for each data or service access
Entropy bits	How many attempts a brute-force attack would need to try before guessing a password
Password length	Once all character types are represented, longer passwords are stronger
Authentication factors	Something you know, something you have, something you are
2FA	Authentication system that uses two factors to authenticate users. For password-based systems, these are normally something you know and something you have
Passwordless system	Authentication system that uses something you are and something you have
Stateful packet filtering	Filtering packets based on the state of the network transport
Contextual packet filtering	Filtering packets based on application state and safe inputs
IDS	Filters packets based on information about common attacks
Defense in depth	Building multiple layers of defense, each of which ideally has different vulnerabilities
DMARC	Domain-based Message Authentication, Reporting, and Conformance
SMTP	Simple Mail Transfer Protocol
MTA	Mail transfer agent
DKIM	DomainKeys Identified Mail, signs email header fields to ensure they are not changed in transport

SPF	Sending Policy Framework, a list of valid email addresses in a domain
Spam filter	Searches mail for keywords, key phrases, attachments, suspicious links, etc.
Spam	Mail to many recipients, could include advertising, scams, etc.
Phish	An email crafted for an individual user; takes advantage of knowledge about that specific user; a social engineering attack
Cipher	An encryption algorithm
Clear text	Unencrypted text
Cipher text	Encrypted text
Symmetric cryptography	The sender and receiver share the same key
Secret key cryptography	The sender and receiver share the same key
Public key	One of the two keys used in asymmetric cryptography, this key can be published or shared publicly
Asymmetric cryptography	Cryptographic system using public and private keys
Private key	One of the two keys used in asymmetric cryptography, this key should be securely stored
Cryptographic hash	A cryptographically created, non-repeatable, signature across a data set; cannot be unencrypted
Cryptographic hash use cases	Authentication, validation, nonrepudiation
VPN	Virtual private network
Proxy	Terminates session; hides source address

20

Part V

Managing Networks

Building a network, or even taking over a network that is already running, is a small part of a network engineer's job. Networks must be configured. Networks must be managed. Networks break and must be fixed.

This part of this book considers configuring, managing, and troubleshooting networks—although not in that order.

Chapter 21 kicks off this part by discussing the concepts and tools of managing a network. The first section of Chapter 21 covers the importance and kinds of documentation, the second section of the chapter considers the observability problem and the law of large numbers. The final section of Chapter 21 covers the practical tools and techniques used to connect to a network device.

Chapter 22 once again begins with theory, in this case the theory of efficient and effective troubleshooting. Formal troubleshooting skills are rare in computer networking. The chapter then considers the troubleshooting process and finally the importance of packet captures.

Chapter 23 walks through configuring and troubleshooting a small network using Cisco devices. This chapter brings all the theory into practice. This is also the last technical chapter in the book.

The chapters in this part of the book are as follows:

Chapter 21: Managing Networks

Chapter 22: Troubleshooting

Chapter 23: Configuring a Network

CHAPTER 21

Managing Networks

This chapter covers the following exam topics:

5. Diagnosing Problems

5.1. Demonstrate effective troubleshooting methodologies and help desk best practices, including ticketing, documentation, and information gathering.

Policies and procedures, accurate and complete documentation, prioritization

5.4. Differentiate between different ways to access and collect data about network devices.

Remote access (RDP, SSH, telnet), VPN, terminal emulators, Console, Network Management Systems, Network Cloud Management (Meraki), scripts

Engineers tend to spend more time thinking about designing and deploying networks than managing them, and yet, most of the time in a network's lifecycle is day-to-day management. Design does directly impact the manageability of a network. Simpler networks with well-defined functional separations are easier to manage than complex networks with many overlapping and mixed functionality.

Beyond design, however, there are many network management concepts a network engineer should know. This chapter introduces concepts like

- Network documentation
- Network lifecycle
- Network management challenges
- Connecting to manage

These topics are important for network engineers, especially those beginning their careers. Most network engineers begin by managing networks, following one of two career paths as their careers mature:

- Moving from managing networks to designing networks and finally to an architecture role
- Moving up in network management to become a master of operating and troubleshooting networks

Both career paths are valuable; both need to understand the basics of managing a network.

"Do I Know This Already?" Quiz

Take the quiz (either here or use the PTP software) if you want to use the score to help you decide how much time to spend on this chapter. Appendix A, "Answers to the 'Do I Know This Already?' Quizzes," found at the end of the book, includes both the answers and explanations. You can also find answers in the PTP testing software.

Table 21-1 "Do I Know This Already?" Foundation Topics Section-to-Question Mapping

Section	Questions
Network Documentation	1
Network Processes and Lifecycle	2, 3, 4
Management Challenges	5
Connecting to Manage	6, 7, 8
Management Systems	9

CAUTION The goal of self-assessment is to gauge your mastery of the topics in this chapter. If you do not know the answer to a question or are only partially sure of the answer, you should mark that question as wrong for purposes of the self-assessment. Giving yourself credit for an answer you incorrectly guess skews your self-assessment results and might provide you with a false sense of security.

1. Network descriptions should never include the following:

   a. The intent behind each configuration choice

   b. The device naming system

   c. Where each cable terminates

   d. How to find the source code used in network automation

2. Why is flexible network design important?

   a. Because network hardware has a very short lifecycle and needs to be replaced regularly

   b. Because new features constantly need to be integrated into the network

   c. Because you can never really gather all the requirements nor anticipate all future requirements

   d. It is critical for the ROI of an organization

3. What should you always include in a change management plan?

   a. A backout plan in case the change fails

   b. The intent behind each configuration change

   c. The MTBF of each piece of hardware included in the change

   d. A mission statement

4. What is technical debt?

   a. The gap between current hardware and the hardware currently in use

   b. Old software that is no longer supported or maintained by the vendor

    c. The gap between how a system really works and how the operator thinks it works

    d. Old hardware that is no longer supported or maintained by the vendor

5. Do long MTBF ratings guarantee network resilience?

    a. Yes, because as long as the hardware does not fail, the network will not fail

    b. Yes, because MTBF is a direct measure of resilience

    c. No, because the MTBF can be offset by the law of large numbers

    d. No, because the MTBF is often measured in a lab and does not represent real-world use

6. Some operators prefer out-of-band management because

    a. Out-of-band management continues working when the network itself fails.

    b. Out-of-band management requires less hardware than in-band management.

    c. Out-of-band management produces more accurate information about the network than in-band management.

    d. Out-of-band management is easier to implement than in-band management.

7. What is the best or most secure way to connect to a router or switch remotely?

    a. Console port

    b. Telnet

    c. SSH

    d. SNMP

8. Why do most operators prefer NETCONF/YANG over SNMP management interfaces?

    a. Because NETCONF/YANG provides more information than SNMP

    b. Because NETCONF/YANG is more secure than SNMP

    c. Because vendors more widely implement NETCONF/YANG

    d. Because SNMP is an older technology

9. What is one disadvantage of cloud-based management systems?

    a. They are not as feature-rich as locally configured and operated management systems

    b. They will always be more expensive than locally configured and operated management systems

    c. They may lock the operator into a single vendor's solutions

    d. They require a lot of bandwidth from the operator's network to the cloud

Foundation Topics

Network Documentation

It often seems no one in network engineering enjoys documenting their networks. What every engineer enjoys, especially at 2 a.m., when the network is down and they are on the phone with technical support, is having access to good network documentation.

Engineers also really like to have thorough documentation on hand when they are planning changes. Documentation can answer questions like

- Which ports are in use, and which are unused?

- Where does a cable run?

- Which routers are running which routing protocol?

- Where are the failure and security domains?

- Where does a virtual topology land? Where are the tunnel head- and tail-ends?

Where will the documentation you need to plan and troubleshoot come from if you do not create it? No "network documentation monsters" will wander around your network, building brilliant documentation for you.

The bottom line is—network documentation is important enough for you to overcome your distaste and do it.

There are five basic kinds of network documentation:

- Network diagrams

- Descriptions

- Baselines

- Failure reports

- Hardware and software

Chapter 10, "Basic Network Hardware," explained network diagrams. The other four documentation types are considered in one of the following sections.

Descriptions

Network descriptions should include anything helpful to a new engineer trying to understand how a network works and why it works that way. Examples include:

- The principles used in designing the network. Documenting what was considered important and what was not can be helpful many years later.

- Applications the network was designed to support and their requirements.

- The *intent* behind each device's configuration. While many parts of a device's configuration will be obvious—IP addresses assigned to each interface, for instance—many parts of a device's configuration will not be intuitive. A good rule of thumb here is *if you had to explain this to a vendor's technical support person at 2 a.m., you should document why it is configured this way.*

- The device naming system.

- The IP addressing system and why this naming system was chosen.

- The expected flow of control plane (routing) information and data through the network.

- The way any automation works, how to find the source code, what servers it runs on, and anything else to make automation easier to understand.

Network operators should not be afraid of writing too much. Anything useful should be written down somewhere easily accessible to every network engineer.

Baselines

Suppose a user calls the help desk and complains about an application. According to the user, the application is taking too long to create a critical report, so can you please fix it?

The problem is "too long" could mean

- The user is late to an important meeting, so the application seems to take a long time to create the report.

- The application is taking longer than usual to complete the report, but the report is still being created within the application's original design specification.

- The application is taking longer than usual to complete the report, but the network is seriously overloaded right now because someone released a new viral cat video.

- The application is taking longer than usual to complete the report because of network problems.

You cannot know if something is broken—or even how it is—unless you know how something was *designed* to work, how it *should* work, and how it *normally* works. These are three very different things.

 Baselining measures how things work, so you have something to compare future performance against.

Network operators should have **baselines** for just about everything involving events and performance, including

- Bandwidth utilization pattern on each link.

- How often a link flaps or fails.

- How long it takes for each section of the network to converge.

- How often a router, switch, optical interface, etc., fails.

- The average delay across each section of the network.

Each baseline should be updated over time so operators can see trends. For instance, if you measure the bandwidth utilization of your Internet connection every week, you can probably figure out when the link might need to be upgraded.

Failure Reports

Every network failure is a chance to learn how the network works, unanticipated hardware and software problems, etc. Those who do not document these things, however, are doomed to repeat the same troubleshooting steps and outages repeatedly.

Every outage should be documented, including the

- **Symptoms:** Documenting the symptoms as accurately as possible can make finding the cause of similar failures in the future much easier.

- **Root cause:** The hardware or software failure that caused the outage should be described as accurately as possible.

- **Temporary fix:** If you deployed a temporary fix, what was the fix, how did you think it would solve the problem until you could put a permanent fix in place, and how did it work?

- **Permanent fix:** What fix did you use to fix the problem permanently?

Failure reports are a gold mine of information while troubleshooting a failure, of course, but they are also very useful when planning changes to the network or designing support for a new application, location, etc. Reports should be contained in a well-designed ticketing system.

Hardware and Software

Have you ever looked inside the front cover of a telephone book (if you can find one anyplace other than an antique store)? Among the items listed is a number to call if your telephone is not working. The telephone book does not, however, explain how you are supposed to call the telephone company to report an outage if your telephone is not working.

Telephone books might seem like a humorous throwback to the past, but the problem of communicating is still genuine when the communication system fails. The modern world is *always online*. We assume vendor documents, troubleshooting tips, and help will always be just a few clicks and an online search away.

But what if you are trying to fix the network because it is down? If the network is down, you might not be able to reach the Internet. If you rely on Internet resources to help you fix your network, you might be stuck.

Network documentation should include local copies of the user manuals for critical hardware and software. You should always have the information you need, regardless of the network's state, to build at least some basic connectivity.

Network Processes and Lifecycle

Networks, individual network devices, and software all have a lifecycle—just like everything else. Figure 21-1 illustrates a typical view of a network lifecycle.

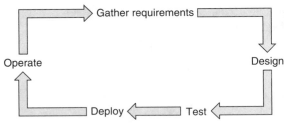

Figure 21-1 *Typical Network Lifecycle*

In Figure 21-1, *gather requirements* includes

- Discover all existing application requirements.

- Discover all existing business requirements.

- Discover all future applications that might run on the network and their requirements.

- Discover all future business plans and how these plans place requirements on the network.

- Discover existing operational problems.

Once you have discovered and validated these requirements, you can design the network. *Design* includes determining or deciding

- The best hardware and software combination to meet the requirements.

- The best way to connect all the pieces to make a network.

- The best way to configure each router, switch, or other network equipment.

- The best way to measure baselines and build documentation.

Once the network is designed, you can build tests, test, deploy, and operate it.

The design process sounds cut and dry—and perhaps a little simple—from the outside. Real life and real networks tend to be a lot messier.

How do you gather *all* the requirements? If you tried to gather *all* the requirements, you would probably find the requirements change before you can gather them all. How do you nail down *every possible* side effect for *every* design decision?

These things are impossible in the real world. Instead of following a clean process, most network engineering teams follow a more piecemeal approach. Each piece of hardware, each link, each module, and the network itself all have lifecycles. These lifecycles act like *wheels within wheels* and interact with one another in often unexpected ways. Figure 21-2 illustrates.

In Figure 21-2, three modules are shown. Suppose *Module 3* is a physical router or switch, *Module 2* is a set of routers in a single rack or location, and *Module 1* is the entire network.

Each module's lifecycle is different, with its own requirements, design, testing, and operation timelines. Each lifecycle's beginning, shown with the arrowheads, starts and ends at a different time. "Bridges" show interaction surfaces where one module interacts with another.

Engineers need to keep track of this hierarchy of lifecycles to build a maintainable network. The lifecycle of each component, each module, and the network's lifecycle need to be tracked, planned, and managed.

Further, there is no single point in time when a design is "done." Instead, networks must be modified over time to fit new applications and purposes. Because the network's environment changes constantly and there is no way to gather every possible requirement accurately, engineers often find it better to build flexible, extensible networks able to support many applications.

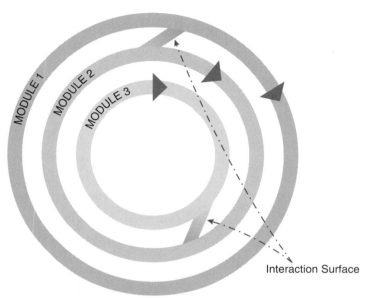

Figure 21-2   *Module Lifecycles*

Managing Change

Change management is the set of formal and informal processes used to manage changes to a network over time. Change management plans have many components, including

- Testing processes that must be followed before network changes can be implemented.

- Documentation standards, including the problem being solved, how it is being solved, why it is being solved this way, expected changes in behavior, etc.

- A backout plan in case a change fails.

A **backout plan** is a simple set of instructions allowing the operator to quickly and easily restore the network to its original, pre-change state.

Changes sometimes occur during **scheduled outages**, where the network is intentionally taken down to make changes, test the changes, and then be brought back into service. These scheduled outages are also called **change windows**.

Most modern networks do not have networkwide scheduled outages. Instead, outages are planned for individual modules.

Testing Techniques

Network engineers often understand tests across multiple stages, but only at a surface level. Figure 21-3 illustrates the different places testing might take place in design and deployment.

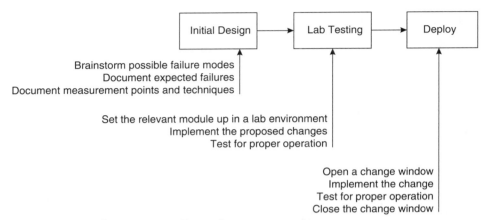

Figure 21-3 *Change Process Example*

Many operators test only for proper operation.

Proper operation testing validates the system produces expected outputs when given expected inputs. This kind of testing is also called *positive testing* because it checks for proper operation only when all the system's components are working correctly, and it checks system operation using only expected inputs.

Organizations should strive to extend this kind of positive testing to much stronger forms of *negative testing*. Negative testing includes intentionally failing individual pieces of hardware and software, misconfiguring devices, injecting bad control plane information, running attacks against the network, etc.

Negative testing can

- Catch failure modes no one thought of in the design phase.

- Help operators gain a better understanding of how the network normally looks versus how it looks in a failed state.

- Find measurements that would be useful in a failure but are not captured in the initial design.

Injecting failures into a network under test or an operational network is called **chaos engineering**. Many engineers and operators fear to inject failures; they fear the network will fail. That, however, is the point.

A second concept in testing is called the **canary**. A *canary test* places a small amount of real-world workload after a change, putting the changes into operation when the operator is confident the network will work correctly with the changes in place. The name comes from the canaries miners used to carry into mines. If you are in a mine with a canary and the canary passes out, it is time to leave; canaries will run low on oxygen and pass out far more quickly than humans.

Figure 21-4 illustrates a single module's complete change control process within a larger network.

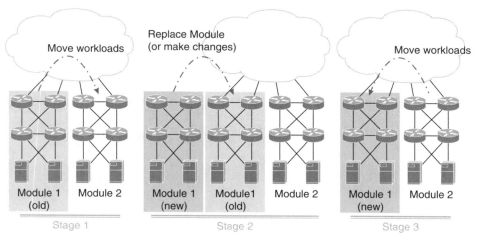

Figure 21-4 *Deployment Process Example*

In *Stage 1*:

- A modified module is designed, emulated in a lab environment, and tested using positive and negative testing.

- A physical replacement module is built, or automation is created to move the module from an old configuration to a new one, etc.

- The change window is opened. If applications and users can be moved without disruption (which is ideal), no change window or network outage is needed.

- All processes and users are moved off *Module 1* and onto *Module 2*.

In *Stage 2*:

- The old *Module 1* is removed from the network and replaced by the new version. If this is just a software or configuration change, the automation system is instructed to make the correct changes.

- Positive and negative testing is performed on the new module. This should include chaos, security, and other kinds of testing.

- Engineers should observe the results of this testing for any signs the new design does not work and to gather information about what failures look like, etc.

- If this testing works, the change window can be closed at this point. Even though the new *Module 1* has no workload, the network can be considered "operational" now.

In *Stage 3*:

- A few applications or users are moved into the new *Module 1*.

- If these applications migrate successfully, the remaining applications and users can be migrated to the new *Module 1*, restoring the network to its original operating condition (with modifications)

This short section gives you a brief overview of the canary process. Many other elements are not considered here, such as setting clear guidelines about when one stage ends and another begins, documentation that must exist before undertaking the canary deployment, how to control module generations, etc.

Technical Debt

One term you are bound to hear a lot if you work around engineers is **technical debt**. Most engineers think of technical debt as some combination of the following:

- Anything old such as hardware, software, or system

- Anything the original vendor no longer supports

- Anything they do not understand

The original meaning of *technical debt* is the buildup of changes in a system over time no one really understands or the gap between how a system works and how the operator thinks it works. When you have 10 or 15 people designing and deploying changes to a large network or making changes to an application's code, it is easy to lose sight of the system's design.

Engineers resolve technical debt through **refactoring** or the intentional rebuilding of system components to fit current requirements, specifications, and testing practices.

For an application, refactoring might mean rewriting the entire application or maybe rewriting pieces of the application so smaller changes fit into a new architectural vision. For a network, refactoring can mean anything from removing older hardware and software to reworking the configuration on every device to fit a new architectural pattern.

Management Challenges

Network management is often difficult in small- and large-scale networks because problems are not always obvious. As RFC 1925m, rule 4 says: "Some things in life can never be fully appreciated nor understood unless experienced firsthand."

This section considers two challenges: the observability problem and the law of large numbers.

The Observability Problem

Physicists and scientists know observing things at a very small scale changes their behavior. In quantum mechanics, this is stated as Heisenberg's Uncertainty Principle, which says there is a fundamental limit to the accuracy of measuring specific pairs of physical properties.

The best-known physical properties are momentum and position. Measuring the momentum of a particle changes its position, and measuring the position of a particle changes its momentum.

Does this apply at a larger scale, say in a network or software? Yes.

The **observability problem** is the impact of the network's operation because you are trying to measure something about the network. For example, assume you are having problems with a particular router, so you set up a monitoring host in the network, as shown in Figure 21-5.

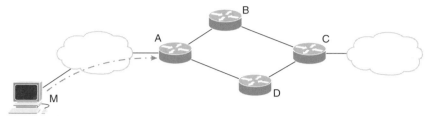

Figure 21-5   *The Observability Problem*

In Figure 21-5, host *M* is configured to capture router *A*'s input queue every time the queue holds 10 packets (the input queue depth is 10). Consider what happens when the 10th packet is placed in the input queue:

- Host *M* sends a packet to *A*, running the correct command to display the queue.

- Router *A* sends the information host *M* requested.

- Host *M* acknowledges receiving this information.

If host *M* is connected through the monitored port, *M*'s packets will count toward the number of packets in *A*'s input queue, which means sometimes *M* will send information when only nine "real" packets are in its input queue. Further, host *M*'s packets will be included in *M*'s response.

Checking the contents of the input queue is an obvious case where observing a network changes the network's behavior. Many others are not so obvious. Configuring debug output can cause an application to run more slowly, resolving a problem or changing the symptoms.

Two rules can help you counter the observability problem:

- Always ask, "How could measuring this change the measurement?" Try to work around projected changes.

- Always instrument the network so you can measure it at any time, but keep measurements to the minimum unless you need them.

Failure Rates in the Real World

Computer and network equipment manufacturers perform rigorous lab testing to determine how long a device should last before failing. This number is called the *mean time between failures* (**MTBF**). For instance, the Cisco 8200 Series Edge Platform has an MTBF of 692,577 hours, or around 80 years. If you install devices that will not fail for 80 years, you should never experience a hardware failure.

Things do not work out this way in the real world.

First, each router, switch, or other network device has optical interfaces, memory modules, and many other components. Each of these also has MTBF ratings; one component failure will cause the entire device to fail. The MTBF of each device component must be combined to understand just how often a device might fail.

Second, at some scale, the **law of large numbers** will overcome even the longest MTBF. If you have 80 Cisco 8200s in your network, one will fail annually across 80 years. They might all fail in the 80th year, or one a year might fail for 80 years. Figure 21-6 shows the most likely failure rate, a skewed bell curve.

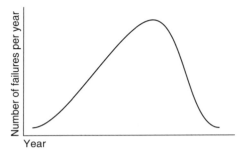

Figure 21-6 *Probable Failure Rates*

While the top of this curve might seem distant, some routers will still fail each year. At higher scales, more routers will fail each year.

Finally, any time humans interact with physical objects, there is always some chance a little too much pressure over there, or a little too much pressure over there, will cause a weak connection or physical component. Humans also conduct high voltages along their skin through static electricity.

Electrostatic discharge (ESD) procedures are designed to drain static electricity off the human body and tools to prevent damage to electronic components. However, even the strictest adherence to ESD processes still leaves room for weakening a component, reducing the time before it fails.

As the volume of hardware increases, the number of human-to-hardware interactions increases, causing more ESD failures.

Connecting to Manage

Chapter 10 covered common management ports: console ports and management Ethernet ports. You can use these ports to connect to a router in several ways—either using in-band or out-of-band management.

In-Band and Out-of-Band Management

In-band management means connecting to and managing network devices through the same interfaces used to forward user traffic. **Out-of-band management** means you connect through ports dedicated to managing the network. Figure 21-7 illustrates these two ways of managing a network.

The operator is using host *A* to manage the network. User traffic flows between server *B* and host *C*. The management workstation can reach routers *D* and *E* in two ways:

- *In-band* through router *D* and router *E* through *D*. On this path, user and management traffic are mixed.

- *Out-of-band* through router *F*. The out-of-band network is connected to different Ethernet interfaces on routers *D* and *E*, either a standard or an Ethernet management port.

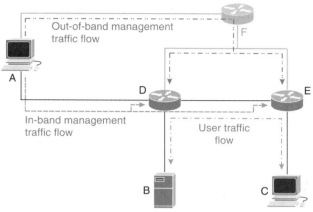

Figure 21-7   *In-Band and Out-of-Band Management*

The primary advantage of building an out-of-band management network is it should continue working even if the network carrying user traffic fails. Using in-band management, on the other hand, does not require additional hardware and wiring.

Connecting Through a Terminal Emulator

You connect to a router or switch from a host—like an Apple Macintosh or Windows computer—or a mobile device through a *terminal emulator*. Terminals originally connected to computers through a serial interface, but over time they have been adapted to connect in other ways, including the console port, the *teletype network (**telnet**)* protocol, and *Secure Shell (**SSH**)*.

The console port provides a serial connection to the router, switch, or other middlebox. You can connect to this port physically using a cable from your computer (or mobile device, in many cases) or remotely through a *terminal server*.

Most network devices, including Cisco routers and switches, include a *virtual terminal* interface type, listed as *vty* interfaces, for connecting to the device through any terminal emulator.

A *terminal server* is a router with serial interfaces. Each serial interface on the terminal service is connected to the console port of a network device.

Telnet and SSH are both IP-based protocols. You need to have an Ethernet, Wi-Fi, or some other port configured on the router or switch to connect using one of these protocols.

> **NOTE**   Chapter 15, "Application Transport, " describes SSH. Chapter 23, "Configuring a Network," explains how to configure a Cisco router or switch for SSH access.

21

Device Management Security Practices

The following three basic rules will allow you to manage network devices remotely while maintaining your network's security:

First, always use SSH to connect to network devices. Telnet is not secure enough to use for day-to-day management of network devices. Use Telnet or the physical console port to configure SSH; then disable the Telnet protocol.

Second, control physical access to the console port by placing the device in a secure room or location.

Third, never allow management connections of any kind from outside of your network. Figure 21-8 illustrates the correct way to access a router or switch from outside the network (through the Internet).

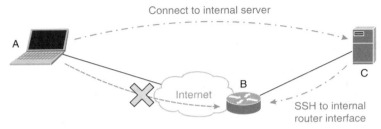

Figure 21-8   *Controlling Network Device Access*

In Figure 21-8, host *A*'s user would like to SSH into router *B*. Router *B*'s filters should be configured to prevent connection on its Internet-facing interface. Blocking direct access to the router from the Internet prevents attackers from attacking this edge router directly—even using known exploits.

Instead, host *A* must connect to server *C* using *Remote Desktop Protocol (RDP)*, SSH, or another method. From there, the user can connect to router *B*'s internal network interface using SSH.

Management Systems

At some scale or level of complexity, all operators move from manually monitoring and managing their networks to using some form of *network management system* (**NMS**). Figure 21-9 illustrates the basic components of an NMS.

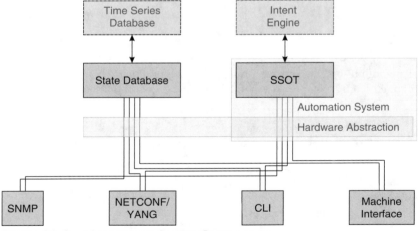

Figure 21-9   *Management System Components*

In Figure 21-9:

- **Time series database:** Not all network management systems have a time series database keeping periodic snapshots of network state and a historical record of network events. The time series database, if one exists, can be used to "rewind" prior network states, which can be helpful in *root cause analysis* or understanding a change's impact.

- **Intent engine:** Not all network management systems have an intent system translating business or operational intent into a network model.

- *State database*: This database contains information about the current state of individual devices and overall network health. Comparing this to the *single source of truth* (**SSOT**) can highlight points where the network is not configured or doing what the operator intends. This state is gathered from many systems, including those shown in Figure 21-9. Some network management systems store this information using a *modeling language*, in a relational database, or some other organized format. The state database is rarely just dumps of data gathered from individual devices.

- *Single source of truth (SSOT)*: The SSOT is the *intended* configuration of each network device. It might contain actual configurations, or it might contain configurations stored in a *modeling language*.

- *Automation system*: This script set pulls data from the SSOT and makes configuration changes on individual devices as needed. These same scripts might pull data off each device to build a database of the current network state.

- **Hardware abstraction:** If the SSOT is stored using a modeling language, the hardware abstraction module converts data to and from the device's configuration format to the modeling language.

The bottom of Figure 21-9 shows four different ways data is collected from network devices and used to configure network devices. These include

- *Simple Network Management Protocol (**SNMP**)*: This older protocol is used for managing network-connected devices. SNMP formats data using *Management Information Bases (MIBs)*. SNMP is widely considered a legacy protocol—many operators are working toward eliminating SNMP from their networks—because it is considered insecure.

- **NETCONF/YANG:** NETCONF is a protocol to carry YANG-formatted data. YANG is a *markup language*, which means it is human-readable and formatted using tags like the *Hypertext Markup Language (HTML)* or *Extensible Markup Language (XML)*.

- *Command-line interface (CLI)*: This is the same CLI operators use to interact with individual routers and switches. Scripts can pull the data from a router's CLI output, *parse* it into databases, *comma-separated value (CSV)* files, etc. Automation modules can also build commands and feed them to a router or switch through the CLI.

- **Machine interface:** Many network devices now have an interface designed for automation. These interfaces allow operators to access device data in its native format. *Google Remote Procedure Call (GRPC)* is one widely used interface.

21

There are many other information sources in a network. Heating and cooling systems, power supplies, and even scripts that periodically ping or traceroute to specific destinations to test for liveness generate data a network management system can consume and act on.

NMS Dashboard

Most NMSs allow operators to quickly gauge the network's or an individual device's health through a dashboard—often called a *pane of glass*. These systems can alert the operator when a device or link fails, when a specific server is no longer reachable, when a device or link is too heavily utilized, and for many other conditions.

Work Process System

Every network operations team needs a way for users to report problems, triage those problems, and then repair them over time. *Triage* determines how important a reported failure is and how hard the failure will be to repair, and then prioritizes the workload.

Modeling Language versus Configuration

What is the difference between a *modeling language* and a configuration as a router's CLI displays it? Figure 21-10 illustrates both forms of configuration.

```
GigabitEthernet0/0 is up, line protocol is up (connected)
   Internet address is 192.0.2.24/24
   Broadcast address is 255.255.255.255



<interface>
  <name>GigabitEthernet0/0/1</name>
  <enabled>true</enabled>
  <ipv4 xmlns="urn:ietf:params:xml:ns:yang:ietf-ip">
    <address>
       <ip>192.0.2.24</ip>
       <netmask>255.255.255.0</netmask>
    </address>
  </ipv4>
</interface>
```

Figure 21-10 *CLI Output Versus Modeled Data*

The upper part of Figure 21-10 shows a snippet of the CLI output from a Cisco router's interface configuration. The lower part of Figure 21-10 shows the same information placed inside a YANG model.

On initial examination, the YANG version appears more complex: there is more text, and some text is enclosed in brackets. The text inside brackets contains *tags*, *markup*, or even *metadata*; they explain the tagged text. For instance:

- The interface address is the text between <address> and </address>.

- The interface IP address is the text between <ip> and </ip>.

- The subnet mask is the text between <netmask> and </netmask>.

While these tags make the text harder for a human to read, they make it much easier for a computer program or script to find the right information. Rather than searching for the term

Internet Address in the output—which might be used for more than just an IPv4 address—the script can look for the correct tags.

Information structured using markup is designed to be easily machine-readable and at least human-readable.

Cloud-Managed Networks

Many network equipment vendors, including Cisco, are now shipping and supporting *cloud-managed networks*. This trend started with large-scale Wi-Fi networks but is spreading to campuses, data centers, and wide area networks. Figure 21-11 illustrates a cloud-managed network's basic components and operation.

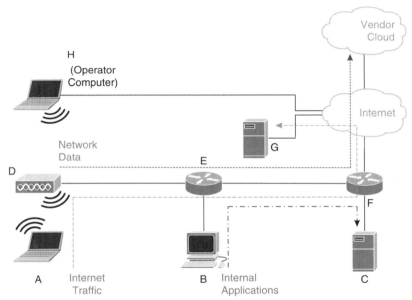

Figure 21-11 *Parts and Operation of a Cloud Management System*

There are three kinds of traffic flows in Figure 21-11:

- Traffic to Internet destinations, such as the traffic from host *A* to server *G*. This traffic is carried through the network normally.

- Traffic to internal destinations, such as the traffic from host *B* to server *C*. This traffic is carried through the network normally.

- Traffic sourced from network devices, like access point *D* and routers *E* and *F*. This traffic contains all the standard information a network management system contains, such as device status, link utilization, etc.

The cloud-managed service works much like a standard, locally managed NMS. Personal and corporate data is not carried into or through the vendor's cloud management service (although sensitive metadata or data about traffic flowing through your network might be).

21

An engineer uses host *H* to connect to the cloud management service. Host *H* does not need to be connected to the corporate network to access the vendor's managed cloud service. Instead, host *H* can reach the cloud management service directly over the Internet.

There are many positive and negative aspects to cloud-managed networks, including

- The vendor's internal experts are watching your network for problems. Since these experts work for the vendor, they have direct access to product development teams.

- Private and proprietary information might be sent into the vendor's cloud; operators must ensure this data is handled correctly and have plans to deal with potential breaches.

- Network management is much easier; the operator does not need to build or buy and operate a network management platform. Most of these systems rely on a *graphical user interface (GUI)* to manage the network, and they are intent rather than configuration based.

- Vendor-based cloud management systems can limit the operator to hardware and software from that one vendor. Many operators avoid single vendor lock-in.

- The vendor can apply custom tools like *artificial intelligence (AI)* to predicting, finding, and fixing problems. AI tools are more effective at a vendor level because they have the state of many networks to operate across rather than a single network.

Cloud-based management systems are one of the most recent innovations in network management.

Chapter Review

Many organizations install a small network without thinking about how they will manage it over time: What does the network lifecycle look like? How should changes be handled? Manual management and configuration work for very small networks, but as organizations grow, their networks grow. There comes a point in the life of a network when it needs to be properly managed.

This chapter considered many elements of network management, starting with documentation. While network diagrams were considered in Chapter 10, other kinds of documents and what you should be documenting were considered in this chapter. The next section of this chapter considered network lifecycle—something very few network engineers think about beyond some basic change control. Canary and chaos testing are essential tools network engineers should be using regularly. "Management Challenges" considered the problem of observing things in a network and the intersection of the large numbers and failure rates.

There are many ways to connect to network devices, but SSH should be your "go-to" tool. Remember, you should never allow outside hosts to access routers inside your network directly. Allowing hosts outside your network access to your devices exposes them to many attacks, increasing the size and scope of your network's attack surface.

Finally, this chapter considered network management systems. Even small networks can benefit from building a strong suite of network management tools from the first day of deployment.

One key to doing well on the exams is to perform repetitive spaced review sessions. Review this chapter's material using either the tools in the book or interactive tools for the same material found on the book's companion website. Refer to the online Appendix D, "Study Planner," element for more details. Table 21-2 outlines the key review elements and where you can find them. To better track your study progress, record when you completed these activities in the second column.

Table 21-2 Chapter Review Tracking

Review Element	Review Date (s)	Resource Used
Review key topics		Book, website
Review key terms		Book, website
Repeat DIKTA questions		Book, PTP
Review concepts and actions		Book, website

Review All the Key Topics

Table 21-3 lists the key topics for this chapter.

Table 21-3 Key Topics for Chapter 21

Key Topic Element	Description	Page Number
List	Five basic kinds of network documentation	429
Paragraph, list	Network descriptions	429
Paragraph, list	Network baselines	430
List	What to document in a network outage/failure report	431
Paragraph, Figure 21-2	Network/module lifecycles	432
Paragraph	Adapting to network environment change volatility	432
Paragraph, list	Change management	433
Paragraphs	Backout plans and change windows	433
Paragraphs	Network testing techniques: proper operation testing, negative testing, chaos engineering, canary testing	434
Paragraphs	Technical debt and resolving technical debt with refactoring	436
Section	The Observability Problem	436
Section	In-Band and Out-of-Band Management	438
Paragraphs	Three basic rules for managing network devices remotely and securely	439
List	Management systems: SSOT, automation, hardware abstraction	441
List	Four ways data is collected from network devices and used to configure network devices	441
Paragraph	Network operation triage	442

21

Key Terms You Should Know

Key terms in this chapter include

network description, baseline, failure report, change management, backout plan, scheduled outage, change window, proper operation testing, chaos engineering, canary, technical debt, refactoring, observability problem, MTBF, law of large numbers, in-band management, out-of-band management, telnet, SSH, NMS, time series database, intent engine, SSOT, hardware abstraction, SNMP, NETCONF, YANG, machine interface, cloud-based management

Concepts and Actions

Review the concepts considered in this chapter using Table 21-4. You can cover the right side of this table and describe each concept or action in your own words to verify your understanding.

Table 21-4 Concepts and Actions

Five kinds of network documentation	Diagrams, descriptions, baselines, failure reports, hardware and software
Network description	Should include just about anything that will help a new engineer understand how a network works, and why it works that way
Baseline	A measurement of how things work right now or normally
Failure reports should contain...	Symptoms, root cause, temporary fix, permanent fix
Gathering requirements	It is not really possible to gather every requirement, nor to anticipate every future requirement
Change management	Formal and informal processes used to manage changes in a network
Scheduled outage	A time period during which a network, part of a network, or service is not available so the operator can implement changes
Proper operation testing	Testing a system while all the components are functioning correctly and with expected inputs
Negative testing	Testing a system by breaking components and giving the system unexpected inputs
Chaos engineering	Intentionally injecting (random) errors into a network or system to see how it reacts
Canary testing	Testing a change by placing increasingly larger amounts of real-world workload on a changed module or system over time
Technical debt	The gap between how an operator thinks a system works and how that system works
Refactoring	Intentionally rebuilding a system to meet current specifications, requirements, and testing practices, even though the system is still operating normally
Observability problem	The impact of the network's operation because you are trying to measure something about the network

Law of large numbers	When there are enough items or events, the improbable becomes likely
MTBM	Mean time between failures
Out-of-band management	Connecting to and managing devices through a separate network
In-band management	Connecting to and managing devices through the same network that carries user traffic
Best remote connection service	SSH
NMS	Network management system
SSOT	Single source of truth
Hardware abstraction	Converts a model of the correct network configuration stored in the SSOT into actual device configurations
SNMP	Simple Network Management Protocol; considered insecure by most network operators
NETCONF	Protocol designed to carry YANG-formatted network device information
YANG	A modeling language designed to carry network state and configuration

21

CHAPTER 22

Troubleshooting

This chapter covers the following exam topics:

5. **Diagnosing Problems**

   5.1. **Demonstrate effective troubleshooting methodologies and help desk best practices, including ticketing, documentation, and information gathering.**

   Policies and procedures, accurate and complete documentation, prioritization

   5.2. **Perform a packet capture with Wireshark and save it to a file.**

   Purpose of using a packet analyzer, saving and opening a .pcap file

Network engineers spend a lot of time troubleshooting—possibly more time than anything else. Networks do not fail constantly, but rather

- Some aspects of any large-scale or complex system will always be less than optimal.

- Understanding a failure's root cause can be complex and take time.

- The design process inevitably includes countering previous failures.

- The design process inevitably includes thinking about how things *might fail* and how the network and operator should react to these potential failures.

Troubleshooting, then, is another one of those *very important skills* for network engineers.

On the other hand, there is little formal training in troubleshooting methods or processes. When faced with a failure:

- Where do you start looking for the problem?

- What is the fastest way to find the problem?

- What is the correct process for making network changes to resolve the problem?

This chapter begins with an overview of failure and resilience terminology before focusing on troubleshooting techniques and tools. These terms, tools, and techniques are not restricted to network engineering; they apply to just about anything that can break and be fixed.

This chapter's second and third sections provide a case study applying these principles in a small network, including what to capture and how to capture it. The final section covers some advice for engineers troubleshooting network problems.

"Do I Know This Already?" Quiz

Take the quiz (either here or use the PTP software) if you want to use the score to help you decide how much time to spend on this chapter. Appendix A, "Answers to the 'Do I Know This Already?' Quizzes," found at the end of the book, includes both the answers and explanations. You can also find answers in the PTP testing software.

Table 22-1 "Do I Know This Already?" Foundation Topics Section-to-Question Mapping

Section	Questions
Failure Terminology	1, 2, 3
Troubleshooting Tools and Techniques	4, 5, 6
Packet Captures	7
Advice to Troubleshooters	8

CAUTION The goal of self-assessment is to gauge your mastery of the topics in this chapter. If you do not know the answer to a question or are only partially sure of the answer, you should mark that question as wrong for purposes of the self-assessment. Giving yourself credit for an answer you incorrectly guess skews your self-assessment results and might provide you with a false sense of security.

1. What is triage?
   a. Determining which failure is the hardest to fix
   b. Determining which failure is the easiest to fix
   c. Determining which failure to work on first
   d. Determining which standard root cause might be the source of this failure

2. Should MTTR include the dwell time?
   a. The MTTR should always include the dwell time.
   b. The MTTR should never include the dwell time.
   c. Whether MTTR should include dwell time is local policy.
   d. MTTR and dwell time are not related.

3. Why does adding redundancy not always increase resilience?
   a. There might not be an existing single point of failure where redundancy is added.
   b. The added redundancy might add enough complexity to make the network react more slowly to failures.
   c. Increasing resilience by adding redundancy might not be required.
   d. The new link might not be used by the control plane anyway.

4. Why is it problematic to start troubleshooting with the part of the network you are most familiar with?
   a. This might not be where the most recent change was made.
   b. This might not be where failures often happen.
   c. You can spend hours looking for something that is not there.
   d. You might not know where the most recent change was made.

5. What are the two stages of the half-split troubleshooting method?

   a. Measure and split

   b. Observe and orient

   c. Decide and act

   d. Observe and blame someone else

6. Which of the following describes a permanent fix?

   a. Increases technical debt

   b. Not well documented

   c. Brings the network back to its pre-failure state

   d. Will need to be replaced in a short time

7. What kinds of information can you get from a packet capture?

   a. Seeing the information that users are requesting from web servers

   b. Finding the paths that packets are taking through the network

   c. Examining the flow of packets between a host and server for errors

   d. The user's birth date and telephone number

8. What is a false positive?

   a. When things look broken although they are not

   b. When things look normal although they are not

   c. Anything that looks "odd"

   d. When you are optimistic and you should not be

Foundation Topics

Failure Terminology

While it is often tempting to start putting a new piece of flat-pack furniture together without bothering to read the long instruction sheet, it is almost always a better idea to understand how the parts are labeled and how they all fit together before using hammers and screwdrivers. Troubleshooting is no different; it is deceptively simple on the outside but easily leads to long sessions of wasted time.

This section begins with the labels—which part is what—and then moves into the half-split troubleshooting process.

What Is a Failure?

The first thing network engineers need to do in terms of failures is decide

- What is a failure?

- Among all possible failures, which one is the most important?

The first question might seem odd. We all know what a failure is when we see it, right? Consider this, however. Which of the following would be considered a failure in a network of 10,000 devices, and which would not?

- None of the 10,000 devices connected to the network can communicate with any other device.

- 5,000 of the 10,000 devices connected to the network can communicate with any other device.

- 2,000 of the 10,000 hosts cannot connect to a specific web server.

- 200 of the 10,000 hosts cannot connect to a specific web server.

- 200 of the 10,000 hosts report poor performance when connecting to a specific web server.

Almost anyone looking at this list will classify the first item as a "failure" but not the last item. However, even the last item on the list might fail if the application is critical. Defining what a *failure* is can be extremely important. The failures in this list might also make a good place to start defining the *triage list*.

Triage determines how important a failure is and in what order operators should work on failures.

The first failure on this list might require calling out every available network engineer to troubleshoot different network parts, while the last might be something an engineer can look at in a couple of days. Triage plays a vital role in organizing the day-to-day work of a *network operations center (NOC)*.

Failure Frequency

Beyond the word *failure*, there are a few essential terms network engineers should know. Figure 22-1 illustrates these critical terms.

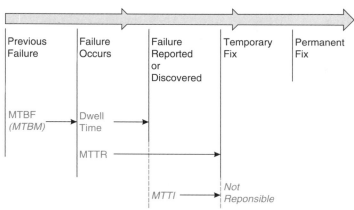

Figure 22-1   *Important Failure Terms*

In Figure 22-1:

- *Mean time between failures* (**MTBF**) is the time between the last and current failures. Engineers often need to consider the MTBF for failures *of this kind*, *any failure of this severity*, and *any failure*. These ways of measuring MTBF help determine if an individual component or part of the network is unstable or the entire network is unstable.

- *Mean time between mistakes* (**MTBM**) is a little tongue-in-cheek, but human mistakes cause most information technology failures. A short MTBM, or a high mistake frequency, might indicate a fragile or overly complex system.

22

- **Dwell time** is the amount of time the failure exists before being detected. The dwell time should be determined as part of the failure post-mortem.

- *Mean time to repair* (**MTTR**) is how long the service, network, etc., was unavailable. The MTTR might be measured from when the failure occurs, so it includes the dwell time, or it might be measured from when the failure is reported or discovered.

- *Mean time to innocence* (**MTTI**) is another tongue-in-cheek term. It describes the time it takes for the network team to prove the problem is not the network.

Network engineers imported many of these terms from other fields, so you will probably hear them in other contexts. For instance, *MTBF* is a common system engineering term, and *dwell time* is a typical security engineering term.

Fragility and Resilience

Key Topic

Fragility and **resilience** can be described in two statements:

- *Fragile systems* fail easily in the face of environmental pressure.

- *Resilient systems* survive environmental pressure.

Environmental pressure might be a link failure, software failure, hardware failure, or even human error.

Network engineers primarily rely on **redundancy** to increase resilience by eliminating *single points of failure*. Figure 22-2 illustrates redundancy.

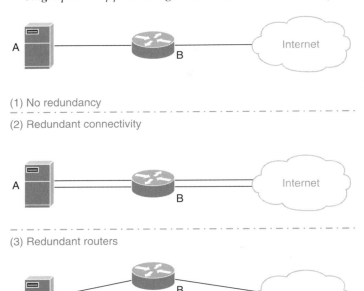

Figure 22-2   *Redundancy in Network Design*

Figure 22-2 shows the same network with different levels of redundancy:

1.   Three single points of failure: server *A*'s network connection, router *B*, and router *B*'s connection to the Internet

2.   One single point of failure: router *B*

3.   No single points of failure

Redundancy is adding network capacity in parallel with existing capacity so the network can route through an alternate path in the case of failure.

A **single point of failure** is where a link or device failing prevents the network from forwarding traffic.

If you can increase resilience by adding more paths in parallel, why not add enough to support any conceivable failure scenario? For example, some network engineers will build enough redundancy to prevent *double* or *triple points of failure* from impacting network performance.

In some cases, additional redundant links are too expensive. Each additional path costs the same amount but adds less additional resilience. A good rule of thumb is

■   Adding a second path increases resilience by about 50% over the single path.

■   Adding a third path increases resilience by about 25% over two paths.

■   Adding a fourth path increases resilience by about 12% over three paths.

In most situations, two paths are adequate. There are almost no situations where four paths are required to provide good network resilience.

Each additional path adds to network complexity, slowing the network's reaction to failures. Networks with too many redundant paths can perform more poorly than a simpler design with just a few parallel paths.

Shared fate is another problem engineers need to plan around. Shared fate exists when a single resource's failure can cause some other group of devices to fail. Figure 22-3 illustrates shared fate.

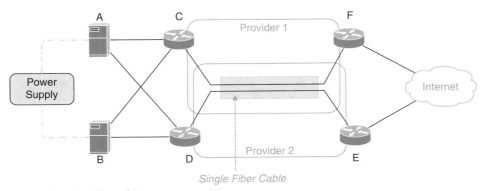

Figure 22-3   *Shared Fate*

The operator designed and built the network in Figure 22-3 so there would not be any single points of failure. From the operator's perspective, there are two servers, each connected to a separate path to the Internet.

The operator might not know there are still two single points of failure in this network. The first single point of failure is the power supply supporting servers *A* and *B*. If this single power supply fails, servers *A* and *B* will fail, so server *A* shares fate with server *B*. The two links to the Internet also share fate at a single point of failure because both providers have chosen to carry traffic through different wavelengths on the same fiber cable.

It is almost impossible to remove every instance of shared fate from a network design, but engineers should be aware of the problems shared fate can cause and avoid it where possible.

Troubleshooting Tools and Techniques

If networks never failed, engineers would not need troubleshooting tools, but networks do break, so engineers need to be able to troubleshoot failures quickly.

The most effective troubleshooting technique blends *start with what you know* with a more formal **half-split method**. Once you find the problem, you need to decide how to fix it and then review what happened, why, how you (or you and your team) did troubleshooting the problem, and how you can improve your troubleshooting performance in the future.

The Half-Split Method

When faced with a problem, most engineers will start with the following:

- The most recent change

- Where most failures have happened in the past

- What the engineer is most familiar with

Starting with the most recent change makes sense as an initial strategy because most network failures occur because of these changes. Likewise, it often makes sense to start where failures have been common.

The third option—start with what you are familiar with—is a bit more problematic. Starting with the most familiar things in the network will allow you to rule those things out quickly. However, starting with the most familiar things can also be like looking for your keys under the streetlight rather than where you dropped them: you might spend hours looking for something that is not there.

While starting with the most recent change or common failures allows you to cover a lot of ground quickly, following them past some initial checks can be counterproductive. You should move to a more formal troubleshooting method after checking recent changes and common failures.

The half-split is the most effective troubleshooting method available—developed through long experience in electronics. Figure 22-4 illustrates the half-split troubleshooting method.

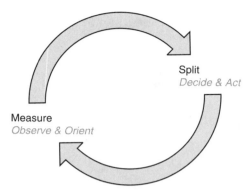

Figure 22-4   *Half-Split Troubleshooting Method*

The half-split method is related to the *Observe, Orient, Decide, Act (OODA)* loop used in military, defense, and general security settings. The OODA and half-split loops give you specific questions to focus on at each point, countering the tendency to wander all over the place when reacting to high-pressure situations.

The half-split method is an intentional troubleshooting method. The half-split method organizes work to split the network into successively smaller pieces. Half-split has two stages: measure and split.

In the *measure* stage, you begin by orienting, asking questions about how things are and what they should look like, including

- What does normal look like here?

- What model can I use to understand what is happening?

- What explanations can I come up with for the difference between what is currently happening and what should be happening?

Orienting means consolidating the available information. *Measuring* includes observing the network and asking questions like

- What can I measure to eliminate or indicate one (or more) of the possible explanations for this problem?

- How do I measure it?

- How might measuring it change the system's operation?

In the *split* stage, you decide where to go in the system or what to do next. Splitting can mean

- Moving closer to the source or destination (left or right)

- Moving into or out of a module (up or down)

Left, right, up, and down are abstract concepts; Figure 22-5 illustrates these four directions.

22

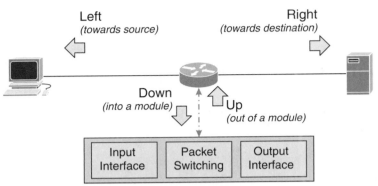

Figure 22-5 *Half-Split Directions*

When you've moved beyond looking at the obvious solutions and into using the half-split method to find a problem, you

- **Select a source:** The source might be a host, server, application, or anything else in the network, but it should ideally be the source of the packets.

- **Select a destination:** The destination might be a host, server, application, or anything else in the network, but it should ideally be where the packets are processed.

- **Choose a point about halfway between the source and destination:** Choosing the halfway point is not always easy, but the starting point doesn't have to be precisely in the middle of the path between the source and destination.

- **Run the loop:** Orient yourself to the point in the network, make observations, and then decide what to do next—move left, right, up, or down, or *solve the problem.*

The half-split method is easier to understand when the theory is paired with an example, like the one in a later section of this chapter.

 Fixes

Once you find the problem, you can fix it. but not all fixes are equal.

A **permanent fix** is one you intend to leave in the network permanently, or at least until the network changes for some other reason. Permanent fixes either

- Bring the network back to the state before the failure.

- Are well-documented, decrease technical debt, and fit within the overall network plan and architecture.

A **temporary fix** is one you use until a better solution can be designed, tested, and deployed. Temporary fixes often increase technical debt and represent "one-off" solutions that cannot or should not be repeated elsewhere in the network.

The Post-Mortem

Post-mortems are a time set aside to go over a network failure, the troubleshooting process, and the solution. Post-mortems should be loosely structured and answer just a few questions, including

- What is the root cause? Why are we sure this is the root cause?

- How can we prevent this failure from happening in the future?

- What was the dwell time? How can we reduce the dwell time?

- How does this change the system architecture?

However, the most important point about post-mortems is to focus on fixing the problem rather than the blame. People make mistakes, and devices fail. Learning is more important than running up the blame score.

Applying the Process: An Example

Troubleshooting is best learned through hands-on experience. Learning the theory is a good start, but real troubleshooting skill comes with *good* practice. Practice does not make perfect. Perfect practice makes perfect.

Figure 22-6 illustrates a small network for walking through a sample troubleshooting process.

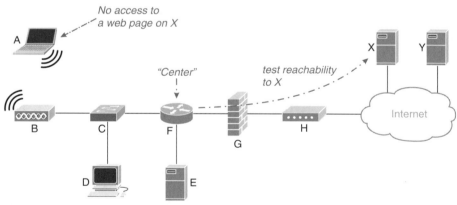

Figure 22-6 *First Stage of Half-Split Process*

In Figure 22-6:

- *A* and *D* are hosts.

- Host *A* is connected via Wi-Fi through access point *B*.

- Host *D* is wired to switch *C*.

- Server *E* is a local network-attached storage (NAS).

- Server *E* is connected to router *F*.

- Router *F* is connected to firewall *G*.

22

- Firewall *G* is connected to MODEM *H*, which then connects through an access provider to the Internet.

- Servers *X* and *Y* are accessible through the Internet.

This first troubleshooting stage begins at router *F* because this is *roughly* the "center" of the path between host *A* and server *X*.

Begin by *pinging* host *X* from router *F*.

If the ping succeeds, *X* is reachable from router *F*, and the problem is likely between host *A* and router *F*.

What if *F* cannot reach *X*? The problem is on *F* itself or somewhere to the right of *F*. If this initial reachability test fails, you could

- Ping server *Y*. If *Y* is reachable and *X* is not, the problem is either with server *X* or someplace "on the Internet" between *F* and *X*.

- Try pinging *X* and *Y* from *G*. If *G* can ping both servers, the problem is on router *F*.

- Try pinging *X* and *Y* from *G*. If *G* cannot ping either server, the problem is on *G* or between *G* and *X* or *Y*.

For this example, router *G* can reach server *X*, so it is time to move someplace else in the network and gather more data. Because the problem appears between host *A* and router *G*, switch *C* or access point *B* would be the new center point. In this case, switch *C* does not have a console of any kind—it is an *unmanaged* switch—so the next stop will be access point *B*, as shown in Figure 22-7.

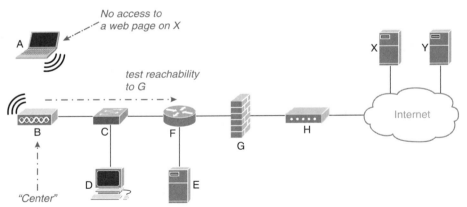

Figure 22-7 *Second Stage of Half-Split Process*

Ping router *F* from access point *B*. If this works, the problem is likely on access point *B* or host *A*.

If this ping does not work, the problem is likely on access point *B*, switch *C*, or router *F*.

How can you test the unmanaged switch *C*? Try pinging router *F* from host *D*. If this works, the problem is before *C*. If host *D* cannot reach *F*, the problem is most likely in switch *C*.

For this example, the ping from access point *B* to router *F* works. To ensure the entire path works, you can also ping from *B* to server *X*. Given the information gathered thus far, this should work. What if it does not work? The problem is most likely at router *F*.

Since the problem seems to be at host *A* or access point *B*, go back to each network point from host *A*, as shown in Figure 22-8.

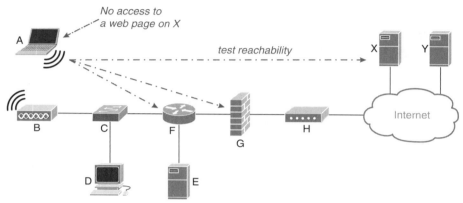

Figure 22-8 *Third Stage of Half-Split Process*

Assume the following for this third stage:

- Host *A* still cannot ping server *X*.
- Host *A* cannot ping firewall *G*.
- Host *A* can ping router *F*.

The information here seems to indicate router *F* is the problem, but we already know, from previous testing, that access point *B* can reach router *F* and even server *X* through router *F*.

It is time to *orient* to the problem and brainstorm a little by asking two questions:

- What kind of problem would cause router *F* to reach *A*, forward packets from access point *B*, and yet not forward packets from *A* toward server *X*?
- What kind of problem would cause host *A* to be able to reach router *F* but not be able to send packets through *F* to server *X*?

The answer to the first question is *packet filters*. The answer to the second question is *host A's default gateway is not set correctly*. How could we tell the difference between these two problems?

The simplest way to tell the difference is to use one of ping's extended features. At router *F*, you can ping host *A* using *F*'s address on its link to firewall *G*.

If this fails, host *A* can reach devices on the same segment, like access point *B* and host *D*, but it cannot reach off-segment destinations like firewall *G* and router *F*'s interface with *G*. Because host *A* uses its default gateway to reach off-segment destinations, the symptoms match a problem with this setting.

22

You can validate this conclusion by checking for packet filters at router *F*.

Figure 22-9 illustrates the half-split troubleshooting process used in this example.

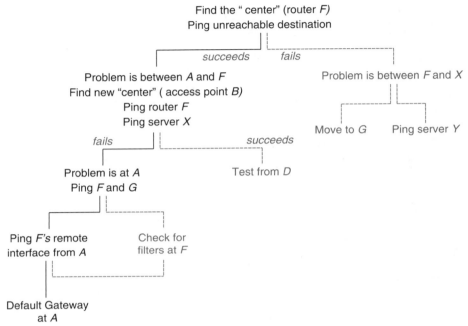

Figure 22-9   *Half-Split Troubleshooting Example*

The half-split method produces a tree of measurements, actions, and possibilities. Drawing a chart like this on paper or a whiteboard while troubleshooting a problem can help you remember what you have already tried, branches you did not take, etc.

Packet Captures

The case study in the previous section used only the **ping** command to capture information about the network. What if the problem were host *A*'s connection to server *X* is slow, while *D*'s connection to server *X* is performing normally? Sometimes, in a case like this, you want to be able to capture packets off the wire and examine the flow for problems.

The most common tool used in the networking industry for capturing and examining packets and flows through a network is **Wireshark**, an open-source, free-to-use tool. (You can install Wireshark from wireshark.org.)

Figure 22-10 shows the screen you will see when you open Wireshark.

This first screen gives you a list of interfaces from which you can capture packets. You can select multiple interfaces using the Shift and Control keys. Once you have selected one or more interfaces, you can select the upper-left icon on the toolbar to start capturing packets. The result will look like the screen capture in Figure 22-11.

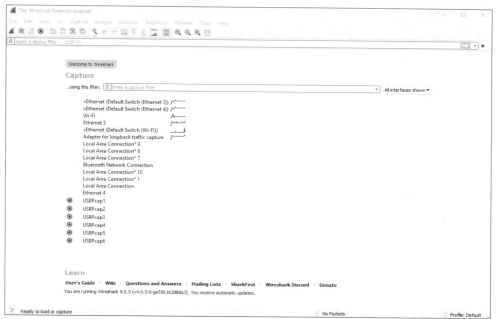

Figure 22-10   *The Wireshark Opening Screen*

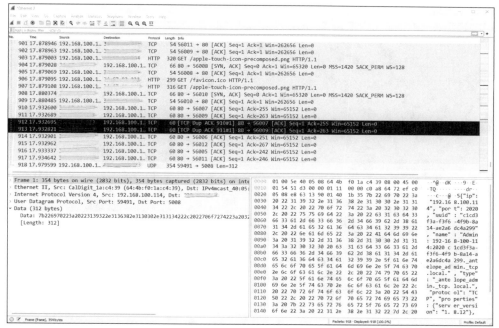

Figure 22-11   *Packet Capture Using Wireshark*

The Wireshark capture screen has three primary components:

- The top window contains a list of the captured packets. You can select an individual packet to examine from this list.

- The bottom-left window provides information about the selected packet. Wireshark's developers have programmed in thousands of different packet formats. Wireshark can show you each value in the packets it knows how to decode.

- The bottom-right window is a *hex dump* of the selected packet. The hex dump can be helpful if you are looking for patterns in the packet or Wireshark does not know how to decode the entire packet.

Because Wireshark captures *every* packet on the selected interface (or interfaces), there will be a lot of information to sort through. Wireshark can capture a subset of the packets, as shown in Figure 22-12.

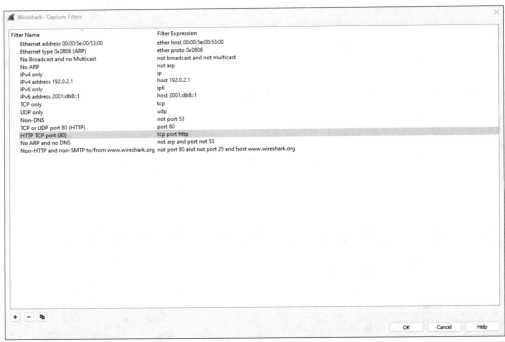

Figure 22-12 *Wireshark Capture Filter Options*

For instance, you can select *HTTP TCP port (80)* if you want to see only traffic to and from a web server. Figure 22-13 shows a capture with HTTP traffic only.

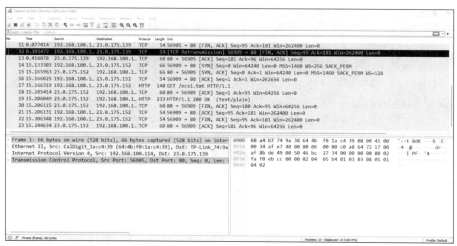

Figure 22-13 *Filtered Wireshark Capture*

This capture shows a connection between a host at 192.168.100.114 and a web server at 23.0.175.139. The packets in this capture include the following:

1. A TCP SYN opening the session from the host to the server
2. A TCP SYN ACK, where the server acknowledges the TCP open
3. A TCP ACK, where the host finishes the TCP three-way handshake
4. The first HTTP GET, where the host requests the main file making up the web page
5. A TCP retransmit (apparently, the TCP session dropped a packet)
6. A duplicate TCP acknowledgment, a result of the dropped packet
7. A standard TCP acknowledgment, which is the server acknowledging receiving the TCP packet containing the HTTP GET

With enough practice, you can trace any packet flow and quickly spot errors such as dropped packets.

You can save packet captures and reopen them for later examination or even to have records of network failures. Wireshark uses the .pcap file format to store packet captures. Most packet capture and analysis software packages use the same .pcap file format.

One valuable Wireshark resource is collections of .pcap files, such as those available at https://netresec.com. These allow you to see what a normal packet flow looks like for

- Virtually every kind of protocol session operation.
- Many kinds of network attacks as they occur.
- The packet captures from penetration exercises.
- Many kinds of malware software sending traffic to command and control systems and installing themselves on devices.

Wireshark, packet capture, and packet analysis are sometimes the only tools to diagnose problems.

22

Advice to Troubleshooters

Troubleshooting is a difficult skill. It is easy to become tangled up in trivia or chase the wrong set of symptoms, and it takes far longer to find and fix a problem than it might seem it should. This section contains some advice from years of experience troubleshooting complex problems in all kinds of networks.

Be careful of **false positives**. Sometimes things will look broken, although they are not. It is easy to see something that looks a little odd, think this odd thing must be the source of the problem, and spend hours pursuing the problem—only to discover the "odd thing" is normal.

Knowing what normal looks like and understanding how protocols work are essential. If you think something is the root of the problem or even related to the problem, ask others and search the Internet for what you are seeing.

Be careful of cutting yourself off. Network engineers saw off the limb they are troubleshooting far more often than they like to admit. Several large-scale outages have been stretched from minutes to days while someone is dispatched to the router's location so someone can plug into the console port. Always think about what you are about to do and its impact on your access to the network.

Be careful of turning on expansive debugging output. Routers, switches, and hosts can crash because of debug output.

Don't focus on MTTI. Your job as a network engineer does not end when you have proven the problem is not in the network. If you are involved in a problem, take ownership, and help where you can. Teams with a wide variety of experience and expertise find and solve problems faster than more specialized teams.

Build relationships with other parts of the organization. You do not—you cannot—know every part of the system. Accept what you do know and be willing to ask questions when you do not know. Existing relationships are much more useful when you are asking for help, so build relationships with adjacent teams before the first outage.

There is nothing more permanent than a temporary fix. Do not allow temporary fixes to become permanent. It often feels much simpler to leave a temporary fix in place. But if you add enough temporary fixes into a network, the entire network becomes a huge unmaintainable mess.

Chapter Review

Troubleshooting is yet another one of those important skills network engineers need to develop and practice over time. It is fine to start with the obvious but quickly move to the formal half-split method. Document where you have looked, what you have measured, and the various theories you have developed about the cause of the problem.

Some other tools discussed in this chapter include the post-mortem—fix the problem, not the blame—and packet captures.

The next chapter is the last technically oriented chapter in this book. It covers configuring a small network from start to finish, showing how to use the CLI to configure Cisco devices and verify their operation.

One key to doing well on the exams is to perform repetitive spaced review sessions. Review this chapter's material using either the tools in the book or interactive tools for the same material found on the book's companion website. Refer to the online Appendix D, "Study Planner," element for more details. Table 22-2 outlines the key review elements and where you can find them. To better track your study progress, record when you completed these activities in the second column.

Table 22-2   Chapter Review Tracking

Review Element	Review Date (s)	Resource Used
Review key topics		Book, website
Review key terms		Book, website
Repeat DIKTA questions		Book, PTP
Review concepts and actions		Book, website

Review All the Key Topics

Table 22-3 lists the key topics for this chapter.

Table 22-3   Key Topics for Chapter 22

Key Topic Element	Description	Page Number
Paragraph	Triage	451
Section	Failure Frequency	451
List, paragraph	Fragile vs. resilient systems and environmental pressure	452
Paragraphs	Redundancy and single point of failure	453
Paragraph, Figure 22-3	Shared fate	453
Figure 22-4, paragraphs	Half-split troubleshooting method	454
Section	Fixes	456
Section	The Post-Mortem	457
Paragraph	Be cautious of false positives	464

Key Terms You Should Know

Key terms in this chapter include

triage, MTBF, MTBM, dwell time, MTTR, MTTI, fragility, resilience, environmental pressure, redundancy, single point of failure, shared fate, half-split method, permanent fix, temporary fix, post-mortem, Wireshark, false positive

Concepts and Actions

Review the concepts considered in this chapter using Table 22-4. You can cover the right side of this table and describe each concept or action in your own words to verify your understanding.

22

Table 22-4   Concepts and Actions

Triage	Determining how important a failure is and in what order operators should work on failures
MTBF	Mean time between failures; the amount of time between the last and current failures
Dwell time	The amount of time the failure exists before being detected.
MTTR	Mean time to repair; how long the service, network, etc., was not available
MTTI	Mean time to innocence; the time it takes for the network team to prove the problem is not the network
Fragile system	Fails easily in the face of environmental pressure
Resilient system	Survives environmental pressure
Redundancy	Adding network capacity in parallel with existing capacity so that the network can route through an alternate path in the case of failure
Single point of failure	Anyplace in the network where a single link or device failing prevents the network from forwarding traffic
Shared fate	When a single resource's failure can cause some other group of devices to fail
Half-split method	Intentional troubleshooting method that organizes work to split the network into successively smaller pieces
Describe the four steps of using the half-split troubleshooting method	Select a source, select a source, choose the halfway point, run the measure/split loop
Permanent fix	One you intend to leave in the network permanently, or at least until the network changes for some other reason, does not increase technical debt
Temporary fix	One you use until a better solution can be designed, tested, and deployed
Post-mortems should discover...	The root cause, preventing the failure, reducing the dwell time, and changes to the system architecture
Post-mortems should not...	Place blame
Wireshark	Open-source packet capture and analysis tool
False positive	When things look broken although they are not

CHAPTER 23

Configuring a Network

This chapter covers the following exam topics:

5. **Diagnosing Problems**

   5.5. **Run basic show commands on a Cisco network device.**

   show run, show cdp-neighbors, show ip interface brief, show ip route, show version, show inventory, show switch, show mac-address-table, show interface, show interface x, show interface status; privilege levels; command help and auto-complete

It is time, once again, to turn from theory to practice by building and configuring a small network. This chapter begins with three small Cisco IOS Software routers, two hosts, and a network-attached storage (NAS) device. It builds a network using these devices from initial configuration through configuring security.

If you have access to physical or virtual Cisco routers, you can follow along with the configuration steps. There will be some differences between a physical and virtual network, such as

- For physical routers, you will need to have a console cable and appropriate terminal emulation software to enable remote access through *Secure Shell (SSH)*.

- For physical routers, you will need to wire the routers together.

- For virtual routers, you will need to build virtual connections between the routers.

If you decide to build this network, you must also translate between the port numbers used in this example to the available physical ports.

You can also read this chapter to understand better configuring and using Cisco IOS Software-based devices. Cloud-based configuration, such as Cisco Meraki, makes deploying and configuring routers and switches simpler, but knowing the basic process for connecting to and configuring a router is still an important skill.

"Do I Know This Already?" Quiz

Take the quiz (either here or use the PTP software) if you want to use the score to help you decide how much time to spend on this chapter. Appendix A, "Answers to the 'Do I Know This Already?' Quizzes," found at the end of the book, includes both the answers and explanations. You can also find answers in the PTP testing software.

Table 23-1 "Do I Know This Already?" Foundation Topics Section-to-Question Mapping

Section	Questions
Initial Access	1, 2, 3
Configuring IPv4	4, 5, 6, 7
Configuring Routing	8
Configuring Remote Access and Security	9
Adding IPv6	10
Adding a Switch	11

CAUTION The goal of self-assessment is to gauge your mastery of the topics in this chapter. If you do not know the answer to a question or are only partially sure of the answer, you should mark that question as wrong for purposes of the self-assessment. Giving yourself credit for an answer you incorrectly guess skews your self-assessment results and might provide you with a false sense of security.

1. What can you do when the router prompt is followed by a greater-than symbol (>)?
   a. View the router's software version.
   b. Configure just the router's interfaces.
   c. Configure the router's hostname.
   d. No commands are available at this level.

2. Which configuration will a router load when it reboots or powers on?
   a. The boot ROM
   b. The startup configuration
   c. The running configuration
   d. A configuration from the floppy disk or USB drive

3. What happens when you press the Tab key once you have typed part of a command?
   a. The router attempts to complete the command.
   b. Nothing.
   c. The router gives you a list of possible commands at this point.
   d. The router will ask you what you are looking for.

4. What is a configuration sub-mode?
   a. Mode for configuring interfaces, processes, etc.
   b. Mode for showing information about interfaces, processes, etc.
   c. Mode for installing routes
   d. Mode for shutting down the router

5. What does **show cdp neighbors** show you?
   a. Routers physically connected to this device
   b. Hosts physically connected to this device

c. Any other CDP-enabled device connected to this device

d. Printers connected to this device

6. What does the letter to the left of a route in **show ip routes** mean?

a. How long this route has been in the routing table

b. Which protocol installed this route in the routing table

c. How the router learned about this route

d. The order in which this route was learned

7. What packets will a router send toward the default route?

a. Any packet whose destination address does not fall within another route

b. Any packet whose source address does not fall within another route

c. Any packet whose destination address does not exactly match another route

d. All packets

8. Why would you want to run a dynamic routing protocol, like OSPF?

a. You do not need to configure static routes to reach every destination on every router

b. Because you want to learn OSPF

c. Because dynamic routing protocols, like OSPF, are easier to configure than static routing protocols, like BGP

d. Because you need to configure OSPF on only one router

9. What default action does an access list take?

a. Permit anything that does not match anything else.

b. Deny anything that does not match anything else.

c. Permit every other packet.

d. Deny every other packet.

10. How do you enable IPv6 on a router's interface?

a. Just assign an IPv6 address.

b. You don't need to do anything; IPv6 is automatically enabled.

c. Use the **ipv6 enable** command.

d. Disable IPv4.

11. What changes will you see in the routing table on any router after adding a switch to the network?

a. None

b. The next hop for some routing table entries will change to the switch's IP address.

c. The next hop for some routing table entries will change from an IP address to an interface.

d. The gateway of last resort will always point to the switch with the lowest identifier.

Foundation Topics

This chapter works through the process of configuring the network shown in Figure 23-1.

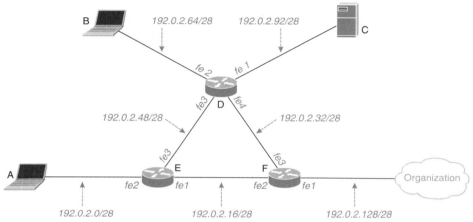

Figure 23-1 *Sample Network*

> **NOTE**   Previous chapters considered configuring hosts. Because of this, *A*, *B*, and *C* will largely be ignored from a configuration standpoint throughout this example.
>
> The IPv4 addresses used in this example and throughout this book are taken from the range of addresses set aside for documentation. You should not use these addresses in a physical or virtual address. For IPv4, use addresses from the pool of private addresses. For IPv6, use addresses from the documentation range for building labs and documentation.

If you follow along, we assume you have three physical or logical routers and three physical or virtual hosts wired up, as shown in Figure 23-1.

> **NOTE**   You will need to use different interface numbers on your devices than those shown in Figure 23-1. Write down the port numbers on a slip of paper and the corresponding port numbers from the diagram to help you remember which port is which.

Initial Access

When you first power on a router, it does not have any IP addresses, and all the interfaces should be disabled or in the *down state*. The only port you can use to connect to the router is the console point, so the console port is where we will begin. Assuming you plug a host into router *F*'s console port and start a terminal emulator, you might see a lot of copyright and version information scroll across the screen. Then you will see something like Figure 23-2.

The first prompt you will see is **router>**. If you see the greater-than symbol (>) at the end of the prompt, you can only see some router information, like interface state and software version; you cannot change the configuration. This is called the *user exec mode*. Because you need to configure this router, you must enter **enable mode**.

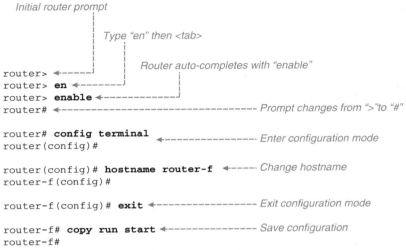

Figure 23-2 *Changing the Router's Hostname*

You can enter this mode by entering the **enable** command. Rather than entering this command directly, however, you can use the Tab key to complete the command. Any time you enter a few letters of a command and press Tab, Cisco IOS Software will finish the command *if you have typed enough letters to identify a single command uniquely.*

This Tab trick works even with multiword commands, like **copy run start**. If you type **co**, then press Tab, then **ru** and Tab, then **st** and Tab, each word in the command will be completed.

> **NOTE** Most operating systems have this kind of **tab completion** functionality in their CLIs.

Enable mode is called an *elevated privilege mode*. While routers can have many different privilege modes or **privilege levels**, this book will use only the following:

- Privilege level 1, indicated by the > symbol. Users can only *read* information at this privilege level, which is also called *read-only mode*.

- Privilege level 15, which is the default level label when entering the **enable** command. Users at this privilege level can *read and write* any device's configuration.

Once you enter elevated privilege mode, you must enter the command **config terminal** to enter configuration mode, enabling you to change the router's configuration. Entering a privileged mode changes the prompt to include (**config**).

Figure 23-2 next shows the **hostname** command, which changes the host's name. This hostname is displayed in the command prompt and many *graphical user interface (GUI)* or cloud-based configuration systems. Operators can quickly tell which router they are connected to by looking at the hostname.

The last command shown in Figure 23-2 is **copy run start**. Routers have at least two different configurations, including

- The **startup configuration** is stored in nonvolatile random access memory (NVRAM). The router loads this configuration when it is powered on or restarted.

- The **running configuration** is the configuration in use right now. This configuration is lost when you reboot or power down the router.

Making changes from the command line changes only the running configuration. If you want the router to keep any changes you make the next time it restarts, you must copy the running configuration to the startup configuration. You can view these two configurations by using the following:

- show running

- show startup

Some examples of **show running** are considered later in this chapter, so we do not go into a lot of detail here.

Why are there two different configurations? Imagine you accidentally enter a command disabling the interface you are using to connect to a router you are working on. As long as you have not copied the running configuration to the startup configuration, powering the router off and back on allows you to access it again. Having two configurations allows you to try configurations without committing them.

If you follow along in a physical or virtual lab, use the same process to set the hostname on routers *D* and *E* to *router-d* and *router-e*.

One common router configuration task is checking the software version number and basic hardware information. Figure 23-3 illustrates the output from **show version**.

The **show version** command provides basic information about the router, including the software version, router serial number, and installed hardware.

Figure 23-3 illustrates five essential parts of the output from **show version**:

- The *software* block tells you which version of Cisco IOS Software this device runs and how to contact Cisco's support.

- The *bootstrap* block tells you information about how and when the router last started. Like all other computers, routers have a *bootstrap image* to bring up the basic hardware and an *operating system* that loads once the hard drive and other hardware can be used.

- The *boot* block tells you when the router was last restarted and why. This section tells you if the router was powered off and back on, restarted from the command line, or was forced to restart because of a crash.

- The *processor* block indicates the router's model number, processor, and memory.

- The *hardware* block often provides information about the physical interfaces.

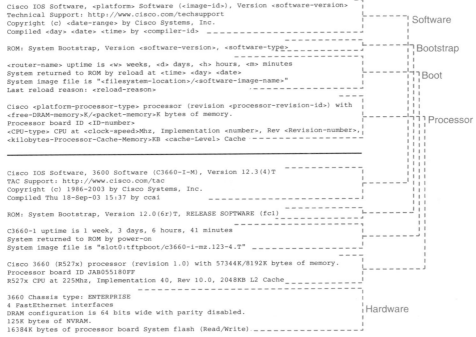

Figure 23-3   show version

Each router has a serial number, power supply, and potentially some installed interfaces. The **show inventory** command provides this information, as demonstrated in Example 23-1.

Example 23-1   show inventory *Command Output*

```
router-f# show inventory
NAME: "Chassis", DESCR: "Cisco ISR4331 Chassis"
PID: ISR4331/K9       , VID: V02, SN: ***********


NAME: "Power Supply Module 0", DESCR: "250W AC Power Supply for Cisco ISR 4330"
PID: PWR-4330-AC      , VID: V01, SN: ***********


NAME: "Fan Tray", DESCR: "Cisco ISR4330 Fan Assembly"
PID: ACS-4330-FANASSY , VID:    , SN:


NAME: "module 0", DESCR: "Cisco ISR4331 Built-In NIM controller"
PID: ISR4331/K9       , VID:    , SN:
```

In **show inventory**:

- *NAME* gives you the part of the router the information describes.

- *Description* gives you a long-form device description, including its model number.

- *PID* is a product identifier.

■ *VID* is the hardware version number.

■ *SN* is the device's serial number.

Configuring IPv4

Once the hostname is configured on the three routers—so you can tell which router you are working on—you should configure basic IPv4 connectivity. You need to configure the IP address on each of the three interfaces on all three of the routers—nine interfaces total.

Figure 23-4 focuses on router *F*.

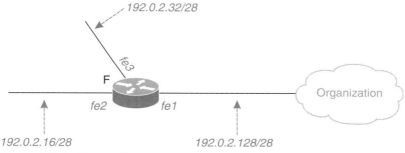

Figure 23-4   *Router F*

There are several points to consider before configuring IP on router *F*.

The Internet-facing interface, *fe1*, should obtain an address from the service provider.

We need to decide which IP address to use within the subnet given in the diagram. Should router *F* have the first address in each subnet or another address within the range? The router's interface is often given either the first or last address in the subnet if the interface connects to hosts, but router *F*'s interfaces, *fe2* and *fe3*, connect to other routers. Some common techniques for choosing interface IP addresses when a link connects two routers are

■ Use the first address in the range for the first router configured, the second address in the range for the second router configured, etc.

■ Use an address indicating where the router is in the topology. For instance, all core routers might use the last IP address in the subnet. All distribution routers might use the second-to-last, etc.

■ Use some random address in the subnet range.

■ Use an address that somehow translates to the router's hostname.

The most common method is the first—assign the addresses in the order the routers are configured, which we will use.

Interface *fe3* should take the first address from 192.0.2.32/28. The first and last addresses, 192.0.2.32 and 192.0.2.47, are broadcast addresses, so we cannot use them. The first usable address in this range is 192.0.2.33, so we will assign this to interface *fe1* on router *F*. Figure 23-5 illustrates the process of assigning an IP address to an interface.

```
router-f> enable
router-f# configure terminal
router-f(config)#

router-f(config)# interface FastEthernet 3  ◄------------------- Enter interface configuration mode
router-f(config-int)#

router-f(config-int)# ip address 192.0.2.33 255.255.255.240 ◄-- Configure IP address
router-f(config-int)# no shutdown ◄--------------┐
router-f(config-int)# exit                         │
                                                   └----------- Bring the interface up
router-f(config)# exit
router-f# copy run start
```

Figure 23-5 *Assigning an Interface IP Address*

Unlike the CLI for a Linux host, routers and switches have **configuration sub-modes** under the primary configuration mode. You can think of these sub-modes as a sort of tree, as shown in Figure 23-6.

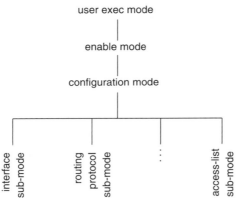

Figure 23-6 *Configuration Modes and Sub-modes*

Once you enter a sub-mode, **exit** will drop you back to the previous level. You can also think of these modes and sub-modes as shortcuts. Rather than entering the interface name each time you want to change an interface's configuration, you can go into the sub-mode for the interface, make the changes, and then exit out of the interface's sub-mode.

Configuration sub-modes allow you to change the configuration for interfaces, processes, etc.

The same process is used to configure and enable the remaining interface addresses as follows:

- Router *F* interface *fe2*: 192.0.2.17 255.255.255.240

- Router *E* interface *fe1*: 192.0.2.18 255.255.255.240

- Router *E* interface *fe3*: 192.0.2.49 255.255.255.240

- Router *D* interface *fe3*: 192.0.2.50 255.255.255.240

- Router *D* interface *fe4*: 192.0.2.34 255.255.255.240

The interfaces on each router where hosts connect are configured the same way, as follows:

- Router *E* interface *fe2*: 192.0.2.1 255.255.255.240

- Router *D* interface *fe2*: 192.0.2.65 255.255.255.240

- Router *D* interface *fe2*: 192.0.2.93 255.255.255.240

We also need to configure each of the host's IP addresses as follows:

- Host *A*: 192.0.2.2/28

- Host *B*: 192.0.2.66/28

- Server *C*: 192.0.2.94/28

Figure 23-7 shows the resulting IP addresses.

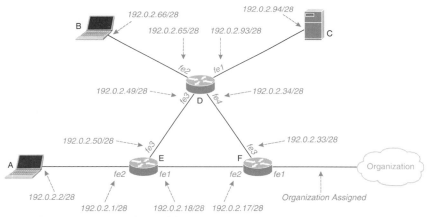

Figure 23-7   *Assigned IP Addresses*

One last interface has no IP address—router *F* interface *fe1*. You need to get this address from the organization you are connecting to rather than using a local number. Assume, for this example, the organization gives you 192.0.2.132/28 and tells you their router's address is 192.0.2.129. In this case, you can configure router *F* interface *fe1*'s address to **192.0.2.132 255.255.255.240**.

Now it is time to check these configurations. Begin with **show cdp neighbors**, which should produce something like the output in Example 23-2.

Example 23-2   show cdp neighbors *Command Output*

```
router-f# show cdp neighbors


Capability Codes: R - Router, T - Trans Bridge, B - Source Route Bridge
                  S - Switch, H - Host, I - IGMP, r - Repeater


Device ID       Local Intrfce   Holdtme    Capability  Platform   Port ID
router-e        FastEth 2       122        R           XXXXX      FastEth 1
router-d        FastEth 3       179        R           XXXXX      FastEth 4
```

Cisco Discovery Protocol (**CDP**) is a lightweight discovery protocol that runs whenever an interface is connected to another device, enabled, and the line interface is up. This **show** command gives you basic information about

■ The devices connected to the local device.

■ The interface through which each device is connected.

■ The remote device's interface through which the remote device connects to this one.

CDP does not run on IP, so it will run and discover connected devices even if IP is not configured.

If you run the command **show interfaces** from the command prompt, you should see something like the output in Example 23-3.

Example 23-3   show interfaces *Command Output*

```
router-f# show interfaces
Fast Ethernet 1 is up, line protocol is up
  Hardware is MCI Ethernet, address is 0000.0c00.750c (bia 0000.0c00.750c)
  Internet address is 192.0.2.132, subnet mask is 255.255.255.240
  MTU 1500 bytes, BW 10000 Kbit, DLY 100000 usec, rely 255/255, load 1/255
  Encapsulation ARPA, loopback not set, keepalive set (10 sec)
 . . .


Fast Ethernet 2 is up, line protocol is up
  Hardware is MCI Ethernet, address is 0000.0c00.850c (bia 0000.0c00.850c)
  Internet address is 192.0.2.17, subnet mask is 255.255.255.240
  MTU 1500 bytes, BW 10000 Kbit, DLY 100000 usec, rely 255/255, load 1/255
  Encapsulation ARPA, loopback not set, keepalive set (10 sec)
 . . .


Fast Ethernet 3 is up, line protocol is up
  Hardware is MCI Ethernet, address is 0000.0c00.950c (bia 0000.0c00.950c)
  Internet address is 192.0.2.33, subnet mask is 255.255.255.240
  MTU 1500 bytes, BW 10000 Kbit, DLY 100000 usec, rely 255/255, load 1/255
  Encapsulation ARPA, loopback not set, keepalive set (10 sec)
 . . .
```

The **show interfaces** command provides basic information about the physical and virtual interfaces connected to this device.

The **show interfaces** command provides a lot of information about the hardware, packet drops, etc., but these are outside the scope of this book. You can look at the configuration of a single interface by including the interface name after the command, like **show interfaces fastethernet1**.

Two fields beyond the IP address and subnet are particularly interesting: the interface and line protocol states.

- *Interface is up* means the interface is not administratively disabled; the interface is not in *shutdown* state.

- *Line protocol is up* means the router is communicating with the router or device connected to the other end of the link.

If the line protocol is down, there is some problem with the cabling or hardware configuration.

The **show ip interface brief** command is also helpful to quickly check the IP configuration, as shown in the output in Example 23-4.

Example 23-4   show ip interface brief *Command Output*

```
Router-f# show ip interface brief
Interface          IP-Address       OK?    Method Status     Protocol
FastEthernet1      192.0.2.132      YES    unset  up         up
FastEthernet2      192.0.2.17       YES    unset  up         up
FastEthernet3      192.0.2.33       YES    unset  up         up
```

Once all the IP addresses are configured, you can try pinging between the routers and hosts. From router *F*, try pinging two of router *D*'s addresses, 192.0.2.34 and 192.0.2.93, as demonstrated in Example 23-5.

Example 23-5   ping *Command Output*

```
router-f# ping 192.0.2.34
Type escape sequence to abort.
Sending 5, 100-byte ICMP Echos to 192.0.2.34, timeout is 2 seconds:
!!!!!
Success rate is 100 percent (5/5), round-trip min/avg/max = 4/6/8 ms
router-f# ping 192.0.2.93
Type escape sequence to abort.
Sending 5, 100-byte ICMP Echos to 192.0.2.93, timeout is 2 seconds:
*****
Success rate is 0 percent (0/5)
```

The ping from router *F* to 192.0.2.34 works, but not the ping to 192.0.2.93. Let's figure out why.

Configuring Routing

Whenever there is a reachability problem, the best place to start looking for the problem is the routing table, which you can see by using **show ip route**. Figure 23-8 illustrates the parts of **show ip route**'s output.

The **show ip route** command displays the router's routing table, including which destinations the router knows how to reach and other information about each reachable destination.

```
router-f# show ip route
Codes: I - IGRP derived, R - RIP derived, O - OSPF derived          ⌐ Route
       C - connected, S - static, E - EGP derived, B - BGP derived   ¦ origin
       * - candidate default route, IA - OSPF inter area route       ¦ information
       E1 - OSPF external type 1 route, E2 - OSPF external type 2 route⌐

Gateway of last resort is not set ⌐ Default Route

C    192.0.2.16 is directly connected, 0:01:00, FastEthernet2 ◄───────────────────────┐
C    192.0.2.32 is directly connected, 0:01:00, FastEthernet3 ◄─────────────────┐      ¦
C    192.0.2.128 is directly connected, 0:01:00, FastEthernet1 ◄──────┐         ¦      ¦
                                                                       ¦         ¦      ¦
                                                                       ¦         ¦      ¦
                                                                       ¦         ¦  First Route
                                                                       ¦         ¦
                                                                       ¦      Second Route
                                                                       ¦
                                                                    Third Route
```

Figure 23-8 *The Routing Table*

The top of the **show ip route** command's output is a list of the sources where the routing table might learn a route. Most of these are routing protocols, but two are locally learned:

- *C* means this route is *connected* or a destination directly connected to a physical or virtual interface on this device.

- *S* means the network administrator statically configures this route.

The following section shows the **gateway of last resort**, also known as the *default gateway*. The default gateway is where the router will send packets if it has no other routing table entry for the packet's destination address.

Finally, each route is listed on a separate line. This line includes information about

- Where the router forwards traffic; in this case, it is *directly connected*.

- How long this route has been in the local routing table.

- What interface the router sends packets to; in this case, it is the three connected interfaces configured earlier in this chapter.

Notice there is a route to 192.0.2.32, which contains 192.0.2.34, so the router knows where to send packets when you ping the address. There is not, however, any routing table entry for 192.0.2.92, which is the network containing 192.0.2.94. When you ping 192.0.2.94, the router has no information about where to send the packets, so the ping fails.

We need to tell router *F* about 192.0.2.92 somehow. The easiest way is to configure a *static route* telling router *F* about 192.0.2.92, including where to send packets to destinations contained in this network. Example 23-6 demonstrates the commands used to configure a static route on router *F*.

Example 23-6 *Configuring a Static Route*

```
router-f# config terminal
router-f (config)# ip route 192.0.2.92 255.255.255.240 192.0.2.34
router-f (config)# exit
```

The **ip route command** creates a static route that will be inserted in the local routing table and forwards packets to the indicated destination.

Pinging from router *F* to 192.0.2.93 now works, as Example 23-7 shows.

Example 23-7   ping *Command Output*

```
router-f# ping 192.0.2.93
Type escape sequence to abort.
Sending 5, 100-byte ICMP Echos to 192.0.2.93, timeout is 2 seconds:
!!!!!
Success rate is 100 percent (5/5)
```

The static route now shows up in router *F*'s routing table, as Example 23-8 shows.

Example 23-8   *Confirming a Static Route*

```
router-f# show ip route
Gateway of last resort is not set
C    192.0.2.16 is directly connected, 0:01:00, FastEthernet2
C    192.0.2.32 is directly connected, 0:01:00, FastEthernet3
C    192.0.2.128 is directly connected, 0:01:00, FastEthernet1
S    192.0.2.92 [1/0] via 192.0.2.34, 0:01:00, FastEthernet3
```

Sourcing the ping from router *F* interface *fe2*, however, causes the ping to fail once more, as Example 23-9 shows.

Example 23-9   ping *Command Output*

```
router-f# ping
Protocol [ip]:
Target IP address: 192.0.2.93
Repeat count [5]:
Datagram size [100]:
Timeout in seconds [2]:
Extended commands [n]: y
Source address or interface: 192.0.2.17
Type of service [0]:
Set DF bit in IP header? [no]:
Validate reply data? [no]:
Data pattern [0xABCD]:
Loose, Strict, Record, Timestamp, Verbose[none]:
Sweep range of sizes [n]:
Type escape sequence to abort.
Sending 5, 100-byte ICMP Echos to 192.0.2.93, timeout is 2 seconds:
.....
Success rate is 0 percent (0/5)
```

What could the problem be? Looking at router *D*'s routing table in Example 23-10 reveals some clues.

Example 23-10   *Using* **show ip route** *to Determine Possible Causes of a Problem*

```
router-d# show ip route
Gateway of last resort is not set
C    192.0.2.32 is directly connected, 0:01:00, FastEthernet4
C    192.0.2.48 is directly connected, 0:01:00, FastEthernet3
C    192.0.2.64 is directly connected, 0:01:00, FastEthernet2
C    192.0.2.92 is directly connected, 0:01:00, FastEthernet1
```

Router *D* does not have a route to 192.0.2.16, which contains 192.0.2.17, the source of the ping packets. You can resolve this once again by creating a static route at router *D*, as demonstrated in Example 23-11.

Example 23-11   *Configuring a Static Route*

```
router-d# config terminal
router-d (config)# ip route 192.0.2.16 255.255.255.240 192.0.2.33
router-d (config)# exit
```

To make every host reachable from every other host, you must configure static routes for every network on every router. There is an easier way, however—running a routing protocol. Detailed routing protocol operation is outside the scope of this book, but configuring the *Open Shortest Path First (OSPF)* protocol takes a few configuration commands, as demonstrated in Example 23-12.

Example 23-12   *Configuring OSPF*

```
router-f (config)# router ospf 1
router-f (config-router)# network 192.0.2.16 0.0.0.15 area 0
router-f (config-router)# network 192.0.2.32 0.0.0.15 area 0
router-f (config-router)# exit
router-f (config)# exit
router-f#
```

```
router-d (config)# router ospf 1
router-d (config-router)# network 192.0.2.92 0.0.0.15 area 0
router-d (config-router)# network 192.0.2.64 0.0.0.15 area 0
router-d (config-router)# network 192.0.2.48 0.0.0.15 area 0
router-d (config-router)# network 192.0.2.32 0.0.0.15 area 0
router-d (config-router)# exit
router-d (config)# exit
router-d#
```

```
router-e (config)# router ospf 1
router-e (config-router)# network 192.0.2.16 0.0.0.15 area 0
router-e (config-router)# network 192.0.2.48 0.0.0.15 area 0
router-e (config-router)# network 192.0.2.0 0.0.0.15 area 0
router-e (config-router)# exit
router-e (config)# exit
router-e#
```

In this set of commands:

- **router ospf 1** starts OSPF process 1. You can run multiple OSPF processes on a router, each routing for different interfaces; the process number allows you to differentiate between the processes.

- **network** *<ip address> <inverse mask>* enables OSPF on any interface with an IP address covered by the **network** statement. For instance, 192.0.2.1 is in the 192.0.2.0/28 network, which can also be written as 192.0.2.0 255.255.240. Inverting the last digit in the network mask gives us .15 rather than .240.

> **NOTE**   OSPF areas are outside the scope of this book.

Example 23-13 shows what the routing table on router *F* now contains.

Example 23-13   *Displaying a Routing Table*

```
router-f# show ip route
Gateway of last resort is not set
C     192.0.2.16 is directly connected, 0:01:00, FastEthernet2
C     192.0.2.32 is directly connected, 0:01:00, FastEthernet3
C     192.0.2.128 is directly connected, 0:01:00, FastEthernet1
O   192.0.2.92 [110/20] via 192.0.2.34, 0:01:00, FastEthernet3
O   192.0.2.64 [110/20] via 192.0.2.34, 0:01:00, FastEthernet3
O   192.0.2.0 [110/20] via 192.0.2.18, 0:01:00, FastEthernet3
```

OSPF learned every reachable destination and advertised it throughout the network so the other routers could calculate paths to them.

One last routing problem to solve is reaching networks in the *Organization* network. Solving this problem is especially difficult because the networks reachable within *Organization* are not given.

The **default route** is designed to solve this problem. Begin by configuring a static default route on router *F*, as demonstrated in Example 23-14.

Example 23-14   *Configuring a Static Default Route*

```
router-f# config terminal
router-f (config)# ip route 0.0.0.0 0.0.0.0 192.0.2.129
router-f (config)# exit
```

The 0.0.0.0/0 route is a special route called the *default*. Routers send any packets they do not know how to forward to this special route. Remember, *Organization* indicated 192.0.2.129 was its router's address. As Example 23-15 shows, router *F*'s routing table shows this new route; the default gateway is now set.

Example 23-15   show ip route *with a Default Route*

```
router-f# show ip route
Gateway of last resort is 192.0.2.129 to network 0.0.0.0
C    192.0.2.16 is directly connected, 0:01:00, FastEthernet2
C    192.0.2.32 is directly connected, 0:01:00, FastEthernet3
C    192.0.2.128 is directly connected, 0:01:00, FastEthernet1
O  192.0.2.92 [110/20] via 192.0.2.34, 0:01:00, FastEthernet3
O  192.0.2.64 [110/20] via 192.0.2.34, 0:01:00, FastEthernet3
O  192.0.2.0 [110/20] via 192.0.2.18, 0:01:00, FastEthernet3
S    0.0.0.0 [1/1] via 192.0.2.129, 0:01:00, FastEthernet1
```

Configuring a static default route works for router *F*, but what about routers *E* and *D*? You can configure a static default in each router, or you can configure OSPF to advertise this default route to routers *E* and *D*, as demonstrated in Example 23-16.

Example 23-16   *Advertising a Default Route Using OSPF*

```
router-f (config)# router ospf 1
router-f (config-router)# default-information originate ?
  always       Always advertise default route
  metric       OSPF default metric
  metric-type  OSPF metric type for default routes
  route-map    Route-map reference
```

The *question mark* (?) at the end of the command means "Tell me what options are available here." The **?** is one of the most valuable additions to the Cisco IOS Software CLI. If you cannot remember a command, put a **?** at the end of what you can remember and let the router help you.

None of these options are essential for this example, so use the **default-information originate** command by itself as demonstrated in Example 23-17.

Example 23-17   *Advertising a Default Route Using OSPF*

```
router-f (config)# router ospf 1
router-f (config-router)# default-information originate
```

Router *E*'s routing table now has a default route, as Example 23-18 shows.

Example 23-18   show ip route *with Default Route*

```
router-e# show ip route
Gateway of last resort is 192.0.2.17 to network 0.0.0.0
C    192.0.2.0 is directly connected, 0:01:00, FastEthernet2
C    192.0.2.16 is directly connected, 0:01:00, FastEthernet1
C    192.0.2.48 is directly connected, 0:01:00, FastEthernet3
O  192.0.2.92 [110/20] via 192.0.2.49, 0:01:00, FastEthernet3
O  192.0.2.64 [110/20] via 192.0.2.49, 0:01:00, FastEthernet3
O  192.0.2.32 [110/20] via 192.0.2.17, 0:01:00, FastEthernet1
O*E2 0.0.0.0 [110/20] via 192.0.2.17, 0:01:00, FastEthernet1
```

NOTE   Advertising the routes within this network to the routers in the *Organization* is outside the scope of this book. You would normally use a routing protocol, like OSPF, to advertise the routes.

Configuring Remote Access and Security

You are not done just because routing is configured and running. Up to this point, you have been using the console port to connect to routers *D*, *E*, and *F*. You want to be able to configure these routers across the network.

To do this, you must configure each router's Telnet protocol. Each Cisco IOS Software device has a set of *virtual terminal* connections called *vty lines*, which you can configure to enable remote access. Example 23-19 demonstrates the commands to enable access for router *F*.

Example 23-19   *Configuring Virtual Terminal Lines*

```
router-f (config)# line vty 0 4
router-f (config-line)# password VeryHardPassw0r1
router-f (config-line)# login
router-f (config-line)# logging synchronous
```

Enabling the *vty lines* is not enough to remotely access the router; Cisco IOS Software will not allow Telnet access unless a local *privilege mode password* is set. To set this password on router *F*, use the commands in Example 23-20.

Example 23-20   *Configuring the Enable Mode Password*

```
router-f (config)# enable secret VeryHardPassw0r2
router-f (config)# exit
```

NOTE   You would typically set up Secure Shell (SSH) to these routers and disable the Telnet protocol, but configuring SSH is outside the scope of this book.

You can increase your network's security by blocking access to the router's interface addresses from outside. There are two ways to do this:

- Block based on the source address, so only addresses connected to the local network can telnet to the router's interface addresses.

- Block based on the destination address, so no device in the *Organization* network can connect to any router's addresses.

We will use the second solution for this example. To begin this process, you need to know the IP address of each router interface, which includes

- 192.0.2.1 (router *E*)

- 192.02.18 (router *E*)

- 192.0.2.50 (router *E*)

- 192.0.2.49 (router *D*)

- 192.0.2.65 (router *D*)

- 192.0.2.93 (router *D*)

- 192.0.2.34 (router *D*)

- 192.0.2.22 (router *F*)

- 192.0.2.17 (router *F*)

- 192.0.2.33 (router *F*)

Given this set of addresses, you can create an *IP access list* using the format shown in Figure 23-9.

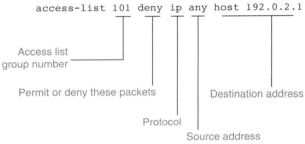

Figure 23-9 *Extended Cisco IOS Software Packet Filter Format*

An **access list** is a set of policies applied to packet forwarding, routing information, and many other places within a router.

In Figure 23-9:

- The *access list group number* identifies a set of associated packet filters to be applied together.

- **Permit** or **deny** describes whether the packet should be forwarded if the packet's contents match the filter or discarded. In this case, packets matching the filter should be discarded.

- The *source address* matches the source address in the IP packet header. In this case, we use a special keyword, *any*, which means match on any source address.

- The *destination address* matches the destination address in the IP packet header. In this case, we only match against the single host address 192.0.2.1.

Example 23-21 shows an access list containing all the router interface addresses using this syntax.

Example 23-21   *Access List Configuration*

```
router-f (config)# access-list 101 deny ip any host 192.0.2.1
router-f (config)# access-list 101 deny ip any host 192.0.2.18
router-f (config)# access-list 101 deny ip any host 192.0.2.50
router-f (config)# access-list 101 deny ip any host 192.0.2.49
router-f (config)# access-list 101 deny ip any host 192.0.2.65
router-f (config)# access-list 101 deny ip any host 192.0.2.93
router-f (config)# access-list 101 deny ip any host 192.0.2.22
router-f (config)# access-list 101 deny ip any host 192.0.2.17
router-f (config)# access-list 101 deny ip any host 192.0.2.132
router-f (config)# access-list 101 permit ip any any
```

Why is **any any** included at the end of the list? Because the default action for a packet that does not match any rule in an access list is to discard it.

How and where is this access list applied to protect routers *D*, *E*, and *F* from outside connections? At any point where the network connects to external devices. In this case, this is router *F* interface *fe1*. Example 23-22 shows this configuration.

Example 23-22   *Applying an Access List*

```
router-f (config)# interface FastEthernet 1
router-f (config-if)# ip access-group 101 in
router-f (config-if)# exit
router-f (config)# exit
```

The **access-group command** applies an access list as an interface packet filter.

You can build a more specific access list by including the protocol like this:

```
access-list 101 deny tcp any host 192.0.2.1 eq telnet
```

The **eq telnet** on the end of the access-list line only matches against the Telnet protocol. Adding this additional command would block Telnet to the router's interfaces while allowing other kinds of connections like SSH or network management.

Adding IPv6

While IPv6 is not entirely displacing IPv4 in many networks, operators are deploying IPv6 more widely daily. Basic IPv6 configuration is no more complicated than IPv4 configuration. You need to

- Enable IPv6.
- Add IPv6 addresses to all the interfaces.
- Run an IPv6-capable routing protocol.

Enabling IPv6 is the first step; this is a single command:

```
router-f (config)# ipv6 unicast-routing
```

The **ipv6 unicast-routing command** enables IPv6 routing. There is a similar configuration command for IPv4 routing, but it is enabled by default.

The second step is adding IPv6 addresses to each interface. The 2001:db8:0::/32 range is set aside for documentation, so we will use addresses from this range. Figure 23-10 illustrates the IPv6 addresses we will use for this network.

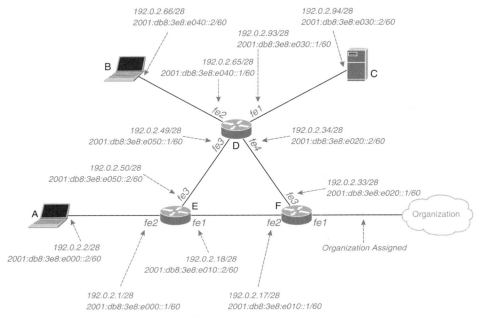

Figure 23-10 *Assigning IPv6 Addresses*

Example 23-23 demonstrates how to assign the IPv6 addresses on router *F*'s interfaces and enable IPv6 on each interface.

Example 23-23 *Enabling IPv6 on a Router's Interface*

```
router-f (config)# interface FastEthernet 2
router-f (config-if)# ipv6 enable
router-f (config-if)# ipv6 address 2001:db8:3e8:e010::1/60
router-f (config-if)# exit
router-f (config)# interface FastEthernet 3
router-f (config-if)# ipv6 enable
router-f (config-if)# ipv6 address 2001:db8:3e8:e020::1/60
router-f (config-if)# exit
```

The **ipv6 enable command** enables IPv6 forwarding on the interface. The **ipv6 address command** assigns an IPv6 address to the interface.

NOTE   Instead of specifying the host portion of the address, you can also use the **eui-64** keyword, which tells the router to draw the host portion of the address from a local physical interface address.

The final step is configuring an IPv6-capable routing protocol, such as *Intermediate System to Intermediate System (IS-IS)* or *Open Shortest Path First version 3 (OSPFv3)*, so the routers can learn about each destination in the network. We will use OSPFv3 here. Rather than using **network** statements to indicate which interfaces the routing protocol runs on, you enable OSPFv3 in the interface configuration, as shown in Example 23-24.

Example 23-24   *Enabling OSPF Routing for IPv6*

```
router-f (config)# ipv6 router ospf 1
router-f (config-rtr)# router-id 192.0.2.17
router-f (config-rtr)# exit
router-f (config)# interface FastEthernet 2
router-f (config-if)# ipv6 ospf 1 area 0
router-f (config-if)# exit
router-f (config)# interface FastEthernet 2
router-f (config-if)# ipv6 ospf 1 area 0
router-f (config-if)# exit
```

The **ipv6 router ospf command** starts an OSPFv3 routing process. The **ipv6 area interface sub-mode command** enables OSPFv3 routing on this interface.

Once IPv6 routing is enabled on routers *D*, *E*, and *F*; IPv6 addresses are configured; and OSPFv3 is enabled, the IPv6 routing table should include what is shown in Example 23-25.

Example 23-25   *IPv6 Routing Table*

```
router-f# show ipv6 route

OI  2001:db8:3e8:e000::/6o
  via 2001:db8:3e8:e010::2, FastEthernet2
C   2001:db8:3e8:e010::/60
  via FastEthernet2, directly connected
C   2001:db8:3e8:e020::/60
  via FastEthernet2, directly connected
O   2001:db8:3e8:e030::/60
  via 2001:db8:3e8:e020::2, FastEthernet3
O   2001:db8:3e8:e040::/60
  via 2001:db8:3e8:e020::2, FastEthernet3
O   2001:db8:3e8:e050::/60
  via 2001:db8:3e8:e020::2, FastEthernet3
```

> **NOTE** Once IPv6 is enabled, the routers are again reachable via Telnet from outside the network. Preventing IPv6 access uses the same process as preventing IPv4 access: build an access list and apply the access list to the correct interface on router F.

Adding a Switch

Figure 23-11 illustrates one final experiment in this small network.

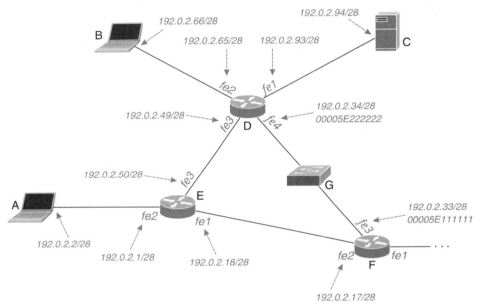

Figure 23-11   *Adding a Switch*

What impact will adding a switch between routers *D* and *F* make? Begin with router *F*'s routing table, as shown in Example 23-26.

Example 23-26   *Routing Table Changes When Adding a Switch*

```
router-f# show ip route
Gateway of last resort is 192.0.2.129 to network 0.0.0.0
C    192.0.2.16 is directly connected, 0:01:00, FastEthernet2
C    192.0.2.32 is directly connected, 0:01:00, FastEthernet3
C    192.0.2.128 is directly connected, 0:01:00, FastEthernet1
O  192.0.2.92 [110/20] via 192.0.2.34, 0:01:00, FastEthernet3
O  192.0.2.64 [110/20] via 192.0.2.34, 0:01:00, FastEthernet3
O  192.0.2.0 [110/20] via 192.0.2.18, 0:01:00, FastEthernet2
S    0.0.0.0 [1/1] via 192.0.2.129, 0:01:00, FastEthernet1
```

There is no difference in router *F*'s routing table. Because switches forward packets based on their physical addresses, routers forward packets based on their IP addresses, and the switch looks like a "bump in the road" to the router.

You can see the switch is there by examining the CDP table, as Example 23-27 demonstrates.

Example 23-27   show cdp neighbors *Command Output*

```
router-f# show cdp neighbors

Device ID       Local Intrfce   Holdtme    Capability  Platform  Port ID
router-e        FastEth 2       122        R           XXXXX     FastEth 1
switch-g        FastEth 3       179        S           XXXXX     FastEth 1
```

Switch *G* replaces router *D* as router *F*'s physical layer neighbor.

Switches are accessed the same way as routers:

- Access the console.
- Set the hostname (in this case to *switch-g*).
- Set a privilege mode password.
- Configure an IP address on interface VLAN 1.
- Configure the virtual terminal interfaces for Telnet access.

Individual switch interfaces do not need to be configured with IP addresses because they do not route IP packets. However, a single IP address is required so you can connect to the switch.

You can see the switch's port status by connecting to the console and using **show interface status**, as Example 23-28 demonstrates.

Example 23-28   *Interface Statuses*

```
switch-g# show interface status

Port    Name    Status      Vlan     Duplex  Speed Type
Fe1             connected   1        a-full a-1000 10/100BaseTX
Fe2             connected   1        a-full a-1000 10/100/BaseTX
```

You can see information about the devices connected to switch *G* using **show cdp neighbors**, as Example 23-29 demonstrates:

Example 23-29   *Show CDP Neighbors from the Switch*

```
switch-g# show cdp neighbors

Device ID        Local Intrfce    Holdtme    Capability   Platform   Port ID
router-d         FastEth 2        122        R            XXXXX      FastEth 4
router-f         FastEth 1        179        R            XXXXX      FastEth 3
```

Finally, because switches forward packets based on their physical layer addresses, you will want to be able to see the switch's switching table, as Example 23-30 demonstrates.

Example 23-30   *Examining the Physical (MAC) Forwarding Table*

```
Switch-g# show mac address-table
Mac Address Table
-------------------------------------------

Vlan    Mac Address     Type        Ports
----    -----------     --------    -----
All     0000.5E44.4444  STATIC      CPU
All     0000.5E55.5555  STATIC      CPU
1       0000.5E11.1111  Dynamic     Fe1
1       0000.5E22.2222  Dynamic     Fe2
```

Chapter Review

There is much more to configuring Cisco IOS Software devices, but this chapter provided a basic overview of the process and mechanics. In this chapter, we completed the following:

- Configured each router's hostname

- Assigned IPv4 and IPv6 addresses to each interface

- Configured IPv4 and IPv6 routing

- Configured an access list and applied it to traffic coming from outside the network

Along the way, we used a variety of **show** commands to examine the results of each configuration stage. Figure 23-12 summarizes router *F*'s configuration.

The next chapter moves into examination preparation.

One key to doing well on the exams is to perform repetitive spaced review sessions. Review this chapter's material using either the tools in the book or interactive tools for the same material found on the book's companion website. Refer to the online Appendix D, "Study Planner," element for more details. Table 23-2 outlines the key review elements and where you can find them. To better track your study progress, record when you completed these activities in the second column.

```
router-f#show running-config

Building configuration...

!
hostname router-f  ◄·—·—·—·—·—·—·—·—·—·—·—·— Sets hostname
!
enable secret VeryHardPassw0r2   ◄·—·—·—·—·—·— Privilege level password
!
ipv6 unicast-routing  ◄·—·—·—·—·—·—·—·—·—·— Enables IPv6 routing
!
interface FastEthernet1
    ip address 192.0.2.132 255.255.255.240 ◄·—·— Assign interface IPv4 address
    ip access-group 101 in  ◄·—·—·—·—·—·—·— Block external access to router interfaces
!
interface FastEthernet2
    ip address 192.0.2.17 255.255.255.240 ◄·—·— Assign interface IPv4 address
    ipv6 enable                         ⌐·|      Assign interface IPv6 address
    ipv6 address 2001:db8:3e8:e010::1/60 |◄—·—   and enable IPv6 routing
    ipv6 ospf 1 area 0    ·—·—·—·—·—·—·—·|
!
interface FastEthernet3
    ip address 192.0.2.33 255.255.255.240 ◄·—·— Assign interface IPv4 address
    ipv6 enable                         ⌐·|      Assign interface IPv6 address
ipv6 address 2001:db8:3e8:e020::1/60    |◄—·—   and enable IPv6 routing
ipv6 ospf 1 area 0        ·—·—·—·—·—·—·|
!
router opsf 1  ◄·—·—·—·—·—·—·—·—·—·—·—·—·— Run OSPF
    network 192.0.2.16 0.0.0.15 area 0 ◄·—·—·— Run OSPF on interface fe2
    network 192.0.2.32 0.0.0.15 area 0 ◄·—·—·— Run OSPF on interface fe3
!                                       ⌐·|
ipv6 router ospf 1                      |◄—·—
    router-id 192.0.2.17  ·—·—·—·—·—·—·|
!
access-list 101 deny ip any host 192.0.2.1    ⌐·|
access-list 101 deny ip any host 192.0.2.18    |
access-list 101 deny ip any host 192.0.2.50    |
access-list 101 deny ip any host 192.0.2.49    |
access-list 101 deny ip any host 192.0.2.65    |   List of router interfaces
access-list 101 deny ip any host 192.0.2.93    ◄·—  for blocking access
access-list 101 deny ip any host 192.0.2.22    |
access-list 101 deny ip any host 192.0.2.17    |
access-list 101 deny ip any host 192.0.2.132   |
access-list 101 permit any any                 |
!                                       ·—·—·—·|
line vty 0 4                            ⌐·|
   password VeryHardPassw0r1             |
   transport preferred all              |◄—·—  Enables remote access using Telnet
   transport input all                  |
   transport output all  ·—·—·—·—·—·—·—·|
!
```

Figure 23-12 *Router Configuration*

Table 23-2 Chapter Review Tracking

Review Element	Review Date (s)	Resource Used
Review key topics		Book, website
Review key terms		Book, website
Repeat DIKTA questions		Book, PTP
Review concepts and actions		Book, website

Review All the Key Topics

Table 23-3 lists the key topics for this chapter.

Table 23-3   Key Topics for Chapter 23

Key Topic Element	Description	Page Number
Paragraph	Entering enable mode	472
Paragraph, list	Privilege modes/levels	472
List	Router startup and running configurations	473
Paragraph, Figure 23-3, list	Checking software version and basic hardware information with the **show version** command	473
Paragraph	Configuration sub-modes	476
Paragraph	Cisco Discovery Protocol (CDP)	478
Paragraph	Displaying physical/virtual interface information with the **show interfaces** command	478
Paragraph	Displaying the router routing table information with the **show ip route** command	479
Paragraphs, Example 23-6	Creating a static route with the **ip route** command	480
Example 23-12, List	Configuring OSPF (**router ospf 1, network** *ip-address inverse-mask* commands)	482
Paragraph	Default route	483
Paragraph, Figure 23-9, list	Creating an IP access list	486
Paragraph	The **access-list any any** keyword/option	487
Paragraph	Applying an access list as an interface packet filter using the **ip access-group** command	487
Paragraph	Enabling IPv6 routing with the **ipv6 unicast-routing** command	488
Example 23-23, paragraph	Enabling IPv6 forwarding/assigning an IPv6 address to an interface with **ipv6 enable** and **ipv6 address** commands	488
Paragraph, Example 23-24, paragraph	Starting an OSPFv3 routing process	489

Key Terms You Should Know

Key terms in this chapter include

enable mode, tab completion, privilege level, **config terminal, hostname**, startup configuration, running configuration, **show version**, configuration sub-mode, **show cdp neighbors**, CDP, **show interfaces, show ip route**, gateway of last resort, **ip route** command, default route, access list, **access-group** command, **ipv6 unicast-routing** command, **ipv6 enable** command, **ipv6 address** command, **ipv6 router ospf** command, **ipv6 area** interface *sub-mode* command, **ip address** command, **network** command (under routing protocol configuration mode), **ip route 0.0.0.0 0.0.0.0**, vty interfaces, **show ipv6 route** command

Concepts and Actions

Review the concepts considered in this chapter using Table 23-4. You can cover the right side of this table and describe each concept or action in your own words to verify your understanding.

Table 23-4   Concepts and Actions

enable	Enters a higher privilege mode
config terminal	Enters configuration mode
Hostname	Sets the device's hostname
Privilege level	Determines the actions you can take on the router; privilege level 0 is also called *read-only mode*; privilege level 15 can configure anything on the router
Running configuration	Configuration the router is running right now
Startup configuration	Configuration saved in permanent memory and loaded by the router when it reboots or powers on
Tab	Autocompletes the command you are typing (if you have typed enough to identify the command uniquely)
?	Lists all the commands available after the one you are typing
show version	Provides general information about the router, including the software version number, router serial number, and installed hardware
Configuration sub-mode	Allows you to change the configuration for interfaces, processes, etc.
ip address command	Configures an IPv4 address for an interface
CDP	Cisco Discovery Protocol; lightweight discovery protocol that runs any time an interface is connected to another device, enabled, and the line interface is up
show cdp neighbors	Shows all CDP-enabled devices connected to this device
show interfaces	Provides basic information about the physical and virtual interfaces connected to this device
ip route command	Creates a static route that will be inserted in the local routing table and used to forward packets to the indicated destination
show ip route	Displays the router's routing table, including which destinations the router knows how to reach, along with other information about each reachable destination
network command	Enables the routing protocol on any interface with an IP address covered by the network statement
ip route 0.0.0.0 0.0.0.0	Creates a default route
Default route	Where a router sends any packet whose destination address does not fall within another route

Vty interface	A virtual terminal interface; you telnet to this interface remotely access a router
Access list	A set of policies applied to packet forwarding, routing information, and many other places within a router
Access list default action	Deny
access-group command	Applies an access list as a packet filter
ipv6 unicast-routing command	Enables IPv6 routing on the device
ipv6 enable command	Enables IPv6 on an interface
ipv6 address command	Assigns an IPv6 address to an interface
ipv6 router ospf command	Starts an OSPFv3 routing process
ipv6 area *interface* sub-mode command	Enables OSPFv3 routing on this interface
show ipv6 route command	Displays the IPv6 routing table

Part VI

Final Preparation

Chapter 24, "Final Preparation," provides exercises and thoughts on studying for the CCST.

Final Preparation

This chapter, along with the books' introduction, suggests hands-on activities and a study plan to help you complete your preparation for the exam.

This book has covered each section of the Cisco Certified Support Technician (CCST) Networking blueprint, going into some detail about the basic building blocks of networks, address formats and uses, endpoints, endpoint configuration, cabling, switching, routing, troubleshooting, and configuration. Reading about these topics will not be enough to prepare you for the certification exam or for building the groundwork for a successful career in information technology.

The first section of this final chapter provides some general advice to engineers gleaned from living in the world of engineering for over 30 years. The second section of this chapter suggests activities to help you consolidate your understanding of each concept. The final section provides a suggested plan for final review and study.

Advice to Future Engineers

Engineering is not just about technology. It is an attitude toward knowledge, problems, and people.

This book works from *how* networks work, and *why* networks work the way they do, to configuration and application. This approach might sometimes seem like the "long way around" to learning network engineering, but this method is grounded in two hard-learned realities:

- Network products, implementations, configurations, and technologies constantly change.

- The problems a network must solve, and the range of possible solutions to those problems, have not changed in 30 years—and are not likely to change in the next 30 years.

The constant change in network engineering can sometimes be exciting, but can also lead to burnout. The key to navigating this change is to focus on the constants underlying the change. Focusing on the constants helps frame and clarify change and helps you learn to ask the kinds of questions that lead to a deeper understanding.

Focusing on understanding first, rather than application first, also opens a new way of thinking about technology—*problems* and *solutions*. These three questions will bring clarity to any technical situation:

- What problem am I trying to solve?

- What are the possible solutions?

- What are the trade-offs for each solution?

Further, moving from *understanding* to *application* creates flexibility. One fear that looms large for many network engineers (although not unique to network engineering) is that change will render their skills obsolete. Building a broad base of understanding will allow you to shift to new areas over time.

Finally, do not forget about people. Engineers can focus so deeply on technology that they miss the people. Find people who know the answers to questions you do not know—because you cannot know the answer to everything. Make time to answer others' questions.

Engineering is still about people.

Learning Consolidation Activities

These activities are designed to help you consolidate what you have learned through this book. Each activity might include knowledge from several different chapters.

1. Install Wireshark and either capture some HTML traffic off your local network or download and open a .pcap file with HTML traffic. For several packets:
   a. What are the source and destination IP addresses?
   b. What is the transport protocol? What is the protocol identifier?
   c. What are the source and destination sockets?
2. Install Wireshark and either capture some HTML traffic off your local network or download and open a .pcap file with DNS traffic. For several packets:
   a. What are the source and destination IP addresses?
   b. What is the transport protocol? What is the protocol identifier?
   c. What are the source and destination sockets?
3. Build physical and logical diagrams for your home network or the network for the building you work in. If you have access, verify the default gateway settings on several hosts are set correctly without looking at the host's configuration.
4. What kinds of connectors do the following Cisco transceiver modules use?
   a. Cisco GLC-SX-MM
   b. Cisco GLC-T
5. Use an online speed test to measure your upload speed:
   a. To a city close to you
   b. To a city far away from you
   c. What is the difference between these two measurements?
   d. Why are these measurements different?
6. Trace a route to a website on the Internet. For each IP address along the path:
   a. Find the name of the service provider.
   b. What kind of provider is this? An access provider, transit provider, exchange point, etc.?

7. Choose two or three domain names. Do the following for each one:
   a. Use an online **whois** tool to discover what you can about each.
   b. Use **dig** to perform a DNS trace to each one. Mark out the response from each kind of DNS server, and note anything you find unusual about the responses.
   c. Use **nslookup** to perform a reverse lookup on the IP address you discovered for each. Do the domain names related to the IP address always match the IP addresses related to the domain names?

8. Describe the services offered by Linode, Digital Ocean, and Amazon Web Services.
   a. What services do they have in common?
   b. What services are unique to each platform?
   c. How would you describe each service?

9. Build a threat model for your home network.
   a. What kinds of attackers might want to break into your home network?
   b. What are the most vulnerable points of entry?

Answer Questions 10 and 11 about the network illustrated in Figure 24-1.

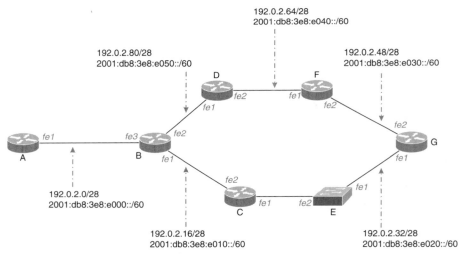

Figure 24-1 *Exercise Network*

10. Assume the IP addresses are configured as shown, and OSPF or some other routing protocol is running on routers.
    a. What IPv4 destinations would router *F*'s routing table contain?
    b. What interface would router *F* use to reach each of these IPv4 destinations?
    c. What IPv6 destinations would router *F*'s routing table contain?
    d. What interface would router *F* use to reach each of these IPv6 destinations?

11. Build the network shown in Figure 24-1 using virtual or real equipment, changing the port numbers as needed.

Suggested Plan for Final Review and Study

This section lists a suggested study plan from the point at which you finish reading this book through Chapter 23 until you take the exam. You can ignore this four-step plan, use it as is, or modify it to better meet your needs.

Step 1.   Review key topics and DIKTA questions: You can use the table at the end of each chapter that lists the key topics in each chapter or just flip the pages looking for key topics. Also, reviewing the "Do I Know This Already?" (DIKTA) questions from the beginning of the chapter can be helpful for review.

Step 2.   Review the exam blueprint and make sure you are familiar with every item that is listed. You can find the blueprint at https://learningnetwork.cisco.com/s/ccst-networking-exam-topics.

Step 3.   Complete *Concepts and Actions*. Open Appendix B from the book's website and print the entire thing or print the tables by major parts. Then complete the tables. Appendix C provides the solutions so you can check your answers.

Step 4.   Use the Pearson Cert Practice Test engine to practice: The Pearson Test Prep practice test software provides a bank of unique exam-realistic questions available only with this book.

Part VII

Exam Updates

Chapter 25, "*Cisco Certified Support Technician CCST Networking 100-150 Official Cert Guide* Exam Updates," will be updated over time so you stay up to date on the latest changes to the exam.

CHAPTER 25

Cisco Certified Support Technician CCST Networking 100-150 Official Cert Guide Exam Updates

The Purpose of This Chapter

For all the other chapters, the content should remain unchanged throughout this edition of the book. Instead, this chapter will change over time, with an updated online PDF posted so you can see the latest version of the chapter even after you purchase this book.

Why do we need a chapter that updates over time? For two reasons:

■ To add more technical content to the book before it is time to replace the current book edition with the next edition. This chapter will include additional technology content and possibly additional PDFs containing more content.

■ To communicate detail about the next version of the exam, to tell you about our publishing plans for that edition, and to help you understand what that means to you.

After the initial publication of this book, Cisco Press will provide supplemental updates as digital downloads for minor exam updates. If an exam has major changes or accumulates enough minor changes, we will then announce a new edition. We will do our best to provide any updates to you free of charge before we release a new edition. However, if the updates are significant enough in between editions, we may release the updates as a low-priced standalone eBook.

If we do produce a free updated version of this chapter, you can access it on the book's companion website. Simply go to the companion website page and go to the "Exam Updates Chapter" section of the page.

If you have not yet accessed the companion website, follow this process below:

Step 1. Browse to www.ciscopress.com/register.

Step 2. Enter the print book ISBN (even if you are using an eBook): **9780138213428**.

Step 3. After registering the book, go to your account page and select the Registered Products tab.

Step 4. Click on the Access Bonus Content link to access the companion website. Select the Exam Updates Chapter link or scroll down to that section to check for updates.

Impact on You and Your Study Plan

This chapter gives us a way to communicate in detail about exam changes as they occur. But you should watch other spaces as well.

For those other information sources to watch, bookmark and check these sites for news. In particular:

- **Cisco:** Check the Certification Roadmap page: https://cisco.com/go/certroadmap. Make sure to sign up for automatic notifications from Cisco on that page.

- **Publisher:** Check their page about new certification products, offers, discounts, and free downloads related to the more frequent exam updates: https://www.ciscopress.com/newcert.

- **Cisco Learning Network:** Subscribe to the CCNA Community at learningnetwork.cisco.com, where I expect ongoing discussions about exam changes over time. If you have questions, search for "roadmap" in the CCNA community, and if you do not find an answer, ask a new one!

As changes arise, we will update this chapter with more detail about exam and book content. At that point, we will publish an updated version of this chapter, listing our content plans. That detail will likely include the following:

- Content removed, so if you plan to take the new exam version, you can ignore those when studying.

- New content planned per new exam topics, so you know what's coming.

The remainder of the chapter shows the new content that may change over time.

News About the Next Exam Release

This statement was last updated in 2023, before the publication of the CCST Networking Study Guide.

This version of this chapter has no news to share about the next exam release.

At the most recent version this chapter, the Cisco Certified Support Technician Networking exam version number was Version 1.

Updated Technical Content

The current version of this chapter has no additional technical content.

Part VIII

Appendices

This part includes the following appendices:

Appendix A: Answers to the "Do I Know This Already?" Quizzes

Glossary of Key Terms

Answers to the "Do I Know This Already?" Questions

Chapter 1

1. b
2. b
3. a
4. b
5. d
6. c
7. a
8. b
9. a

Chapter 2

1. b, c
2. b
3. a
4. d
5. b, e
6. d
7. c
8. b
9. c

Chapter 3

1. d
2. a, b
3. c
4. d
5. a
6. a

7. c
8. d
9. d

Chapter 4

1. c
2. c, d
3. c
4. b
5. c
6. d
7. a, d
8. d
9. a, d
10. d

Chapter 5

1. b
2. d
3. b
4. c
5. c
6. a
7. d
8. c
9. b

Chapter 6

1. a
2. c
3. a, d
4. b, c
5. c
6. c
7. b
8. a

Chapter 7

1. c
2. b
3. d
4. a
5. b
6. c
7. b
8. d
9. a

Chapter 8

1. c
2. c
3. a
4. d
5. b
6. b, d
7. c
8. b
9. a

Chapter 9

1. a
2. b
3. b
4. c
5. c
6. d
7. c
8. b

Chapter 10

1. c
2. a
3. b

Appendix A: Answers to the "Do I Know This Already?" Questions   513

A

4. c
5. d
6. b, c
7. b
8. b

Chapter 11

1. a
2. c
3. c
4. b
5. b
6. a, c
7. a
8. b

Chapter 12

1. b
2. a
3. b, c
4. d
5. b
6. c
7. b
8. a, c

Chapter 13

1. b
2. a
3. d
4. d
5. b
6. a
7. c
8. a, c
9. d

Chapter 14

1. b
2. b
3. a
4. c
5. b
6. c
7. b
8. b
9. a
10. d

Chapter 15

1. a, c
2. b, c
3. c
4. b
5. c
6. b
7. c
8. b
9. b

Chapter 16

1. c
2. a, c, d
3. d
4. b
5. a
6. c
7. c
8. b
9. c
10. b
11. b

Appendix A: Answers to the "Do I Know This Already?" Questions   515

A

Chapter 17

1. c
2. a
3. c
4. b
5. b, c, f
6. d
7. a
8. b
9. c

Chapter 18

1. b
2. a
3. c
4. a
5. d
6. b
7. b
8. c

Chapter 19

1. b
2. c
3. d
4. a, c
5. c
6. b
7. d
8. c
9. d

Chapter 20

1. b
2. c
3. b
4. a

5. c

6. d

7. c

8. a

9. c

10. c

11. b

Chapter 21

1. c

2. c

3. a

4. c

5. c

6. a

7. c

8. b

9. c

Chapter 22

1. c

2. c

3. b

4. c

5. a

6. c

7. c

8. a

Chapter 23

1. a

2. b

3. a

4. a

5. c

6. c

7. a

8. a

9. b

10. c

11. a

GLOSSARY OF KEY TERMS

NUMERICS

* The output of ping and traceroute when a device is unreachable.

2FA Two-factor authentication; an authentication system that uses two factors to authenticate users. For password-based systems, these are normally something you know and something you have.

5G Fifth-generation cellular network.

802.11 IEEE working group that standardizes Wi-Fi.

A

AAA A system that uses authentication, authorization, and accounting to ensure resources are properly accessed and used.

abstraction The act of removing information to reduce the amount of state or information; this could be aggregation or summarization in a network.

acceptance cone The range of angles from which a fiber-optic cable will accept light signals.

access control The use of AAA systems to control access to a data store or application.

access list A set of policies applied to packet forwarding, routing information, and many other places within a router.

access point The point used to connect a Wi-Fi–connected device to an Ethernet network; sometimes combined with a router.

access provider An organization that sells Internet access to individual users and organizations.

access-group command A command that applies an access list as a packet filter.

aggregation The act of shortening the IP address prefix length to represent a larger set of interfaces (hosts) or subnets.

amperage Electrical volume.

Android An open-source mobile device operating system; originally developed by Google.

anycast A packet that the closest host with a given service or application running should receive and process.

APC Angled Physical Connect; optical fiber where the fiber is cut to reduce light reflection towards the transmitter.

Apple iOS Apple's mobile device operating system.

application firewall (AF)   A packet filtering application designed to support a specific application.

ARP   Address Resolution Protocol; a protocol that maps physical interface addresses to IPv4 addresses.

ARP table   The set of physical to logical address mappings known by a host.

asymmetric cryptography   A cryptographic system using public and private keys.

asymmetric routes   The paths that traffic transmitted to and received from a destination follows.

attack surface   Every point where the network connects to the outside world.

attenuation   The loss of signal from traveling through a cable.

authoritative server   A server that resolves a domain name to an IP address, service, etc.

auxiliary port   A serial port used to access a device's command-line interface.

availability   Making certain that data is available to authorized users.

availability zone   A set of resources within a cloud that should fail separately from (not share fate with) other availability zones within the same region.

B

back-end server   A server that combines information from many sources to fulfill a user's request.

backhaul   Carry data from a cellular radio tower into the service provider's network.

backout plan   A plan for how to stop a change before it is completed and restore the network to its original state.

band   The range of frequencies used in a wireless transmission.

bandwidth   The maximum amount of data a signal can carry.

base station   Equipment used to send and receive cellular radio transmissions.

baseline   A measurement of how things work right now or normally.

BDF   Building distribution frame; the place where outside wiring normally enters a commercial building.

beachhead   The initial point at which an attacker gains access to a network; the place where the attacker expands their control and access.

beam forming   Shaping a wireless signal to make it directional.

breach   Unauthorized disclosure of data.

bridge learning   The process by which a switch learns a given physical address is reachable on a given port by examining the source addresses of frames it receives.

bridge table   A table of interfaces through which physical addresses can be reached.

broadcast   A type of packet that every host within a given part of the network should receive and process.

broadcast address   The all 0s address, or the first address in the subnet and the all 1s address, or the last address in the subnet.

bus topology   A network topology in which all hosts are connected to a single long wire, generally coax.

butterfly fabric   Five-stage fabric design.

C

C2 system   Command and control system; used by an attacker to maintain access to a network.

cable cutting   Discontinuing television channels received through a cable television service and using streaming services over an Internet connection instead.

canary   The process of testing a change by placing increasingly larger amounts of real-world workload on a changed module or system over time.

carrier   The signal on which information is modulated.

carrier frequency   The center frequency of a signal, or the frequency that is varied to carry information.

CDP   Cisco Discovery Protocol; a lightweight discovery protocol that runs any time an interface is connected to another device, enabled, and the line interface is up.

change management   Formal and informal processes used to manage changes in a network.

change window   The time during which a network is planned down for changes.

channel   A small set of frequencies within a spectrum.

chaos engineering   Intentionally injecting (random) errors into a network or system to see how it reacts.

chassis device   A network device with line cards.

cipher   An encryption algorithm.

cipher text   Encrypted text.

clear text   Unencrypted text.

CLI   Command-line interface; either the Terminal or PowerShell app on Windows 11.

Clos fabric   Three-stage fabric design based on the work of Charlie Clos.

cloud direct connect   A physical link between the customer's and cloud provider's network.

cloud region   A group of data center fabrics connected by high-speed links, generally within a single geographic region.

cloud-based management   A management system that runs in a public or private cloud system.

cloud-native   A type of application designed and developed to be deployed in a cloud environment.

coax   A two-layer electrical conductor.

cold aisle   The place where network equipment draws cooled air.

CoLo   Colocation facility; a place where providers and customers colocate networking and information technology hardware.

confidentiality   Protecting information from access by unauthorized parties.

config terminal   A command that enters configuration mode.

configuration sub-mode   Allows you to change the configuration for interfaces, processes, etc.

connectionless transport   A simple service to transmit data across a network.

connection-oriented transport   A more complex transport service providing retransmission in the case of dropped packets or errors; it provides flow control.

console port   A serial port used to access a device's command-line interface.

content distribution network (CDN)   A kind of provider that caches and distributes data to users globally.

content provider   An endpoint of the Internet; an organization that stores and processes data, and provides services.

contextual packet filtering   Filtering packets based on application state and safe inputs.

Control Panel   Windows 11 GUI application used for finding and setting a host's IP address.

CPE   Customer premises equipment; equipment owned by the provider but installed on the customer's property.

CRAC   Computer room air conditioner; a unit that cools air inside the data center room.

crossover   A cable that connects the transmit wires of one device to the receive wires of another device, and vice versa.

cryptographic hash   A cryptographically created, nonrepeatable signature across a data set; cannot be unencrypted.

cryptographic signature   A cryptographically created, nonrepeatable signature across a data set; cannot be unencrypted.

CSMA/CA   Carrier Sense Multiple Access with Collision Avoidance; the method used to multiplex a Wi-Fi channel, or share the same transmission frequency among several transmitting devices.

CSMA/CD   Carrier Sense Multiple Access with Collision Detection; the method used by Ethernet to allow multiple hosts to share a single segment.

D

data collection The process of collecting data through monitoring or logging network information; also relates to collecting information on individual users.

data exfiltration The process of copying critical or private information from within the network to an attacker's server.

DCI Data center interconnect; a platform that connects multiple DC fabrics.

DDoS Distributed denial of service; the act of overwhelming a system's resources so it cannot be accessed.

DDoS reflection attack A type of attack that overwhelms a system's resources so it cannot be accessed using traffic reflected from some public service such as DNS.

decibels A logarithmic measurement scale.

default route The place where a router sends any packet whose destination address does not fall within another route.

defense in depth The process of building multiple layers of defense, each of which ideally has different vulnerabilities.

deidentification Suppression, noise injection, aggregation, and segmentation; it reduces the chance of an individual user being identified in a data set.

delay The amount of time required for a packet to traverse a network.

demarc The point where the provider's network ends and the customer's network begins.

detection The process of monitoring a network for unusual events or behavior.

DHCP Dynamic Host Configuration Protocol; a protocol that assigns an IP address, default gateway, and name server to a host.

dictionary The set of rules matching a field's location (in the case of fixed-length fields) or type (in the case of a TLV) to a definition of the data being carried.

DIG Domain Information Groper; an application that recurses through a domain name to uncover the entire resolution process.

direct DDoS attack A type of attack that overwhelms a system's resources so it cannot be accessed using traffic directly sourced from a large number of hosts or devices.

disclosure The act of making data available to a process or user for analysis.

dispersion The act of breaking light into many smaller beams, weakening the overall signal.

distance-vector routing protocol A protocol that finds loop-free paths through a network.

DKIM DomainKeys Identified Mail; a method that signs email header fields to ensure they are not changed in transport.

DMARC Domain-based Message Authentication, Reporting, and Conformance.

DNSSEC   A method of signing DNS records so recursive servers and hosts can verify the information in the record is correct.

DOCSIS   A standard for carrying data or IP networking traffic across a cable television network.

DoH   DNS over HTTPS; a protocol designed to protect DNS queries sent from hosts to recursive servers.

domain name   A name that can be translated into am IP address, location of a service, or some other piece of information through the DNS.

domain name resolution   The process of looking up a domain name through the DNS to discover the IP address of the resource or further information provided by DNS.

DoS   Denial of service; a type of attack that overwhelms a system's resources so it cannot be accessed.

dwell time   The amount of time the failure exists before being detected.

E

enable mode   Privileged mode on a router; it allows you to view and configure all options.

encapsulation   The act of adding a header to data to carry metadata such as the source and destination addresses.

encryption   The act of using mathematical transformations to prevent observers from accessing data.

End User (EU)   A device connected to the cellular network.

entropy bits   Random bits used in cryptographic operations to prevent repeatability.

environmental pressure   Changes in the environment that cause a system to either become stressed and close to failure, or to fail.

ephemeral port   A port number assigned to an application randomly by the local networking stack.

error control   The method of detecting errors in transmission and determining how to respond to these errors.

EUI-48   A physical address format standardized by the IEEE.

exploit   A tool designed to allow a threat actor to take advantage of a vulnerability.

exploitability   The ease with which a vulnerability can be exploited.

F

fabric   A specialized kind of network that is repeatable and nonplanar.

failure report   A description of a failure, troubleshooting process, root cause, temporary fixes, and permanent fixes.

false positive   The state that occurs when things look broken, although they are not.

fan-out   The number of connections from a single router in a data center fabric.

FC connector   Ferrule Connector; a fiber-optic connector with a screw-down mechanical connection.

F-connector   A cable television connector. This kind of connector is normally used with a coaxial cable.

FEXT   Far-end crosstalk; interference measured at the far end of the cable.

fiber optic   A glass fiber that carries light signals.

firewall   A collection of services including NAT, packet filtering, and stateful packet filtering.

five-tuple   The source address, source port number, protocol number, destination address, and address port number; it is used to identify a flow.

fixed-length encoding   An encoding method where the position and length of the data are set by the protocol specification and cannot be changed by the transmitter.

flashing green status light   A light that typically (but not always) means the port is transmitting or receiving traffic.

flow control   A way of controlling the rate a transmitter sends traffic to a receiver; when you tell your older relative to slow down because you cannot understand them.

fragility   The state of a system when it cannot continue operating in the face of a changing environment.

fragmentation   The act of breaking a packet into multiple smaller packets so they can be carried across a smaller MTU link.

frame   Data encapsulated to be carried from interface to interface.

frequency   The rate of change in the polarity of an electrical signal.

frequency modulation   A way of changing the frequency of a signal to carry information.

front-end server   Web server; it formats data for a user to consume.

FTP   File Transfer Protocol; a protocol designed to transfer large files between hosts.

FWA   Fixed wireless access; the use of Wi-Fi or cellular telephone technology to carry IP data from a building to the global Internet.

G

gateway   A device that forwards packets; gateways often terminate a session, like a proxy, but operate at the application level.

gateway of last resort   The place where a router sends any packet whose destination address does not fall within another route.

GBIC   Gigabit interface converter. A kind of pluggable interface.

geosynchronous   Having satellites positioned further from the Earth's surface so Earth station antennas do not need to be adjusted to track their movements.

GET   An HTML command where the client asks the server for a piece of data.

goodput   The amount of data transferred without error, in order, etc., across a network.

GPON   Gigabit passive optical network; passive optical networking technology used in last-mile networks.

grammar   The set of rules determining the order in which data is transmitted, how sessions are set up, how sessions are torn down, etc.

guest network   A network with access to the Internet but not internal devices, such as hosts and printers.

H

half-split method   An intentional troubleshooting method that organizes work to split the network into successively smaller pieces.

hardware abstraction   A model of the network devices in an intent-based system.

hardware abstraction layer (HAL)   A set of functions and applications that separate software running on a host from the host's hardware.

HEAD   The beginning of an HTML file.

host   A computer system that hosts applications, like Windows, Linux, or macOS.

hostname   A command that sets the device's hostname.

hot aisle   The place where network equipment expels hot air.

HTML   Hypertext Markup Language; a language used to transport data between web servers and browsers (or web clients).

HTTP   Hypertext Transfer Protocol; a protocol designed to build a client/server relationship between a web server and web browser; it is used to carry all the data needed to build a web page.

hub-and-spoke topology   A network topology with a small number (usually two) of hub devices providing connectivity to a larger number of remote sites.

hybrid cloud   An environment that uses public and private cloud facilities in parallel.

I–J

IaaS   Infrastructure as a Service; compute, memory, and network connectivity are provided as a service (does not include databases, applications, etc.).

IANA   Internet Assigned Numbers Authority; the organization that manages the assignment of numbers, like IP addresses, in the global Internet.

ICAAN   Internet Corporation for Assigned Names and Numbers; the organization that manages the assignment of numbers and names in the global Internet.

identity store   A database of users and the data or systems they are authorized to access.

IDF   Intermediate distribution frame; any wiring closet, equipment room, or wiring structure that handles connectivity between any two other points in the network.

IDS   Intrusion detection system; a kind of middlebox that detects intrusions and other security breaches; it filters packets based on information about common attacks.

ifconfig   macOS and Linux CLI application used for finding and setting a host's IP address.

in-band management   A way of connecting to and managing devices through the same network that carries user traffic.

integrity   An operator's confidence that data has not been intentionally or unintentionally changed while being stored or processed.

intent engine   A model of the desired outcome in an intent-based system.

interference   Unintended modifications to an electrical or wireless signal; interference creates transmission errors.

Internet exchange   IX; a system that provides local connectivity between access providers, and a regional hub of Internet activity.

IoT   Internet of Things; anything like a printer, light switch, or thermostat connected to the Internet.

IoT gateway   A device that converts IoT protocols to IP so the data can be carried across the global Internet.

ip address command   A command that configures an IPv4 address for an interface.

ip route 0.0.0.0 0.0.0.0   A command that creates a default route.

ip route command   A command that creates a static route which will be inserted in the local routing table and used to forward packets to the indicated destination.

ipconfig   A Windows 11 command-line application used for finding and setting a host's IP address.

iPerf   A software packet designed to measure a network's performance.

IPv4   Internet Protocol version 4; the most widely used network transport protocol in the global Internet.

IPv6   Internet Protocol version 6; the next generation of IP protocol, currently in the process of being deployed in the global Internet.

ipv6 address command   A command that assigns an IPv6 address to an interface.

ipv6 area interface sub-mode command   A command that enables OSPFv3 routing on this interface.

ipv6 enable command   A command that enables IPv6 on an interface.

IPv6 link local address   An address auto-calculated by a host for use on a single link; a link local address is not guaranteed to be unique across an entire network or the global Internet.

ipv6 router ospf command   A command that starts an OSPFv3 routing process.

IPv6 SLAAC   A method of auto-calculating an IPv6 address from a prefix and physical interface address.

ipv6 unicast-routing command   A command that enables IPv6 routing on the device.

ISMI   International Mobile Subscriber Identity; a number that contains the information required to identify a cellular network subscriber so they can connect to the wireless network.

ISO   International Organization for Standardization; an international organization that sets engineering standards in many areas, including computer networks.

IXP   Internet exchange provider; provides regional connectivity and colocation facilities.

jitter   Variance in the arrival times of packets in a flow.

K–L

kernel   The central functions of an operating system.

key   The piece of information that a sender uses, along with an encryption algorithm, to encrypt a piece of data, and the receiver uses, along with the same encryption algorithm, to unencrypt the data.

last mile   The network connecting individual buildings and users to the global Internet.

lateral movement   The movement within a network to find important resources once the network is breached.

law of large numbers   A principle that states when there are enough items or events, the improbable becomes likely.

LC connector   Little connector; a device used for high-density fiber-optic installations.

LEO (low Earth orbit)   The orbit of satellites positioned close to the Earth's surface to reduce delay.

letters in a port number   Letters that generally indicate the speed of the interface.

lifecycle controls   A plan to properly de-identify, and ultimately destroy, data once it is collected.

line card   A card containing interface ports and a separate forwarding engine.

link-state routing protocol   A protocol that finds loop-free paths through a network.

local routing table   The set of destinations, next hops, and outbound interfaces used to forward traffic by a host.

logical address   An address assigned to a logical interface and used as a packet's source and destination address.

logical interface   A higher-layer interface defined in software and related to a physical or virtual interface.

logical network diagram   A schema that contains information about network addresses, control planes, and where links are connected; follow the flow of the traffic.

M

MAC address   Media Access Control address; a physical address format standardized by the IEEE; generally the same format and style as an EUI-48 address.

machine interface   An interface designed for access by a computer program rather than by a person.

malware   A self-replicating application designed to disrupt a computer system.

MAN   Metropolitan area network; normally a ring.

management port   A low-speed Ethernet port used to connect a device to an out-of-band management network.

marshaling   Formatting data so the sender and receiver can exchange information.

masquerade   A virtual network address translation device in the Linux networking stack.

metadata   Data about a collection of data.

metrics   The cost of crossing a link.

metro fiber   A fiber ring designed to provide connectivity within a metropolitan area.

MITM   Man-in-the-middle attack; the attacker inserts themselves between the transmitter and receiver.

mobile core   The "intelligence" of a cellular network.

mobile device   Generally a smaller device, capable of being handheld, that can connect to the Internet.

modem   A device that converts long-haul optical and electronic signals into local Ethernet and Wi-Fi signals.

modulation   The process of varying a carrier signal to carry information.

monitoring   Providing the information that network administrators need to determine, in real time, whether a network is running optimally.

MPO connector   Multiple fiber push-on/pull-off connector; a common kind of fiber connector.

MTA   Mail transfer agent.

MTBF   Mean time between failures; the amount of time between the last and current failures.

MTMB   Mean time between mistakes; the amount of time between operational and configuration mistakes causing outages.

MTR   An enhanced form of traceroute.

MTTI   Mean time to innocence; the time it takes for the network team to prove the problem is not the network.

MTTR   Mean time to repair; how long the service, network, etc., was not available.

MTU   Maximum transmission unit; the largest packet that can be transmitted over a link.

multicast   A group of hosts should receive and process this packet.

multi-cloud   An environment that uses services from multiple public cloud providers in parallel.

multimode   Lower-powered light source and a larger core.

multiplexing   Using a single physical channel to transmit multiple signals, or signals between multiple senders and receivers.

N

namespace   A set of functions including applications, kernel functions, and network functions on a Linux host.

NETCONF   A protocol designed to carry YANG-formatted network device information.

Network Address Translation   NAT; the translation of a range of IP addresses into a single IP address and use of ephemeral port numbers to differentiate between the addresses.

network command (under routing protocol configuration mode)   A command that enables the routing protocol on any interface with an IP address covered by the network statement.

network description   An explanation that should include just about anything that will help a new engineer understand how a network works and why it works that way.

NEXT   Near-end crosstalk; the amount of interference a cable can reject.

NIM   Network interface module; a pluggable module for installing ports or features into a network device.

NMS   Network management system.

nonauthoritative answer   An answer to a DNS query served from the local cache rather than directly from an authoritative service.

nonblocking   A type of network that will refuse traffic at the edge if the traffic cannot be carried to the destination.

noncontending   A type of network that will not drop traffic so long as the link to no single attached device is overloaded.

nonplanar   A type of network that cannot be drawn without links crossing.

nonrepudiation   The ability to prove that a sender actually transmitted a piece of information.

nslookup   A utility available on almost every host for manually resolving domain names.

NTP   Network Time Protocol; a high-precision time distribution protocol based on accurate external clocks.

numbers in a port number   Numbers that generally indicate the physical module, slot, and sequence number of the port.

O

OADM   Optical add/drop multiplexer; a device that adds or drops a single wavelength or color of light from a WDM system.

observability problem   The impact of the network's operation because you are trying to measure something about the network.

oDoH   Oblivious DNS over HTTPS; an encrypted DNS query system that uses proxy servers to hide the querier's identity.

off-premises   A place other than the user's site where network, computing, and storage are physically located, such as in a public cloud provider's data center or a colocation facility.

on-premises   A place on the user's site where network, computing, and storage are physically located.

open peering   Provider-customer peering in which the provider does not charge for access to the global Internet.

OSI   Open Systems Interconnection; a suite of computer networking protocols.

OSI seven-layer model   A widely used model for network communications.

OtT   Over the Top; when voice and video traffic is carried over the data network rather than in parallel with the data network.

out-of-band management   A way of connecting to and managing devices through a separate network.

P

PA address space   The address space assigned by a provider to their customer; it can be used to route through the global Internet but must be returned to the provider if the customer ends the contract.

PaaS   Platform as a Service; a service that replicates everything an organization would provide through internal IT systems.

packet   Data encapsulated to be carried from host to host.

packet capture   A tool used for capturing and examining packets and flows through a network. The most common packet capture tool is *Wireshark*, which is an open-source, free-to-use tool.

partitioning   Breaking a single data source into multiple parts and storing each part in a different data source.

passwordless   A type of authentication system that uses something you are and something you have.

peering point   A facility where providers and their customers interconnect.

PEP   Policy enforcement point; the place where a policy described by the policy engine is enforced.

permanent fix   The type of fix that you intend to leave in the network permanently, or at least until the network changes for some other reason; it does not increase technical debt.

phish   Mail to many recipients; it could include advertising, scams, etc.

phishing   A form of electronically based social engineering sent to a well-researched individual user.

physical address   An address assigned to a physical interface and used as a frame's source and destination address.

physical interface   A physical point of connection where electrical or optical signals are converted to and from data.

physical network diagram   A schema that contains the physical location of hardware and physical cable connections; follow the flow of the wires.

PI address space   Provider-independent address space; it is assigned by a regional registry and may be used to route on the global Internet regardless of the provider.

PII   Personally identifiable information; handling and use of PII is often regulated.

ping   An application that sends a series of packets to a destination to determine if the destination is reachable.

plenum   The air return system in a building.

pluggable interface   A kind of interface where the physical cable connector is separated from the transmission electronics so a single connector can be used for multiple kinds of media.

PMTUD   Path Maximum Transmission Unit Discovery; a process used to determine the largest packet that can be transmitted across a link.

PoE   Power over Ethernet; a technology that is used to power small network-connected devices.

policy administrator   The person or organization making the rules about accessing resources.

policy engine   A system that contains organizational policies for user access to resources.

PoP   Point of presence; a provider's facility in a metropolitan area, city, or other region.

port   The address of an individual application running on a host.

port address translation (PAT)   The use of ephemeral ports to extend the IPv4 address space.

POST An HTML command where the client sends data to the server.

post-mortem A time set aside to go over a network failure, the troubleshooting process, and the solution.

PowerShell A terminal application in Windows 11.

prefix The network or aggregate portion of an IP address.

primary data use The use of data for the purpose given in the privacy consent and notice.

privacy consent The request for a user to accept the privacy terms before they can access a resource.

privacy notice An announcement notifying a user about the ways collected data may be used before they access a resource.

private address space The address space set aside for use within a private network; it cannot be advertised or routed on the global Internet.

private cloud A cloud service operated by the organization/user.

private key One of the two keys used in asymmetric cryptography; this key should be securely stored.

privilege level A setting that determines the actions you can take on the router; privilege level 0 is also called *read-only mode*; privilege level 15 can configure anything on the router.

proper operation testing Testing a system while all the components are functioning correctly and with expected inputs.

protocol A way of doing things that enables communications. It includes a dictionary and grammar to regulate the formatting of data, order of operations, etc.

protocol layers A model that breaks the problem of transferring data between computers into smaller problems, and solves these problems with a set of protocols, some of which depend on other protocols within the suite.

protocol specification A description of how to implement a protocol.

proxy A device that terminates a session; hides the source address.

public address space Address space that may be advertised and routed on the global Internet.

public cloud A cloud service operated by a public service provider.

public IP address An IP address that can be used to route packets on the global Internet.

public key One of the two keys used in asymmetric cryptography; this key can be published or shared publicly.

punch-down tool An instrument used to connect telephone and computer network wiring to a wiring block.

Q–R

QUIC   A transport protocol built on top of User Datagram Protocol (UDP) with all the characteristics of TCP, but that also includes encryption.

rack-mounted cable organizers   Devices that include ladders, fingerboards, shelves, and lacing bars.

rack unit (RU)   A standard measure of equipment height; 1.75 in or 44.45 mm.

RAN   Radio area network; part of the cellular network system.

ransomware   A type of malware that encrypts the data on a system and requires the user to pay for a key to unencrypt it.

reassembly   The process of combining several fragments so the data in the original, nonfragmented, packet can be retrieved.

recursive server   A DNS server that recurses through each domain, starting with the right side of the domain name, to resolve the domain name to a piece of information.

red status light   A light that typically (but not always) means the port is malfunctioning.

redirect   Inform a host to use a different router to send traffic to a destination.

redundancy   The situation that occurs when network capacity is added in parallel with existing capacity so that the network can route through an alternate path in the case of failure.

refactoring   Intentionally rebuilding a system to meet current specifications, requirements, and testing practices, even though the system is still operating normally.

regional cloud hub   A regional connection point through which customers can connect to a cloud service; often contained in colocation space.

regional registries   Organizations that manage the assignment of numbers and names in a region.

relay   A router that forwards DHCP or other packets to the correct server for processing.

repeater   A network device that electrically reshapes and regenerates a signal; in wireless networks, it repeats a Wi-Fi signal to extend the range of the Wi-Fi network.

reserved addresses   Addresses that cannot be routed on the global Internet.

resilience   A system's ability to continue operating in the face of changing conditions or environment.

right-of-way   The agreement that is made when a land owner allows an outside entity to use part of their land for some specific purpose, such as burying a cable.

RINA model   Recursive InterNetwork Architecture; a model of computer communications focused on the problems being solved rather than protocol interactions.

ring topology   A simple two-connected network topology using two ports on each device.

riser   A virtual conduit or facility for carrying cables between floors of a commercial building.

risk   Any potential event, such as an attack, that can disrupt an organization's operations.

ROADM   Random optical add/drop multiplexer; a device that adds or drops any wavelength of color of light from a WEM system.

root server   A server that knows which server to ask for information about each top-level domain (TLD).

route server   A server that carries routing information between routers connected to an IXP fabric.

routing loops   Loops in which a set of routers forward traffic among themselves.

routing protocol   A protocol that finds loop-free paths through a network.

routing table   A table containing destinations, next hops, and interfaces used to forward traffic.

running configuration   A configuration that the router is running right now.

S

SaaS   Software as a Service; software that can be provided as a service over the cloud.

SC connector   Square connector; a fiber-optic connector.

scheduled outage   A planned network outage or downtime for maintenance or changes.

secondary data use   The use of data for some purpose other than that given in the privacy consent and notice.

secret key   A key that is shared only between the sender and receiver.

segment   Data encapsulated to be carried from application to application.

segmentation   Also called partitioning; the act of splitting data into multiple stores to prevent a single user or process from accessing all of it.

server room   A room dedicated to operational servers within a building. There is normally only one server room in a building.

session key   A secret key used for encrypting traffic on this session.

Settings app   A Windows 11 GUI application used for finding and setting a host's IP address.

settlement-free peering   The interconnection that occurs when two providers peer without charging one another a settlement.

SFP   Small Form-factor Pluggable; a kind of pluggable interface.

SFTP   Simple File Transfer Protocol; a file transfer system similar to FTP within SSH; it provides encrypted file transfer between hosts.

shared fate   When a single resource's failure can cause some other group of devices to fail.

shift left   Move security and privacy as close to the design phase as possible.

show cdp neighbors   A command that displays all CDP-enabled devices connected to this device.

show interfaces   A command that provides basic information about the physical and virtual interfaces connected to this device.

show ip route   A command that displays the router's routing table, including which destinations the router knows how to reach, along with other information about each reachable destination.

show ipv6 route command   A command that displays the IPv6 routing table.

show version   A command that provides general information about the router, including the software version number, router serial number, and installed hardware.

SIM card   Subscriber identity module; a device that contains the information required to identify a cellular network subscriber so they can connect to the wireless network.

single point of failure   Anyplace in the network where a single link or device failing prevents the network from forwarding traffic.

single-mode   Higher-powered light source and a smaller core.

SMTP   Simple Mail Transfer Protocol.

SNMP   Simple Network Management Protocol; a relatively insecure method of managing network devices.

social engineering   Tricking a user into giving an attacker access to a protected resource.

socket   A coding-centric term describing the same thing as a port. The address of an individual application running on a host.

Solid green status light   A light that typically (but not always) means the port is connected and functioning correctly.

source address spoofing   Sending traffic from some source address other than the one assigned to the device or host.

spam   A form of electronically based social engineering sent to a large number of users.

spam filter   Software that searches mail for keywords, key phrases, attachments, suspicious links, etc.

spectrum   The complete set of frequencies available to create a link (transmit data over wireless signals).

speed test   A system that tests the speed of connection from a network to the Internet.

SPF   Sender Policy Framework; a list of valid email addresses in a domain.

spine-and-leaf fabric   A fabric design with spine and leaf nodes.

SSH   Secure Shell; a secure terminal protocol and application that is a replacement for Telnet; provides secure terminal access to a remote system like a server, router, or switch.

SSH key   A pre-shared public/private key pair used to establish SSH sessions.

SSID   A set of services connected to the same segment or broadcast domain on a Wi-Fi network.

SSO   Single sign-on; a system that allows you to sign on to many different resources using a single username and password or other authentication method.

SSOT   Single source of truth.

ST connector   Straight Tip connector; a fiber-optic connector.

star topology   A network topology in which each host has a separate wire connecting to a central point, such as a hub, switch, or router.

startup configuration   A configuration saved in permanent memory and loaded by the router when it reboots or powers on.

stateful packet filtering   Filtering packets based on the state of the network transport.

STP   Spanning Tree Protocol; a protocol that finds loop-free paths through a switched network.

stratum   The number of hops away from an accurate time source an NTP server is.

subdomain   A domain name within another domain name; a domain that is part of another domain.

subject   The person, device, or process attempting to access a resource.

subnet   A group of hosts or networks.

supply chain attack   A cyberattack used to gain access to a network through some element of their supply chain.

symmetric cryptography   An algorithm in which the sender and receiver share the same key.

System Settings app   A macOS GUI application used for finding and setting a host's IP address.

T

tab completion   The act of pressing the Tab key to complete a command in the CLI if available.

TCP   Transmission Control Protocol; a transport protocol with error control and flow control.

TCP/IP model   An early model of computer communications developed in parallel with the TCP/IP protocol suite.

TDR   Time-domain reflectometer; a device used to discover the location of a cable break.

technical debt   The gap between how an operator thinks a system works and how that system works.

telnet   A terminal protocol as well as a terminal application.

temporary fix   A solution you use until a better one can be designed, tested, and deployed.

threat   A potential violation of security.

threat actor   A person or organization behind a threat or attack.

three-way handshake   A process whereby two hosts exchange initial parameters and ensure the connection works in both directions.

throughput   The total amount of data delivered by a network.

time series database   A database that records events sequentially.

TLD server   Top-level domain server; a server that knows which server to ask for information about each domain name.

TLV   Type-length-value; an encoding method where the type and length of the data are carried across the network as part of the data stream; this allows the data to be moved within the packet or have a variable length.

topological reach   The topological area within a network where a network makes sense without any further context.

traceroute   An application that sends a series of packets to a destination to determine the path that packets take to reach this destination.

transit provider   A device that carries packets across diverse geographic regions.

triage   The act of determining how important a failure is and in what order operators should work on failures.

TTL   Time-to-live; a mechanism used to prevent a packet from being forwarded eternally in a forwarding loop.

tunnel   A place to hide packet contents and headers from intermediate devices by adding a layer of encapsulation.

twisted pair   A pair of electrical conductors twisted around one another to reduce interference.

two-connected topology   A type of network with more than one path between any two reachable destinations.

U

unicast   A transmission in which one individual host should receive and process this packet.

unlicensed spectrum   Radio transmission or frequency bands that anyone can use to transmit data, without a license, although within specific power and range rules.

UPC   Ultra Physical Contact; an optical fiber where the fiber is cut to optimize light transmission.

upstream connectivity   Access providers contact with transit providers to provide them upstream connectivity to the global Internet.

user space   A space where each application has its own memory space, and accesses hardware interfaces through sockets or a HAL.

V

virtual host   A collection of services that appear to be a host but are running virtually in parallel with other virtual hosts on a single physical host.

voltage Electrical pressure.

vty interfaces A virtual terminal interface; you telnet to this interface remotely access a router.

vulnerability A possible point of attack against a defensive system.

W

wattage Electrical power; the combination of pressure and volume.

wavelength The length of a single cycle in a signal; it is related to the color of light.

WDM Wave division multiplexing; carrying different signals on different colors of light through an optical fiber.

WDM/D A passive filter that selects one wavelength from a set in a wave division multiplexing system.

web server A host that stores the files that make up a web page and responds to user requests for these files.

web service Software or a set of hosts that, combined, make up a service.

well-known port A port number assigned to an application (such as a web server) through standardization.

Wi-Fi A standard wireless transmission method.

Wi-Fi connected device A device connected to a Wi-Fi network.

Wi-Fi mesh Multiple Wi-Fi access points connected through a backhaul to create a mesh.

windowed flow control A system where the sender is given a window of information it can send before needing to pause until the receiver acknowledges its receipt.

Wireshark An open-source packet capture and analysis tool.

wiring closet A storage space dedicated to communications hardware and wiring. There is normally one wiring closet per floor in a multistory building.

X–Z

YANG A modeling language designed to carry network state and configuration.

yellow status light A light that typically (but not always) means the port is connecting or malfunctioning.

zero trust A security system requiring users to authenticate for each data or service access.

zoned access A type of access in which patch panels are installed throughout the floor of a building to increase flexibility.

Index

B

C

D

I

M

T

X-Y-Z